May 6th final

Contemporary Data Communications
A *Practical Approach*

Emilio Ramos
Al Schroeder

Richland College

Macmillan Publishing Company
New York

Maxwell Macmillan Canada
Toronto

Maxwell Macmillan International
New York   Oxford   Singapore   Sydney

Cover art: Marjory Dressler

Editor: Charles E. Stewart, Jr.

Cover Designer: Thomas Mack

Production Buyer: Pamela D. Bennett

This book was set in Bookman and was printed and bound by Arcata Graphics/Martinsburg. The cover was printed by Phoenix Color Corp.

The Publisher offers discounts on this book when ordered in bulk quantities. For more information, write to: Special Sales Department, Macmillan Publishing Company, 445 Hutchinson Ave., Columbus, OH 43235, or call 1-800-228-7854.

Macmillan Publishing Company
866 Third Avenue
New York, New York 10022

Macmillan Publishing Company is part of the
Maxwell Communication Group of Companies.

Maxwell Macmillan Canada, Inc.
1200 Eglinton Avenue East, Suite 200
Don Mills, Ontario M3C 3N1

Library of Congress Cataloging-in-Publication Data

Ramos, Emilio
    Contemporary data communications : a practical approach / Emilio Ramos, Al Schroeder.
        p. cm.
    Includes index.
    ISBN 0-02-408021-7
    1. Computer networks.   2. Data transmission systems.   I. Schroeder, Al. II. Title.
    TK5105.5.S385 1994
    004.6' 16--dc20
                                                      93-1505
                                                       CIP

Printing: 1 2 3 4 5 6 7 8 9   Year: 4 5 6 7 8

Preface

Introduction

As you read this textbook you will find that it follows a different strategy than traditional data communication books. This strategy is based on a different view of the field of data communications. Our view departs from traditional approaches, but we think it is more appropriate for today's marketplace.

The graduating student in the field of Computer Information Systems will be required to have a comprehensive understanding of contemporary connectivity topics. These topics include LANs, connectivity among different platforms, and microcomputers as integral parts of the connectivity strategy. Although there are many good books in the field of Business Data Communications, the material in such books is very broad and often too general to have applicability.

Students at this level need to get a good understanding of the solutions to the communication problems that they will face as soon as they leave the doors of the college. The CIS student must be exposed to a variety of computer operating environments, operating systems, and LAN connectivity problems and solutions, in addition to some traditional communication concepts.

We feel that, for the rest of this decade, a book for the introductory communication course must include more information on the operating environments that CIS students will be using in the business world. Traditionally, instructors expect the students to have such knowledge before taking a course in data communications. It is our experience that this assumption is not always valid. Although students are exposed to MS-DOS or some other microcomputer operating system, their knowledge of the computer operating environment is very limited and not related to the data communication process. We feel that a data communication course at the introductory level needs to be relevant to the marketplace that students enter upon completing their college studies.

Objective of This Text

This book provides information in a format that is clearer and more concise and relevant than traditional communication textbooks. Such textbooks go into the telecommunication process in great detail. Our book also covers this traditional market in a more general format, but it concentrates on the practical aspects of data communications from the personal computer point of view. We take this approach since we believe that this market is where our students are most likely to find employment.

We think that the topics in this book address the needs of the student. It includes discussion of several popular operating environments and how they are used to generate and transmit information. It explains traditional data communication concepts that the student will have to deal with in the workplace. It includes a study of networking concepts and the role of the personal computer in the networking environment, including the exciting world of multimedia.

Organization of the Text

The book is divided into three major sections:
1. The Operating Environment
2. The Data Communication Environment
3. The Microcomputer and Local Area Network Environment

The textbook has a total of 13 chapters. In addition, we have provided extensive ancillary materials in an Instructor's Manual/ Test Bank to accompany the book. These include Lecture Outlines, Answers to End of Chapter Questions, and Transparency Masters.

Appendices

Appendix A summarizes the most commonly used commands of the UNIX vi editor. This section can be used by students who have access to a UNIX based computer while studying chapters 1 and 2 of the text.

Appendix B contains a listing of software and hardware vendors of data communication and networking equipment and services.

A glossary containing commonly used terms is included at the end of the book. Additionally, an index containing both subjects and acronyms is provided.

Acknowledgments

We would like to thank our colleagues and students for supporting our efforts during this project. We also are grateful to the following reviewers of our text: Catherine Bakes, Kent State University; Philip Enslow, Georgia Institute of Technology; Lolita Gilkes, Richland College; Stephen Jordan, Cooke County College; Irene Liou, University of Baltimore; Sue Luckey, Moorehead State University; Hasan Pirkul, Ohio State University; Richard Ramirez, Iowa State University; Jim Trumbly, University of Oklahoma; Richard West, University of California at Berkely; George Whitson, University of Texas at Tyler; and David Yen, Miami University (Ohio).

Many thanks to all the people at Macmillan Publishing who helped turn the idea of this book into a reality.

To my loving son, Christopher

ER

Contents

Chapter 2. Operating System Concepts 45

Chapter 3. Computing Configurations   109

Chapter 5. Advanced Communication Hardware 173

Chapter 6. Communication Media   207

Chapter 7. Communication Networks and the Central Office   239

Part Three. The Microcomputer and Local Area Network Environment 295

Chapter 8. Microcomputer Connectivity 297

Chapter 9. Network Basics   345

Chapter 10. Local Area Networks   397

Chapter 11. LAN Installation   435

Chapter 13. Multimedia Technology and Networks 509

Appendix A. A Quick View of the UNIX vi Editor 535

Part One

The Computer Operating Environment

Basic Computer Resources

Objectives

After completing this chapter you will:

1. Understand the hardware components that make up the basic computer environment.
2. Have a general understanding about how the internal components of the computer perform their functions.
3. Understand the role of software in the overall computing environment.
4. Be able to distinguish the different attributes or devices used for communication by the computer.

Key Words

ALU	Application Software
Bus	Central Processing Unit (CPU)
Co-processor	Expansion Bay
FAX	Floppy Disk
Hard Disk	I/O Ports
ICU	Input Devices
Interface Board	Operating System
Output Devices	Programming Environment
RAM	ROM
System Software	

Introduction

Although the main focus of this book is data communication, it is important that the student understand the computer environment and some of the most commonly found options in hardware and software that he or she is to find in the market place. This understanding is crucial in order to have a better comprehension of the multitude of choices that will have to be contended with in the data communication field. It is important to discuss the use of modems, gateways, serial communication, and other communication topics. However it is also important that the student understand how the devices that sit externally to the system interact with the system inside. Knowledge of current technologies and options must be part of any data communication course.

Although it is expected that such knowledge is acquired in previous courses prior to a data communication course, actual experience suggests the contrary. In any event, revising some of the basic concepts of the computer environment that in most cases is the beginning and end of the communication process is conducive to better learning and easier retention of the complex and newer concepts that will be introduced in later chapters.

This chapter discusses the basic computer resources in terms of hardware and software. It explains the components found in any basic computer including the bus, CPU, memory, interfaces, and others. Additionally, it discusses the differences between application software and system software and their relationship to the hardware. It ends with a discussion of how all the different components are linked in order to have a successful computer process.

Computer technology was one of the most important topics of discussion during the decade of the 80s, continues to be in the 90s, and it will continue to be well into the future. The computer revolution during the past decade has been compared to some of the other great events such as the invention of the automobile and the telephone. Few of man's creations have been able to touch every facet of people's lives as extensively as the computer.

The technology advances in the micro-electronics industry have revolutionized our personal lives and the manner in which we operate in society. The presence of computers is around us in every shape and form. It can be found at the grocery store checkout counter, the teller machine at the bank, as the medium of communication at the office, and of course, in the home as an extension of the office or as a means of communication to the outside world.

Computers are available in many different shapes, sizes, and processing capabilities. However, they share some commonalities in the basic way they function. But it is the microcomputer, or personal computer as it is sometimes called, that has captured the attention of millions of people. The ability to take power away from the expensive and large mainframe computers and put it on our desks has made the personal computer an instant success. The microcomputer area is the fastest growing sector of the computer industry. With prices of entire systems well within the reach of the average person, the personal computer has become one of the main business communication mediums in the home and at the office.

As the power of microcomputers has increased dramatically over the last few years, their cost has decreased. Today, microcomputers with multiuser operating systems are performing jobs that used to be delegated to mainframes and minicomputers. It is for these reasons that we will concentrate on the features and power of high-end microcomputers as the main source of examples in this book. Although mainframe and minicomputer concepts and communication uses will be explored throughout the book, it is the availability and relative low cost of the microcomputer that makes it an ideal platform to explore the world of data communications. Additionally, because the basic operating environment of high-end microcomputers is virtually identical to that of minicomputers and mainframes, the concepts explored through this book can also be applied to those working environments.

Basic Resources

The basic computer system is a collection of components that work concurrently to achieve a goal. It can be thought of as a black box that has the capacity to accept input, manipulate the input, perform mathematical and logical operations, and print and store the results of these operations. Regardless of the type of computer, it performs basically the functions outlined above. Fig. 1-1 shows a complete desktop computer system. In it, you can see a box that contains the circuitry necessary to perform most of the operations required from a computer system. Additionally, there are input devices (mouse and keyboard), output devices (printer and monitor), a communication device (the modem underneath the telephone), and storage devices (floppy diskettes).

Fig. 1-1. A typical microcomputer system.

The computer system can be divided into software and hardware subsystems. The hardware consists of the physical parts that make up the computer. Some of these parts are the keyboard, the metal box that protects the electronic circuits, the electronic circuits themselves, the monitor, and other electronic devices. In more general terms, the hardware can be categorized by the function that each component performs into:

1. Central Processing Unit
2. Main Memory
3. Supporting Circuitry
4. Input Devices
5. Output Devices
6. Secondary Storage Devices

The software consists of the instructions that tell the computer what to do. Software can be categorized according to the purposes for which it was created and is used. The major categories are:

1. System Software
2. Application Software

Hardware Resources

The Central Processing Unit

The central processing unit, also referred to as the CPU or the processor, is responsible for performing the calculations and logical operations that a program requires of the computer. A program is the instructions stored in memory that instruct the computer to perform its basic functions (see Fig. 1-2). These functions are: add, subtract, multiply, divide, compare, copy, start input, and start output. The CPU also decides which instructions are executed and controls communications among the hardware devices. The instructions that the CPU must deal with consist of an operation code and one or more operands. The operation code is the instruction to be performed, and the operands correspond to memory locations that are part of the operation (see Fig. 1-3).

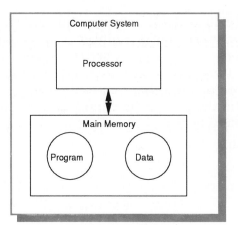

Fig. 1-2. Computer components.

Fig. 1-3. Operation code.

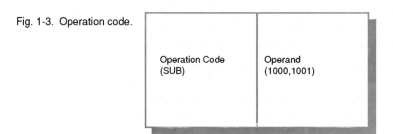

The central processing unit contains four major components in addition to its supporting circuitry (see Fig. 1-4). These components are the instruction control unit (ICU), the arithmetic logic unit (ALU), registers, and the clock.

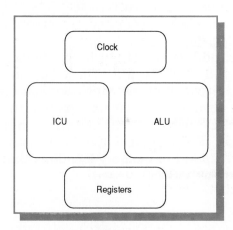

Fig. 1-4. CPU components.

The ICU is responsible for fetching instructions from memory to the other components of the CPU. The ALU is responsible for all mathematical calculations and logical operations that need to be performed. The registers are special holding areas where data, intermediate results, and other information are temporarily stored during processing. The clock generates electronic pulses at precise times. These pulses are used to synchronize the operation of the computer.

Machine Cycles

All of the components of the central processing unit need to work in a precise and timely manner if the computer is to be reliable in its operation. The clock is the component that generates the electrical pulses that allow the other members of the CPU to work together. The instructions that the computer needs to execute occur during what is called machine cycles.

The machine cycle starts when the clock generates an electrical pulse that activates the ICU. The ICU determines the instructions that will execute next. The instructions are stored in main memory (also called primary storage). The location of the next instruction to be executed is found in a special location in the CPU called the instruction counter (Fig. 1-5). The ICU checks the instruction counter, locates the address of the instruction that

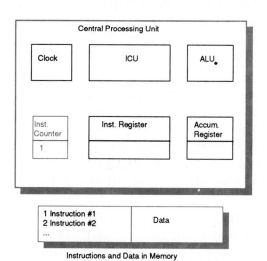

Instructions and Data in Memory

Fig. 1-5. CPU with the Instruction Counter set to 1 indicating next instruction to be executed.

needs to be executed, and fetches the instruction located at that address, placing it in one of the registers in the CPU called the instruction register (Fig. 1-6). Then the instruction counter is incremented, pointing to a new instruction.

Fig. 1-6. Data is placed in the Instruction Register.

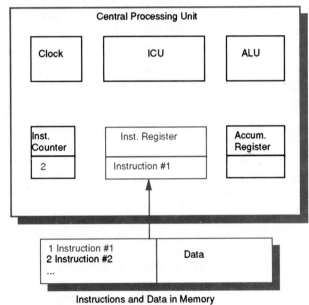

Instructions and Data in Memory

The ALU is the component of the CPU that is capable of executing the instructions. Therefore, the ALU takes the instruction from the instruction register and executes it. Any intermediate results are stored in a special register called the accumulator (see Fig. 1-7).

Now the clock generates a new electrical pulse. This activates the ICU and starts a new machine cycle. Using the instruction counter, the ICU fetches the next instruction to the instruction register (Fig. 1-8) and the instruction counter is incremented once again. The ALU executes the instruction in the instruction register and adds data from memory to the accumulator (see Fig. 1-9 on page 12).

Next, the clock provides another electrical pulse, the ICU fetches the next instruction, the instruction counter is incremented, and the instruction is executed by the ALU. Instructions are fetched during instruction time, I-time, and executed during execution time, E-time (see Fig. 1-10). The above process is

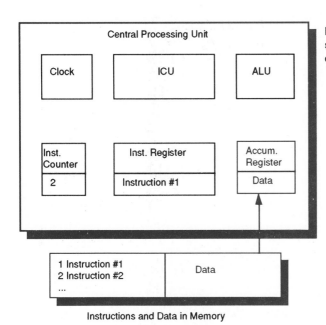

Fig. 1-7. Intermediate results are stored in the accumulator.

Instructions and Data in Memory

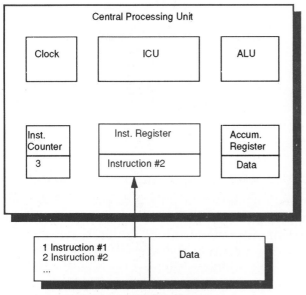

Fig. 1-8. The ICU fetches the next instruction to the instruction register.

Instructions and Data in Memory

repeated until all the instructions of the program stored in memory are executed or the program provides a terminating instruction.

Fig. 1-9. The ALU executes the instruction in the instruction register and adds data from memory to the accumulator.

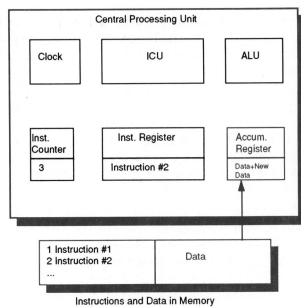

Instructions and Data in Memory

Fig.1-10. The instruction execution cycle.

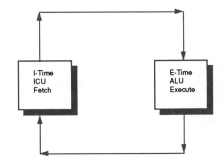

Notice that the clock is the device that "drives" the execution of instructions by providing electrical pulses at precise intervals that are used as event generating. The rate at which the clock produces the electrical pulses determines the processing speed of the computer. Faster generation of the clock pulses allows the computer to process instructions faster. The clock speed is measured in Hertz. A Hertz is the number of instructions that can be completed in one second. Since computer clocks normally process millions of instruction in one second, the speed of the clock needs to be expressed in millions of cycles per second or megahertz (Mhz). Therefore, a computer with a clock speed of 20 Mhz is faster than a computer with a clock speed of 15 Mhz.

However, comparing the processing speed of different machines based only on the clock speed could be very misleading. There are several other factors that affect the overall speed of the computer besides the clock speed. Some processors process 8 bits at a time, while others process 32 bits at a time. An 8-bit processor operating at 20 Mhz is not faster than another processor operating at 10 Mhz but processing 32 bits at a time. This is because the second processor can move more data per cycle than the first processor. Additionally, not all instructions are executed in the same amount of time. Some instructions may require several cycles in order to be executed.

When comparing machines using the clock speed as the only base of comparison, make sure that the other internal components of the two computers are basically the same. In this situation, clock speed is more accurately a good measure of the increased processing capabilities of one machine over the other. Additionally, the other components of the computer can play an important role in the overall response time (time transpired between entering a transaction and getting a response from the system) of the computer as we will see later in this chapter.

In the microcomputer field, the Intel and Motorola corporations dominate the design and sale of CPUs. On the Intel side, the most popular CPU chips produced are the 8088, 80286, 80386, 80486, and the P5 or 80586 as it is sometimes called. The 8088 is a chip with a 16-bit word size for the CPU, 8-bit bus, and a clock running at 4.77 Mhz. The 80286 ranges in clock speed from 6 Mhz to as high as 33Mhz, it has a CPU word size of 32 bits, and a 16-bit bus. The rest of the CPUs have 32-bit CPUs, clock speeds of 16 Mhz to over 50 Mhz, and bus sizes of 32 bits. Each new design improves the instruction set of the previous CPU and incorporates new techniques to improve the throughput of the machine.

On the Motorola side, the CPU design has gone through the same type of improvements that Intel CPUs have experienced. The first of these processors was the 68000. It was followed by the 68020, 68030, and the 68040. These processors also have different ranges of clock speeds and are comparable in processing power to that found in the Intel processors.

The Co-Processor

Although the power of CPUs has increased dramatically over the past few years, the complexity and the number of programs that a computer needs to perform have also increased. In order to make hardware more efficient in the use of existing resources, computer manufacturers often include a co-processor with their machines. The role of the co-processor is to take some of the processing away from the main processor and, with the aid of specially built circuitry, process those instructions more efficiently than could be done by the main CPU. One co-processor commonly found in personal computers is a mathematical co-processor. This device (when instructed by the software) can perform mathematical computations that are normally the responsibility of the main processor, faster and more accurately. However, a computer system doesn't take advantage of the co-processor just because one is installed in the system. Software needs to be written specifically to address the instruction set of the co-processor.

Main Memory

Main memory, also called primary storage, is composed of a large number of storage addresses and locations. Each of these locations has a unique address number and they all hold basically the same amount of information, a byte. A byte can be thought of as the amount of memory required to store a character. Each byte is composed of eight bits, a bit being the minimum amount of information that can be stored inside the computer. Bytes are grouped together to form a word. Some computers have 8-bit words (1 byte), while more powerful machines have 32-bit words (4 bytes) or 64-bit words. Words are used for storage instead of bytes, because a single byte is too small to store meaningful-size numbers. However, the total amount of memory that a computer has is measured in bytes. Typically a personal computer has between 640 kilobytes, Kb, and 1 megabyte, Mb. A kilobyte is 1,024 bytes. Therefore, if a computer has 640 Kb, then it actually has 655,360 bytes of total memory.

RAM

Memory is usually divided into random-access memory (RAM) and read-only memory (ROM). RAM is used by programs to store instructions and data during execution or run time. These instructions tell the microcomputer what to do whenever a specific application is running. Data typed into the computer is also stored in RAM for further processing by the CPU. Instructions in RAM can be accessed very quickly. The contents of RAM can be changed by the user and the application programs any time. However, when the power supply to the computer is turned off, all the instructions stored in RAM are lost unless previously saved to some secondary storage device.

ROM

ROM contains instructions that tell the computer what to do during the startup or booting process. Booting is the process the computer goes through when it is first turned on. During this time the hardware goes through self-checks and uses a minimum set of instructions to begin communicating with the user. The instructions to perform all of these operations are stored in ROM. The contents of ROM are established at the factory, and the application and system software use the instructions stored in it. These instructions cannot be altered; hence the name "read only." However, some newer computers come with special erasable ROM chips whose contents can be changed with the use of special software provided by the computer or ROM manufacturer. This proves to be an easy and efficient manner to upgrade computer ROM instructions and maintain a state-of-the-art system.

Supporting Circuitry

Computer Bus

As stated before, data and instructions flow between the components of the computer in response to processor commands. For this to take place, all the elements that need to communicate with each other must be physically linked. The physical link is called the bus. The bus is a set of parallel wires that are capable of carrying multiple bits at a time.

Some of the bus lines transmit power to other devices. Other lines carry data, instructions, or addresses. Some computers have a single bus that is used for multiple purposes. Other computers have multiple buses for instructions, data, or addresses.

However, regardless of the number or specialty of the buses inside a computer, the job of the bus lines is the same regardless of the computer system. They connect or link the internal hardware devices of the computer.

Expansion Bays and Cards

Most computer systems contain expansion ports or bays that are simply open connectors that are linked directly to the computer bus. These expansion bays accept expansion cards (see Fig. 1-11) that have been manufactured explicitly for the computer system. These cards are designed to enhance the functionality of the computer by providing additional hardware for input/ output, video, memory expansion, connectivity to other computers, co-processor additions, and other uses. The number of expansion bays differs from machine to machine, and the number of connectors in the expansion cards also differs according to the type of bus that they are designed to interface with.

Fig. 1-11. Cards, also called firmware, are added to computers to enhance their capabilities. This is an Ethernet card from an IBM computer.

Installing an expansion card into a computer system requires opening the protecting case, locating an empty expansion bay, and placing the expansion card into the open bay or slot. Some cards can work after this relatively simple procedure. Other cards require hardware switches to be set on the computer itself, the card, or both. Additionally, some cards require the installation of software that helps the computer manage the resources provided by the expansion card.

The I/O Ports

The input/output (I/O) ports are connectors normally found at the back of most computers. Although different types of I/O ports perform the same function (input and output), they are labeled according to how they perform their functions. Some of the most common types of I/O ports found are serial port, parallel port, and SCSI port. The serial port is used for serial communications between computers or between a computer and a peripheral such as a printer. The parallel port is the most common manner to attach a printer to a microcomputer. The SCSI (small computer system interface) port is a device made popular by the Macintosh computer. It is used to connect the computer to other peripherals such as CD-ROM players and hard disks.

Sometimes users call one of the ports the interface. For example, a user may refer to a serial port as the serial interface. This is an error. The port itself doesn't constitute an interface. Because the electronic signals used to control communication between the computer and the keyboard, the computer and printers, and the computer and other peripherals, are different, each peripheral has its own interface. One side of the interface communicates with the computer through the port. The other side of the interface depends on the device that it is attached to and translates the instruction from the computer into the native language of the device. If a computer needs to talk to a printer using a parallel port, both the computer and the printer need to have a parallel port and an interface for the communication to be successful. The job of the interface is translation between the device that it is attached to and external devices that may be attached to its port. The I/O ports are explained in more detail later in this book.

Input Devices

Input devices are used to accept data from external sources such as users. The input received is converted by the input device's interface into signals that the CPU can understand.

The most popular input devices are:

1. The Keyboard
2. The Mouse
3. Touch Screen
4. Voice Entry
5. Scanner

The Keyboard

All computers have some type of keyboard. Advanced or extended keyboards contain function keys that indicate functions to be performed on entered data. Also, some function keys act as interrupt keys. Additionally, most keyboards contain numeric key pads, and they control keys used to transmit sequences that can be acted on by a program. Specialized keyboards contain foreign language characters and job specific characters (see Fig. 1-12).

Fig. 1-12. This keyboard for an IBM PS/2 personal computer has a numeric keypad at the right side. Twelve program function keys are at the top. (Courtesy of IBM Corporation)

Light Pen

This device is used to select options from menus appearing on the screen. When the pen is aimed at the video display screen, the light image can be read by the computer and the coordinates of the point are determined by the system. The coordinate system is translated into a selection displayed on the screen.

Mouse, Joy Stick, and Trackball

The mouse is a small input device that fits in the palm of the hand (see Fig. 1-13). The mouse allows the user to control the screen cursor by moving the mouse on a table surface. On top of the mouse are one or more buttons. When the screen cursor is on a selection, a mouse button is pressed. This triggers an event that indicates to the computer that a user made a selection. Based on the screen coordinates of the object selected, the application program running in the computer takes a specific action. The action is normally associated with some software option.

The joy stick moves the cursor by moving the stick in a specific direction. A trackball is similar to the mouse except that the cursor is moved by rotating a ball mounted in a fixed holder. The cursor moves in the direction of rotation of the ball.

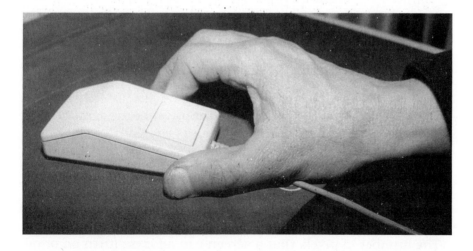

Fig. 1-13. This mouse can be moved around on the desktop to control the location of the cursor on the screen of a monitor. The buttons are used to send signals to the computer. (Courtesy of H. G. Haigney)

Voice Entry

Data can be entered into the system by using a microphone. Special voice-recognition software is required in the system.

Page Scanner

A page scanner can scan an image and translate it into a digital format. The image can be stored in one of many graphical formats for inclusion into a document. Additionally, the graphical image created by the scanner can be processed by character recognition software that translates the graphical character into text characters, producing a file that can be loaded into a spreadsheet or word processor.

Output Devices

Output devices allow the display of data and information on some media for viewing by the user. If the output takes the form of print on paper, then it is called a hard copy. If the output is on the monitor, it is called soft copy. The most common output devices are monitors and printers, although facsimile machines have become popular output devices for computers in recent years.

Monitors

Monitors are output devices that can use cathode ray tube (CRT) technology, also employed in the commercial TV industry. The image produced on these screens is sent from the computer to the CRT electronically. Inside, the CRT has an electron beam that strikes a phosphorus-coated screen on the monitor. When the coating is struck by the beam, light is emitted by the electrons in the phosphorus. The higher the intensity of the beam, the brighter the picture. It is the phosphorus-emitted light that produces images on the screen.

Computer monitor screens are normally divided into addressable dots that can be illuminated. Each addressable dot is called a pixel or picture element. As an electron beam inside the CRT scans each pixel, its intensity can be varied to turn the pixel on or off.

The number of pixels that a screen can address (turn on or off) determines the resolution of the monitor. More pixels on the screen will produce a higher resolution. In the IBM PC family of personal computers, there are several standard monitors that can be used for displaying output. The quality of the output depends not only on the type of monitor being used, but also on the graphics display adapter that drives it. Fig. 1-14 shows a picture of a basic VGA monitor. The different types of display modes found in the IBM PC family of computers are: monochrome adaptor or MDA, color graphics adaptor or CGA, enhanced graphics adaptor or EGA, video graphics array or VGA, super video graphics array or SVGA, extended graphics array or

Fig. 1-14. A VGA monitor.

XGA, and a new nonstandard graphics array, sometimes called professional graphics array or PGA. The quality of the image increases down the list from MDA to PGA.

Printers

Printers can be grouped into two major categories:

1. Impact Printers
2. Nonimpact Printers

Impact printers (see Fig. 1-15) produce an image on paper by driving a series of pins against a ribbon (dot matrix printers), by hitting fully formed characters that are stored on a platter against a ribbon (daisy wheel printers), or by hitting fully formed characters that are stored on a belt against a ribbon (line printers).

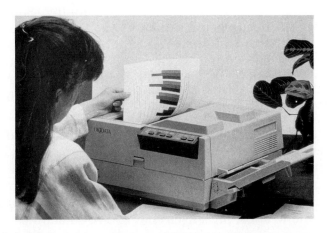

Fig. 1-15. A desktop laser printer. (Courtesy of Okidata, an Oki America company)

The pins on a dot matrix printer are normally arranged in the shape of a rectangle, typically from nine to twenty-four pins high and from one to five pins wide. More pins mean better quality of the letter produced on paper. Dot matrix printers operate at a variety of speeds, from fifty characters per second to more than one thousand characters per second. They can produce text and graphical output and print in a bidirectional mode. That is, they can print from left to right and from right to left.

Nonimpact printers use technologies such as thermal printing and laser technology. Thermal printers, like dot matrix, have a print head consisting of wires. They get hot and leave an imprint on heat-sensitive paper. Laser printers are top-of-the-line devices, having excellent print quality, speed, and quietness of operation. They use technology similar to that of a photocopier. The output produced by a laser printer is composed of consistently dense characters and graphics, suitable for business output and presentations.

Other Output Devices. The Facsimile Terminal (FAX)

A facsimile terminal (see Fig. 1-16) is able to transmit an exact picture of a hard-copy document over telephone lines and satellite circuits anywhere in the world.

FAX machines are divided into four major groups according to their technology and speed. Groups 1 and 2 are older analog machines, whereas groups 3 and 4 are digital technology machines. Most newer FAX machines are groups 3 or 4. Group 3 machines can transmit a page in approximately one minute or less. Group 4 machines can transmit an 8 1/2 by 11-inch page in approximately 20 seconds. Additionally, group 4 FAX machines have a higher image transmission quality. Some newer models of FAX machines use "plain paper" to produce a hard copy of a digital transmission. This type of machine, also known as a laser FAX, can double as a scanner for the computer or as a plain paper copier. Its circuitry is based on laser printer engines, and it can serve as a multipurpose machine on a network.

Signals from a digital facsimile device can be read into a computer and stored because they are made up of bits. This has led to the development of FAX boards that can be added to microcomputers. With these boards, any document created on a personal computer can be transmitted to any FAX machine through phone lines. Messages sent by FAX machines can also be received by the FAX boards inside microcomputers, and a picture of the document can be stored on a disk or sent to an attached printer.

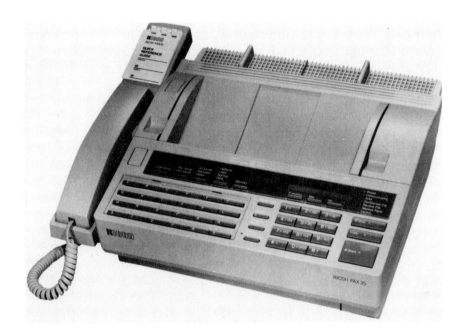

Fig. 1-16. This FAX35 facsimile machine can transmit a page of data in 15 secs. It contains a 30-page memory for sequential broadcasting and a 124-station autodialer. (Courtesy of Ricoh Corporation

Storage Devices

Since the information stored in RAM can be lost if the computer is turned off or if a power failure takes place, computer systems require the use of a secondary or permanent storage system. By placing data and programs into secondary storage, they can be loaded back into RAM at a later time for more viewing or modification. The two major types of storage devices for micro-computers are the floppy disk (diskette) and the hard disk.

Floppy Disks
The floppy disk, also called diskette, floppy, or simply disk, is one of the principal storage devices for the microcomputer. It is available in different sizes, with 5 1/4 inches and 3 1/2 inches

in diameter being the most common. A floppy disk consists of plastic (Mylar plastic), coated with an oxide material. This material is similar to the coating used in cassette technology. The Mylar plastic disk is enclosed in a protective jacket that consists of paper or plastic. The jacket has an opening to expose a portion of the disk surface so that the disk drive can read and write information from and to the disk. Floppy disks can store between 360 Kb and 2.8 Mb of information. On most personal computers the floppy disk drive is labeled drive A or drive B.

Hard Disks

A hard disk, or fixed disk as it is called, stores data on platters which are permanently mounted inside the computer and cannot be removed. On hard disks, the read/write mechanism, all moving parts, and the metal disks which store the information are enclosed in a sealed metal case. This avoids contamination of the storage surface by dust or any other foreign particle. The hard disk can store from 20 Mb to several hundred megabytes of information. In addition to the larger storage capacity over the floppy disk, the hard disk has data access times that are much faster than those found in floppy disks, making the hard disk faster by several orders of magnitude. Fig. 1-17 shows a hard disk that is typically found on microcomputers.

Fig. 1-17. The case has been removed from this fixed disk to show the hard disk and a read/write head. (Courtesy of Seagate)

Other Secondary Media

The least expensive of all secondary media is the cassette. This is the same cassette used for recording music. In this case, a special tape recorder connected to the computer receives the data from the system and stores it in the cassette. They are inexpensive and compact, but their slow speed and linear storage format make them impractical for situations where quick access to data is necessary. Cassette systems are used mainly for backing up data and storing the cassette in a safe place.

Magnetic tape is similar to cassette tape in terms of the technology. The tape is accessed through fast drives, with data transfer rates similar to disks. They have high data capacity but can store data only in a linear manner. This makes their practicality for everyday use limited.

Compact disk technology came of age in the late 80s and early 90s. Sometimes referred to as CD-ROM, (see Fig. 1-18), it can hold large amounts of information, and it can store audio and video data in a digitized format. It is the preferred method of delivering software products that require large storage such as encyclopedias, clip-art libraries, and other reference material.

Fig. 1-18. Compact disk player and storage media.

Laser video disks use similar technology to that found in CD-ROM systems. The advantage of laser video disk is that it can store approximately 30 minutes of full motion video per side.

This makes it the preferred method of storage for creating and delivering multimedia presentations that require full motion video that needs to be accessed randomly.

Software Resources

Software consists of the instructions that tell the computer what to do. As stated before, computer software can be divided into two major areas:

1. System Software
2. Application Software

System software programs contain instructions that control the function of the computer and the communication between the computer components and the users. Within the system software we can find the operating system, utility programs, and computer languages used to create application software.

Application software consists of programs that were developed to solve specific problems. Some examples of application software are word processors, spreadsheets, databases, and telecommunication programs.

The Operating System and System Applications

The operating system is a set of programs that controls the hardware of the computer. A program is a series of instructions that indicates the computer process that must take place. The operating system allows the user to communicate with the hardware without the need to understand the inner workings of the machine. Without the operating system, the user would have to learn machine language, which consists of zeros and ones. Computing would never have reached the masses without the aid of the operating system. There are many popular operating systems in the market, among them MS-DOS and UNIX for machines based on Intel microprocessors (IBM PS/2 and compatibles), Multifinder for the Macintosh, UNIX for many minicomputers, VMS for minicomputers made by Digital Computer Corporation, VM for IBM mainframe, and others.

Operating systems, as mentioned before, are composed of many different programs. It would be inefficient and a waste of resources to load the entire operating system into memory at once. This would leave little or no room for application programs, and in some cases it would be impossible to do so. Therefore, the operating system is normally divided into its memory resident portion and system programs.

The memory resident portion is a series of instructions that are loaded into RAM and reside there until the system, the user, or the application that is currently running requests the services of the instructions. In the microcomputer area, COMMAND.COM is an example of this type of program. The microcomputer requires that this file be in memory when the user wants to communicate with the hardware. The command COPY is another example of a memory resident operating system utility.

The rest of the programs that make up the operating system reside on the hard disk and are loaded into memory only when their services are requested. In this fashion, they act like any other application program and must share resources with any other programs that are resident in memory. One example of this type of system program is FORMAT.COM. This program formats new disks so they can be used on IBM PCs and compatible microcomputers.

Additionally, third party vendors provide utilities and other system programs that enhance the computer operating system. Some of these programs, also called system programs, perform such tasks as defragmenting a hard disk that has empty spaces. This process makes the disk more efficient in locating files and programs. Other system programs manage programs that need to reside in RAM concurrently. This type of program ensures that one program doesn't corrupt the instructions or data of any other programs that reside in RAM simultaneously. Other programs check for viruses, manage memory, provide file transfer to other systems, and so forth.

Although the line delineating application and system programs is in many occasions indistinguishable, the above programs and similar ones generally fall into the category of system applications if they are designed to enhance the operating system of the computer.

Programming Environments

An altenative to buying a program in order to solve a problem is to write one. The type of language will determine to some extent the type of solution that is being sought. The programing environment available today can be classified into low level languages and high level languages. Low level languages include all programming languages that use one mnemonic (memory-aiding) instruction for every machine-level instruction. One such language is assembly language. When using assembly language to create a program, the programmer uses an instruction like AR (for add registers) instead of the equivalent binary operating code of 00110101. The operands use labels such as A and B, instead of the binary numbers that represent the address of data. This simplifies the task of creating code for the computer.

Once the main program in assembly language (source code) is created, an assembler program is used to convert the source code into an object module (see Fig. 1-19). The object module is a machine code version of the source program. This object module can be loaded into memory and executed.

Fig. 1-19. Conversion process from source code to object module.

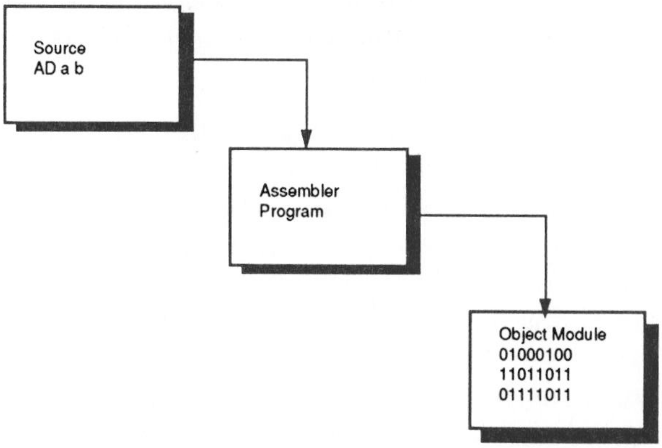

Source
AD a b

Assembler
Program

Object Module
01000100
11011011
01111011

Because an assembler language programmer must write one mnemonic for each instruction that needs to be executed, assembly programs are machine specific, making transporting them to a different system difficult at best.

In order to have programs in a format that is more machine independent and therefore increases the programmer's efficiency, high level languages were developed. These are called compiler languages and many have been around for many years. Some of the most popular are FORTRAN, BASIC, Pascal, and COBOL. Using one of these languages, the programmer writes source code, obeying the language syntax. The source code is compiled (converted into an object module) and then executed. If the same program needs to be used in a different machine, then the same source code with or without modifications can be recompiled for the next machine provided that a compiler for the same language exists. This allows the programmer to write one program and execute it on many different computers.

Using high level programming languages, programmers can create object modules that can be placed in an object-module library. Since object modules are in machine language, there is no major difference between one that is produced by a FORTRAN program and one produced with an assembler. Some modules can be loaded into memory and executed directly; others have references to subroutines that are not part of the object module. Programmers can use these modules from within their programs to perform the tasks that the object module was designed for. When the programmer completes the source code for the new program and compiles it, the new object module can be linked, using a link editor, with the object module stored in the library and combined into a larger program. The linkage editor creates a complete load module that can be placed into memory and executed. This process is depicted in Fig. 1-20.

Fig. 1-20. The complete process for creating a load module.

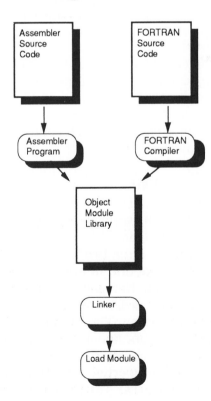

In this manner, the programmer can be isolated from some of the more mundane tasks of programming, such as communicating with the hard disk or printer, and concentrate on solving the problem at hand. Whenever the program needs access to the mentioned peripherals, the program makes a call to the code that exists in the object module in the library and passes control to it. After the library module completes the request, control is passed back to the main module and the program continues its execution.

Some programming languages look like high level languages yet they retain the speed of low level languages. A language that is considered by many to fall into this category is the C language. In shows all the flexibility of a high level programming language, yet it is easier to interface it with assembly language routines than most other high level languages.

Another type of programming language environment is a new breed of languages that are becoming more popular all the time. These are what are called object oriented and visual programming languages. These types of languages depart from the linear programming methodologies of the past and concentrate on new techniques that free the programmer from having to write new routines every time a function needs to be performed or a problem solved. Using this type of programming environment, "objects" already created to solve a previous problem are reused in their present format or their "properties" are the original objects. In this manner, the programmer can create a solution to a problem in a fraction of the time required with conventional or traditional languages.

In addition, some object oriented languages allow the programmer to "paint the screen" with the objects that are going to participate in the program. The term "painting the screen" means that the programmer places the objects on the screen by using a mouse and clicking on icons that represent the object desired. The objects already have many properties built in that allow the object to respond to messages sent to them by other objects in the program. Each object is given some code through a scripting language in order to make it perform some action in addition to the actions that it normally takes based on the self-contained properties of the object. The programmer modifies existing properties, creates derivatives of the original objects, provides short new properties, and then compiles the program. The result is an executable program that solves the problem in addition to having an elegant user interface. Two of these types of programs are Visual-Basic for IBM PCs and compatibles and Hypercard for the Macintosh.

There is a drawback to this type of programming environment. Programs created in these environments normally consume more system resources than those created by traditional programming languages. However, with the increased power of processors and their relatively low cost, the additional resources required are easily justified when compared with the savings in time and effort that these environments provide.

Each of the above programming environments has supporting utilities that make it a self-contained environment. They all have editors, debuggers, linkers, libraries, and compilers.

Application Software

Hardware is useless by itself. It requires instructions to tell it what to do. The instructions are stored in programs. If a program is created to solve a specific problem, then it is normally called an application program or application software. Although there are many types of application programs, the most commonly used are:

1. Word Processing
2. Spreadsheet
3. Graphics
4. Database
5. Telecommunications

Word processing is used to type memos, letters, and other documents. The user enters words by typing on a keyboard and the computer stores them in memory. The user can then change any of the text, change margins, add boldfacing, add underlining, and provide other enhancements to the document. Finally, the letter or document can be stored on a disk or printed on a printer.

The spreadsheet is used by people who work with numbers, such as accountants or statisticians. Numbers, formulas, and text can be entered into the spreadsheet, and questions such as "what if" can be asked of the program. The results are displayed on the computer monitor or on a printer.

Graphic programs allow users to see graphical representations of series of numeric values. The graphs can be produced by using data created by a spreadsheet or database. The ability to see numerical values in a graphical representation allows managers to have a better understanding of the information required to make better business decisions.

Databases allow users to enter, retrieve, sort, and update data organized in a manner that is efficient. With these types of programs a manager can produce quick reports from large amounts of data stored on a computer. Also, some database programs allow many types of inquiries to be performed, and the information can be accessed and displayed in many different formats.

As mentioned before, there are many other application programs on the market. Games used for entertainment fall into this category. Also, products such as flight simulators are considered application programs. But for most businesses, the majority of their needs are solved by programs that fall into one of the categories described above, or that employ a combination of several of the categories such as an accounting program.

Data

Programs stored in a computer at some point in time need to manipulate data. This data is stored on hard disk, floppy disk, or some other hardware device as patterns of bits in the same way as the programs that manipulate it. However, storing data on a hardware device is not good enough to ensure normal and efficient computer operations. Computer systems tend to have many disks and tapes, each containing thousands or, in most cases, millions of bytes representing the data for dozens of applications. A computer system must be able to store, locate, and retrieve the data required by a specific program. This is what is called system data management.

It seems that data and the instructions on a program should be accessed in the same manner. However, in most cases, all the instructions required for a program are loaded into memory. But, the data required by a program is loaded in a selective manner by the running application. That is, only certain data elements are required at any given moment. Therefore, the system needs to locate the data and it also needs to differentiate the individual data elements that make up the data.

A data element is an individual meaningful unit of data. Sometimes the element is called a field. A program may need one
specific field such as salary, temperature, or social security
number to perform an operation in order to solve a problem.
Most systems are capable of addressing an individual field by
accessing it as a binary digit, decimal number, real number,
character, or string of characters.

Data Structures

In order for the computer to retrieve data from storage, it has to
know the location. Computer programmers employ several data
structures to help with this requirement.

The simplest of all data structures employed is the list. A list
contains elements in a predetermined order. Fig. 1-21 shows an
example of a list. In the list, elements can be located by the
numbers on the top that are separated by commas. For example,
the element located in the second column, third row, can be
located by using the address 3,2. Programming languages
support the list structure through arrays. Once a list is completed it can be written to disk and later read back to process the
information.

1,1	1,2	1,3
34	54	37
2,1	2,2	2,3
21	43	33
3,1	3,2	3,3
12	21	11

Fig. 1-21. A list with data.

However, if there is a need to process only a few elements from
a very large list, then using this data structure becomes inefficient. To begin with, even though only a few elements are
desired, the entire list must be in memory. Then, the programmer will need to separate the elements of the list.

A better structure to handle this case is another type of data
structure, the file (see Fig. 1-22). In a file, all data is composed
of bits, the bits are grouped to form bytes, the bytes are grouped
to form fields, the fields are grouped to form records, and the

Fig. 1-22. A file containing data.

Field 1	Field 2	Field 3
Data 1	Data 1	Data 1
Data 2	Data 2	Data 2
Data 3	Data 3	Data 3

records are grouped to form files. The file is then processed record by record. The programmer creates a program that reads one record, separates the record into its individual fields, and processes the data in the fields. When the record is no longer needed, the next record is read. Since only one record is stored in memory at one time, there is no waste of memory resources. And since files can be large, then the size of the data structure is not limited by the amount of memory, rather by the amount of secondary storage, which is normally much larger than the amount of memory in the system.

How is the data located in a file by the system? The techniques used vary according to the application and the training of the programmer. However, they all share a commonality, that is the relative record number. Remember that a disk is divided into tracks and sectors much the same way an old fashioned LP record has tracks. It is possible to create a list that contains the relative position of each record with respect to the first record. And for each record we can record not only the relative position of the record, but also the track and the sector number where each record resides. For example, assume that we have 10 records that belong to a particular file. Assuming that each record occupies a sector, we can create an index like the one shown in Fig. 1-23 that lists the relative record number of each record and also lists the track and sector in which this record can be found. In this manner, the third record in the file is located on track 12, sector 3.

The storing system could get rather complex if we want to store multiple records in one sector or if the records have variable length. However, algorithms can be created to handle these cases also. The algorithms available allow the retrieval and

Relative Record Number	Location on Disk
0	12 1
1	12 2
2	12 3
3	12 4
4	12 5
5	12 6
6	12 7
7	12 8

Fig. 1-23. This list shows the location on disk of records indexed by relative record number.

storage of data sequentially or in random order. Normally a key is used to organize the records in the file. This key is associated with the relative record number and in turn the relative record number is associated with track and sector positions on the disk.

It is important to note that some computer designers don't rely on the relative record number for accessing data in a file. Several operating systems don't use the record structure. Instead, data on the disk is treated as simple strings of bytes. In this case, programmers address data by relative byte number.

Traditionally, especially in the mainframe area, different applications often require access to the same data. Because of this, some data elements are stored in multiple places creating a redundancy problem. In addition, the logic of programs created to access the data can be too closely linked to the data. Then if the data needs to be modified, the programs will have to go through extensive modification also. What is clearly needed is a mechanism that centralizes data logically and provides for a high degree of data independence. The application that provides this benefit is the database. By using a database, all programs that need to access the data must go through the database management system (DBMS) itself. This insulates programs and programmers from the physical structure of the data, reducing redundancy and creating a highly independent mechanism for accessing data stored in files.

Linking the Components

Data is stored inside the computer as patterns of bits. These patterns are the same throughout the machine. If a character is represented by the group of bits 01001011, then this pattern represents that given character throughout the machine. Using this bit group to represent other characters is not allowed. This rule applies only to the machine itself and not to the peripherals or any I/O unit.

Keyboards generate characters every time a key is pressed. Printers, as outlined before, represent characters as patterns of dots or print positions on a print wheel. Each peripheral device represents or interprets data in its own manner. In order for these dissimilar devices to communicate with each other and the computer, some type of translation is necessary. The device that performs the translation is the interface board.

It is the interface board that takes signals from the peripheral device and translates them in a format that is understandable by the computer that will be the host (see Fig. 1-24). In addition, each interface board is device dependent. Consider the keyboard, for example. The electronic signals generated by the keyboard when a key is pressed are very different from the signals generated by the printer when a print job is taking place. Each device must have its own unique interface board that performs the translations for communication to occur. There must be a translation when input is taking place and another when output is being generated. However, since the device dependent functions are assigned to interface boards, both (the circuitry for the input and output functions) can be attached to the same computer. Typical interfaces for printers come in the form of a serial and a parallel or Centronics interface.

Fig. 1-24. Interface board connecting computer components.

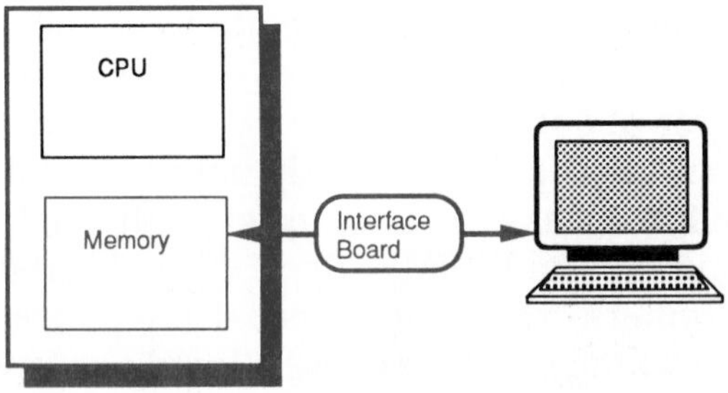

CPU

Memory

Interface Board

Secondary storage devices also have to be linked to the system through interfaces. The interface used for disk drives or other secondary storage actually controls the device. It is responsible for accepting the commands required to seek, read, and write to the disk. It manages the mechanism that controls the read/write head and also manages the flow and timing of the information in and out of the disk drive. Multiple devices can be attached and controlled by the same board. Therefore, at any given time, only one disk drive can be active.

Some interfaces contain buffers to speed up the processing of information in and out of the peripheral. A buffer is a portion of memory that is dedicated to hold data that flows to and from the peripheral to which is assigned. The memory can be allocated from the computer's main memory or it can be in the form of microchips specially built into the interface or computer system itself. When using a buffer, the computer sends information to the buffer and reads information from the buffer. Since the buffer is made up of computer memory, it is much faster than the mechanical devices (such as a disk drive) that it is assigned to. This speeds up the overall processing of data.

Assigning an interface to each peripheral attached to the computer is a practical manner of communication in the microcomputer world. However, in the minicomputer and mainframe arena, a single computer may have hundreds of peripherals attached to it. If an interface were assigned to each device, the cost of the system might be prohibitive. Therefore, mainframes and most large minicomputers perform input and output through channels and control units.

Certain functions that are common to most peripherals are assigned to data channels (see Fig. 1-25). These channels perform device independent functions. The device dependent functions such as moving a disk mechanism are performed by I/O control units. Each physical device has its own control unit. The channel communicates with the computer, and the I/O

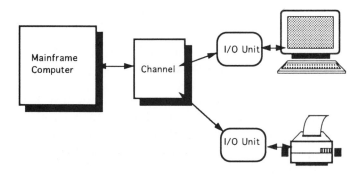

Fig. 1-25. Channels are used by a mainframe computer to communicate with peripherals.

control unit communicates with the device. Both of them together, the channel and the I/O control unit, perform the translation.

Regardless of the system, it is the bus with its bus lines that is responsible for carrying the data from the interfaces and I/O ports to the memory and the CPU for storage and execution. The number of lines that make up the bus determine the amount of data that can be transferred to and from the individual components that make up the entire system.

Bus sizes come in 8 bits, 16 bits, and 32 bits. Larger bus sizes provide faster throughput of the data and shorter overall response time. The bus size, the clock speed, and the size of the word in the CPU provide a closer measure of the overall processing power of the computer than the clock speed alone.

For example, a computer with a CPU word size of 32 bits, a 20 Mhz clock and a 16-bit bus will be slower than the same machine with a bus size of 32 bits. The percentage of power increase depends on the type and quality of information that needs to be processed.

All of the components of the machine, including the bus, CPU, interface units that reside on the computer, memory circuitry, ROM chips, expansion bays, and others, reside on a rectangular plastic board. This board, called the motherboard, in most cases houses the entire logical and calculating circuitry that makes up the computer system. In many cases, especially in the case of microcomputers, when a component of the system fails, it is cheaper to replace the entire motherboard than to try to locate and fix the problem. The motherboard houses the "real" computer. The rest of the devices found inside the computer housing are the power supply, speaker, and storage devices.

Looking Ahead

This text doesn't concentrate on the abstract theoretical concepts that many books on this subject tend to concentrate on. Nor does it claim to cover all of the topics that relate to data communications and telecommunications. It assumes that you have some basic knowledge of computers, perhaps in the form of a computer literacy course, and presents the most commonly encountered elements and concepts in the field of data communications. It also tries to provide such material from the perspective of the microcomputer field, although the roles of mainframes and minicomputers are discussed when appropriate.

However, before the main topics of data communications are discussed, you must understand not only the hardware environment that you will be working with, but also the software environment and how it affects data communication. That is the function of the next chapter. It will discuss the basic functions of the operating system and provide some concepts of the most popular operating system in the field. Additionally, it discusses graphical user interfaces and their influence in the field of data communications. Although it is tempting to skip the next chapter and dive into the main topics of the book, it is recommended that you read the next chapter thoroughly. You may find a few things that you didn't expect. In addition, you will be able to better relate future concepts to your current working environment.

Summary

The basic computer system is a collection of components that work concurrently to achieve a goal. It can be thought of as a black box that has the capacity to accept input, manipulate the input, perform mathematical and logical operations, and print and store the results of these operations.

The system can be divided into software and hardware subsystems. The hardware consists of the physical parts that make up the computer. Some of these parts are the keyboard, the metal box that protects the electronic circuits, the electronic circuits themselves, the monitor, and other electronic devices. In more general terms, the hardware can be categorized by the function that each component performs into:

1. Central Processing Unit. This component consists of the ALU, ICU, registers, and counters to keep track of which instruction needs to be executed next. The computer clock is used to keep precise timing so all the components can work in unison in order to have a successful computer operation.

2. Main Memory. It consists of RAM and it is where data and instructions are stored before they are processed by the CPU.

3. Supporting Circuitry. Consists of the bus, interfaces, and other electronic devices that support the processor in its duties.

4. Input Device. Consists of any device that provides the main computer with input data to be stored in main memory. Some of these devices are the keyboard, mouse, light pen, voice entry devices, and scanners.

5. Output Device. Consists of electronic equipment that is used to produce some type of output. The most commonly used output devices are the monitor and printer.

6. Secondary Storage Device. This device is used to store information from RAM in a more permanent form. Examples of these devices are the hard disk, floppy disk, tape systems, and CD-ROM players.

The software consists of the instructions that tell the computer what to do. Software can be categorized according to the purposes for which it was created and is used. The major categories are:

1. System Software. System software programs contain instructions that control the function of the computer and the communication between the computer components and the users. Within the system software we have the operating system, utility programs, and computer languages used to create application software.

2. Application Software. Application software consists of programs that were developed to solve specific problems. Some examples of application software are word processors, spreadsheets, databases, and telecommunication programs.

All of the software mentioned above at some point in time needs to manipulate data. This data is stored on hard disk, floppy disk, or some other hardware device as patterns of bits. There are many data structures that the programmer can take advantage of to facilitate the computational process. Two of these structures are the list and the file. However, to facilitate changes in the format of data regardless of the program used to access it, a database should be employed.

All of the devices mentioned above are controlled by the system and application software. However, since each device has its own language and way of communicating, interfaces are used in microcomputers to link the I/O devices to the computer bus and the rest of the computer components. Mainframes use similar devices but they take advantage of channels and I/O control units to streamline the I/O process.

Questions

1. Briefly discuss the function of the operating system.
2. What are the components of the CPU?
3. Why are interfaces used?
4. What devices are responsible for the translation process in mainframes?
5. What are system programs?
6. What is the role of the computer bus?
7. How can we obtain a good estimate of the processing speed of a computer?
8. Describe a machine cycle.
9. What is the purpose of expansion bays?
10. Why is data independence important in system design?

Projects

1. Locate a computer and, with permission of your instructor, open the protective shell and find and sketch the basic hardware components found on the motherboard. Draw and label blocks that represent the CPU, co-processor, memory, ROM, interface units, expansion bays and connecting bus, I/O ports, and secondary storage devices. Use a paint or CAD package for your sketch if possible. Otherwise use a

template to create symbols. Additionally, mention in your diagram any other peripheral devices that may be attached to the system.

2. Visit your school's student computer laboratory or data center and find out what type of hardware and computers are available at this center. Try to answer the questions below and type your report using a word processor. If your report requires the use of diagrams use a graphics package to draw your sketches and incorporate them into the final report.

    a. What types of mainframes or minicomputers are present?
    b. What type of personal computers are available?
    c. What size bus, CPU word size, processor type, and clock speed do the computers possess?
    d. Are the computers networked? If so, what type of network is being used?
    e. What type of expansion boards are used in the microcomputers?
    f. What type of operating system is being employed?
    g. What type of third party system software is being used? What is the purpose of the software?
    h. What type of application software is being used?

3. If possible, obtain a copy of software used to measure processing speed of microcomputers or devise your own. Set up several types of microcomputers with different options in them and test the system under the following conditions.

    a. Loading a large word processor file.
    b. Recalculating a large spreadsheet.
    c. Writing a file to the hard disk.
    d. Sorting at least 100 records in a database.

Collect the statistical data produced, and present a report that describes the process undertaken, the steps you performed, and the configurations tested. Then provide the result in numerical and graphical formats, comparing the different machines.

Operating System Concepts

Objectives

After completing this chapter you will:

1. Understand the purpose of the operating system and its relation to the hardware that it supports.
2. Have a basic understanding of the MS-DOS operating environment.
3. Have a basic understanding of the UNIX operating environment.
4. Have a basic understanding of the Macintosh operating environment.
5. Understand the purpose of graphical user interfaces.
6. Understand how Microsoft Windows implements the GUI concept in the MS-DOS world.

45

Key Words

Booting	Booting Sector
Bootstrap	CPU
Directory	File System
Finder	Format
GUI	Input/Output Control Unit
Mouse	MS-DOS
Operating System	Paths
RAM	ROM
UNIX	Windows

Introduction

The first chapter introduced the basic hardware that serves as the foundation to establish data communications between computers. Before we embark on understanding the different aspects of the communication process, it is important to have an understanding of the software environment that runs the computer. This is important since many of the operating environments in the personal computer and minicomputer world such as Microsoft Windows NT, OS/2, and others, have embedded networking and communication capabilities that are the starting point for more sophisticated networking schemas. Although data communications between computers will require additional hardware devices, protocols, and other elements, it all starts with the computer and the operating system that governs the computer. This chapter briefly describes the basic purposes of the operating system and provides examples of three commonly used operating environments in the personal computer and minicomputer world.

The operating system serves as the interface between the computer hardware and the user along with application software. It shields the user and programmers from having to deal with the computer at the machine-language level in order to have effective communication. In addition, the operating system manages all the resources of the computer such as disk space and memory allocation. Basically, we can subdivide operating systems into single-user and multiuser operating systems. The next section describes the basic functions of the operating system application. It includes a brief view of the most popular operating systems in the microcomputer and minicomputer world, including the graphical shells that serve some of them.

Basic Functions of the Operating System

Software Interface

Since many of the makers of networking products and network operating systems have merged or created close ties with the creators of traditional operating systems, the individual computer operating system contains many of the networking components required to achieve a complete solution. This trend continues as computer corporations realign themselves in the market in order to be more competitive. For example, Novell now owns the traditional operating system maker Digital Research, Microsoft creates Windows for Workgroups and Windows NT, and IBM produces OS/2 with its own networking capabilities.

Because of such close integration between the computer operating system and the network, it is important to understand the computer operating environment before trying to study networking itself. Although the material in this chapter is covered in greater depth in other courses of the CIS/CS curriculum, many students study networking without knowing the workstation operating system and its operating environment. The material that follows tries to remedy this situation, and even for the knowledgeable student it serves as an overview of topics that must be understood before networking concepts are explored.

The Command Processor

As stated before, one of the operating system functions is to serve as an interface between the user and the computer system. The part of the operating system that is responsible for this process is the command processor. Recall that the operating system of a computer is not a single computer program. It is composed of many different system applications. Some of the programs need to be memory resident at all times, and some reside on secondary storage until they are needed. This last set of programs sometimes includes system utilities.

One of the programs that needs to reside in memory is the command processor. The command processor intercepts commands that the user inputs and translates them into a format that the computer can understand (see Fig. 2-1). Additionally, the command processor translates responses from the computer into a format that the user can understand.

Fig. 2-1. The Command Processor.

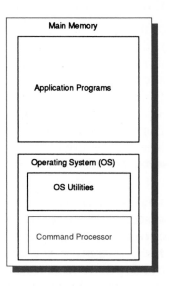

The command processor interfaces with the users through the use of a command language. The programmer or user types commands directly into the computer or application in a syntax that is established by the command language. The syntax is in the form of commands such as LOAD, COPY, DELETE, and FORMAT. The commands are intercepted by the command processor as they are typed from the keyboard or as the application is running. It then sends a request to the operating system. If the command processor receives a command that it cannot understand, it notifies the user of the error.

Obviously, the command processor is a complex and, in many cases, a large program. Because of this, it is composed of routines that are individually responsible for performing a particular task or process that is requested by the user. For example, one of the subroutines is in charge of interpreting commands typed by the user. Other subroutines are in charge of executing programs, and others respond to commands like LOAD (see Fig. 2-2).

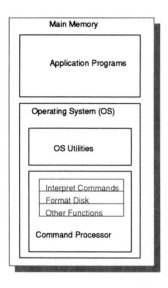

Fig. 2-2. Commands being executed by the Command Processor.

Let's go through an example of copying a file from one location on the disk to another to see how the operating system handles such tasks. Assume that we have a generic computer that responds to the COPY command as the instruction that tells the system that a file needs to be copied from one location to another. Fig. 2-3 shows the logical state of the system as the user types the command COPY FILEA FILEB. In this case FILEA is the name of the original file and FILEB is the name of the new copy of the file. At this point the command processor receives the command from the user and control is transferred to the subroutine in charge of interpreting and translating the user's command.

After checking the syntax of the command, it identifies the function to be performed, and control is passed to the subroutine that is responsible for the function (Fig. 2-4). The function of copying an image of a file to a different location of the disk is performed and control is returned to the user as the command processor waits for the next instruction. This type of process is what is called command driven. Operating systems such as MS-DOS and UNIX fall into this category.

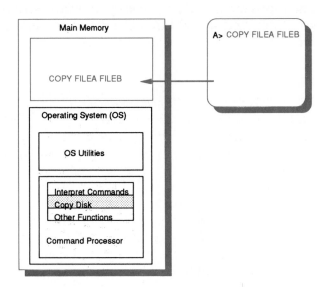

Fig. 2-3. Logical state of the system as the user
types the command COPY FILEA FILEB.

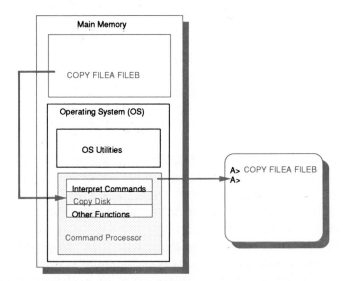

Fig. 2-4. Commands being processed by the
Command Processor.

In some situations, parts of the command processor are offloaded from memory while other processing takes place. When
this process ends, the entire command processor needs to be

loaded back into memory. That is why, in many situations, the message "Can't find COMMAND.COM" or something similar takes place when using microcomputers.

Utilities

In command driven operating systems, facilities or utilities are usually provided to help the user with repetitive tasks that need to be performed often. One of these facilities is batch files. Batch files are composed of commands that would be typed directly into the system and interpreted by the command processor. They resemble small programming languages that are executed in a sequential or linear format. For example, assume that on a daily basis a check of inventory needs to be performed and then a backup copy of the main file needs to be created. The commands required to perform these tasks could be typed directly into the system or placed into a batch file named DAILY.BAT as follows

LOAD INVNT

RUN INVNT

COPY INVNT.DAT INVNTBCK.DAT

Now that the batch file exists, the commands in it can be executed by typing the name of the batch file from the command line as

DAILY

and letting the command processor translate each command and perform the appropriate action.

Another type of utility is called the shell. A shell is a software routine that surrounds the basic core of the operating system in order to provide an easier interface to the user and to exploit the functionality of the operating system (see Fig. 2-5). The shell is another layer of insulation between the user and the hardware of the computer. Many shells are graphical in nature. That is, they use icons and menus to represent different system functions that can be performed. The user is relieved from remembering the syntax expected by the command processor and relies instead on visual cues in order to perform the same functions that were previously requested from the keyboard. Microsoft Windows is an example of such a shell. This type of shell or graphical user interface (GUI), as it is sometimes called, is discussed at the end of this chapter.

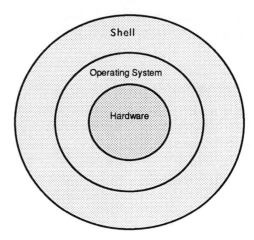

Fig. 2-5. The Operating System Shell.

Hardware Interface

Operating systems were born out of the need to control the input and output process. Placing data into an output device is a complex and difficult task. For example, if a file needs to be saved on a hard disk, the system first has to initiate a seek to find an empty track, locate the track, and then begin to write data to the track. If the track and sectors that make up the track get full, a new track with empty sectors needs to be located to store the rest of the file. Of course, the system needs to manage the location of all the tracks and sectors used to store the file. This could be a burden for a programmer if he or she were to perform each of these operations manually. And, in the case of multiuser systems, making sure that someone else's data is not destroyed in the process is not an easy task.

This is where a modern operating system's input/output control system, or IOCS, comes into the picture. The input/output control system is the part of the operating system responsible for communicating with peripheral devices (see Fig. 2-6). Recall that each peripheral has its own set of internal commands, and the logic used by these devices differs from that used by the computer itself. Another problem arises in the fact that programmers don't want to be concerned about the physical access requirements of peripherals or their internal logic. Instead,

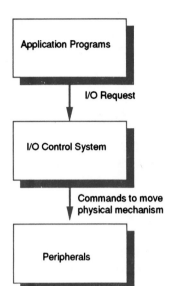

Fig. 2-6. The input/output control system.

I/O Request

Commands to move
physical mechanism

programmers want to issue logical commands such as READ and expect the system to perform all the translation, physical, and logical movements required to locate and read the data.

Also, different devices have unique physical and logical structures. For example, assume that a computer program needs to communicate with a disk drive. The program may need to process data stored on the disk using a specific byte arrangement. However, the disk may have been formatted and arranged to accept data using a set number of bytes per sector. If the program saves its data using less bytes than the specific arrangement per sector that the disk has, space is wasted. Storing 100 bytes into a 512-byte sector wastes 412 bytes. The solution is to create blocks of data where multiple records are stored in a single block. Then the system could be instructed to read a block of data and the software would be responsible for differentiating among the records.

The job of the IOCS, on input, is to accept logical commands from the system and perform whatever operations are required to provide the application or user with the proper data or information. On output, the IOCS combines several small records or divides large records so they can fit into the arrangement of the storage device efficiently. It places the data on the disk and provides information to keep track of where the data is located. This is done regardless of the differences in access logic that the program or application uses.

Resource Management

The function of the operating system is managing not only input and output but all the other resources that are required for the successful use of the computer system. After data is saved to secondary storage, its location and size must be recorded if we are to locate it for future use. The file system is the part of the operating system that is responsible for such tasks. The file system helps users to keep track of data and programs stored on the disk.

Each file has a starting location and any other tracks and sectors that it may occupy. These addresses are located on the disk directory (see Fig. 2-7). If a command is issued to load a

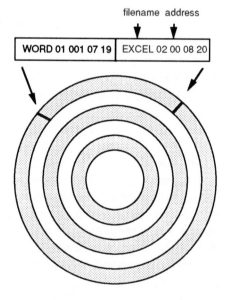

Fig. 2-7. Address locations on the disk.

particular file, the system looks in the disk directory for the starting address of the file, and locates it for the user. The entire process is demonstrated in the following example.

Assume that a user has a program called Works stored on the hard disk and wants to execute it. At the command line the user types

LOAD WORKS

The command processor interprets the command and indicates to the system that it is a program located on the disk that needs to be placed in memory. The file system is alerted that it needs to locate the program. The disk directory is then loaded into memory and it is searched for the name of the requested file. Once the name is located, the starting track and sector are identified. At this point, the information is relayed to the input/output control system. The IOCS generates the physical and logical commands to copy the program instructions from its location on the disk into main memory. Now the program is resident in memory, control is returned to the user, and the command processor waits for the next command. The next command is

RUN WORKS

After translating this command, the command processor passes control to the run routines of the operating system, which in turn execute the program.

When data is written to the disk, the file system records its name and disk location in the disk directory. Therefore, the file system is also responsible for allocating space on the disk. When a program is deleted, its entry is removed from the subdirectory and the tracks and sectors that it occupied are made available to the system. The data that made up the file still exists on the disk, but its reference in the disk directory has been erased. Therefore, with the proper software a file that has been erased could be recovered by placing another entry in the disk directory that maps to the file locations on the disk. However, if a file is erased, and more files are saved to the disk, the chance of recovery is small. This is because when the entry for the file is erased and new data saved to the disk, the system can put new data on top of the old data. This will destroy the original contents of the file.

Memory Management

Recall that the operating system is a collection of programs, some of which must reside in memory. Therefore, the operating system must compete with application software for memory space. Fig. 2-8 shows a screen that describes how memory is partitioned on an IBM PC using MS-DOS. The bytes occupying the lower parts of memory are set aside to hold control information for the operating system. The input/output control system occupies the next locations in memory, and next is the area occupied by the command processor. The rest of memory is the application area and it is here that programs and data reside.

```
C:\HJ2>mem

Memory Type          Total =   Used  +  Free
-----------          -----     ----     ----
Conventional          640K      50K     590K
Upper                 155K     122K      33K
Adapter RAM/ROM       304K     304K       0K
Extended (XMS)       7013K    2269K    4744K
-----------          -----     ----     ----
Total memory         8192K    2826K    5366K

Total under 1 MB      795K     173K     622K

Largest executable program size       589K   (603520 bytes)
Largest free upper memory block        33K    (33440 bytes)
MS-DOS is resident in the high memory area.

C:\HJ2>
```

Fig. 2-8. Memory allocation of an IBM PC compatible.

When the computer is dedicated to a single user and a single application, managing the memory resources is a relatively simple task. But what happens when there are many users and a limited amount of memory? What happens if several applications need to be loaded in memory at the same time and there isn't enough memory to hold all the applications at once?

The answer is the use of virtual memory, memory overlays, and swapping. Virtual memory allows the system to use available disk space as an extension of memory. Assume that we have a multiuser system and only 1Mb of RAM is available to users. The system can use the hard disk to hold data and instructions that normally reside in memory while they are not being used. In this manner, only instructions and data that are being executed reside in memory, making it available to more users. When the system gets to a location in the program where additional information is needed, the contents of memory are sent to the disk and swapped for the information that the program needs to continue running.

Memory overlays work in a very similar manner. Suppose that a user is given only 128Kb to work with, but he or she needs to run a program that occupies 256Kb. The solution is to break the program into modules. Then only the modules that are required to satisfy the user needs, at a particular point in time, are loaded into memory. When the application reaches a location where an instruction from a module that is not in memory is required, the module in RAM is swapped with the one on the disk that contains the required instructions (see Fig. 2-9). These processes allow computers to run programs that are much bigger than the memory allocation of the system. However, these gains come at the expense of speed. Since the disk is a mechanical device, it takes much longer to save and retrieve information than it takes the CPU to process the information.

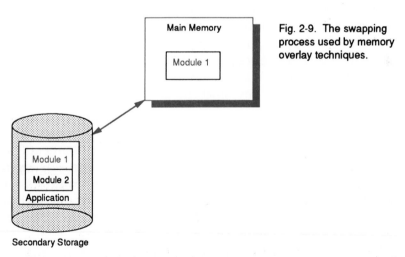

Fig. 2-9. The swapping process used by memory overlay techniques.

All of the processes described above must be managed carefully to execute the program properly and to avoid affecting other users of the system. The operating system is responsible for managing all programs in memory and resolving any conflicts that may arise when multiple applications need to share the same memory space.

Linking the Components

The communication between main memory and the CPU is controlled by the computer's clock. Each electrical pulse of the clock is an event-generating process during which memory addresses are used to read and write from and to RAM. The common path of communication is the bus. Peripherals, on the other hand, have their own processors and work independently from the basic computer processor. How does the system know that it needs to send information to a peripheral or how do peripherals tell the system that it needs to return information while an application is running? The answer is the use of interrupts.

An interrupt is an electronic signal that is sent to the processor. When the system detects an interrupt, it saves the information of the current process and transfers control to a program in the device that sent the interrupt. After the device completes its process the previous process is reactivated and execution continues from where it left off.

Users can send interrupts simply by pressing certain keys on the keyboard. Some combinations of keys, such as pressing the control and break key at the same time, send an interrupt to the hardware which in most cases tells the system to stop executing the current process. Other commonly used interrupts are the escape key, the print key, and the pause key.

Software can also generate interrupts. Most operating systems support programs that can send interrupt requests to the system to perform a specific function. However, using software interrupts requires good knowledge of the operating system receiving the interrupt, otherwise unpredictable results can take place. Interrupts are used to check the system for hardware options, detect component malfunctions, software errors, and other processes.

Booting

When the computer is turned on, it performs self-check functions, and the operating system is loaded into memory, making the computer ready to use. Application programs are then loaded and started by users typing a command or selecting an option from a menu. How is this process taking place?

In computer terms, booting the system refers to starting the computer. The operating system resides on a disk when the computer is not on. When power is turned on, the CPU executes instructions in a special read-only memory chip (ROM), called the bootstrap ROM. Unlike RAM chips, the bootstrap ROM does not lose its contents when the power is turned off. The bootstrap ROM contains instructions for checking the system and to enable the CPU to access the main part of the operating system located on the disk. Here, there is a special program called the boot (see Fig. 2-10). The boot is stored in the first few sectors of a disk called the boot sectors. These sectors are read automatically and their contents loaded into memory. After this is loaded, the rest of the operating system can be loaded into memory and its components executed by the CPU. Then it is said that the operating system is booted. If a computer is turned on, it is called a cold boot or cold start. If the computer was reset by pressing a combination of keys or through software, it is called a warm boot or warm start.

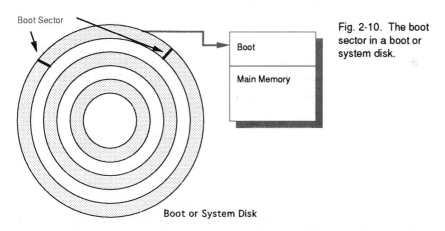

Fig. 2-10. The boot sector in a boot or system disk.

The rest of this chapter provides an introduction to three of the most commonly found operating systems for microcomputers and minicomputers. It is meant to serve as a tutorial as well as a reference chapter. Although a comprehensive look at these operating systems would require a separate book on each, the next sections provide a general overview for the student who is not familiar with one of the systems. Instead of just reading the material, find a computer or a terminal that has access to each of these operating systems and try the commands that are described in each section.

The MS-DOS Environment

MS-DOS, or PC-DOS as it is sometimes called, is the dominant operating system used in IBM PCs and compatibles. It is a collection of programs that act as a supervisor controller for all functions performed on these types of microcomputers. For all practical purposes PC-DOS and MS-DOS are functionally identical. PC-DOS is supplied with machines manufactured by IBM, and MS-DOS is used by the rest of the clone makers. For the rest of this book when we refer to MS-DOS we also imply PC-DOS.

Although later versions of MS-DOS contain a menu driven shell that can be accessed with a mouse, MS-DOS is still a command driven language. The general syntax of the MS-DOS command is as follows.

> D> COMMAND Parameters
>
> D refers to the default drive that the user is working with.
>
> > is the system prompt. It indicates that the command processor is ready to accept input.

COMMAND is where the actual command for the operating system will be placed. Here commands such as COPY and DIR are typed in. The command can be followed by one or more delimiters. Depending on the type of parameter that follows the command, the delimiters can be a space, comma, semicolon, equal sign, and the tab key.

Parameters are options that a command may have. These options are specific to the command being provided to the system. The entire command line can be typed in upper case or lower case.

We can divide the MS-DOS commands into resident and nonresident. Nonresident programs, also called transient, reside on the disk and are invoked and loaded into memory only when necessary. Some of the internal MS-DOS commands are COPY, DIR, and DEL. Some of the transient commands are DISKCOPY, FORMAT, and MODE.

There are three special files that handle the translation of user commands. These files are COMMAND.COM (the command processor), IBMBIO.COM, and IBMDOS.COM. COMMAND.COM serves as the primary interface between the computer and the user. All commands that the user types from the keyboard are translated by this program into a format that the computer can understand. The last two programs are sometimes called MS-DOS Hidden Files. They are called hidden because they are invisible to the user and cannot normally be modified by the user. They perform input and output tasks and convert input and output requests into a form that the computer can understand.

Starting MS-DOS

The process of turning the microcomputer on and loading the operating system from disk into main memory is what we already described as booting the system. This process varies from machine to machine, but the basic steps can be generalized as:

1. Placing a disk that contains the operating system into a floppy disk drive. Generally, the drive which is designated to accept the MS-DOS diskette is drive A. If the computer has a hard disk, then the floppy disk would not be used, and there should be no disk in drive A.

2. The microcomputer is turned on. Instructions are loaded first from ROM into main memory, then the rest of the operating system is loaded into main memory.

3. The instructions loaded from ROM, also called the boot instructions, transfer control of the microcomputer to the operating system. In most cases, at this point the computer instructs the user to enter the correct date and time.

4. Finally, the operating system prompt is displayed. This prompt is an indication to the user that the system is ready to accept commands from the keyboard (see Fig. 2-11). At this point, application software can be loaded into memory and executed.

Fig. 2-11. Starting
screen from an IBM
PC compatible.

```
Current date is Fri 5-16-1992
Enter new date (mm-dd-yy):
Current time is 17:42:36.34
Enter new time:


IBM DOS Version 5.0
        (c) Copyright International Business Machines
                Corp 1981, 1988, 1991
        (c) Copyright Microsoft Corp. 1983-1992

A>
```

The system prompt can be one of several letters, A>, B>, C>, D>, or E>. A and B are reserved for floppy drives and the rest are used for hard disks or RAM drives. A RAM drive is a portion of conventional memory that is set up to act as a hard disk. Using RAM drives can speed up the I/O process but uses main memory space. The system prompt is also a pointer to the drive that commands typed from the keyboard will reference (called the default drive). If the system prompt displays A> and the command DIR is given, followed by pressing the ENTER key, the directory of the disk in drive A will be displayed on the screen. To make the system "point" to another drive, name the drive in the command (e.g., DIR C:) or change the drive reference (e.g., C:, then ENTER) to make C the default drive.

Some applications require that a specific version of MS-DOS be present in order to run properly. If you are not sure which version is installed in your system, type the command

> VER

and press the ENTER key. This command uses no parameters and displays the version of operating system that you are currently using.

Formatting a Disk

After a data disk is purchased, it must be formatted once in order for the disk drive to use it as a secondary storage medium. Formatting is a function that MS-DOS performs on all new disks to subdivide the surface of the disk and number the segments for easy reference. In the same manner that a mail carrier needs to know the address of where to deliver mail, MS-DOS needs to know the addresses on the disk so it can put data in its proper place. The formatting process essentially writes a pattern of sectors on the disk surface, records a copy of the boot routine (if it is instructed to do so) on the first sectors, and prepares control information about the disk.

Once a diskette is formatted, a disk drive can write information on the disk and read information from the disk. However, the command used to format a disk can be dangerous. If you format a disk that was already formatted, then any data residing on the disk will be destroyed by the formatting operation. Make sure that there is no valuable data on the disk before the formatting operation is invoked. To format a disk the command is as follows:

> FORMAT   D: /option

where D: is the letter that identifies the drive where you want the formatting to take place. The /options can be any of the following

> /v: label. This option asks the user for a label for the volume to place on the disk.

> /q. Deletes the file allocation table and root directory of a previously formatted disk.

> /u. Specifies an unconditional format operation for a floppy or hard disk. Unconditional formatting erases previous data on the disk and prevents later "unformatting" of the disk.

> /f: size. This option specifies the size of the floppy disk to format. The possible sizes are 360, 720, 1.2, 1.44, and 2.8.

> /b. This option reserves space for system files.

> /s. This option copies operating system files to the new disk, making a bootable disk.

> /t: tracks. Specifies the number of tracks on the disk.

> /n: sectors. Specifies the number of sectors on the disk.

> /1. Formats a single side of a floppy drive.

> /4. Formats a 5.25-inch, 360K disk on a 1.2 Mb disk drive.

> /8. Formats a 5.25-inch disk with 8 sectors per track.

For example, to format a 720-Kb disk located in drive A and place a label on the disk, the command is

> FORMAT A: /f:720 /v

The File System

Every file saved on a disk must have a name which is used by the operating system to locate the data stored in the file. The file name is provided by the user before data is saved to the disk. Normally a program will prompt the user for a file name when the user chooses the save option from within an application.

The names of files in MS-DOS consist of two parts, the file and the extension. A file name can consist of letters and alphanumeric characters (e.g., numbers). It can be up to eight characters in length, should begin with a letter, and must not contain any spaces. The name is followed by a period and then a three character extension. The extension is sometimes provided by the software that saves the file. Some extensions provide a clue as to the type of file they represent. Some common types of extensions are:

1. COM and EXE. These extensions are used by executable and binary files. Files that have these extensions are normally programs that can be executed from the command prompt by typing their name and pressing the ENTER key.
2. BAT. These types of files are batch files. They contain MS-DOS commands and are executed by typing their name and pressing the ENTER key.
3. DAT. This extension is normally used with data files.

File names should be chosen to represent the type of data stored in them. If a word processing file is to store a resume, then RESUME.DOC is a better name than FILE1. Selecting appropriate names facilitates retrieving the files later because it is easier to identify their contents.

Directories

A disk groups files into directories. Each directory in turn can be subdivided into subdirectories. Directories are most important when a hard disk is involved. Managing the directories on the hard disk is a key function of the MS-DOS file system. When a file is written to disk, its name, disk address, creation date, size, and other information are recorded in the disk directory. When the data needs to be retrieved, the computer loads the directory into memory and searches for the name of the file. When the file is modified, the file system automatically updates the directory entry.

Every disk has at least one directory. When the disk is formatted, the system creates a root directory where all other files and directories will be stored. Subdirectories can be created from the root directory in order to better organize files. The directories and subdirectories form a structure called a directory tree. Subdirectories can be created within subdirectories if necessary (see Fig. 2-12).

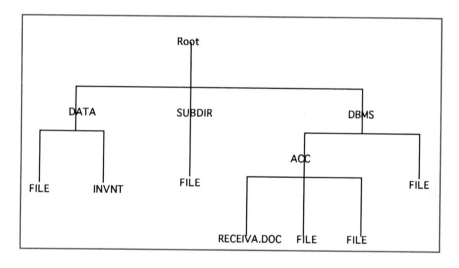

Fig. 2-12. Directory and subdirectory tree.

For all practical purposes, all directories except the root directory are subdirectories. However, in order to differentiate a directory within another directory, the latter is called the directory or parent directory and the first is called the subdirectory or child directory. The names of directories follow the same rules as those imposed on file names. The major difference comes in the extension given to the directory and in the name of the root directory. The name of the root directory is \. The rest of the directories can have any name that follows the convention already stated including an extension, except that it shouldn't be a COM, EXE, or BAT extension.

Paths

The path provides a pointer or directions to the location of a file within a directory structure or tree. The path is the search route that the operating system must follow, starting at the root directory, to locate files in another directory. For example, referring to Fig. 2-12, to get to files in the ACC directory, MS-DOS must go through the following directories \, DBMS, and ACC; therefore, the path that will produce the desired result is

\DBMS\ACC

The first back slash references the root directory. The second back slash separates the directory ACC from its parent directory, DBMS. To specify a file in the ACC directory, the path is

\DBMS\ACC\RECEIVA.DOC

It seems that it would be easier to have all files under a single directory. However, as the number of files increases, using subdirectories simplifies managing the file system in much the same way an office uses file cabinets and file folders to organize the office.

To view the contents of the working directory the command is

DIR

This command displays all the files in the directory that you are currently working with (see Fig. 2-13). If there are many files in the directory, then you may not be able to see all the file names before they scroll off the screen. A variation of the above command with the /P option provides a screen full of names and

Fig. 2-13. Result
of the execution of
the DIR command.

```
C>DIR

COMMAND   COM   05-10-92  5:55p
CONFIG    SYS   05-10-92  5:56p
AUTOEXEC  BAT   05-18-92  1:32p
MSWORKS   <DIR>  05-21-92  2:21p
WINDOWS   <DIR>  05-20-92  8:06a
     5 file(s)    58260 bytes
              44177408 bytes free

C>
```

then pauses until a key is pressed from the keyboard. Then a new screen is displayed. This process is repeated until all the files have been displayed. The command is

DIR/P

To see the contents of other directories in the current or any other disk drive the command is

DIR   D:NAME   /X

Where D: is the drive specifier, NAME is the name of the subdirectory that you want to explore, and /X is one of the options such as /W to display the contents of the directory in multiple columns or /P for page mode. For example, to see the directory contents of a disk in drive A, the command is

DIR   A:\   /P

To view all directories on a disk, make sure that you move the drive pointer to the location where the MS-DOS files are located. If the operating system files are in a subdirectory called DOS in drive C, then the command is

CD \DOS

where CD stands for change directory. If the operating system files are on a disk in drive A, and you are currently in drive C, then to change to drive A, type

A:

Once you are in the same directory as the operating system files, type the command

TREE

MS-DOS displays a directory tree showing all the directories that exist on the current disk. To see the tree structure, starting at the root directory, the command is

TREE \

And to see the file names in each directory of the tree, include the /f switch as in

TREE \   /f

Creating Directories

To create directories, the command MKDIR or MD is used. If the working directory is the root (\), to create a directory called INVNT, the command is

MKDIR INVNT

If the directory that you need to create resides inside another directory, then you could move the file pointer to the subdirectory with the CD command or use a longer form of the MKDIR command as in

MKDIR D:PATHNAME

where D: is a drive specification and PATHNAME is the path of the directory that will contain the new directory that you plan to create.

If you want to delete a directory, the command is RMDIR or RD followed by the path and name of the directory that is to be deleted as in

RMDIR D:PATHNAME\DIRNAME

For example, to remove a directory named INVNT stored in drive C under the subdirectory DATA, the command is

RMDIR C:\DATA\INVNT

This command will remove the subdirectory provided that there are not files within the INVNT subdirectory. If any files are in the subdirectory, they must be deleted before the directory can be removed.

Creating Files

Files in the MS-DOS environment are normally created by application programs and MS-DOS text editors. There is a command that can be used to copy text directly from the keyboard to a file. This is the COPY command. This process is normally used when the file to be created is relatively small. The command is

COPY CON D:PATH\NAME

where CON indicates that the data will come from the keyboard, D: is the drive designator, PATH is the path to the subdirectory where the file will be placed, and NAME is the name of the file to be created.

As an example, to create a file and place it in the root directory in drive C, the command is

COPY CON C:\TEST.DAT

At this point you can type any data that you desire. When all data is typed in, the CONTROL and Z keys are pressed simultaneously and the ENTER key is pressed. This closes the file, and the system places the file in the root directory.

Another format of the copy command allows users to copy files or groups of files from one location to another. The syntax of this more general command is

COPY   S:PATH\NAME   D:PATH\NAME

where S: indicates the source drive of the original drive, and D: is the destination drive where the copy will be placed. As an example, consider a file called BIRTHS.DAT in drive A that needs to be copied to the subdirectory PERSONS in drive C. The command to perform the process is

COPY   A:\BIRTHS.DAT   C:\PERSONS

One directory can be copied into another by using the COPY command and typing the path and name of each directory separated by spaces as in

COPY   A:\   C:\TEMP

The command above copies the contents of the root directory in drive A to the subdirectory named TEMP that is located in the root directory in drive C.

Groups of files can be copied with the use of wild cards. A wild card is represented by an asterisk (*) and allows the system to ignore any characters that the wild card is replacing. For example, the command

COPY   C:\TEMP*.DOC   A:\

instructs the system to copy all files in drive C, subdirectory TEMP, that have the extension DOC, to drive A. This will be performed regardless of the names of the files. Wild cards can be used in many different formats. For example,

COPY C:\TEST*.* A:\

instructs the system to copy all files from the root directory in drive C that begin with the letters TEST and ignore the rest of the name. This will copy files with names such as TEST1.DOC and TESTING.DAT to drive A.

There is a special wild card character, the question mark (?), that is used to represent any single character in a file name. For example, assume that you have three files named TEST1.DOC, TEST2.DOC, and TEST3.DOC. To copy all of these files as a group from drive C to drive A, the command is

COPY   C:\TEST?.DOC   A:\

To display the contents of any given file on the screen, you can use the command

COPY D:PATH\NAME CON

For example, to display the contents of the file TEST1.DOC on the screen the command is

COPY C:\TEST1.DOC CON

Another way of performing this task is to use the TYPE command. To perform the same function as above you could have typed

TYPE C:\TEST1.DOC

TYPE reads the file and displays it on the screen. Program files, those with EXE or COM extensions, are special files and their contents cannot be viewed on the screen with the TYPE or COPY commands. This type of file can be loaded into memory and executed by typing the name of the program file. For example, if a file exists on the hard disk called ACC.EXE representing an accounting program, the program can be executed by typing the name of the program ACC and pressing the ENTER key.

If you create a file and no longer want it, you can delete it with the DEL command. The command

DEL ACC.EXE

will delete the entry for the file ACC.EXE from the disk directory. The data is still on the disk, but the reference to it in the disk directory is deleted. Therefore, for all practical purposes the file is no longer available.

Redirection

Most MS-DOS I/O commands assume a standard input and output device. This standard input and output can be changed with the use of redirection characters. A redirection character changes the place that a command gets information from or sends information to. For example, the command DIR normally sends output to the screen. However, if we want to send the output to the printer, which in MS-DOS is known as PRN or LPT1, the output could be redirected with the use of the redirecting character > as in

DIR>PRN

To copy the contents of the disk directory to a file named DDATA in drive A, the command is

DIR>A:DDATA

If the program ACC.EXE needs input from the file RECV.DAT, then another redirecting character (<) can be used to send data to the ACC program as in

ACC<RECV.DAT

To add the output from a command to the end of a file without losing the contents of the file, the >> symbol is used. For example, the command

DIR>>DLIST.TXT

will append the directory listing to the end of the file DLIST.TXT without destroying whatever was in DLIST.TXT originally.

A filter command divides, rearranges, or extracts portions of the information referenced. For example, to find the contents "Pacific Ocean" in the text file OCEAN.DOC, we can use the FIND command as a filter as in

FIND "Pacific Ocean" < OCEAN.DOC

The following command saves the occurrences of "Pacific Ocean" in a file called NEWOCEAN.DOC.

FIND "Pacific Ocean" < OCEAN.DOC > NEWOCEAN.DOC

Another filter is the SORT command. It alphabetizes a text file or the output of a command. For example,

SORT < OCEAN.DOC

will sort the file and display the results on the screen.

A pipe causes a command's default output to be used as the default input to another command. The character for a pipe is a vertical bar (|). An example is the MORE command as in

DIR | MORE

The output produced by the command DIR is sent to the MORE filter instead of the screen. The MORE filter displays one screen at a time and then pauses until the user presses a key before displaying the next screen.

Batch Files

Although the majority of applications in the MS-DOS environment are interactive, there are occasions when a number of commands need to be repeated several times from the MS-DOS command line in order to perform some function. One way to complete the process at hand is to type the commands every time they are required. However, a better way is to place all of the needed commands in a batch file. A batch file has the extension BAT and it can be executed by typing the name of the file itself.

To create a batch file you can use the MS-DOS editor. If there are only a few commands, the following command will allow you to type the instructions directly from the keyboard. The command is

COPY CON FILENAME.BAT

Any commands that you type are placed in the file indicated in FILENAME. When you are finished creating the file, press the CONTROL and Z keys simultaneously. This will close the file and place it on the disk. To execute the file, type the name of the file and press the ENTER key.

There is a special batch file that the system executes every time the computer is booted. It is called the AUTOEXEC.BAT file. Any commands placed in this file will be automatically executed when the machine is turned on or when a warm boot takes place.

Additional Commands

There are many other commands that you may find useful if you need to use an MS-DOS-based system. We will not explore all these commands here; however, a quick scan of the reference manual may suffice in understanding their purpose. These commands are as follows:

DISKCOPY. Copies one disk to another of the same type.

RECOVER. Allows you to recover files that have been deleted.

PRINT. Helps in printing files to printers.

CHKDSK. Checks the disk for bad clusters and repairs them.

DATE. Displays the system date and allows you to change it.

TIME. Displays the system time and allows you to change it.

COMP. Compares two files and reports any differences.

ERASE (DEL). Allows you to delete files.

HELP. Provides help with the syntax of MS-DOS commands.

The UNIX Environment

UNIX was developed at Bell Laboratories in the 1970s by Ken Thompson and Dennis Ritchie. It has wide acceptance in the business and academic worlds. One of the most immediate differences between MS-DOS and UNIX is that the latter supports multiple users, while MS-DOS is a single-user system. Like other operating systems, UNIX is a collection of software programs. The UNIX kernel is the heart of the system. The kernel is where all the controlling activities take place. The rest of the software components of UNIX are programs that call on the kernel's services. When a program or user requests the services of the UNIX kernel, it takes the steps required to fulfill the requests. For example, if a program requests file services, the program gives the kernel a system call. The kernel supervises the access of the data on the hard disk where the files reside. The kernel extracts the data and delivers the data to a memory buffer area. The program picks up the data from the buffer and processes it.

To isolate the user from having to interact with the system at too low a level, UNIX has two standard shells that process user commands (see Fig 2-14). The shell lies between the user and the kernel. The shell is in essence the command interpreter. The two most commonly used shells are the Bourne and C shells. The Bourne shell was developed at Bell Laboratories and the C shell was developed at Berkeley.

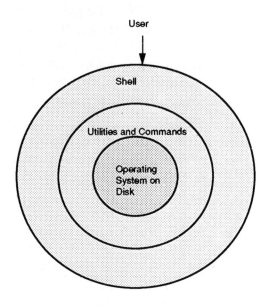

User

Fig. 2-14. The relationship between the operating system shell and the UNIX kernel.

Shell

Utilities and Commands

Operating System on Disk

A UNIX command has the following syntax,

$ command [-options] [parameters ...]

$ is the system prompt for the Bourne shell. The C shell's prompt is the % character.

The "command" is the actual syntax of the command that the user wants to execute.

The minus sign (-) separates the options from the parameters.

The options are one or more single letters that indicate a specific function that the command must perform.

The parameters are normally file names or paths.

The ellipsis (...) indicates a possible list of file names.

UNIX commands may seem cryptic at first, but a closer look reveals that each command is actually meaningful. For example, to see a listing of files in the working directory, the command is ls.

The Personal Computer and UNIX

Personal computers are considered entry-level UNIX systems. To run UNIX on a microcomputer, it should be a high performance machine based on a 32-bit CPU and bus. These types of computers, with the UNIX system installed, become functional multiuser systems supporting between 8 and 16 users.

There are several versions of the UNIX operating system for microcomputers. Among the most popular are XENIX and UNIX System V/386. However, many companies offer UNIX or a work-alike for microcomputers including IBM with its AIX offering. Apple's computer, the Macintosh, can also support UNIX. Apple's offering is called A/UX which boasts a graphical user interface.

In order to practice the commands described in the rest of this section, you will need access to a UNIX or work-alike system, an account in the system, and a password.

Logging On the System

UNIX users don't have to concern themselves with booting the system and setting basic system parameters. Such tasks are performed by a system administrator or super user. When a user sits in front of a terminal, the system should be running.

A UNIX session begins with the user typing a login id and, after the id is typed, pressing the ENTER key. The system will request a password. Type the password and press the ENTER key. The password and id are provided to you by the supervisor. If the id and password you typed are correct, the system will display a screen similar to that shown in Fig. 2-15.

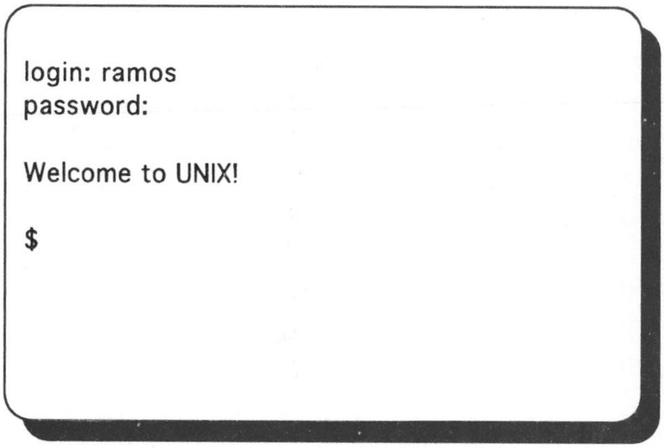

```
login: ramos
password:

Welcome to UNIX!

$
```

Fig. 2-15. Welcome screen of the UNIX operating system.

Once you are in the UNIX system, you can change your password by typing the following command at the system prompt.

passwd

Some systems mail an electronic message to new users to welcome them to the environment. If your system has such a function, you may see the message

You have mail.

after you login. To read the message you can type

mail -r

If you forget your id name or where you are in the system the command

who am i

will display your current login id. To see all users currently logged on the system, type

who

As mentioned before, there are two commonly used shells in UNIX, the C shell and the Bourne shell. If you are in the Bourne shell and want to use the C shell, type the command

csh

If you are in the C shell and want to use the Bourne shell, the command is

sh

To terminate a shell and return to the original shell that you used last, press the CONTROL and D keys simultaneously.

The File System

Names

UNIX , like most other operating systems, allows users to name, save, and retrieve files using names identified by the user. A file name can be up to 256 characters in length and must not begin with a dash (-). In addition, UNIX is case sensitive, therefore the system will distinguish between upper and lower case letters. Files can have extensions. All extensions begin with the first period that the system finds in the file name, and have a length of 14 characters including the period itself. The extensions are used by some of the applications running in the system. For example, the C compiler expects all of its source files to have the .c extension.

Files can also be made invisible. Invisible files in UNIX start with a period and they are not listed when the directory is displayed.

Directories

Like MS-DOS, UNIX has a hierarchical directory structure. There is a root directory which is indicated by the (/) character. Any directories growing off the root are called "children." Each "child" directory can become a "parent" directory and have "children" directories of its own. The process can be repeated as often as needed to create a structure to satisfy the user's needs. Fig. 2-16 shows how such structures look using a hierarchical tree graph. The root directory has several children, one of which is user. However, user is itself a parent of several other directories, which in turn are parents of more directories.

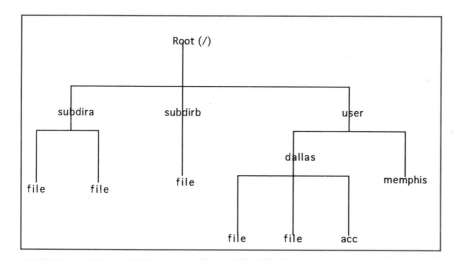

Fig. 2-16. Hierarchical tree graph.

Paths

In order to identify a file that may reside in a directory located deep inside the directory tree, paths are used. The structure of a path in UNIX is

/dir/dir/dir .../file

The first slash (/) is a reference to the root directory.

The dir letters would normally be the names of the subdirectories that are the "ancestors" of the directory where the file name resides.

The file is the name of the file that the user wants to use.

Using Fig. 2-16 as a reference, to access the acc program the path would be

/user/dallas/acc

When you login to UNIX, your working directory (the one where the system places you after login) becomes your home directory. If a file resides in your working directory, a path is not required. To make another directory the working directory, the command is

cd

For example, referring to Fig. 2-16, to make memphis the working directory and assuming that you are in the directory dallas, the command is

cd /user/memphis

To see which directory you are working on presently, type the command

pwd

and press the ENTER key. The system will display the path and name of the directory that is presently your working directory.

To list the files in the working directory, the command is

ls

To see all the files, including invisible files, type the above command along with the -a option. Fig. 2-17 shows what a listing may look like after typing the above command. You may notice that there are two files, one with a single period (.), and another with a double period (..). The single period stands for the working directory and the other stands for the parent directory. They are used for typing shorthand forms of the paths to the directories. The complete syntax of the ls command is

ls [-options] [directory ...]

The options and their meaning are:

a. All entries

d. Directories only

g. Group identification

l. Long form

r. Reverse alphabetical order

s. Show size

t. List files according to the time of modification

u. Show last time accessed

Try the ls command with the above options to see their effect on the output.

```
$ls -a
.       .user    .login    .mail    .profile
..      .acc     .logout
$
```

Fig. 2-17. Result of the ls command.

Creating Directories

To create a directory under the UNIX operating system, the command is

mkdir dirname

For example, to create the directories accts and persnl, the syntax is

mkdir accts persnl

In this fashion, multiple directories can be created at once. If the directory accts created above is no longer needed, the command to remove it is

rmdir accts

Creating Files

As in many other operating systems, most files are created by application programs. Word processors, spreadsheets, text editors, and databases are some of the programs that you will find working in the UNIX environment. UNIX provides a line editor (ed) and a full screen editor (vi) for this purpose. Although a comprehensive study of vi and ed is beyond the scope of this book, you will find in Appendix A a listing of the most commonly used commands of the vi editor, as well as a sample session on how to edit a file. Basically, to invoke vi and create or edit a file, the command is

> vi letters.doc

Please refer to Appendix A for further explanation.

Working with Files

To see the contents of a file, a program designed to read it could be used, or you can view its contents by typing the following command:

> cat filename

For example, to see the contents of a file name accts which was typed in vi, the command is

> cat accts

You should now see a screen displaying whatever you typed in vi when the file was created. If the file is too large to fit on a screen it may scroll too fast for you to see its contents accurately. In this case, UNIX provides a command to display the file one screen at a time. The command is

> more filename

where filename is the name of the file whose contents you want to examine. If a file is in a directory other than your working directory, you must use a pathname before the name of the file. Assume that your working directory is persnl and that you would like to display the contents of a file named accts that resides in the receiv subdirectory. The command to perform this is

> cat /receiv/accts

This will work provided that the receiv subdirectory is a child of the root directory. If the receiv subdirectory was a child of your working directory then the command would be

> cat receiv/accts

To copy files from one location on the disk to another, the command is

> cp sourcefile targetfile

where sourcefile is the name of the file that you want to duplicate. Targetfile is the name of the new file that is going to have the contents of the sourcefile. Of course, if one of the files was located in a different directory than your working directory, then the file name must be preceded by the path where the file is or will be located. Files can be renamed using the mv command, and rm removes links to files.

When you perform an operation that affects a file, you may be able to use wild cards. The wild card characters in UNIX are the question mark (?) and the asterisk (*). The question mark is used to represent any single character in the name of the file. The asterisk represents multiple characters. For example, to copy all files that begin with the characters acc from the working directory to a directory named backup, the command is

cp acc* /backup

Pipes, Filters, and Redirection

Your terminal is the standard input/output device for your UNIX activities. Any of the commands described above will send its output to your terminal screen. Most commands are not aware of their source of input, nor are they aware of their output's destination. If you want the output of any UNIX command to go to a different location than its default output device, you must use the redirecting characters. These characters are

<. It directs the source to a specified file or device.

>. It directs the destination to a specified file or device.

>>. It directs the destination to an existing file and appends new output to it.

|. This is the pipe character. It pipes standard output to another command or to a filter.

For example, to send the listing of the working directory to a file named dirlist the command is

ls>dirlist

If you now display your working directory, you will see the dirlist file in it.

A filter accepts input from the standard input device, modifies it, and places the results in the standard output device. The sort is an example of a filter. The sort utility reads records from a file or files and alphabetizes them. For example, if a file named accts needs to be sorted, then the command is

> sort accts

A pipe makes the standard output of one utility be used as the standard input for another utility. For example, in the command

> cat receiv | sort

the standard output is routed to sort, where the file contents are displayed in alphabetical order.

Shell Scripts

Many processes on a UNIX-based system need to be performed several times during the business day or week. In such instances, it is more efficient to execute all of these commands at one time. This task can be accomplished by placing all the needed commands in a batch or shell script.

A shell script file is analogous to a BAT file in the MS-DOS environment. The language used for creating the file is a sophisticated interpreted language that contains its own variables, expressions, decision, and repetitive structure. Creating such scripts is beyond the scope of this book, but if you will be a UNIX user, it is a feature that you should become familiar with.

Graphical User Interfaces (GUI)

Functions of a GUI

A graphical user interface is a collection of programs designed to provide user-friendly access to the computer and to computer applications. In contrast to the traditional command and menu driven environments, graphical user interfaces provide a graphics-based operating environment. This type of interface is considered to add flexibility and ease of use to the computer environment. The Apple Macintosh computer series has long been known for its graphics-oriented operating environment, X-Windows is a standard in the UNIX world, and Microsoft Windows has adopted a similar style. The trend is clearly moving in the direction of graphical user interfaces (called GUI) for all types of microcomputer usage. Along with ease of use, it bridges the gap between stand-alone programs by providing internal integration among applications. It provides the capability of integrating stand-alone applications such as word processors and spreadsheets.

GUIs for MS-DOS Systems

Microsoft Windows is the premiere GUI for IBM personal computers and compatibles. It allows the close integration of stand-alone applications such as Microsoft Word and Microsoft Excel, thus allowing you to use the integrated applications such as Microsoft Works or to integrate stand-alone applications such as Microsoft Word for Windows and Excel.

The Windows software includes program management, file management, and print management software, as well as a variety of accessory programs. The program management software facilitates running and integrating application programs such as Word for Windows and Excel. The file management software facilitates creating, deleting, and storing files. The print management software manages the printing of files. Accessory programs include such things as text editing, graphics, calculator, calendar, and cardfile management.

Windows includes other features that enhance the usability of the computer system. A particularly powerful feature is the ability to move data from one application to another through the clipboard storage facility. Other features include the ability to have multiple applications running simultaneously (multitasking), and the ability to have multiple applications viewed side by side or in foreground and background.

The Macintosh Environment

The Macintosh computer system uses a graphical oriented "desktop" that allows users to perform most functions by selecting items on the screen with a mouse. Regardless of which Macintosh computer is being used, starting the Macintosh is about the same. In most cases the system is booted automatically from the hard disk if it is specified as the startup disk. The startup disk is a special disk that contains the commands necessary for the computer to perform its functions. The startup disk contains the System Folder and the Finder. Both make up part of the Macintosh operating system and a discussion of them is beyond the scope of this book. If the computer does not have a hard disk (all new models of the Macintosh come with a hard disk), the startup disk will be one of the floppy disks that came with the machine. Due to the low cost of hard disks in the market, and since all new Macintosh systems have a hard disk, the rest of this book will assume that Works is stored on the hard disk and that the hard disk is the startup disk.

The Macintosh Desktop

Depending on the type of Macintosh available, the procedure to turn on the machine will vary slightly. On some models, there is a switch on the back of the machine, on others a special key on the upper part of the keyboard is the ON switch. In either case, when the computer is turned on, the first display that is available to the user is the Macintosh desktop. Fig. 2-18 shows a picture of the desktop. The content will be different from computer to computer depending on what is stored in the system, but generally the layout is the same.

The desktop contains a background area, which is the target area represented in Fig. 2-18. It contains a menu bar across the top, an icon for each disk on the system, and a trash can icon. It also contains a window displaying the contents of the system disk, that we will call the Opening System Disk window.

The Background

The patterned surface within the border in Fig. 2-19 is the background for all of the objects on the desktop. All items are placed on the desktop in the same manner as a person places papers, books, and artwork on top of a desk. The objects available on the desktop are icons, menu bars, windows, and dialog boxes.

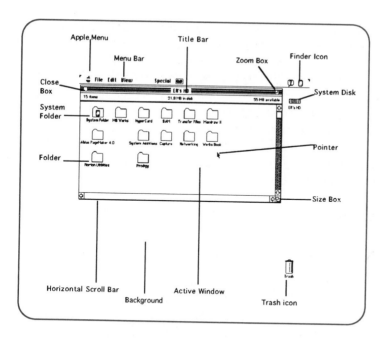

Fig. 2-18. The Macintosh desktop.

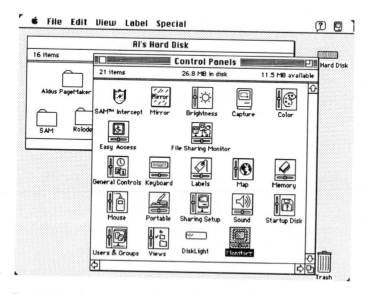

Fig. 2-19. Screen showing the background of the desktop.

The Mouse

The mouse is a major component of the Macintosh computer system. It is used to manage the windows and to select icons and menu items. The mouse is rolled on a flat surface. As the mouse moves, the mouse pointer moves on the screen in a corresponding direction. The pointer symbol is an arrow symbol when the system is booted. In most application programs, the pointer will appear as the arrow, but it will be displayed in other forms also, including a vertical bar, a cross, and a hand. There are six different mouse actions required to perform most functions on the Macintosh. These are point, click, press, drag, double click, and shift-click.

Point

To move the pointer to an icon, roll the mouse on the flat surface until the pointer on the screen is on the icon desired. The direction of movement of the mouse on the flat surface is imitated on the screen. The movement technique is used to point to windows, bars, menu items, and any symbol or identifier on the desktop.

Click

To click the pointer on an icon, the pointer must overlap the chosen icon. With the pointer over the chosen icon, press the mouse button and release it quickly. This selects the object. The object selected changes color to indicate that it is now active. To deselect an icon, move the pointer to another part of the desktop and click the mouse button. If you are pointing to something else, this will make it active. Pointing to a blank area in the active window and clicking the mouse button will leave no icons active.

Press

Pressing the mouse button means holding it down while an action takes place. Pressing is commonly done to select a menu item and then a submenu item. It can also be used to select an icon and move it to another area of the desktop.

Drag

Dragging means placing the mouse pointer over an object, pressing the mouse button, and holding the button down while the mouse is moved across a flat surface, thus moving the object across the desktop. The effect of dragging depends on the application running when the dragging takes place. If an icon is selected in the Finder window (the main window), and it is dragged, the effect is to move the icon across the desktop until the mouse button is released. Dragging the mouse inside a text document highlights the characters that it is dragged over. A window can be dragged by placing the pointer on the title bar, pressing the mouse button, and then dragging the window to its new location and releasing the mouse button.

Double Click
Double clicking means pressing and releasing the mouse button twice in rapid succession. Double clicking on an icon selects the icon and performs an action on the selected option. In the Finder, double clicking on a folder opens the folder. Double clicking on a program icon launches (executes) the program. Double click-ing on a file loads the program that the file belongs to and loads the file into memory.

Shift-Click
The last mouse technique is shift-clicking. This technique allows the selection of multiple elements. For example, to select three folders in Fig. 2-18, press the shift key and hold it down while moving the mouse pointer to overlay all of the icons and then release the mouse button. Once all the icons are selected, dragging one of them moves all of them at the same time.

The Icons

Types of Icons
An icon is a graphic representation of an option. Fig. 2-19 shows a disk icon, the trash can icon, the Opening System Disk window with several folder icons, and a folder window containing several program icons.

All disk icons will typically be displayed on the upper right side of the desktop. Any disks currently in use by the system will be displayed. Even though you may have only one floppy drive, there may be several floppy disks in use by the system at the same time, and there is typically one hard disk in use. Each disk is named to identify it. The icon for a hard disk is a small rectangular box, and the icon for a floppy disk is in the shape of a floppy disk jacket. The active disk will be shaded or colored differently. When the system is booted, the system disk will be the active disk. Generally, the system hard disk will be the only disk on the system when it is turned on unless the computer contains multiple hard disks.

The trash can icon is on the lower right side of the desktop and is always present, even though it may be hidden from view by a window. It is used to delete unwanted files from the disks. Any files to be deleted are first placed in the trash can icon. Then the trash is emptied by selecting an Empty Trash command from a menu.

Other icons generally reside in the windows and there are three types. Folder icons, seen in Fig. 2-19, look the same and indicate a folder containing other folders and/or files. Except for the system folder, which contains a symbol inside it, folder icons do not contain pictures.

The second type of icon, seen in Fig. 2-19, is a program icon. Although many program icons form a rectangle, each one is a different picture. And some, such as the SAM Intercept icon in Fig. 2-19, do not form a rectangle.

The third type of icon is a document. Document icons are typically characterized by a rectangular format with the upper right corner folded over (dog-eared), but may also take on a different shape. They commonly contain pictures depicting the type of document file.

How Icons Are Used

Document icons identify documents containing data. Documents can include text, database, spreadsheet, and communications, each of which is characterized by a separate document icon. These are used to store and process data.

Program icons represent programs that can be executed (launched) to perform a specific application. For example, the Sound program pictured in Fig. 2-19 provides the sound messages to you in response to incorrect actions. The user can modify the volume and message in the program, which will be launched by the other programs to send the message.

Folder icons are containers, holding documents, programs, and other folders. The Apple File Exchange folder shown in Fig. 2-20 contains programs, documents, and other folders. By creating a hierarchical structure of folders, the desktop can stay organized; programs and their corresponding files will be easier to manage.

A folder within a folder is said to have a child/parent relationship, with the outer folder being the parent and the folder in it the child.

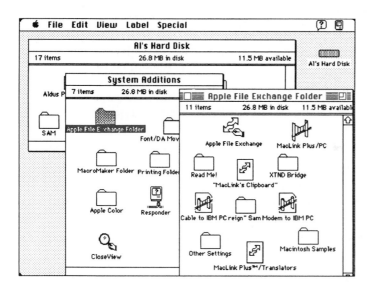

Fig. 2-20. The Apple File Exchange folder.

Menu Bar

At the top of the desktop is the menu bar. The menu bar contains options for pull-down menus with commands or selection items on them. The Apple menu on the left (picture of an apple) is always present, and it includes items pertaining to system control and operation. The Apple menu shown in Fig. 2-21 contains icons for programs written by Apple and other companies. These programs can be run from within any application running on the Macintosh. One of these programs, the Control Panel, is a special desktop accessory that allows the customizing of the Macintosh environment such as the color of the background, the type of sound the computer plays when an action takes place, and the type of monitor used.

The other menu items will vary, depending on operation status and the program running at the time. The options available on them will also vary, depending on system and program status.

Fig. 2-21. Icons in the Apple menu.

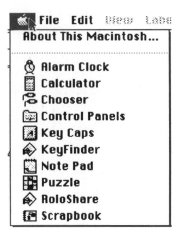

The menus contain commands that are used to create folders, empty the trash can icon, and many other commands used in operating the Macintosh.

To access any of these menus, move the mouse pointer to the menu and press and hold the mouse button, causing a pull-down menu to appear (see Fig. 2-22). In this menu, one of the choices, New Folder, is used to create new folders to place on the active window (the one currently in use).

Fig. 2-22. Pull-down menu with options to manage the desktop.

Windows

A window is a rectangular portion of the screen that displays some type of information. Programs use windows to display the results of calculations, queries, or any other action required of them. A window contains a work area, a title bar, a vertical scroll bar, a horizontal scroll bar, a close box, and a size box. It may also contain other characteristics that are associated with a particular function. For example, the window shown in Fig. 2-23 has a line under the title bar with specific information regarding the disk. Although many windows may be on the desktop, only one is active. It is characterized by shaded lines on the title bar.

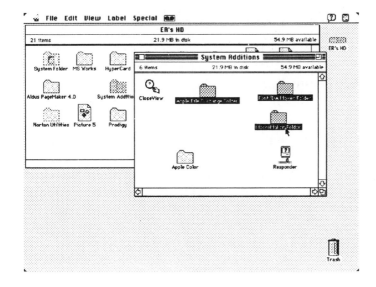

Fig. 2-23. Windows used in a GUI.

In Fig. 2-24 there are two windows displayed on the desktop. The active window is the one with the title Control Panels. Clicking the mouse on another window makes it active and the previously active window becomes inactive. The active window will always appear in the foreground (all of it showing), with other overlapping windows in the background (appearing to be behind it). The size and position of any window can be changed, and any one of them can be made the active window (the one that the user wants to work with) at any moment.

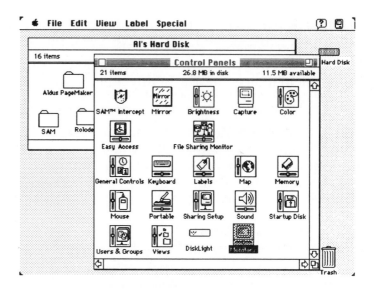

Fig. 2-24. Multiple windows displayed on the desktop.

Title Bar

The title bar is the bar across the top of the window. It contains the name of the disk, folder, data file, or program that the window represents. On the left end of the bar is a small box, called the close box. Selecting this box will close the window and remove it from the desktop. On the right end of the bar is a small box within a small box. This is called the zoom box. Selecting the box will zoom the window to the size of the desktop. Selecting the box again will return the window to its original size. The close box and zoom box are selected by moving the pointer to the box and clicking the mouse button. If the window is not active, the bar will be clear. If the window is active, the bar will have lines running through it, giving it a shaded effect. When the window is active, the bar can be used to move the position of the window on the desktop. This is done by placing the pointer on the bar, pressing the mouse button, and dragging the window to its new location, then releasing the mouse button.

Vertical Scroll Bar

The bar on the right side of the window is the vertical scroll bar. It contains an arrow at the top, pointing up. Clicking the mouse button with the pointer on the arrow will move the data down one line in the work area (move the window up one line). Pressing the mouse button with the pointer on the arrow will scroll the data down through the window (move the window up through the data). The bar contains an arrow on the lower end that points down. This arrow is used in the same way, causing the data to move up in the window (the window appears to move down). If there is only one page (window) of data, the bar will be clear. If there is more than one window, the bar will be shaded.

When the data is more than one page (window), a box will be displayed on the bar, indicating the relative position of the data in the window to all the data. For example, if there were five pages of data, and you were on the third page, the box would appear to be about three-fifths of the way down the scroll bar. You can use the box to scroll through the data by placing the pointer on the box, pressing the mouse button, and dragging the pointer in the desired direction. Releasing the mouse button terminates the scrolling process. You can also place the pointer ahead of the box, in either direction, and click the mouse button, causing the data to scroll a page (window) through the data in that direction. For data with multiple output pages (paper pages), such as a letter, the box will contain a number that indicates the actual output page number, given the current specifications.

Horizontal Scroll Bar

The horizontal scroll bar is the bar on the bottom of the window. It contains the same characteristics as the vertical scroll bar and works the same way. If the data is not wider than the window, it will be clear. If the data is wider, it will be shaded and will include the arrows and the box.

Size Box

The small box in the lower right corner of the window, linked to another small box, is called the size box. It is selected by placing the pointer on it and pressing the mouse button. Moving the pointer in any direction with the box selected will resize the window, making it wider, narrower, taller, or shorter. This box is used to help manage the display of multiple windows on the desktop by resizing them as appropriate.

Dialog Box

Dialog boxes are distinguished from windows in that they have no title bar or scroll bars. They are used by programs to communicate information to and from the user. A dialog box may contain as little as a message and a button to acknowledge receiving it, or it may have many boxes and buttons, along with messages to the user.

Three types of boxes are used in a dialog box. A text entry box is used to enter data into the program. A text entry box is rectangular in shape, with the length of the rectangle defining the visible entry size. A check box (in the shape of a square) is used as a toggle switch to turn an option on or off. If it has an X in it, selecting it will erase the X and turn the option off. If it is empty, selecting it will place an X in it and turn the option on. A list box contains a list of names. The list is used as a reference list or a selection list from which to choose the desired item.

There are two types of buttons used in dialog boxes. A rectangular or oval type button is used to select a command option from the dialog box. The second type, called a radio button, is a round button used to select alternative options. The round button represents a toggle switch and is clear if it is off and shaded with a dot if it is on. Sometimes turning on one radio button in a dialog box will cause another one to be turned off (in mutually exclusive options).

You will also see messages and icons in dialog boxes. The messages are used to describe status, define options, and identify boxes and buttons. The icons are used to provide options in picture form, rather than through boxes and buttons.

Managing Files and Folders

All documents created with application programs will have to be stored on a hard or floppy disk. Otherwise, when the power to the computer is turned off, all work will be lost.

From time to time, old files will be deleted from the disk or copied to other disks in order to have multiple backup documents in case an accident destroys the originals. All documents created are called files, and the processes required to create, store, delete, and copy them are called file management.

Before you use the computer, make sure that a floppy disk has been prepared to accept files. When the first letter of a document is typed or when you choose "Create New File" from a menu, the file is automatically created in main memory. As explained before, main memory is volatile (its contents are erased when the power to the computer is turned off). For this reason, the file stored in memory will need to be saved on a disk for more permanent storage. This process should be repeated often since power failures can take place at any time. It is frustrating to work on a document for two hours and see it disappear if, for some reason, the power is interrupted.

All files should be copied onto a disk other than the original or working disk. This process is called backup. The reason for backing up files is that the original disk may get damaged and information stored on it can be lost. Even though there are programs on the market that help you recover files after an accident erases them, sometimes they can't be recovered. There-fore, all files stored on the working disk should be backed up at the end of each session, and the backup disk should be stored in a safe place. If any files are damaged, the backup disk can be used to restore the files to their more recent state.

Creating Folders and Files

Files on a Macintosh disk are organized into folders. Folders are the counterparts of a file cabinet drawer in a file cabinet. In an office, file folders are organized by function or subject and stored in appropriate cabinet drawers. The same process applies to a computer disk.

Although files and programs do not have to be placed into folders, doing so organizes the desktop and makes finding and accessing programs and data files easier.

Folders can be created by clicking on the File pull-down menu, dragging the mouse until New Folder is selected, then releasing the mouse button. This creates an empty folder where files and programs can be placed. The default name of the new folder is "untitled folder" as in Fig. 2-25. As soon as the folder is created, typing a new name that represents the future contents of the folder will replace the default name.

Files, on the other hand, are created by application programs such as word processors, spreadsheets, databases, and others. Usually, to create any type of data file on the Macintosh, a program must first be launched, then a new file created and saved to disk before a file icon shows on the desktop. Program files are placed on the desktop by copying or moving a program file icon from another disk onto the desktop.

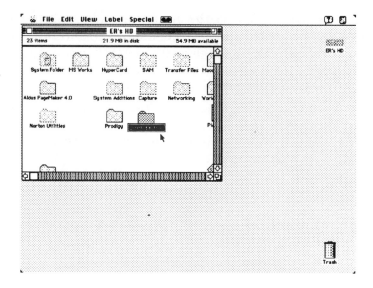

Fig. 2-25. Creation of a new folder.

Moving and Copying Files and Folders

To move files and folders from one area of the desktop to another, the desired item is selected and the icon is dragged to the final place on the desktop. Fig. 2-26 shows a program icon "Teach-Text" being moved from a window named "ER's HD" to a folder

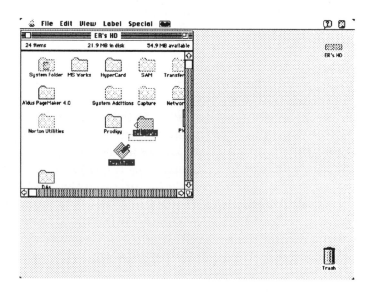

Fig. 2-26. Moving program icons.

named "Test Data." When the program icon is dragged, an outline of the figure moves with the mouse pointer. Placing this outline over the new folder and releasing the mouse button causes the program to be placed in the folder.

The process of copying what an icon represents is similar to moving, except that copying is performed from one disk to another. First the icon is selected. Then the icon outline is dragged and positioned over the outline of the disk icon where the copy is to be placed, as in Fig. 2-27. The mouse button is released and the copy takes place.

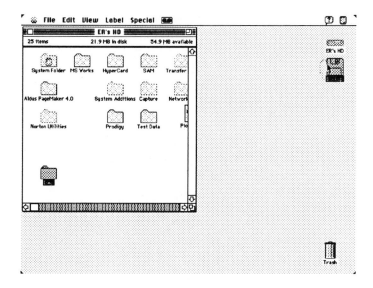

Fig. 2-27. Copying the files represented by an icon.

Deleting Files and Folders

The process of deleting a file or a folder is the same. The item to be deleted is dragged to the trash can icon. When the object is placed over the trash can, it changes color. When the mouse button is released, the item is placed in the trash can, and the trash can will change sizes, showing a bulge. Items placed in the trash can may be retrieved by opening it. When the user is certain that the items in the trash can icon are to be erased, the Special pull-down menu is accessed and the Empty Trash option is selected. This action erases the files represented by the icons from the disk.

Renaming Files and Folders

To change the name of a folder, click on the name at the bottom of the icon. The icon will become active and the name will appear shaded or colored. You can type the new name to replace the old name. Or you can create an insertion point in the existing name by clicking the mouse with the pointer next to any character, and then edit the name. Clicking on anything outside the name box or pressing the RETURN key completes the process. A file name is changed using the same procedure.

The Windows Environment

Microsoft Windows provides for access by both mouse and keyboard. Most of the commands sent via the mouse can also be sent from the keyboard. A major strength of the environment, however, is the ability to manage much of the system activity using the mouse. This text will focus on using the mouse to manage the environment, while providing reference to some of the keyboard alternatives.

Since it would be impractical if not impossible to operate Windows without a hard disk, the remainder of this book will assume that the hardware used includes a hard disk and that Windows is stored on the hard disk. It is not necessary to have Windows manage the entire disk nor all the software on it. Windows can share the system with other software that is managed from DOS or from another operating environment.

The following sections will explain the characteristics of the Windows environment, as seen by you. The screen displays what is described as a desktop, and communication with the system is accomplished through items placed on the desktop.

The Windows Desktop

Windows is launched by typing WIN from the DOS prompt. This will execute the program and take you into the Windows operating environment. The program manager will be opened and displayed, and you can begin using the software. Many systems are configured to launch the Windows software when the system is booted, automatically placing you in the Windows environment. In either case, you can leave Windows and go to DOS by closing the program manager.

When Windows is running, the screen (monitor) area occupied by Windows is referred to as the desktop. The conceptual analogy is that you are working at a desk, and the screen represents the desktop. Items can be placed on the desktop, moved around on the desktop, and removed from it.

The Background

The surface within the border in Fig. 2-28 is the background for all of the objects on the desktop. All items are placed on the desktop in the same manner that a person places papers, books, and artwork on top of a desk. The objects available on the desktop are icons, menu bars, windows, and dialog boxes.

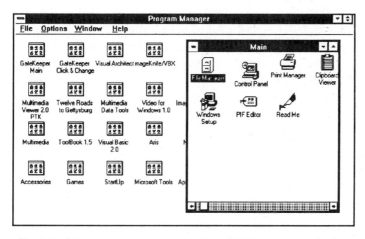

Fig. 2-28. Windows and background of Microsoft Windows.

The Mouse

The mouse is a major component of the Windows operating environment. It is used to manage the windows and to select icons and menu items. The mouse is rolled on a flat surface. As the mouse moves, the mouse pointer moves on the screen in a corresponding direction. The pointer symbol is an arrow symbol when the system is booted, but changes shapes depending on the operation and location of the pointer. There are five different mouse actions required to perform most functions. As with the Macintosh environment, these are point, click, press, drag, and double click. Additional terminology such as window, scroll bar, and others is the same as in the Macintosh environment.

Managing Programs

When Windows is launched, the Program Manager is usually opened on the desktop, with group icons displayed in it. Some of the group icons may be opened and some may be closed.

The opening display can be modified by rearranging the group icons to the desired location and saving the settings. The Save Settings command is on the Options pull-down menu. Choosing it prior to leaving Windows will place a check mark next to it and will save the display format when leaving Windows. If you do not want to save the modified format, be sure that the item is not checked.

Opening and Closing Groups of Programs

Regardless of the current format of the display, groups of programs can be opened and closed as needed. A group can be opened by moving the pointer to the group icon and double clicking the mouse button. This will open the group as a window with the application program displayed in it. A group can be closed by selecting the control-menu box, then choosing the Close item. This will reduce the group window to a group icon within the Program Manager window.

Arranging Group Icons and Program Icons

Windows can be resized or moved as necessary to position them on the desktop. You can also use menu commands to arrange windows, groups, and programs.

You can arrange the closed group icons by choosing the Arrange Icons option from the Window pull-down menu. This command will position the group icons in a uniform fashion in the lower portion of the Program Manager window. If the programmed arrangement is not satisfactory, you can move the icons individually to position them where you want them.

You can arrange the opened groups within the Program Manager window by choosing the Cascade item or the Tile item from the Window pull-down menu. The Tile option will arrange the opened windows adjacent to each other within the space available, resizing them as necessary to fit into the space. The Cascade option positions the opened group windows so that each title bar is visible.

Arrangement and management of opened windows is important when using the program manager and when running programs. You should always be aware of which windows are open and what they contain. It is important to remember that, as windows are opened and closed, some windows may be totally hidden from view. The currently active window will always be in the foreground.

Within a window the program item icons can sometimes appear cluttered because of adding and deleting applications. Or you may simply prefer a different arrangement. With the group icon open and active, select the Arrange Icons item from the Window pull-down menu. This will organize the icons within the window. If the arrangement is inappropriate, you can move them individually as desired.

Running an Application

To launch (run) an application, open the group icon that contains it. Then locate the program icon within the window and move the pointer to it. Double click the mouse button to launch the program.

Once the program is running, you can reduce it to an icon by using the minimize button on the right end of the title bar. The program icon will appear outside the program manager on the lower side of the desktop. Double clicking on the icon will open the program window.

Termination of the application program will depend on how the program itself provides for termination. It is commonly done by selecting Quit or Exit from a pull-down menu, but may be done in other ways. Leaving Windows will terminate execution of all programs currently running under Windows.

Help

Help is available in Windows. It is common to see a Help option on the menu bar or in a dialog box. Selecting it will provide a list of available categories from which to choose. Among the items available on the Help pull-down menu is one explaining how to use Help. It is a good place to gain an understanding of the help feature.

Most areas of Windows include several features, along with an explanation of how to use help. An alphabetical listing of available help topics is typically available. A dialog box to search for help on a specific topic is usually there. Help information about the application being used is also commonly included.

Summary

The basic function of an operating system is to serve as an interface between the hardware (the computer) and the user of the system. In addition, the operating system manages resources for the user and provides these resources to applications as they are requested. Although all the functions of the operating system are closely integrated, they can be subdivided into

1. Hardware interface
2. Software interface
3. Resource management
4. Memory management

Two of the most common operating systems for the personal computer are MS-DOS and the Macintosh operating system sometimes called the Finder. UNIX is a popular operating environment for minicomputers that can also be found in the personal computer world. Several versions of UNIX are available for personal computers. Among them are XENIX for IBM and compatibles and A/UX for the Macintosh personal computers.

A graphical user interface is a collection of programs designed to provide user-friendly access to the computer and to computer applications. In contrast to the traditional command and menu driven environments, graphical user interfaces provide a graphics-based operating environment. This type of interface is considered to add flexibility and ease of use to the computer environment.

Questions

1. Briefly describe the basic functions of the operating system.
2. How has the operating system contributed in making access to the computer a reality for the average person?
3. What is booting?
4. What are the purposes of batch files?
5. How can a file's contents be displayed on the screen for a user working in the UNIX environment?
6. What is a script file?
7. What is the Finder?
8. Describe the directory structure used by the Macintosh computer.
9. What is a GUI?
10. Why are GUIs beneficial for end users?

Projects

Media Conversion and File Transfer

Media conversion refers to the transfer of data and information from one physical entity to another. A document typed on a word processor may need to be shared with other users that have incompatible systems. In such situations, time and effort can be saved if there is some methodology by which the document can be transferred from one system to a different system without having to retype the document.

Incompatibility creates problems in the following situations:

1. New computers are added to an office and the new machines are incompatible with the old machines at the operating system level or at the physical (hardware) level.
2. Various departments or employees within a department use different and incompatible equipment.

3. Users produce documents on home computers or portables with disks that can't be used at the office.

4. Documents need to be transferred among companies that have different equipment.

5. Users have the same equipment, but use different software programs to produce their documents. A document from one package is often incompatible with other packages.

Conversion Problems

Physical Media Conversion

Since the introduction of the first personal computer, different types of storage media have been available with the introduction of new advanced products. Initially, personal computers used magnetic tape (cassette) to store documents. Then the first floppy disks were available in the Apple II, IBM PC, and other home computers. These initial disks were capable of storing up to 160,000 bytes per disk. However, data written on a disk by one type of computer (e.g., IBM PC) could not be read by drives on a different computer (e.g., Apple II). There wasn't an effective means by which documents could be easily exchanged among users of the different computers.

In today's business world, the most common types of media conversion that are required among PC users are as follows:

1. Conversion from an 8-inch disk to a 5 1/4-inch disk (IBM format).

2. Conversion from a 5 1/4- inch disk to a 3 1/2-inch disk (IBM format).

3. Conversion from a 5 1/4-inch disk low-density to a 5 1/4-inch disk high-density (IBM format).

4. Conversion from a 3 1/2-inch disk double-density to a 3 1/2-inch high-density (IBM format)

5. Conversion between IBM formats and Apple Macintosh format.

The incompatibility between the IBM format and the Apple formats lies in the process used to store data on the disk by the respective computer manufacturers. IBM and Apple use different techniques for placing document data on the floppy disks.

Therefore, a document saved with an IBM version of a word processor can't be read directly by the Apple version of the word processor.

Document Conversion

Although users may use the same computer to produce documents, they may use different types of software products. Each document-generating program has its own unique manner of formatting and saving the document with formatting codes.

As an example, consider a document created with WordPerfect. If this document needs to be incorporated into another document that is being prepared with Word, the formatting codes for bold face, underline, and so forth created with WordPerfect will not transfer to Word. Word will try to interpret the formatting codes as part of the data and produce a document that is incorrect. If the document is transferred without any formatting codes, then the problem of formatting is placed on a single user.

Protocol Conversion

Protocol conversion deals with documents that are transferred among computers that use different protocols such as ASCII and EBCDIC. Also, it applies to documents sent over communication lines. A document created on an ASCII-based computer will have to be translated by some protocol converter before it can be understood properly by an EBCDIC-based computer.

Solving Conversion Problems

The easiest way to solve conversion problems is to have a single vendor for all equipment used in the office. In many situations, though, this is impossible. Even with a single vendor, there are file and media conversion problems. However, a single vendor environment is effective in minimizing conversion problems. Some solutions to the conversion problems outlined above are presented next.

1. Conversion from an 8-inch disk to a 5 1/4-inch disk (IBM format).

   Conversion from a 5 1/4-inch disk to a 3 1/2-inch disk (IBM format).

   Conversion from a 5 1/4-inch disk low-density to a 5 1/4-inch disk high-density (IBM format).

Conversion from a 3 1/2-inch disk double-density to a 3 1/2-inch high-density (IBM format).

The easiest way to solve these problems is to have a machine with one type of drive (such as an 8-inch drive) and a drive of a different type (such as a 5 1/4 high-density drive). In this case, the data from one disk is copied to the other using the operating system commands for copying and data transfer. When two drives of the desired type are not available, telephone lines or direct connection through the serial port of the computer can be used, along with a communications program.

2. Conversion between IBM format and Apple Macintosh format. This type of conversion can be performed by using the Macintosh superdrive that is standard on all new Macintosh computers, and using the Apple File Exchange program. By selecting the Apple File Exchange folder under the System Additions folder, a screen is displayed that shows on one side the files and folders on the Mac, and on the other files and directories on the IBM PC. Highlighting the names of the files to transfer and the direction of transfer, that is IBM->Mac or Mac->IBM, causes the transferring to take place.

The above process works well when the number of files to be transferred is small. However, if a large number of files needs to be transferred between an IBM PC or compatible and a Macintosh, a commercial software product such as Maclink Plus/PC may prove to be a more efficient solution. This product allows an IBM PC or compatible and a Macintosh computer to transfer files using the telephone lines or a direct connection. The process for both options is the same, the only difference is that, with the first, a phone number must be dialed. The project at the end of this chapter uses Apple File Exchange to transfer documents between incompatible media.

3. Document conversion. Converting a document from one format to another can be accomplished with the use of format-converting software. Several commer-

cial software packages such as Keyword 7000 can convert a document from one format such as Wordstar to another format such as DisplayWrite.

Additionally, some word processors, spreadsheets, and other document-generating software programs are capable of reading many different formats. This provides enhanced flexibility to the users since a document can be generated with one type of word processor and loaded into another without the loss of formatting.

4. Protocol conversion. Documents that are produced in one protocol can be transferred to another computer using a different protocol with the aid of a protocol converter. A protocol converter is a device that connects between a computer and the communication line to other systems. The protocol converter performs all the character conversions necessary for the receiving computer to obtain the proper codes for the characters that make up the document.

5. Hard copy to electronic format conversion. There are situations where a document that is already on paper needs to be converted into electronic format. One device that can be used for this purpose is a scanner. A scanner can transfer written text or a picture on paper into an electronic document. The document can be saved in a variety of formats and incorporated into other documents.

Also, a figure or text scanned into an electronic document can be sent as a FAX document using a computer equipped with a FAX board. A FAX board allows a PC to act as a FAX machine. That is, it can send and receive documents, unattended, through the telephone lines. The main difference between a stand-alone FAX machine and a computer equipped with a FAX board lies in how the document is placed in the FAX machine for sending. A stand-alone FAX machine can receive documents that are on any type of paper. To send a FAX using a FAX board and a computer, the document must first be converted into electronic format.

Additional Project on Media Conversion

Using any MS-DOS-based text editor create the following document:

```
Dear Fred,

This is a great day to try converting a
document from one personal computer to
another. This document is being created in a
DOS-based computer and later will be trans-
ferred to the Macintosh computer using the
Finder operating environment.

I hope that you are as successful in
transferring documents as I hope to be.


Sincerely,

Bob
```

Save this document on a floppy disk. Go to a Macintosh computer and, using the Apple File Exchange facility, copy the file into a folder on the Macintosh. Print the document.

Create the same document in the Macintosh and transfer it to a floppy disk that is being formatted for an MS-DOS machine. After the file is copied to the disk, take it to an MS-DOS-based machine and print the document. Ask your instructor for directions on using the Apple File Exchange facility if necessary.

Computing
Configurations

Objectives

After completing this chapter you will:

1. Differentiate among single-user, multitasking, and multiuser systems.

2. Understand the importance of a multiuser system in data communications.

3. Know the basic definition of WANs, MANs, and LANs.

4. Understand the role of the microcomputer in the data communication process.

5. Know the difference between a microcomputer, minicomputer, and mainframe.

6. Understand the role of front end processors and mainframes in the communication process.

Key Words

Front End Processor	LAN
Mainframe	MAN
Microcomputer	Minicomputer
Multitasking	Multiuser
Multiuser DOS System	Network
Single User	WAN

Introduction

The basic hardware resources and the operating environments available to manage the hardware were explored in previous chapters. Now it is important to understand some of the configurations that these components may comprise in data communication. This chapter starts by exploring the use of the microcomputer beyond its single-user original design. As the power of the processor in personal computers increases, so do the needs of the user. Today's powerful microcomputers are replacing low end minicomputers in the workplace. We can find microcomputers supporting as many as 16 users running the UNIX operating system or some multiuser version of the MS-DOS operating system. These systems should not be overlooked in the data communication design of a company. They are powerful systems that on most occasions are as efficient and more cost effective than a local area network schema. It is important to know their capabilities and how they could be used to solve the data communication and processing needs of users.

Additionally, the chapter explores the basic concepts of wide area network, metropolitan area network, and local area network. Although these concepts will be discussed more thoroughly in later chapters, this is a good place to introduce their definitions and the role that microcomputers play in these systems. Finally, minicomputers and mainframes can't be ignored as an integral part of the overall data communication strategy. Although many corporations are streamlining their data communication operations by distributing their needs among minicomputers and powerful microcomputers, the mainframe has a role to play in data communication.

The chapter serves as a preamble to more sophisticated data communication concepts that are explored in subsequent chapters. It is important that the student understands the basic operating environment that he or she is most likely to encounter in the real world. Additionally, it is equally important to point out that not all data communication needs are solved with the implementation of a network. As we'll see in subsequent chapters, networking is not easy nor inexpensive. Alternatives should always be explored. Within this context, multiuser systems can play an important role in solving the data communication needs of users.

The Microcomputer

Stand-Alone Microcomputers

The microcomputer or personal computer is typically a computer with a single central processing unit designed to support a single user. It contains a limited amount of memory and supports a limited number of peripherals. The peripherals consist of one or two floppy disks, one or more hard disks, a keyboard, a screen, and often a printer.

Early microcomputers were nothing more than sophisticated "toys" that computer enthusiasts enjoyed playing with. These types of people required little or no support in order to use the machine. The microcomputer became a mainstay of the business community when IBM introduced the IBM PC. Although sophisticated for its time, the IBM PC had limited resources. It couldn't execute large programs or manipulate large amounts of data. During the past decade, the versatility and processing power of the central processing unit that is at the heart of the IBM PC was increased. With this increase in processing power, software developers brought to the market more powerful software that also increased the functionality of the microcomputer in the workplace. The IBM PC evolved into the IBM AT, and then into the PS/2 line of computers. In addition, many clone manufacturers have developed microcomputers (called IBM compatibles) that are capable of running the software designed for IBM microcomputers, and at the same time providing increased power and flexibility.

Apple Computer Corporation, which introduced a personal computer before IBM, also developed the power of their line of microcomputers. Their system started with the Apple II family, and has evolved through the GS series, Apple Lisa, Apple Macintosh, the Quadra, and others. With each new generation, the power and speed of computation was at least doubled.

This trend of increased computational speed and decreased price of the hardware shows no signs of abating. On the contrary, the evolution of the personal computer continues at a fast pace with new processors with millions of transistors appearing everyday. These new CPUs continually overshadow the performance of the ones they replace. At the same time, the price of existing hardware drops as drastically as the performance of new microprocessors increases.

In addition to the computational speed of the CPU, modern microcomputers have also increased the amount of main memory they can address. From an early 128 Kb of RAM, today's machines can access millions of bytes of RAM and are capable of much more if there is room in the system to put it in. Also, hard disk and floppy disk capacity have increased over the years. A typical hard disk for a personal computer can address 150 Mb of storage or more at a cost of several hundred dollars.

All of this increase in speed and power has created what is called a computer revolution. Although the power of machines has increased dramatically through mass production and new production techniques, their price has steadily dropped. Most people in the United States who need a personal computer can afford one. And since, generally, it is intended as a single-user machine, security is not usually a problem.

Multitasking Microcomputers

A microcomputer with a powerful processor can be used to run multiple programs at the same time. This function is called multitasking on a microcomputer. In reality multitasking capabilities are not so much dependent on the hardware as they are dependent on the operating system that runs the computer. MS-DOS was not designed to be a multitasking operating system. When running it on a personal computer, you must provide additions or modifications in order for the system to be able to run multiple programs at the same time. However, multitasking doesn't necessarily mean multiuser. A multiuser operating system not only has to be multitasking but also needs to be able to support more than one user concurrently.

Several working environments are available for MS-DOS-based microcomputers to become multitasking personal computers. Two of the most popular are QuarterDeck's DesqView and Microsoft Windows. Windows allows more than one program to run in memory and share resources at the same time. Some caution must be taken here since it is easy to get the impression that multiple instructions may be running in parallel. That is not the case. The processor of microcomputers running under the Windows operating environment executes only one instruction at any given time. However, under Windows control, the processor shares CPU time with the instructions of multiple programs.

UNIX is a true multitasking operating system (a public domain version of UNIX called 386BSD is available). In the microcomputer world UNIX runs on machines that have a processor based on the Intel 80386 or higher, or a Motorola 68030 or higher central processing unit. UNIX on this type of system provides low cost multitasking capability. Several versions of the UNIX operating system have been ported to the microcomputer environment. Among the best known are SCO UNIX for the Intel-processor-based machines and A/UX for Motorola-processor-based machines.

Multiuser Microcomputers

Although microcomputers were designed as a single-user system, with the proper hardware and software they can be converted into powerful multiuser systems. Perhaps one of the best ways to make a microcomputer a good multiuser system is to acquire hardware that has a powerful processor, such as Intel's 80386 or 80486 or Motorola's 68030 and 68040, and install a multiuser operating system, such as UNIX, on it. A computer equipped in this manner can easily become a host system for up to 16 users or more depending on the types of applications that need to be executed.

To provide access to the applications running on the host, inexpensive terminals can be purchased and, through built-in serial ports, the terminals can be connected to the host system. Since UNIX was designed for this purpose -- that is, multitasking and multiuser -- it is not difficult to create a system set up as described above. However, what if you need to run MS-DOS applications instead of UNIX applications?

Several companies offer multiuser operating systems that allow several MS-DOS applications to share the same processor and files, providing services to more than one user. These products use one of two techniques to provide this type of service to users. Some of these products are additions to the MS-DOS environment that require DOS in order to run. Two examples of this type of product are VM/386 and 386/MultiWare. Other systems replace the MS-DOS operating system completely. Examples of these products are Concurrent DOS 386 and PC-MOS/386. These operating system replacements are supposed to be compatible with any MS-DOS application program that uses standard DOS calls for its functions.

The physical installation of one of these systems is basically the same as the one described above. Once the operating system is installed in a highly powerful personal computer, low cost terminals are connected to the host system through serial ports. This schema works well when the application running is text based rather than graphics based. If graphics are used, the response time of the system is slowed down since the serial transmission between the terminal and the computer is slow (see chapter 4).

Although these systems perform many of the functions found in bigger multiuser environments such as file exchange and printer sharing, they don't have all the capabilities that a stand-alone MS-DOS-based machine normally has. Additionally, numerous low cost networking schemes provide many of the functions that these operating environments have. Yet they serve a market niche for those users who require a centralized, multiuser environment, capable of running basic MS-DOS programs.

One of their most common problems is dealing with the color and high-resolution graphics required of most desktop systems. In a multiuser DOS system, creating a small graphic image can take as long as 10 seconds. Complex high-resolution images, assuming that the monitor is capable, can take several minutes. This is due to the slow communication link between the computer and the terminal. However, newer technology has advanced the transmission capabilities of these systems, making them more efficient when high-resolution graphics are required.

There are basically two ways that the graphics problem has been resolved (see Fig. 3-1). One is to use a fiber optics link between the computer and the terminal. In this manner, and with appropriate hardware, the link becomes an extension of the computer bus. One provider of this type of technology is Sun-River Corporation.

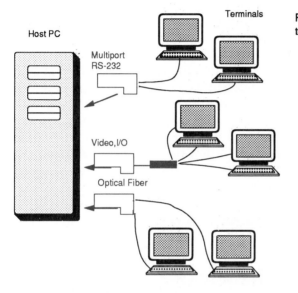

Fig. 3-1. Attaching multiple terminals to a host PC.

Another way to provide high performance graphics in an MS-DOS multiuser environment is to use special hardware and circuits that extend the keyboard, parallel and serial ports, and video ports beyond the host computer's motherboard. This technique combines the functions of the above computer components in an expansion board located in the host computer. Then signals go out over a cable to a controller box located next to the terminal. This box has connections for the keyboard, video, and parallel and serial ports. One company that uses this approach is Advanced Micro Research with its AMR Video Graphics Network. The cable used in this schema can be fiber optics or twisted pair. The fiber optic cable has the advantage of being much faster than the twisted pair cable, but it is more costly.

It is important to note that this type of system normally supports four to eight users. If graphic-intensive applications are required, the number will have to be small, otherwise the system performance deteriorates rapidly. If text-only applications are being executed, the number of users can increase. However, with new processors such as Intel's 80486 and the right hardware, these types of systems will be able to support as many as 16 users running normal MS-DOS applications.

Multiuser systems based on microcomputers can be relatively inexpensive solutions to many data communication needs. They don't require the high cost physical environments that many minicomputers and mainframes must have in order to operate properly. In addition, since they are centralized systems, they have good security measures. Connecting them to existing systems or networks gives them added flexibility. This provides room for growth since you can start with a multiuser system and grow into a media-sharing local area network. Linking with other networks gives the users of the multiuser system the same resources as anyone else in the network. For many small offices or companies, a multiuser system based on a powerful micro-computer can be the most efficient and cost effective manner to provide file and resource sharing. Also, since some of these systems allow the user to run MS-DOS software, the investment in software and in the system is protected.

A Quick View of Networks

A computer network is a collection of workstations or computing devices, also called nodes, connected by some type of physical medium. A node in a network can be microcomputer, main-frame, terminal, printer, or any other "intelligent" device (a device capable of some type of logical processing). In modern networks, the most commonly found device is a microcomputer.

The medium of communication of a network in many instances determines the transmission capabilities of the network. Typical mediums of communication are coaxial cable, telephone wires, optical fiber, microwaves, and others. Each of these has its own capabilities in terms of speed of transmission and amount of data that can be transmitted at one time, with optical fiber being the fastest.

The geographical area covered by a network determines whether the network is called a wide area network (WAN), metropolitan area network (MAN), or a local area network (LAN). Wide area networks link systems that are too far apart to be included in a small in-house network. Metropolitan area networks connect across distances greater than a few kilometers but no more than 50 kilometers (approximately 30 miles). Local area networks usually connect users in the same office or building. In some cases, adjacent buildings of a corporation or educational institution are connected with the use of LANs.

Wide Area Network (WAN)

WANs cross public right-of-ways and typically use common-carrier circuits (see Fig. 3-2). They use a broad range of communication media for interconnection that includes switched and leased lines, private microwave circuits, optical fiber, coaxial cable, and satellite circuits. Basically, a wide area network is any communication network that permits message, voice, image signals, or computer data to be transmitted over a widely dispersed geographical area.

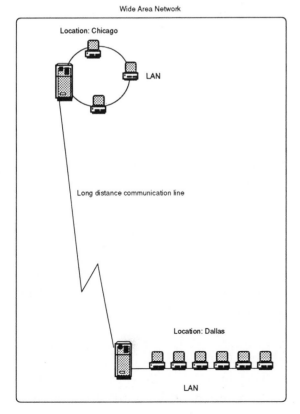

Fig. 3-2. A wide area network made up of other networks located over a large geographical area.

Metropolitan Area Network (MAN)

MANs connect locations that are geographically located from 5 to 50 kilometers apart (see Fig. 3-3). They include the transmission of data, voice, and television signals through the use of coaxial cable or optical fiber cable as their primary medium of transmission.

Customers of MANs are primarily large companies that need to communicate within a metropolitan area at high speeds. MAN providers normally offer lower prices than the phone companies and faster installation over a diverse routing, and include backup lines in emergency situations.

Fig. 3-3. A metropolitan area network.

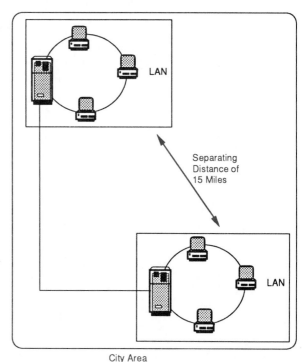

Separating Distance of 15 Miles

City Area

Local Area Network (LAN)

LANs connect devices within a small area, usually within a building or adjacent buildings (see Fig. 3-4). LAN transmission media usually do not cross roads or other public thoroughfares. They are privately controlled with respect to data processing equipment, such as processors and terminals, and with respect to data communication equipment such as media and extenders.

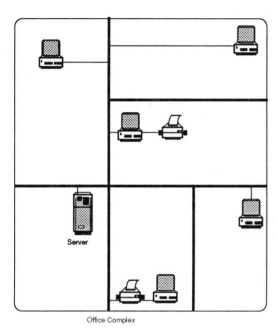

Fig. 3-4. A local area network in an office complex.

Server

Office Complex

The Role of the Microcomputer Workstation and Client/Server Computing

As mentioned above, the typical node in a network is a microcomputer workstation. A microcomputer workstation is a general purpose microcomputer or specialized input/output workstation with "smart" circuitry and a central processing unit. Technically, there is a difference between a microcomputer workstation and a microcomputer. The workstation includes the tools necessary for a professional to perform his or her daily work. These tools are specialized software applications such as CAD systems and mathematical modeling systems. In addition, today's workstations have the ability to multitask software programs. This means they can run multiple programs simultaneously and can switch among them as the user needs to. The microcomputer may not have all of these capabilities built in. It may be used only for word processing or database access. Regardless of which system we are discussing, the microcomputer is an integral part of communication networks. It can be used as part of a local area network or as a terminal device connected to a host system. Fig. 3-5 shows a picture of a typical microcomputer system.

Fig. 3-5. A typical microcomputer system.

Microcomputer workstations are being increasingly used in networks since they can perform many processing functions internally before the data is passed on to a host system. Some of the ways in which they are used are:

1. Data stored in central systems is transmitted (downloaded) to the microcomputer. The data can be processed by the microcomputer using a word processor, database, spreadsheet, or some other software application. After processing, the data is transmitted back to the central system for further processing or storage.

2. Data stored on the microcomputer can be submitted as a batch job to the host system as required.

3. Applications on the microcomputer can be assisted by the processing power of the host system. For example, a scientific database can reside in part on

the microcomputer system, but when large calculations or repetitious calculations are required, the microcomputer can rely on the host system for assistance.

4. Large projects can be divided among several microcomputers. The completed pieces can then be assembled on the host system.

5. Microcomputers can work as terminals to the host computer. In this role they emulate the native terminals of the central system.

6. Microcomputers that are part of a local area network can share storage and printer devices on the network or devices on the central system.

Sometimes when microcomputers are part of a network that uses one or more hosts to provide the microcomputers with the files and data necessary to perform calculations, the microcomputers are called clients. The host providing the data or files is called the server. In this type of architecture, many disk-intensive tasks stay on the file server. Using this technique, the traffic on the network is reduced, but the load of the server's processor is increased.

Additionally, personal computers can easily attach to the networking world described above in three distinct ways:

1. The personal computer can use a terminal emulation program to attach to a minicomputer or mainframe which in turn attaches to the network world.

2. The personal computer can be attached to a LAN and the LAN can be attached to the world by a router or a gateway.

3. The personal computer can be using UNIX and attach to the networking world using some type of networking protocol.

These different methodologies of connecting a microcomputer to other users locally and over long distances are explored throughout the rest of the chapters in this book.

Beyond the Microcomputer

Front End Processors

Front end processors are normally minicomputers, although they could be microcomputers. They are often employed at the host end of a communication circuit to perform control and processing functions required for the proper operation of a data communication network. Fig. 3-6 illustrates the location of a front end processor in a communication network. The front end processor provides an interface to the communication circuits.

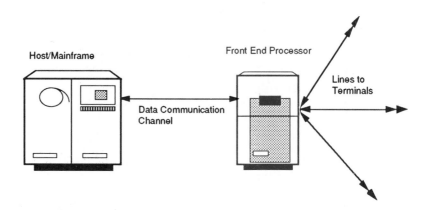

Fig. 3-6. The front end processor in a communication network.

It relieves the host computer of its communication duties, which allows the host to perform the data processing function more effectively.

The typical duties of the front end processor (FEP) are message processing and message switching. In message processing, it interprets incoming messages to determine the type of information requested. Then it retrieves the information from an on-line storage unit, and sends it back to the inquiring terminal without involving the host system. In message switching, the front end processor switches incoming messages to other terminals or systems on a network. It can also store messages and forward them at a later time.

Functions of the Front End Processor

The functions of the front end processor include, but are not limited to, the following:

1. Circuit polling and addressing terminals. Polling involves asking each terminal if it has a message to send. Addressing involves asking a terminal if it is in condition to receive the message.

2. Answering dial-in calls and automatic dialing of outgoing calls.

3. Code conversion from ASCII to EBCDIC or EBCDIC to ASCII.

4. Circuit switching. This allows an incoming circuit to be switched to another circuit.

5. Accommodating circuit speed differences.

6. Protocol conversion, such as asynchronous to synchronous.

7. Multiplexing (see chapter 4).

8. Assembly of incoming bits into characters.

9. Assembly of characters into blocks of data or complete messages.

10. Message compression for more efficient communications.

11. Activating remote alarms if errors are detected.

12. Requesting retransmission of blocks of text containing errors.

13. Keeping statistics of network usage.

14. Performing diagnostics on attached terminals.

15. Control of editing that includes rerouting messages, modifying data for transmission, etc.

16. Buffering messages before they are passed to the host computer or user terminal.

17. Queuing messages into I/O queues between the front end processor and the host computer.

18. Logging of messages to tape or disk.

19. Identifying trouble or security problems.

There are many vendors of front end processors. Some of the best known models are the IBM 37xx family of communication controllers and the NCR COMTEN 3600 series of front end processors.

Minicomputers and Mainframe Computers

The differences between a minicomputer and a mainframe computer are at times difficult to determine, depending on the system being discussed. Mainframe computers are considered central computer systems that perform data processing functions for a business or industry. They sometimes employ multiple processors to increase their throughput capacity. Of course, many minicomputers can also fit that definition. On that side of the spectrum, many microcomputers are more powerful than some minicomputers. Typically, a minicomputer is a multiuser system and a microcomputer is not. However, many microcomputers are not capable of supporting multiple users. Therefore, trying to define a clear line between microcomputers, minicomputers, and mainframes is difficult. If a system supports several hundred users, and has several gigabytes of storage capacity, it probably should be called a mainframe.

In some networks, several mainframe computers can be found sharing the responsibility of processing information as a distributed system. In such systems the hardware, software, processing, and data are normally dispersed over a geographical area. The individual technologies are connected through some type of communication network. As part of this network, mainframe computers can perform networking functions as well as the more traditional processing functions.

A mainframe computer that is built to perform "number crunching" routines may not be suitable to perform communication routines. The type of processing required for communications differs greatly from that required to perform mathematical calculations. For a computer that is built to perform traditional data processing functions, additional or auxiliary hardware is required. The type of auxiliary hardware will depend upon the configuration of the network.

 There are three types of configurations, the _first_ of which consists of a computer that is not part of any local or wide area computer network. The circuitry required to handle all communications is built into the machine. Fig. 3-7 shows a typical configuration for this type of centralized system. This configuration uses dedicated hardware to handle the interaction between the host system and the data entry terminals.

The mainframe computer can store users' programs as well as the software to handle communication with the users. The type of configuration shown in Fig. 3-7 can be found in manufacturing environments and in dedicated database systems. Even though we refer to the computer as the mainframe computer or host computer, this central system is often a minicomputer system.

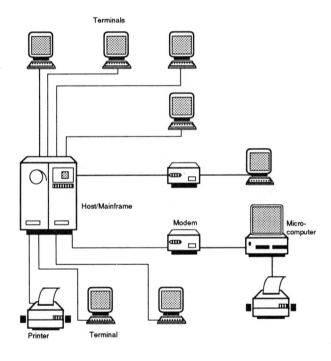

Fig.3-7. A centralized system using a mainframe as the host.

 The second type of configuration is a network that employs microcomputers, minicomputers, and mainframe computers connected through some type of local area network (LAN). Fig. 3-8 depicts this type of system. The network is usually confined to the business office or business complex where the processing is taking place. Users can communicate to the outside world by sending their message to an outside system through the local telephone exchange or some other medium. The local exchange then routes the message through long distance networks until it reaches the local exchange of the receiving system. Finally, the message is routed to the receiving computer or local network. These systems are important, and there are several chapters in this book that further explore the concepts.

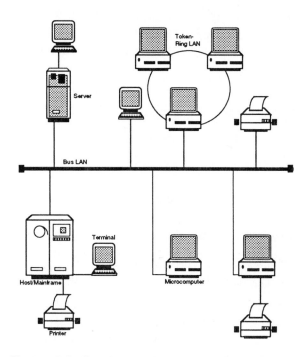

Fig. 3-8. A distributed communication and processing system.

 The final type of configuration is one that employs a large general purpose computer along with a front end processor. Fig. 3-9 shows a diagram of this configuration. The front end processor is known by names such as line controller, communications controller, or transaction processor. The function of the FEP is to interface the main computer to the network where the users' communication equipment resides. It can be a nonprogrammable device that is built to handle a specific situation. Or the front end processor can be programmable and it can handle some processing functions in addition to input/output activities.

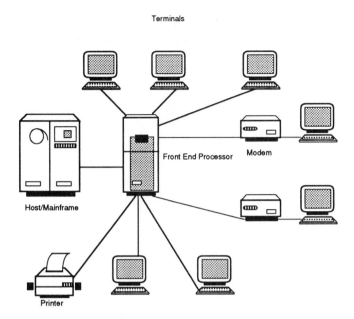

Fig. 3-9. A communication system employing a mainframe and a front end processor.

During the past few years, network designers have opted to remove as much processing as possible from the host computer. The idea is to distribute the processing hardware along a network, making the entire system more efficient.

Fig. 3-10 shows an example of this type of network distribution. The front end processor handles the control of all communication functions. The data channel between the front end processor and the host system handles the movement of data into and out of the main processing computer. Remote terminal controllers handle users' terminals. Microcomputers process data locally and later transmit the results to the host system. Telephone exchanges, multiplexers, and other devices are used throughout the network to handle communications efficiently between users and the host computer. Further in this book, chapters on networks and local area networks explain the terminology and concepts in more detail.

The trend in computer technology is toward faster, smaller, and distributed network systems. However, the central or host system plays an important part in network strategies. The processing and data throughput power of minicomputers and mainframes is superior to that of microcomputer systems. This makes the mainframe or the minicomputer a key component of a successful network configuration. In addition, many network managers rely on a central or host system for security, backup, and maintenance purposes.

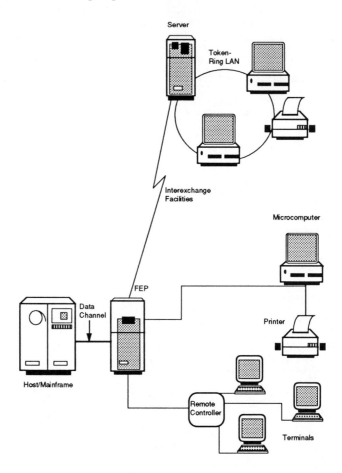

Fig. 3-10. A distributed networking solution.

Summary

Microcomputers were designed to perform the task of servicing a single user at any given time. However, the increase of processing power of microcomputers has allowed these systems to run multiple programs at the same time. In order for a personal computer to execute several applications and allow them to share resources, a special operating environment, other than MS-DOS, needs to be present. Two of these environments are UNIX and Microsoft Windows.

Additionally, with the proper hardware and operating system, a microcomputer can be converted into a powerful multiuser system that can accommodate as many as 16 users without much degradation in performance. Multiuser systems based on microcomputers can be a good solution for the data communication needs of a small office or company.

A computer network is a collection of workstations or computing devices, also called nodes, connected by some type of physical medium. The nodes in a network can be microcomputers, mainframes, terminals, printers, or any other "intelligent" device. The medium of communication of a network in many instances determines the transmission capabilities of the network. Typical mediums of communication are coaxial cable, telephone wires, optical fiber, microwaves, and others.

The geographical area covered by a network determines whether the network is called a wide area network (WAN), metropolitan area network (MAN), or a local area network (LAN). Wide area networks link systems that are too far apart to be included in a small in-house network. Metropolitan area networks connect across distances greater than a few kilometers, but no more than 50 kilometers (approximately 30 miles). Local area networks usually connect users in the same office or building.

A typical node on a network is a microcomputer workstation. Microcomputer workstations are being increasingly used in networks since they can perform many processing functions internally before the data is passed on to a host system. Mainframes and minicomputers can also be nodes in a network. Increasingly, minicomputers are used as front end processors for a mainframe. In addition to many other capabilities, the front end processor relieves the mainframe from its communication duties, which allows the host to perform the data processing function more effectively.

Questions

1. What does multitasking mean?
2. What does multiuser mean?
3. How can a microcomputer become a multiuser system?
4. Describe a wide area network.
5. Describe a local area network.
6. What is a mainframe computer?
7. What is the function of a front end processor?
8. Does multiuser imply multitasking? Explain.
9. In what circumstances is a microcomputer-based multiuser system a good solution?
10. Describe one technique used to provide high-resolution graphics processing to a microcomputer-based multiuser system.

Projects

This project provides the student with the theory and hands-on practice in setting up and using a microcomputer and a modem to access a bulletin board service. Although the data communication concepts to hookup a computer to a modem have not been introduced, the project is simple enough that the student should be able to complete it. In addition, it provides hands-on experience with a graphical interface environment. The EBBS number must be provided to the student in order to complete the assignment. To find the number of any EBBS in the area, contact a local computer user group. It is important that students understand the uses and benefit of the EBBS since they are being used by corporations as services to their employees and as a means to do business.

Bulletin Boards

The electronic bulletin board system (BBS or EBBS) consists of a computer system that is used to store, retrieve, and catalog messages sent in by the general public with the use of a terminal or microcomputer and a modem. The telephone company provides the link between the person using the BBS and the computer that is the host of the BBS. The main reason for their existence is for people to leave messages for others.

Components of an Electronic Bulletin Board

To connect to an electronic bulletin board you will need several elements. These elements include:

1. Modem
2. Telephone lines
3. High-capacity computer
4. EBBS software
5. System operator

Popular Electronic Bulletin Board Systems

Quite a few commercial and public BBS are in operation across the USA. Some offer a large variety of services and are also called information services. Some of the best known are

1. Dow Jones News/Retrieval Services
2. CompuServe
3. GEnie
4. DIALOG
5. Prodigy

Dow Jones News/Retrieval Services

The Dow Jones News/Retrieval Services is a collection of business, economic, financial, investment, and general interest news oriented toward the uses and needs of businesses. It is operated by the *Wall Street Journal*.

It contains the full text of several major business publications such as the *Wall Street Journal* and *Barron's*. This service provides some of the most comprehensive business and financial news of all information services in the industry. In addition, it provides its members with brokerage services, e-mail facilities, national and international news, travel information services, weather, and other general interest services.

To sign up for this information service system, call or write to

Dow Jones News/Retrieval

Dept LB, Box 300

Princeton, NJ 08543

609-520-4650

CompuServe

CompuServe Information Service is a public on-line service that provides private communications, database services, network services, and general interest services for businesses, financial institutions, government agencies, and individuals.

The range of topics available is rather large and includes e-mail, news, sports, weather, travel, electronic shopping, entertainment, home services, family services, education, technology services, and business services. In addition, CompuServe is used as a gateway to other services.

To sign up for this information service system, call or write to

CompuServe

5000 Arlington Centre Blvd.

Columbus, OH 43220

800-848-8199

GEnie

GEnie is an acronym for General Electric Network for Information Exchange. It provides services for e-mail, news, entertainment, home services, reference services, business services, and other general interest services.

To sign up for this information service system, call or write to

GEnie

GE Information Services, Dept. 2B

401 North Washington St.

Rockville, MD 20850

800-638-936

DIALOG

DIALOG provides access to over 150 million records of information. They include financial information, statistical information, and bibliographic reference information. The information provided by DIALOG comes directly from private, public, and government publishers.

To sign up for this information service system, call or write to

DIALOG Information Services

3460 Hillview Ave.

Palo Alto, CA 94304

800-334-2564

Prodigy

Prodigy is a general information service provider with topics that include news, sports, finance services, business services, e-mail, recreational services, travel, home banking, electronic shopping, access to the Dow Jones News/Retrieval, bibliographic information, and other services.

Prodigy is one of the fastest growing information services, and it has been tailored toward the home user who wants to explore and use professional services at low costs.

To sign up for this information service system, call or write to

Prodigy Membership Services

445 Hamilton Ave.

White Plains, NY 10601

800-284-5933

Connecting to an Electronic Bulletin Board System

The Communications Process

Computers process information in digital form. That is, information is in the form of individual bits or digits. A bit is the smallest unit of data that the computer can represent. Normally, personal computers use seven or eight bits to represent the individual characters that make up the alphabet and other special characters.

lk to each other, the information exchanged
sing the individual bits that make up the
\puters are in close proximity, then coaxial
connect them.

apart, then telephone lines are typically
\ines. If the phone company is used as
nputers, then another small problem
'ravel through the phone lines are
_omputer cannot interpret. Moreover, the
...ot carry digital signals. In order for two
\o communicate over phone lines, a modem must be

The hardware and software required to connect your computer
to the outside world are as follows:

1. Your personal computer.
2. A modem connected to your computer.
3. A telephone line.
4. A host (receiving) computer with a modem.
5. Communications software (e.g., the communications
   tool in Microsoft Works for the Macintosh or the
   communications tool in Microsoft Windows).

The Modem

A modem is an electronic device that converts (modulates) the
digital signal of computers into audible tones that can be
transmitted over telephone lines. The received data is then
reconverted (demodulated) from the audible tones into digital
information. Most modems for personal computers can dial
numbers for you, redial busy numbers, automatically answer
calls, and set the proper communication speed.

Modems can be external or internal. An external modem is
placed next to the computer, connected to its serial port with the
use of a serial cable, and to the phone line with a telephone cord.
An internal modem is placed inside the computer by using an
available expansion slot. Then it is connected to the phone line
with the use of a phone cord. Once the modem is connected to
the computer and the phone line, its function is controlled by the
communications tool in Works. Your modem will come with
instructions on how to unpack it and an explanation of the type
of port it can connect to. Refer to these instructions to make sure
the modem is properly installed.

Software Communications Terminology

By following the general steps outlined below, you will be able to communicate with electronic bulletin boards or services (EBBS). Before an actual connection is used, your modem and software need to have the same settings as the receiving or host computer that you are trying to access. These settings are common to all communications setups; they are:

1. Baud rate. This is the rate of transmission of data and it is a measure of the number of signal events per second. Typical settings are 300, 1200, 2400, 4800, and 9600. As the baud rate increases, the rate of transmission also increases and the time you have to spend waiting for information to appear on the screen decreases. Some EBBS services charge more per hour when you use higher baud rates.

2. Data bits. This is the number of bits that make up a character. Most mini- and mainframe computers use seven bits.

3. Stop bits. This is the number of bits used to indicate the end of a character. In most cases, one stop bit marks the end of the character.

4. Handshake. The term refers to the manner in which the communicating computer knows when the other machine is sending or receiving data, or when it is doing some other task that might interfere with the transmission signals. This is also referred to as the communications protocol. The protocol refers to all the conventions that must be observed in order for the computers to communicate with each other. If two computers communicate over phone lines, then X-On/X-Off is used. If the machines are connected with coaxial cables, then Hardware is used.

5. Parity. This is a method of checking for errors in data communications. If the number of data bits is eight, then parity should be None. Otherwise, you need to refer to the host machine and find out which type of parity it is using, then set this selection appropriately on your computer.

Setting up the Hardware

External modems have an RS-232 or serial connector that is normally found at the back of the modem. An RS-232 cable will be required to connect this type of modem to the RS-232 or serial port on the back of the PC. You will need to use the appropriate serial cable for your computer. The IBM PC and compatible microcomputers use a cable that has end connectors that are different from the connectors found on Apple computers.

The rest of the exercise uses the Macintosh as the base computer; however, an IBM PC or compatible using the communications tool in Windows will also work.

Check with your local dealer or your instructor to find the right cable.

1. Connect the modem and the PC using the serial cable.
2. Connect a telephone cable from a wall outlet to the phone connector normally found at the back of the modem.
3. Turn the modem on. The front lights of the modem labeled MR (modem ready) and either LS (low speed) or HS (high speed) should be on. These lights may vary from modem to modem.

If you have an internal modem,

1. Remove the protective case of the computer and install the modem in one of the empty slots located at the back of the machine.
2. After it is securely placed in the expansion slot, replace the computer cover.
3. Now connect a phone cord to the phone connector port found at the rear of the modem.

The next step is to obtain a bulletin board phone number and then set up the communications software to connect the computer to the EBBS.

There are many communication software packages on the computer market. Some of the more common are Crosstalk, ProComm, and Smartcom. There are also public domain and shareware communication programs that perform many of the functions of the more expensive packages. You can contact your local computer dealer or computer magazines for a listing of such programs. Additionally, many integrated programs such as Microsoft Works contain communication software built-in along with other productivity programs. This type of application program can also be used to perform most, if not all, of the communication requirements that you may have.

Regardless of which communication program you have, the application will contain a screen similar to Fig. 3-11. The screen in Fig. 3-11 displays the type of terminal emulation desired, the baud rate or speed of transmission, and the other items previously discussed in this section. Some additional items are the phone type and the handshake. The phone type indicates whether the modem will use touch-tone or a rotary dialing method. The handshake indicates the protocol that will be used. If a modem is used to connect two systems, typically X-On/X-Off is selected. If the two computers are connected directly through a cable, then hardware is selected.

The value of each parameter is found by calling the bulletin board operators or by trial and error. The values shown in Fig. 3-11 will work in most cases. If one of the parameters is initially set incorrectly, the screen will contain "garbage" characters. In this case, change the number of bits, stops bits, and parity until the screen looks right.

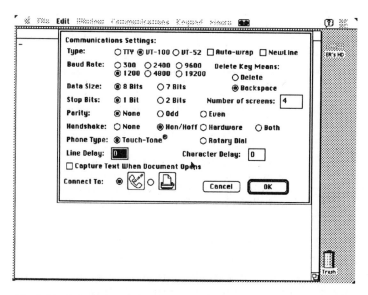

Fig. 3-11. Communication settings.

The software that you use will have a provision to type the phone number of the data line for the EBBS. You may have a screen similar to Fig. 3-12 or your dial menu may be different. In either case, the function is to type a phone number and indicate that the computer is to dial it. Type the phone number for the EBBS at this point and instruct the software to dial the number. This last function is usually accomplished by pressing a key combination that tells the modem to dial the number automatically.

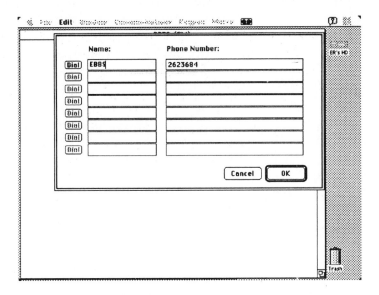

Fig. 3-12. Dialing options.

After the number is dialed (and assuming a response from the EBBS host computer), an entry screen will appear. The EBBS will display a general menu of services that are available to users. The type and amount of service provided depend on the type of EBBS. If it is a large commercial EBBS system such as DIALOG or PRODIGY, numerous services are available. If the EBBS is set up by an individual or small group of individuals to service a local user group, the number of services is limited. Normally, these services include electronic mail, conferencing, games, and special interest sections. To use the EBBS, follow the instructions below.

4. In most instances typing the first letter of a menu item and pressing the ENTER key will activate the desired menu.

5. At this point you can navigate throughout the EBBS at your own pace. To perform a desired function, most EBBSs have on-line instructions that indicate the procedure to follow.

6. When the session is over, select Exit and hang up from the communication software menu.

Some commercial services such as PRODIGY offer many different types of options and menus to choose from. Fig. 3-13 shows the initial menu of PRODIGY and some of its choices.

Fig. 3-13. Menu options from a commercial BBS.

Part Two

The Data Communication Environment

Basic Communication Concepts and Hardware

Objectives

After completing this chapter you will:

1. Differentiate between the various modes of data transmission.
2. Understand the ASCII code system and its importance.
3. Understand the concept and use of modems in the communication process.
4. Use and design interfaces for serial (RS-232) ports.
5. Understand multiplexing technology.

Key Words

ASCII	Async Communication
Control Characters	Full-Duplex
Half-Duplex	Modem
Multiplexer	Parallel Communication
RS-232 Interface	Serial Communication
Simplex	Smart Modem
Sync Communication	

Introduction

Data communication hardware and software come in many different forms and levels of sophistication. However, at the basic level of transmissions a few concepts and devices are standard across all computing and data communication platforms. The mode of transmission is one of these concepts. Regardless of the devices transmitting, the modes in which the data is transmitted remain basically constant. In this case data can be transmitted in half-duplex or full-duplex, and it can be a serial or parallel transmission. Data can be sent asynchronously or synchronously. These are the concepts that this chapter explores along with a description of the standard digital codes that constitute the data being transmitted.

In addition to the mode of data transmission, this chapter explores the concepts and uses of modems. Since modems are a basic and common way of communication in the microcomputer world, they deserve special treatment. Also, the port used to connect the modem to the computer, the RS-232 or EIA-232 as it is sometimes called, is explored and analyzed in detail. Finally, multiplexers are introduced as a means to lower the costs of transmitting data.

Modes of Transmission

There are many different ways in which the transmission of data can be classified. However, data transmission is normally grouped into three major areas according to:

1. How the data flows among devices.
2. The type of physical connection.
3. The type of timing used for transmitting data.

Data can flow in simplex, half-duplex, or full-duplex mode (see Fig. 4-1). The physical connection can be parallel or serial (see Fig. 4-2), and the timing can be synchronous or asynchronous.

Simplex. Data travels only in one direction.

Fig. 4-1. Data transmission modes.

Half-duplex. Data can travel in both directions, but only in one direction at a time.

Full-duplex. Data can travel in both directions simultaneously.

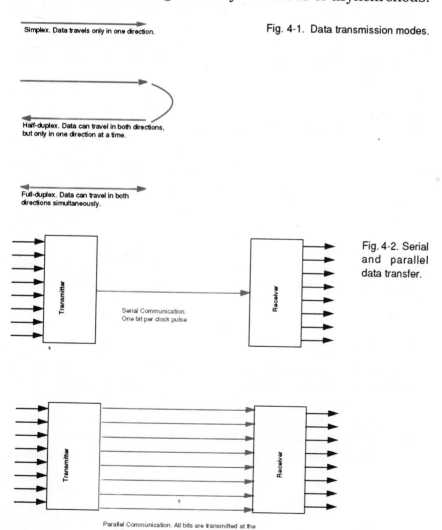

Transmitter

Serial Communication.
One bit per clock pulse

Receiver

Fig. 4-2. Serial and parallel data transfer.

Transmitter

Receiver

Parallel Communication. All bits are transmitted at the same time.

Data Flow

In simplex transmission, data flows in only one direction on a data communication line. Examples of this type of communication are commercial television and radio transmission. A television station normally broadcasts a signal from an antenna connected to a production studio and it is received by a television receiver in the home. Once the signal is received by the television set, it is displayed but no data is sent back to the production studio.

In half-duplex mode, transmission is allowed in either direction on a circuit, but in only one direction at a time. This type of transmission is widely used in data processing applications. If a computer is communicating with a terminal in this mode, then only one of them can be transmitting at any given time. Once the terminal sends data to the computer and the message is received, then the computer can send data back to the terminal. During this last phase, the terminal becomes the listener and the computer the sender. If two devices are communicating in half-duplex and both transmit at the same time, then the data sent is not received or simply becomes "garbage" in the lines.

Full-duplex mode allows for the transmission of data in both directions simultaneously. Most terminals and microcomputers are configured to work in full-duplex mode. This type of transmission requires more software and hardware control on both ends. This mode allows the computer and the terminal to send at the same time. Specialized software and hardware make sure that the messages are delivered to their destinations in a legible format. Although this is the most complex of the three modes, it is also the most efficient.

Physical Connection

Although data transmission can be classified according to the format of the data flow through the communication wires, it can also be classified as to how many bits of information are transmitted with every clock pulse. If data transmission is classified in this manner, then two possibilities arise. One is parallel communications and the other is serial communications.

The input/output ports of a data processing device can transmit data bit by bit or send an entire byte in a single parallel operation employing eight lines, one for each bit. The benefit of parallel transmission is its simplicity. A byte is placed on the output port of a device and a single pulse of the computer clock transfers the data to a receiving device. However, because of the number of wires involved, it is expensive and impractical over long distances. Parallel communication is achieved through the use of a parallel port or Centronics interface normally located at the back of the computer.

In serial transmission the data is sent one bit at a time using a single conductor to provide communication between devices. Standard telephone lines can be used to transmit data serially. Although transmitting data in this mode is slower than parallel transmission, it is currently a widely used data transmission mode. This is especially true in the case of communications between a microcomputer and a minicomputer or mainframe. In many situations, the microcomputer is simply working in a terminal emulation mode. That is, it is working as if it was the native terminal of the minicomputer or mainframe. In such cases, most managers want to use the least expensive communication schema. If the microcomputers are in close proximity to the host, serial communication is normally employed.

Timing

The type of timing used for the transmission of data is the last of the major categories for classifying data communications. Here, timing refers to how the receiving system knows that it received the group of bits that form a valid character. Two major timing schemas are used. One is asynchronous communication and the other is synchronous data communication.

Asynchronous communication is characterized by the use of a start bit preceding each character transmitted. In addition, there are one or more stop bits which follow each character. In asynchronous transmission, sometimes called async, data comes in irregular bursts, not in steady streams.

The start and stop bits form what is called a character frame. Every character must be enclosed in a frame. The receiver counts the start bit and the appropriate number of data bits. If it does not sense the end of a frame, then a framing error has occurred and an invalid character was received. When this happens, smart systems ask that the sender retransmit the last group of bits.

Asynchronous transmission is relatively simple and inexpensive to implement. It is widely used by microcomputers and commercial communication devices. However, it has a low transmission efficiency since at least two extra bits must be added to each character transmitted. Also, asynchronous communication takes place at low speeds, ranging from 300 to 19,200 baud.

The start and stop bits in asynchronous transmission add overhead to the bit stream. There is an alternate method of serial communication that doesn't use start and stop bits. It is called synchronous serial communication. With synchronous transmission, data characters are sent in large groups called blocks. These blocks contain synchronization characters that have a unique bit pattern. They are placed at the beginning and middle of each block with the synchronization characters ranging in number from one to four. When the receiver detects one of these special characters, it knows that the following bit is the beginning of a character maintaining, in this manner, synchronization.

This type of transmission is more efficient than asynchronous communication. As an example, assume that 10,000 characters are going to be sent serially. If the characters are sent via asynchronous transmission, then 10,000 char x (8 data bits + 2 bits per char) yields 100,000 bits that are sent in asynchronous communications. Using synchronous communication, the calculation (10,000 char + 4 synchronous char) x 8 bits per char yields 80,032 bits that are sent.

In this example, the synchronous transmission has a 22 percent increase in transmission efficiency over asynchronous transmission. The efficiency of synchronous over asynchronous transmission increases as the block of data gets larger. Many terminals use synchronous communication, including the IBM 3270 series. However, the actual efficiency of the transmission will also depend on many other factors such as how many times bits must be retransmitted.

Standard Digital Codes

As mentioned before, computers process information in digital form. That is, information is in the form of individual bits or digits with a bit being the smallest unit of data that the computer can represent. Normally, personal computers use seven or eight bits to represent the individual characters that are stored inside the computer. Individual characters for the English language that are stored in a computer include:

> Lower- and uppercase letters of the alphabet (a...Z)
>
> Digits (0...9)
>
> Punctuation marks (., ?, :, ...)
>
> Arithmetic operators (*, -, +, /, ...)
>
> Unit symbols (%, $, #, ...)

In addition to these characters, there is a set of special characters that some computer makers include with their machines. These are mostly graphical and language-specific characters.

For many years, the computer industry has tried to standardize the representation of digital codes. As a result, two major code representations exist in the market today. The most popular and widely recognized is the code system employed by computer manufacturers in the United States and many other countries called the American Standard Code for Information Interchange (ASCII). The other major code is the Extended Binary Coded Decimal Interchange Code (EBCDIC), which is used by IBM mainframes and compatibles. Most other types of mainframes, minicomputers, and microcomputers employ the ASCII code.

ASCII is a seven-bit code in which 128 characters are represented. EBCDIC uses eight bits to represent each character. Table 4-1 shows the standard ASCII code representation. In addition to the standard 128 ASCII characters, there is a set of 128 special characters used by IBM personal computers and compatibles called the Extended ASCII. The characters represented in Extended ASCII vary among computer manufacturers and are used to represent foreign characters or graphic characters.

In this chapter we will concentrate on explaining the ASCII representation since it is the most popular. The ASCII code in Table 4-1 contains 128 unique items. The table shows 32 control characters and 96 printable characters. Table 4-1 uses the hexadecimal system to represent the ASCII value of each character. To find the ASCII value of a character the process is as follows. Assume that the ASCII value of "A" is required. The column number of "A" is four, therefore four is multiplied by 16 giving 64. The row number of "A" is one, so one is added to the previous result. The total is 65 and that is the ASCII value of the character "A." Notice that the rows jump from 9 to A, B, C, D, E, and F. In this case A represents 10, B is 11, C is 12, D is 13, E is 14, and F is 15. Using this example it is easily verified that the ASCII value of the character "O" is 79, because 4 x 16 = 64, and 64 + 15 = 79.

	0	1	2	3	4	5	6	7
0	NUL	DLE	SP	0	@	P		p
1	SOH	DC1	!	1	A	Q	a	q
2	STX	DC2	"	2	B	R	b	r
3	ETX	DC3	#	3	C	S	c	s
4	EOT	DC4	$	4	D	T	d	t
5	ENQ	NAK	%	5	E	U	e	u
6	ACK	SYN	&	6	F	V	f	v
7	BEL	ETB	'	7	G	W	g	w
8	BS	CAN	(	8	H	X	h	x
9	HT	EM	)	9	I	Y	i	y
A	LF	SUB	*	:	J	Z	j	z
B	VT	ESC	+	;	K	[	k	{
C	FF	FS	`	<	L	\	l	|
D	CR	GS	-	=	M	]	m	}
E	SO	RS	.	>	N	^	n	~
F	SI	US	/	?	O	_	o	DEL

Table 4-1. The ASCII code.

The printable characters can be generated by pressing the corresponding key on the keyboard, or by pressing the shift key and the appropriate key. The control characters are generated by pressing a key labeled Control or CTRL on the keyboard and a corresponding key. For the rest of this chapter, the character ^

will be used to denote the CTRL key. These control codes are used for communicating with external devices such as modems, printers, and additional codes.

The control codes can be further subdivided into format effectors, communication controls, information separators, and others as described below.

Format Effectors

The format effectors provide functions analogous to the control keys used in document preparation. Each code name is followed by its hexadecimal representation, then a colon, and finally the key combination that can generate the code. A description of each follows.

> BS (backspace) 08H:^H. It moves the cursor on a video display or the print head of a printer back one space.

> HT (horizontal tab) 09H:^I. This is the same as the Tab key on a keyboard or typewriter.

> LF (line feed) 0AH:^J. It advances the cursor one line on a display or moves the printer down one line.

> CR (carriage return) 0DH:^M. It returns the cursor on a display or moves the printer head to the beginning of the line. This code is sometimes combined with the line feed to produce a new line character that is defined as a CR/LF sequence.

> FF (form feed) 0CH:^L. It ejects a page on a printer. It also causes the cursor to move one space to the right on a video screen.

> VT (vertical tab) 0BH: ^K. It line feeds to the next programmed vertical tab on a printer. It causes the cursor to move up one line on a video screen.

Communication Controls

Another series of control codes is used for communication. These controls facilitate data transmission over a communication network. They are used in both async and sync serial protocols for data transfer handshaking.

The communication control codes are:

SOH. It indicates the start of a message heading data block. Workstations in a network check the data following this header to determine if they are the recipients of the data that will follow the heading. Sometimes this character is used in asynchronous communications to transfer a group of files without handling each file as a separate communication session.

STX. It indicates the start of text.

ETX. It indicates the end of text.

EOT. It indicates the end of transmission.

ENQ. It indicates the end of an inquiry.

ACK. It indicates acknowledgment by a device.

NAK. It is negative acknowledgment.

EXT. This is an interrupt.

SYN. It is synchronous idle.

ETB. It indicates the end of a block.

These control codes are used in building data-transfer protocols and during synchronous transmission.

Information Separators

The information-separator codes are:

FS. It is used as a file separator.

GS. It is used as a group separator.

RS. It is used as a record separator.

US. It is used as a unit separator.

Most of the communication control and information-separator codes are not relevant to the material presented in the rest of this chapter. However, they are shown here for general information purposes.

Additional Control Codes

Of the remaining codes used by computers, the most important are:

NUL (null) OOH: ^@. It is used to pad the start of a transmission of characters.

BEL (bell) 07H:^G. It generates a tone from the speaker on the video monitor or the computer.

DC1, DC2, DC3, and DC4 (device control): ^Q, ^R, ^S, ^T. These codes are used to control video monitors and printers. Of these four, the first (DC1) and the third (DC3) are of special interest. DC1 is generated by ^Q, and it is called X-On. DC3 is generated by ^S, and it is called X-Off. If a computer sends information to a printer too fast, then the printer's buffer gets full before it can print the characters stored in it. The result is that characters are lost before they can be printed. In this situation, the printer sends a ^S (X-Off) to the computer before the buffer is completely full. This causes the computer to stop sending characters. When there is room in the printer buffer for more characters, a ^Q (X-On) is sent to the computer. This indicates to the machine that it can resume sending characters. This use of X-On and X-Off is called software handshaking.

ESC (escape) 1BH: ^[. Video terminals, computers, and printers interpret the next character after the escape code as a printable character.

DEL (delete) 7FH. It is used to delete characters under the cursor on video displays.

When two computers communicate with each other, the information will be exchanged by passing the individual bits that make up the characters. The flow of information is controlled by the use of control codes between communicating devices. The conventions that must be observed in order for electronic devices to communicate with one another are called the protocol. The bits that make up these control characters flow through some type of communication medium.

If the communicating devices are in close proximity, then the medium of communication can be coaxial cable, twisted-pair cable, or optical fiber. If the computers are far apart, then microwave, satellite, or telephone line connections are used to connect the machines. The phone company provides one of the most common and inexpensive methods of connecting machines. However, if analog phone lines are used, a modem must be employed.

Modems

Normally data communication between terminals or microcomputers and other host systems is done over some type of direct cabling. Direct means that the cable goes directly from one device to the other. However, sometimes the distance between the devices is too large to have a direct connection. In such cases a device, called a modem, can be used to facilitate the transmission process using telephone lines.

Fig. 4-3 depicts the connection of a remote terminal or microcomputer to a host system via standard telephone lines. The terminal and host systems are connected through telephone lines with a modem at each end of the connection. As stated earlier, a modem is an electronic device that converts (modulates) the digital communications between computers into audible tones that can be transmitted over telephone lines. The

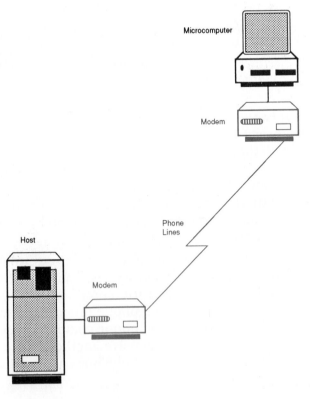

Fig. 4-3. Connection between remote terminal and host through the telephone lines using modems.

Microcomputer

Modem

Phone Lines

Host

Modem

received data is then converted (demodulated) from the audible tones into digital information. This is the origin of the name modem (MOdulator-DEModulator).

Modems not only facilitate the transmission process, but many of them have smart features built in. For example, many modems can dial phone numbers automatically. Additionally, they can redial busy numbers and automatically set the proper communicating speed. These features and others are discussed later in this section.

Although modems can be classified in many different ways, one way to classified them is according to the location of the modem with respect to the computer that it serves. Modems can be external or internal. An internal modem (Fig. 4-4) is placed inside the computer by using available bus expansion slots or bays. Then it is connected to a phone line with the use of a standard phone cord.

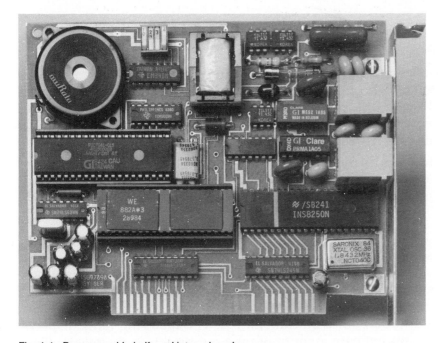

Fig. 4-4. Programmable half-card internal modem.

An external modem (Fig. 4-5) is placed next to the computer and connected to one of its serial ports with the use of a serial cable and to the telephone line with a phone cord. Once the modem is connected to the computer and the telephone, its function is normally controlled by software residing in the computer.

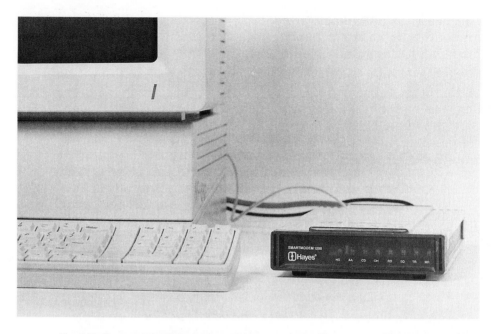

Fig. 4-5. Hayes external modem.

Modems transmit data at various speeds. The speed of data transfer through a modem can range from 300 bits per second to 9600 bits per second on microcomputers. On mainframe networks, modems commonly operate at speeds of up to 1.5 million bits per second, and sometimes higher.

The speed of the modem determines the time required to transfer files. A higher speed of transmission means lower transfer time. The file transfer time can be estimated by using the formula:

Time = (characters to be transmitted x bits per character) / (modem speed in bits per second)

As an example, assume that a 100-page document is to be transmitted over telephone lines. Further assume that each page contains approximately 3300 characters and each character requires seven bits for storage. This means that there will be 2,310,000 bits to be transmitted. The following table displays the approximate amount of time required to transmit the file.

Bits per second	300	1200	4800	9600
Time (seconds)	7700	1930	480	240

These are approximate times. The actual time required to transfer a file depends on many factors such as noise in the communicating lines, how the data is packed, and how many times a character must be retransmitted when an error occurs. However, the times shown in the table can be used to obtain an idea of how the transmission time is reduced by increasing the speed of the modem.

Types of Modems

There are several types of modems, each with a unique set of functions that makes it suitable for a specific job. Some of the most common types are optical, short haul, acoustic, smart, digital, and V.32 modems. Of all of these, smart modems are the most commonly found in the microcomputer market.

Optical Modem

An optical modem transmits data over optical fiber lines. This type of modem, at the sender's end, converts electrical signals from a computer into pulses of light to be transmitted over optical fiber lines. At the receiver's end, the modem receives the light pulses and converts them back into a signal that the computer can understand. It operates using asynchronous or synchronous transmission modes.

Short Haul Modem

This type of modem uses paired wire cable to transmit electrical signals when the distances involved are approximately 20 miles or less. A short haul modem transmits at speeds of 9600 bits per second up to 5 miles, 4800 bits per second up to 10 miles, and finally at 2400 bits per second for distances of 10 to 20 miles. Normally, this type of modem is used to connect computers between different offices in the same building.

Acoustic Modem

This is an older type of modem, also called an acoustic coupler. It interfaces with any phone set and is used for dialing another computer.

Smart Modem

A smart modem can perform functions by using a command language. The language can be accessed through communication programs and adds functionality to the modem. Among microcomputer users, the Hayes modem has become a standard. This device can automatically answer or dial other modems, switch communication parameters, set the modem's speaker volume, and perform many other functions under software control.

Digital Modem

If, instead of using analog conversion, the communication circuits use digital transmission, then a digital modem is used. This type of modem modifies the digital bits as needed. Its function is to convert EIA-232 digital signals into signals more suitable for transmission.

V.32 Modem

A V.32 modem works at full duplex at 9,600 bits per second over normal telephone lines. It is typically used to back up leased phone lines on networks. That is, if data transmission through a leased line is interrupted, a V.32 and normal phone lines could be used as a temporary replacement for the leased line.

Features of Modems

Most newer modems have features that facilitate their use by inexperienced computer users. These features include the ability to change the speed of transmission, automatic dialing and redialing numbers, and automatic answering of incoming calls.

Speed

Modems are designed to operate at a set speed or a range of speeds. The speed can be set via switches on some modems or fall under program control. Typical speeds for modems under microcomputer control are 300, 1200, 2400, 4800, and 9600 bits per second.

Automatic Dialing/Redialing

Some modems can dial phone numbers under program control. If the modem encounters a busy line, it automatically redials the number until a connection is made.

Automatic Answering

Modems can automatically answer incoming calls and connect the dialing device to a host system. This is especially useful when setting up a private or home electronic bulletin board (see projects at the end of this chapter). In this case, you want the modem to answer calls automatically when a potential user calls in.

Self-Testing

Most new modems have a self-testing mode. Each modem has electronic circuitry and software in ROM that allow the modem to check its electronic components and the connection to other modems, and to report any problems to the user. This includes memory checking, modem-to-modem transmission tests, and other self-tests.

Voice-Over-Data

Modems also allow the simultaneous transmission of voice and data. This allows a conversation to take place while data is being transmitted over the same phone line.

Other

Newer modems contain many other features in addition to the ones outlined above. Some of these features are:

      Auto-disconnect

      Manual connect/disconnect

      Speaker

      Full- or half-duplex

      Reverse channel

      Synchronous or asynchronous transmission

      Multiport

The RS-232 Port

Modems normally connect to the computer through an RS-232 or serial port. On most microcomputers, the connections between external modems, computers, and other devices conform to this RS-232 standard. The RS-232 is a connector that is found on the back panel of most computers. Fig. 4-6 shows a diagram of a 25-pin RS-232 connector.

Fig. 4-6. 25-pin RS-232.

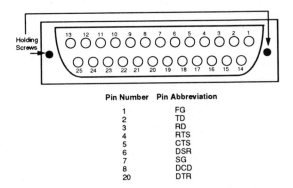

Pin Number	Pin Abbreviation
1	FG
2	TD
3	RD
4	RTS
5	CTS
6	DSR
7	SG
8	DCD
20	DTR

The important pins to consider are pin numbers 1, 2, 3, 4, 5, 6, 7, 8, and 20. Following is a description of these connectors with the capitalized abbreviations corresponding to the modem front panel.

Pin 1. Frame ground: FG. It is used to connect the frame of the terminal or modem to earth ground. It protects the device from dangerous voltages. Normally, this pin is left unconnected.

Pin 2. Transmit data: TD. Outgoing data travels from the terminal or computer to the modem via pin 2.

Pin 3. Receive data: RD. Incoming data travels from the modem to the terminal or computer via pin 3.

Pin 4. Request to send: RTS. This is used to indicate to the terminal or computer that the modem has activated its carrier and that data transmission can start.

Pin 5. Clear to send: CTS. This pin is taken to an active level when the terminal or computer is ready to accept data.

Pin 6. Data set ready: DSR. An active DSR indicates to a device that it is connected to an active modem.

Pin 7. Signal ground: SG.

Pin 8. Data carrier detect: DCD. This pin is used by the modem to inform the computer or terminal that a remote connection has been made.

Pin 20. Data terminal ready: DTR. An active DTR indicates to the modem that it is connected to an active device.

Handshaking is the manner in which the communicating computer knows when the other machine is sending or receiving data, or when it is doing some other task that might interfere with the transmission signals. This is also referred to as the communications protocol. Handshaking can be accomplished through the use of software by using control characters (X-On and X-Off). Pins 4, 5, 6, 8, and 20 are used for hardware handshaking. That is, these pins are used to make sure that there is cooperation between the devices exchanging data.

Another type of RS-232 connector is the nine-pin RS-232 connector found on some microcomputers. By using nine pins instead of twenty-five pins, space is saved on the back panels of computers and peripherals. The layout of the pin connections on this type of RS-232 differs from manufacturer to manufacturer. Fig. 4-7 shows the layout of the nine-pin RS-232 connector found on the IBM PC-AT.

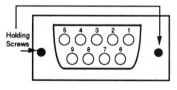

Fig. 4-7. Nine pin RS-232.

Pin Number	Pin Abbreviation
1	DCD
2	RD
3	TD
4	DTR
5	SG
6	DSR
7	RTS
8	CTS
9	RI

The nine-pin connector in Fig. 4-7 has an extra pin (pin 9, RI) beyond the eight defined above. This is the ring indicator. This pin becomes active when the modem has received the ring of an incoming call.

The process of using a modem to connect a microcomputer or terminal to a host system is as follows:

1. When the communicating devices are powered up, the terminal's DTR signal and the modem's DSR signal are activated.

2. When the terminal is ready to send data, it activates its RTS signal.

3. The modem activates the CTS signal of the analog carrier.

4. The user's modem dials the phone of the remote modem and waits for its response.

5. When the user's modem senses communication over the phone line, it activates its DCD signal.

6. A high level DCD signal tells the microcomputer or terminal that it is connected to a remote device and the data exchange can begin.

Multiplexers

Although modems are used to connect computers over large distances and direct cable is normally employed over short distances, the number of cables required to satisfy all users can at times be overwhelming. In addition, leasing lines from the phone company to communicate between two offices located far away from each other can be expensive. Multiplexers help in solving some of this economic cost by allowing the transmission of multiple data communication sessions over a common wire or medium.

Function

Multiplexing technology allows the transmission of multiple signals over a single medium. Multiplexers (see Fig. 4-8) allow the replacement of multiple low-speed transmission lines with a single high-speed transmission line. The typical configuration includes a multiplexer attached to multiple low-speed lines, a communication line (typically four-wire carrier circuit), and a multiplexer at another site that is also connected to low-speed lines. Fig. 4-9 depicts this configuration. In addition, the figure shows a remote site that is connected to a multiplexer through the use of modems. The remote site contains terminals, micro-computers, modems, and printers attached to a multiplexer. The host site has a multiplexer, FEP, and a host CPU.

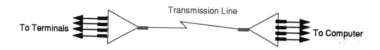

Fig. 4-8. Multiplexers can lower the number of wires required for communication between two locations.

The operation of the multiplexers, frequently called MUXs, in Fig. 4-9 is transparent to the sending and receiving computers or terminals. The multiplexer does not interrupt the normal flow

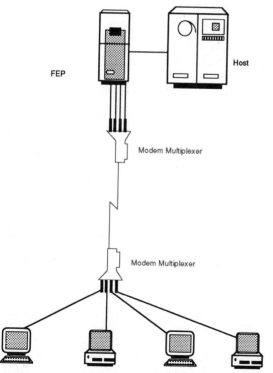

Fig. 4-9. Multiplexer operation is transparent to sending and receiving computers.

Terminals and Workstations

of data. Multiplexers allow for a significant reduction of the overall cost of connecting remote sites, since the number of lines required to connect the sites is decreased.

Techniques

Multiplexing techniques can be divided into frequency division multiplexing (FDM), time division multiplexing (TDM), and statistical time division multiplexing (STDM).

Frequency Division Multiplexing (FDM)

Users of existing voice-grade lines (phone lines) can multiplex low-speed circuits into the standard voice-grade channels by using FDM. In FDM, a modem and a frequency division are used to break down the frequency of available bandwidths of a voice-grade circuit, dividing it into multiple smaller bandwidths. The bandwith is a measure of the amount of data that can be transmitted per unit of time. The bandwidth is determined by the difference between the highest and lowest allowed frequencies in the transmission medium.

As an example, assume that a telephone circuit has a bandwidth of 3100 Hz, and a line capable of carrying 1200 bits per second (bps). Suppose that instead of running a terminal at 1200 bps, it is desired to run three terminals at 300 bps. If three terminals are going to use the same communication line, then some type of separator is required in order to avoid crosstalk (interference of signals from one to another). This separator is called a guardband. For transmission at 300 bps the standard separation is 480 Hz. Therefore, in the above situation, two guardbands of 480 Hz each are required (see Fig. 4-10). Since the guardbands now occupy 960 Hz, and the original line had a bandwidth of

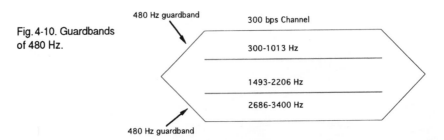

Fig. 4-10. Guardbands of 480 Hz.

480 Hz guardband

300 bps Channel

300-1013 Hz

1493-2206 Hz

2686-3400 Hz

480 Hz guardband

3100 Hz, then the frequency left for the 300-bps transmission is 2140 Hz. If three terminals are required, then 2140 Hz divided by three gives a frequency of 713 Hz to be used per channel.

With FDM it is not necessary for all lines to terminate at a single location. Using multidrop techniques, the terminals can be stationed in different locations within a building or a city.

Time Division Multiplexing (TDM)

Time division multiplexers are digital devices and therefore select incoming bits digitally, placing each bit into a high-speed bit stream in equal time intervals. (See Fig. 4-11.) The sending multiplexer will place a bit or byte from each of the incoming lines into a frame. The frames are placed on high-speed transmission lines, and a receiving multiplexer, knowing where each bit or byte is located, outputs the bits or bytes at appropriate speeds.

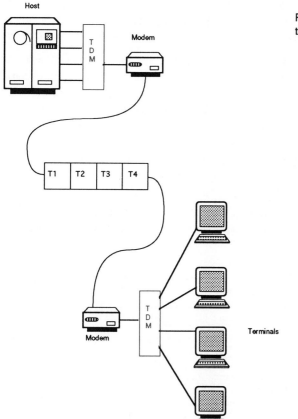

Fig. 4-11. Time division multiplexing.

Time division multiplexing is more efficient than frequency division multiplexing, but it requires a separate modem. To the sending and receiving stations it always appears as if a single line is connecting them. All lines for time division multiplexers originate in one location and end in one location. TDMs are easier to operate, less complex, and less expensive than FDMs.

Statistical Time Division Multiplexers (STDMs)

In any terminal-host configuration the terminals attached to the host CPU are not always transmitting data. The time during which they are idle is called down time. Statistical time division multiplexers are intelligent devices capable of identifying which terminals are idle and which terminals require transmission, and they allocate line time only when it is required. This means line time is provided only when a terminal is transmitting. This allows the connection of many more devices to the host than is possible with FDMs or TDMs (see Fig. 4-12).

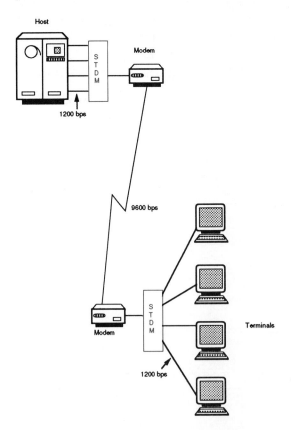

Fig. 4-12. Statistical time division multiplexing.

The STDM consists of a microprocessor-based unit that contains all hardware and software required to control both the reception of low-speed data coming in and high-speed data going out. Newer STDM units provide additional capabilities such as data compression, line priorities, mixed-speed lines, host port sharing, network port control, automatic speed detection, internal diagnostics, memory expansion, and integrated modems.

The number of devices that can be multiplexed using STDMs depends on the address field used in an STDM frame. If the field is 4 bits long, there are 16 terminals (2 to the power of 4) that can be connected. If 5 bits are used, 32 terminals can be connected (2 to the power of 5).

Configurations

Multiplexers can be used in a variety of configurations and combinations. Cascading is a typical configuration used to extend circuits to remote entry points when there are two or more data entry areas. Fig. 4-13 shows an example of cascading multiplexers. In the figure, data entry terminals in a geographical location are multiplexed, and a single carrier sends the data to a temporary receiving location. The data is then demultiplexed

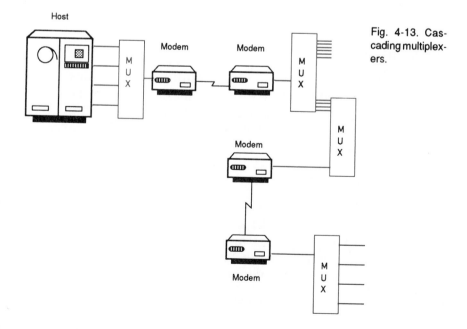

Fig. 4-13. Cascading multiplexers.

and multiplexed by a third multiplexer before being sent to the final destination. Then a multiplexer receives the data and distributes it among the ports of the host system.

The number of ports that a multiplexer can accommodate varies. Commonly there are 4, 8, 16, 32, 48, or 64 ports. The price of a multiplexer will vary with the number of ports in it and the sophistication of the device.

Types

Newer multiplexers are difficult to define. Some devices have a large array of options and functions that make them work in a specific format under some working conditions. They can be switched to a different type when the conditions change. We will make an attempt to outline some standard types that can be found in the market place. However, keep in mind that some multiplexers can perform the functions of several of the types outlined below.

Inverse Multiplexer

An inverse multiplexer provides a high-speed data path between computers. It takes a high-speed line coming out of a computer and separates it into multiple low-speed lines. The multiple low-speed lines are then recombined by another inverse multiplexer before making connection with the receiving computer.

T-1 Multiplexer

A T-1 multiplexer is a special type of multiplexer combined with a high-capacity data service unit that manages the ends of a T-1 link. A T-1 link is a communication link that transmits at 1.544 million bits per seconds. Therefore, T-1 circuits can carry 24 channels of 64,000 bits per second.

Multiport Multiplexer

A multiport multiplexer combines modem and time division multiplexing equipment into a single device. The line entering the modem can be of varying transmission speeds. The multiport multiplexer then combines the data and transmits it over a high-speed link to another receiving multiplexer.

Fiber Optic Multiplexer

A fiber optic multiplexer takes multiple channels of data, with each channel transmitting at 64,000 bits per channel, and multiplexes the channels onto a 14 million bits per second fiber optic line. It is similar in operation to a time division multiplexer, but operates at much higher speeds.

Summary

There are many different ways in which the transmission of data can be classified, but data transmission is typically grouped into three major areas according to:

1. How the data flows among devices.
2. The type of physical connection.
3. The type of timing used for transmitting data.

Data can flow in simplex, half-duplex, or full-duplex mode. The physical connection can be parallel or serial, and the timing can be synchronous or asynchronous. Regardless of the mode of transmission, the data being transmitted is described by coding standards. One is the ASCII standard used by all microcomputers, and non-IBM mainframes and minicomputers. The other standard is the EBCDIC standard which is used by IBM mainframes and some of their minicomputers.

In the case of serial communications over telephone lines, modems have to be used. A modem is an electronic device that converts (modulates) the digital communications between computers into audible tones that can be transmitted over telephone lines. The received data is then converted (demodulated) from the audible tones into digital information. There are several types of modems each with a unique set of functions that makes it suitable for a specific job. Some of the most common types are optical, short haul, acoustic, smart, digital, and V.32 modems. Of all of these, smart modems are the most commonly found in the microcomputer market.

Modems connect to the computer, normally through an RS-232 or serial port. On most microcomputers that use the ASCII code, the connections between external modems, computers, and other devices conform to this RS-232 standard. The RS-232 is a connector that is found on the back panel of most computers.

In order to lower the cost of data communications, multiplexers are employed. Multiplexers allow the replacement of multiple low-speed transmission lines with a single high-speed transmission line. The typical configuration includes a multiplexer attached to multiple low-speed lines, a communication line, and a multiplexer at another site that is also connected to low-speed lines.

Questions

1. What is data transmission in full-duplex mode?
2. Why is the synchronous mode more efficient than the asynchronous mode?
3. Since parallel transmission is faster than serial transmission, why don't we perform all data communication using parallel transmission?
4. What is the purpose of the ASCII standard?
5. Describe the function of a modem.
6. In the case of microcomputers, which modem are we most likely to use when sending data over phone lines? Why?
7. Describe three different types of modems?
8. What is the purpose of the RS-232 port?
9. Briefly describe the process of handshaking.
10. What is the purpose of multiplexing technology?
11. Which type of multiplexing technique is more efficient? Why?
12. Describe two types of multiplexers.

Projects

The projects in this chapter are intended to familiarize the student with the basic hardware required to connect computers and printers using standard RS-232 ports. The basic equipment required to perform the projects is outlined in project 1. As an additional challenge, the instructor may provide unknown or lesser known serial printers and instruct the student to design the interface between the printer and a microcomputer.

Interface between an External Modem and a Microcomputer

There are two methods of connecting an external modem to your computer. The first method is to purchase a serial cable from a local computer store, and connect the RS-232 or serial connector at the back of the computer with the serial connector at the back of the modem. This is the easier method. The second method is to construct your own serial cable. The tools required to make this cable are as follows:

1. Soldering iron and solder material.
2. Nine-wire (or more) cable.
3. Two serial connectors of the right gender. The gender can be "male" or "female." The male has pins coming out of the connector. In most cases the connector required for the PC will be female and that for the modem will be male. However, the gender of the connectors is not standard among all equipment manufacturers.
4. Wire strippers.
5. Clamps to hold the wires and connectors.
6. Breakout box (optional).

After all the tools and materials are gathered, use the connections outlined in Fig. 4-14 to connect a modem and a terminal.

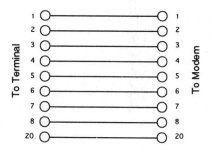

Fig. 4-14. Pin diagram for connector between a modem and a terminal.

Serial Interface between Two IBM or IBM-Compatible Microcomputers

To connect one computer directly to another without a modem, a modem eliminator or null modem is required. A null modem is a cable that has at a minimum the wires that connect pins 2 and 3 on both computers crossed over. Pin 2 on both computers is responsible for sending data, and pin 3 receives data. As you can imagine, if both of these pins were not crossed, then both the computers could talk but neither would be listening. Make these two connections now.

Making the connecting cable is only one aspect of connecting two microcomputers. Communication software will be required to perform the communication functions. The project in chapter 4 explores this topic further and provides some hands-on experience. A general null modem can be created by crossing pins 2 and 3, 20 and 6, and connecting 8 to 6 on the RS-232 cable as in Fig. 4-15.

Fig. 4-15. Pin diagram for connector between two IBM or IBM-compatible microcomputers.

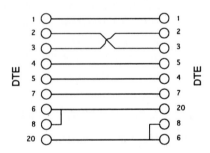

Advanced Communication Hardware

Objectives

After completing this chapter you will:

1. Understand the use of concentrators, protocol converters, PBXs, cluster controllers, and matrix switches in a data communication system.

2. Understand the different line adapters that can be placed on a network and their application to data communication lines.

3. Understand the need for security in a data communication line and the equipment that can be used to enforce it.

4. Know the purpose of a breakout box.

5. Know how to create and debug serial communication interfaces (if projects are complete).

Key Words

Channel Extender	Cluster Controller
Concentrator	Digital Line Expander
Encryption	Line Monitor
Line Splitter	Matrix Switch
PBX	Protocol Converter

Introduction

Today's data communication systems have increased in sophistication and take advantage of equipment that was formerly reserved for voice communication systems only. Multiplexers, protocol converters, PBXs, matrix switches, and concentrators are among these devices. Additionally, the educated data communication system user and manager must understand the different devices that can be used to monitor these systems and the transmission media available to them.

It is important to point out that, although newer tendencies in the data communication market are toward networks, a networking solution is in many situations not the best or the only solution to a data communication problem. The uneducated manager may try to solve any communication problem by using local or wide area networks, since these are solutions that usually seem to work. However, a network is not easy to install nor is it always the most cost effective solution for creating a media-sharing environment. Today's data communication managers must be aware of many devices that solve common data transmission problems quickly and effectively. Some of the most commonly found equipment that can be used stand-alone or in a network is described in this chapter, along with some devices that can be used to add additional security to a data communication environment.

This type of thinking, along with the knowledge of the diversity of devices that can be used in different situations, indicates an informed manager who can make smart decisions. This type of individual is a rare commodity in a field that is crowded with so-called experts who don't have proper training in the field of data communication. Any data communication manager can make decisions, but only knowledgeable and open-minded managers can make decisions that are efficient and cost effective. With this in mind, let's take a closer look at some of the data communication equipment that is commonly found in the market place.

Concentrator

The previous chapter discussed various types and functions of multiplexers. Standard multiplexers are bit- or byte-oriented devices with limited storage capabilities and little computing logic. There are occasions when it is desirable to perform some type of processing on the information traveling through the communication medium for purposes of error detection and editing. In this case, handling the information on a bit-per-bit or byte basis is inadequate. For the processing functions that we are discussing, the information must be handled on a message basis, or on a store-and-forward basis. Store-and-forward means that the message is received at a location, it is validated, and an acknowledgment is sent back to the sender. A device that can perform this type of operation is the concentrator.

A concentrator is a line-sharing device with a primary function that is the same as a multiplexer. It allows multiple devices to share communication circuits. In addition, a concentrator is an intelligent device that sometimes performs data processing functions and has auxiliary storage. Some of the earlier concentrators were statistical multiplexers. That is the reason some vendors call a concentrator a statistical multiplexer or stat mux. In addition to having a CPU, concentrators are used one at a time, whereas multiplexers are used in pairs. Also, a concentrator may vary the number of incoming and outgoing lines, while a multiplexer must use the same number of lines on both ends.

A typical concentrator configuration is depicted in Fig. 5-1. The example shows multiple terminals using a concentrator to access several host systems. Concentrators perform data compression functions, forward error correction, and network-related functions in addition to acting as line-sharing devices. They are considered data processing devices, and newer types of concentrators are built around microcomputers and minicomputers. However, "pure" concentrators don't perform any type of routing of data on a network. They just take data from a central location and distribute it to some remote site and take data from the remote site and send it to the central location. Any routing of data from one terminal to another terminal or from one workstation to another workstation is performed by message switching equipment or front end processors. Above, we use the word "pure" to emphasize that the job of a concentrator does not typically include performing data switching functions. But there are some modern concentrators that do perform switching functions. This is the result of equipment manufacturers trying to cover as much of this market as possible. As the hardware becomes less costly, equipment manufacturers try to pack as much power in their devices as possible in order to appeal to a larger audience. The result is equipment that performs the duties of multiple devices.

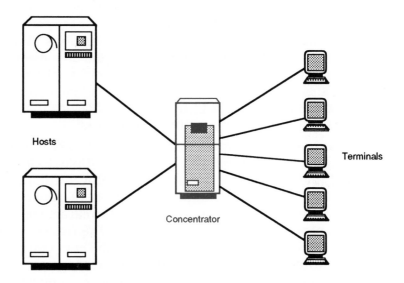

Fig. 5-1. Concentrator placement in a data communication system.

Cluster Controller

A cluster controller is designed to support several terminals and the functions required to manage the terminals. A modern cluster controller performs many of the functions of a front end processor and is in most cases a smaller version of a front end processor. In addition, it buffers data being transmitted to or from the terminals, performs error detection and correction, and polls terminals (see Fig. 5-2). Polling is a technique by which the controller checks to see which terminals are ready to send data. If a terminal needs to send a packet of data to a host, the cluster controller ensures that the packet gets to its destination. In addition, some cluster controllers can be attached to more than one communication line, allowing one user to have multiple sessions that access multiple computers. Normally, a special key combination switches the user from one host computer to another. Also, not only can a user be attached to multiple computers, but some cluster controllers allow the user to have multiple sessions with the same computer. In this manner, a user can be executing a database query and performing file transfer or some other function in different but simultaneous sessions.

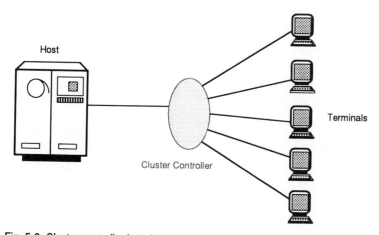

Fig. 5-2. Cluster controller in a data communication system.

Examples of popular cluster controllers are the IBM 3174 and 3274 cluster controllers. These controllers can handle up to 32 terminals and normally interact with 3278/79 terminals or terminal emulators. In the case of the 3174 or 3274, the most common configuration for large-scale systems is to attach groups of cluster controllers through a telecommunication line to a front end processor. Common IBM front end processors are the 3705 and 3725. Also, these devices can be nodes in a network, enhancing the capability of the equipment and making their life cycle longer in an era when data communications equipment must coexist with other equipment in network configurations. This concept is explored in later chapters. It is an important point to explore, because of the number of microcomputers being used to communicate to cluster controllers.

Until recently, 3270 or other types of terminals were the main source of communication between users and IBM mainframes. But as the price of microcomputers dropped during the last decade, people used microcomputers with some type of emulation system as a replacement for the communication terminal. Microcomputers gave users the ability to send large amounts of data to the cluster controller that was originally designed to handle short transactions. The end result is an overloading of the cluster controller, with response time increasing in some situations to as much as 20 minutes. This problem is alleviated by using networks, as we will discuss in chapter 9, and distributing the load of the data communications equipment. The use of the microcomputer as a communicating device between the user and the mainframe also made the protocol converter a popular device.

Protocol Converter

In order for electronic devices to communicate with one another, a set of conventions is required. This set of conventions is called the protocol. A protocol determines the sequence of codes required for data exchange and the bit or character sequences required to control the exchange.

Since computers and other electronic devices sometimes have their own proprietary protocols, protocol converters are used to interconnect two dissimilar computers or terminals so they can talk to each other. As an analogy, imagine a person who speaks only English and another person who speaks only Russian trying to communicate with one another. For the communication to be effective, a translator who understands both languages serves as the bridge between both persons. The protocol converter assumes the role of the translator in the electronic data exchange. Although we discuss only some of the most commonly used protocols in data communications, many more exist. The protocol converter provides an effective means of translating information or packets of data (a message that is subdivided into smaller data units for a more efficient transmission) between dissimilar devices that need to exchange data. Fig. 5-3 shows the IBM 3708 protocol converter which handles up to eight dial-in lines simultaneously.

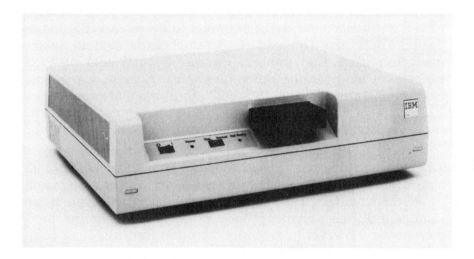

Fig. 5-3. The IBM 3708 protocol converter handles up to eight dial-in lines simultaneously. Many conversion options are available. (Courtesy of IBM Corporation)

Protocol converters also convert character codes. As mentioned in chapter 4, two character codes used in the computer environment in the United States are the ASCII and EBCDIC standards. The EBCDIC code is used by IBM in midrange and mainframe systems. The ASCII code is used by virtually every other computer manufacturer. Therefore, to connect an IBM personal computer that uses the ASCII system to an IBM mainframe, an ASCII-to-EBCDIC converter is required (see Fig. 5-4).

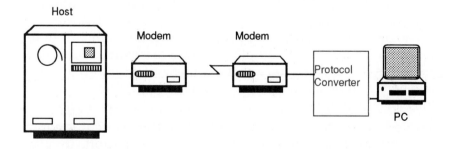

Fig. 5-4. Connection between PC and host mainframe.

Protocol converters can be hardware or software designed. A hardware protocol converter is treated as a "black box" on the communication line. It performs its function in a manner that is transparent to the system. For example, third party vendors offer asynchronous-to-synchronous protocol conversion boxes. This allows an inexpensive async terminal to access an IBM mainframe. There are also add-on circuit boards that fit inside microcomputers that perform communications and protocol conversion at the same time. These boards allow a personal computer to emulate a 3278 or 3279 terminal and connect to a 3174 or 3274 controller via a coaxial cable. Some of the cards have the controller built in and can access the mainframe directly.

The other method of protocol conversion is achieved through software. Typically, this software resides in the host system and converts incoming data to the language that the host system can understand. This is an inexpensive manner of achieving protocol conversion. However, it requires attention from the host computer, reducing the amount of time it can apply to other tasks. Whenever possible, hardware protocol converters are used, but be aware that many protocol converters also perform other functions, such as multiplexing and concentrating. Because of these multiple options in a single device, purchasing decisions must be made carefully to avoid duplication or needless acquisition of features. This is especially true as the sophistication of the equipment increases, such as in the PBX.

Private Branch Exchanges (PBX)

A private branch exchange is an electronic switchboard within an organization, with all the telephone lines of the organization connected to it (see Fig. 5-5). Normally, several of the telecommunication circuits of the PBX go from this switchboard to the telephone company's main office. These are called trunk lines when they are devoted to voice transmission. If they are used for data communication, they are known as leased lines, dedicated lines, or private lines.

Private branch exchanges, like the centralized switching equipment found at the phone company, are computers that are specially designed to handle voice telephone calls. However, since they are computers, they can also handle data communications in a digital format. Their flexibility in this area, especially when it comes to connecting a terminal or microcomputer to a host system, makes them a popular device used in data communication. But, as we will see shortly, the PBX as a hub for connecting data communication equipment is effective only when the required rate of transmission is low. Before we discuss the capabilities of the private branch exchange, it is important to know some of the history behind the development of the PBX so you may understand the capabilities of any existing PBXs at your site.

Fig. 5-5. This Northern Telecom PBX is configured for 600 telephone lines. Line cards can be added or removed for smaller or larger configurations.
(Courtesy of Northern Telecom, Inc.)

PBX History

PBX systems have been in offices for a number of years. As organizations developed and grew, PBX equipment was upgraded and enhanced to meet users' demands. The evolution of PBX equipment can be categorized into several generations.

The first generation of PBXs was placed in service prior to the mid-1970s. They carried only voice and were capable of handling only analog signals. Their design was electromechanical, and they used analog circuitry for switching signals.

The second generation of PBXs was designed between the mid-1970s and the mid-1980s. These were also voice-only PBXs, but they digitized voice signals before transferring them through the switch. This PBX equipment could be modified to carry digital data signals as well as voice. However, the transfer rate for data signals was slow.

The third generation of PBXs has been in existence since the early 1980s. They have the capability to move voice and data at relatively high speeds. Incoming analog signals are converted to digital signals, and therefore offer greater flexibility and capabilities. Most of today's PBXs are from this generation.

The fourth generation of PBXs is characterized by having all voice and data switching capabilities combined in a LAN distribution system. They can serve as voice phone switches, electronic mail, voice mail, and data switches for LANs. However, their implementation has been slow due to the high cost of each line in the system.

Capabilities

Newer digital PBXs, such as the IBM 9751, Northern Telecom's Meridian, and the AT&T System 75 and 85, are designed around 32-bit microprocessor chips that control the entire system. They contain many features, including the following:

1. They can transmit voice and data simultaneously. Obviously, all PBXs can handle voice communications, but most of them have the capability to handle data communications. With this feature, a user with a terminal or a microcomputer can access devices or host computers that are connected to the PBX. In the case of a microcomputer, some type of terminal

emulation is normally used to communicate with the host. To access the host, the user dials the number of the site where the host is located. In some systems, system names can be given instead of the number; the PBX's software interprets the name provided and finds the destination requested. If the host has an available line, the user's microcomputer is connected to the host. When the user is finished with the transmission, the line is made available to another user. In this fashion, other intelligent devices, such as smart facsimile machines and printers, can be made available to users, along with the microcomputer. These facilities can also be made available to users who must dial in from other offices or their homes. Once a line is available to one of these users, he or she has the same capabilities as any user in the office.

2. They can perform protocol conversion, allowing equipment from different vendors to communicate. Modern PBX systems have built-in protocol conversion capabilities that allow microcomputers to connect to host computers with dissimilar protocols without the need of additional equipment. Using an async or sync line provided through the PBX, a microcomputer can be attached to an IBM host, placing the burden of protocol conversion on the PBX instead of the host. Although this type of scenario is not effective when high transmission speeds are required, it is a solution for many users who need only terminal emulation and connection to a host.

3. They can control local area networks from within the switchboard. Private branch exchanges can be used as the connecting hub for several local area networks. In this case, networks that are isolated and need to exchange data with other networks using existing phone wires can use the PBX as a central hub that switches data from one network to another using an available line.

4. They have voice and electronic mail. One of the necessities of the modern office is the need for employees to communicate continuously. Private branch exchanges can provide voice mail for a customer or another user to access the PBX using a telephone,

access a private voice mail box by typing a set number of digits from the telephone pad, and then leave a voice message to the owner of the voice mail box. The owner can then retrieve messages in any order, delete messages, forward messages, or save messages.

Additionally, PBXs offer electronic mail. The concept of electronic mail is similar to that of voice mail, but instead of leaving a voice message using a telephone, a terminal or computer is used to leave a written message. The owner of the electronic mail box has the same capabilities as the owner of voice mail boxes in terms of managing the mail stored by the system.

5. Asynchronous and synchronous transmission can be performed simultaneously. With this capability, a corporation can have multiple hosts, some of which may require async data transmission and some that require sync data transmission. The private branch exchange can handle both types of transmission simultaneously, allowing inexpensive async terminals access to their native host in addition to performing the translation required (in some cases) to use an async type terminal on a host requiring sync transmission. Although many PBX systems place the burden of async-to-sync conversion on other devices, they still allow both types of transmission over the same switching lines.

6. Automatic routing is available, ensuring that calls are routed through the least costly communication system. This is an important feature when a long distance call is made and large amounts of data are being transmitted. The ability to find the least costly route can save thousands of dollars annually to corporations that must maintain data lines with remote offices or sites.

7. They can switch digital transmission without the use of modems. Recall that in order for a computer to send data over ordinary telephone lines, a modem is required. When a private branch exchange system is used, any switching of data from one line of the PBX to another of its lines can be done without the need of

screen, printed to paper, or stored on an auxiliary device for further analysis. Fig. 5-6 shows the placement of a line monitor in the data communication circuit.

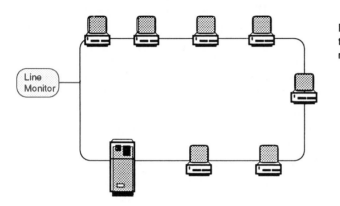

Fig. 5-6. Line monitor in a data communication system.

There are two categories of line monitors, active and passive. Active line monitors can generate data, are interactive, and can emulate various types of monitors. Passive line monitors gather data and store it for analysis at a later time. Modern line monitors provide information about traffic volume, idle status, and errors that take place in the communicating medium. These statistics are normally stored in some secondary storage medium for further analysis and are displayed in a graphical format at the same time that they are being stored.

The hardware monitor is a special type of line monitor. It measures voltage changes in the line and reports changes. Using a hardware monitor, any type of system such as a front end processor, concentrator, and data communication line can be closely monitored. Additional monitors, such as network monitors, are discussed in later chapters, but any monitor of system performance that installs or interfaces between the user's equipment and the data communication line is considered a line monitor.

A typical line monitor can work with data speeds of up to 64,000 bits per second, and has video displays and memory, supports synchronous and asynchronous transmission, has breakout box capabilities (see later section in this chapter), and is capable of being programmed. Using this capability, a system administrator can instruct the line monitor to look for specific signals or to look at the function of individual devices. The purpose is to diagnose problems that a user may report or to find "bottle-necks" in the transmission process in order to improve response time.

Microcomputers can be enhanced to function as line monitors. A PC adapter board, internal RS-232, and software can convert a standard microcomputer into an active and intelligent line monitor and response time analyzer. This is a common procedure in the monitoring of local area networks. Using sophisticated software and an interface card, a personal computer can now perform monitoring functions that expensive line monitors have been performing until recently. In addition, the personal computer can process data as it collects it or store it and process it later.

Channel Extender

A channel extender links remote stations to host facilities. It connects directly to the host system and operates at high speeds. It functions like a small front end processor. In addition to connecting remote work stations and computers to a host, it can support auxiliary devices, including printers, disk drives, and microcomputers. Fig. 5-7 shows the placement of a channel extender in a communication circuit.

Although channel extenders are essentially scaled-down front end processors, they are slower and less powerful than FEPs. However, as the cost of hardware decreases and the software in these devices becomes more sophisticated, channel extenders will be competing more directly with front end processors.

Channel extenders provide a method for improving response time and offloading data communication processes from networks, and they provide a less expensive alternative to front end processors. Through the use of channel extenders, the distance limitation of 400 feet between the terminal and mainframe is overcome. This allows for the implementation of distributed processing beyond the basic physical location of the mainframe. This allows several mainframes, minicomputers, and microcomputers to be located many miles apart, yet function as if they were in close proximitry. This type of connection can be accomplished by using channel extenders and a T-1 line to connect the computers over long distances. The T-1 line provides the high-speed connection, and the channel extender provides the capability of taking the data signals beyond their 400-feet limit.

Fig 5-7 shows how distributed processing can be achieved beyond the typical 400-feet limitation for a mainframe data channel interconnection. The mainframe channel can be extended to another mainframe channel by using a channel extender. This device can also connect microcomputers and terminals at remote locations. Moreover, local area networks can be connected to the mainframe channel through a channel extender.

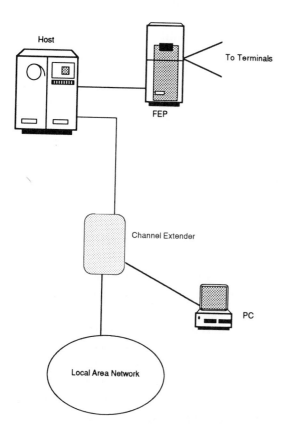

Fig. 5-7. Channel extender location in a data communication system.

Port-Sharing Device

A port-sharing device allows multiple terminals or stations to use a single port on a front end processor or mainframe system. This type of equipment is used when the capacity of the front end processor or host system needs to be exceeded. For example, it is possible that at a given installation the number of ports available on the host are already used. Therefore if the host system has 32 ports, then 32 incoming lines may already be attached to devices or allocated to users. What happens if an additional device is required or if new users need to be added to the system? The obvious solution is to expand the system or acquire a bigger system to accommodate all the required devices and users. But what if the processing capabilities of the system are adequate and just the number of ports needs to be increased? Or what if several devices need to share a common port? In this case the solution may be to install a port-sharing device.

For example, if the number of users in the system increases to 48, or more printers need to be attached, a port-sharing device constitutes a temporary fix until a more appropriate solution is designed. Using a port-sharing device, printers or terminals that are not going to be used simultaneously can be made to share a port and therefore decrease the cost of adding new ports that may be idle during much of the time.

Another example of the use of channel extenders applies to an office or corporation that uses personnel who share a single job. In this case, one or more individuals may perform the same job at different times during the business day or week. However, these individuals may have their own terminals and offices. It seems redundant to equip each employee with a terminal and a line attached to an individual port on the host system. It is a better use of resources to use a port-sharing device or a matrix switch to provide these users with shared access to the resources in the host using a single line or multiple line attached to a port-sharing device. Since only one user will be accessing the host at any given time, this schema will work effectively. In many cases, channel extenders can serve as sophisticated port-sharing devices.

Port Selector

Working alongside the port-sharing device, port selectors allow a user to be automatically attached to the first available port on a host system. Where the port-sharing device allows the connection of many terminals to a single port (only one at a time), the port selector may take a single line and can attach this line to any number of ports that are assigned to the port selector (see Fig. 5-8).

It is normally used in conjunction with dial-up lines where there may be a large number of lines available for connection from the outside, but only a few ports are available for these dial-up users. When a user calls into the system, the port selector searches for an available port on the host. If one is found, the user is connected to that port. If a port is not found, the user is notified of the situation or a busy signal is transmitted back to the user, and he or she is asked to try later.

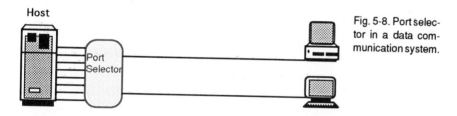

Host

Port Selector

Fig. 5-8. Port selector in a data communication system.

Modern port selectors can handle incoming calls that use different transmission speeds and different communication protocols such as ASCII and EBCDIC. In addition, they can switch users to dial-up circuits or dedicated lines, perform statistics on the use of the host ports, and provide feedback when a port is not available for the user.

Line Splitter

A line splitter works in similar fashion to a port-sharing device with the difference being the location of the line splitter. A line splitter is normally found at the remote end of a communication line, where the terminal or workstation is located (see Fig. 5-9). Port-sharing devices are normally located at the host end of the communication line.

Line splitters act as switches that allow several terminals to connect to a modem to access the host system. Even though multiple terminals are attached to a line splitter, only one communication line exists. Therefore, only one terminal can be communicating with the host at any one time.

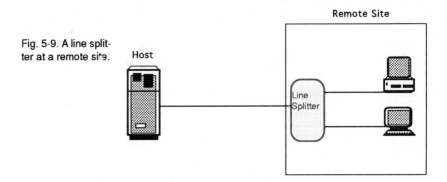

Fig. 5-9. A line split-
ter at a remote site.

As an example of using this technique, assume that four users need access to the host system from a remote location at different times during the working day. One solution is to provide each user with an individual line and a modem in order to access the host system. Therefore, four communication lines and at least five modems are required. Four of the modems are the users' and at least one is needed for the host. This solution, although efficient, could be costly depending on the needs of the users.

Another solution is to use a single line and modem and use a line splitter at the site where the users are located. In this scenario, the line splitter acts as a switch providing one of the users access to the line and modem at any given time. This is a less costly solution than the one mentioned above. However, keep in mind that only one user can access the modem and the data communication line at any given time. The other users must wait for the line and the modem to be given up by the user who is performing the communication before they can transmit data. If a single data communication line must carry the signals of more than one transmission, then another device, the digital line expander, may be used to increase the efficiency of the data line.

Digital Line Expander

A digital line expander allows users to concentrate a larger number of voice and data channels into the bandwidth of a standard communication channel. This is done through the use of hardware and software techniques that make use of the entire bandwidth capability of a standard voice circuit.

For example, if a communication site has only two leased lines between two remotely located terminating points, it can save money by using a line expander to increase the carrying capacity of those lines. One digital line expander can provide up to eight intermixed voice and digital data transmission circuits over a single digital communication circuit. This will obviously reduce the overhead cost of the company and increase the effectiveness of the leased lines. However, as in many other situations, this increase in capacity doesn't come free. If the number of transmissions is increased, the speed of the transmission must be decreased in order to make room for the additional data flowing through the circuit. If a line has a transmission speed of 57,600 bits per second, we couldn't send two transmissions at 57,600 bits per second. But, we could send three data signals travelling at a speed of 19,200 bits per second simultaneously, using a digital line expander. Another device that enhances the efficiency of a data communication line is a data compression device.

Data Compression Device

A data compression device can increase the throughput of data over a communication line by compressing the data (see Fig. 5-10). By reducing the amount of memory that a file or message uses, the net throughput of a line can be increased, since more data is being sent per second. This technique is somewhat similar to compression techniques used in expanding the storage capabilities of a hard disk. Compression software, following a specific compression algorithm, intercepts the data that needs to be transmitted and reduces its space requirements. The end result is that the same information is packed into a smaller number of bytes and then stored, or in this case sent through the

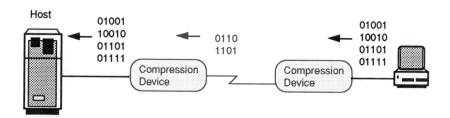

Fig. 5-10. Increasing throughput using data compression.

data transmission lines. At some point, the same algorithm must be used again to decompress the data and restore it to its original state.

A data compression device is a microprocessor-controlled device that uses several techniques for data compression. One type of compression technique is to count the number of repeating characters that are in sequence and send this count instead of sending each character. This is called run length encoding.

A more sophisticated technique is called Huffman encoding. The Huffman encoding algorithm uses tables of the most commonly transmitted characters within a language and adjusts the number of bits needed to transmit each character, based on the relative frequency of the character in the language.

Although a thorough discussion of compression algorithms is beyond the scope of this book, suffice it to say that data compression devices use software techniques to reduce the space requirement of data. Then by sending fewer characters, yet maintaining the integrity of the information, the efficiency of transmission is increased. You may have already seen this type of transmission in a less sophisticated format. Many bulletin boards have their files in compressed format, using one of several popular compressing programs such as PKZIP. The compressed file is then transferred from the host machine, where the bulletin board resides, to the user's computer. Here, using a decompression program such as PKUNZIP, the user decompresses the file, restoring it to its original form. After decompression, the user can use the file the way it was designed to be used. This is a technique commonly employed in the microcomputer communication arena. Fig. 5-11 shows a file before it was compressed by PKZIP and the resulting compressed file and size. As you can see, there is a large decrease in the size of the file after compression. This new compressed file will take less time to transmit than the original file.

Security Devices

The concept of sharing resources and files is one of the great appeals of communication networks and centralized computer systems. However, there are times where user access to records and files must be limited to prevent unauthorized access of such

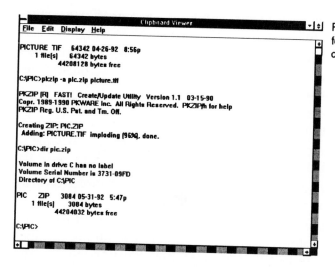

Fig. 5-11. File size before and after software compression.

items or to prevent inadvertent damage of any critical data. Additionally, data travelling through communication circuits is prone to interception, and the devices attached to these lines are also in danger of intrusion by unauthorized users. Securing these data transmission lines is an important aspect of data communications today. For the purpose of preventing unauthorized access to computing equipment, several pieces of hardware can assist in protecting data flowing through communication circuits. These devices are call-back units and encryption equipment. Additional equipment used in the management and protection of data communication, such as metering software and monitoring equipment, is discussed under the topic of networks.

Call-Back Unit

A call-back unit is a security device that calls back the user after he or she makes a login attempt. After the call is answered, the call-back unit hangs up the phone, and the phone number of the originating call is looked up in a table. If the phone that the user is on is an authorized number in the table, then the call-back unit calls the user back and expects the terminal or user's computer to answer the call. If the call is completed properly, the system permits the user to login.

The actual procedure that the call-back unit goes through to secure lines is as follows:

1. A person attempting to access the system makes a connection from a remote terminal or microcomputer using communication software.

2. The person is required to provide an identification number (ID) and a password.

3. The connection is severed after the ID and the password are entered.

4. The ID and password are checked in a table to verify that the user is authorized.

5. If the user is authorized, the call-back unit calls the user's registered phone number. The phone number is stored inside the host and authorized by the company's security personnel.

6. The user's modem is accessed and the session between the terminal and the host begins.

Call-back units provide access only to authorized users, inhibiting access by hackers, unless they are using an authorized phone. However, these units have some problems. First, the host system becomes responsible for the cost of the connection. Second, if a person is on a business trip and tries to access the host system with a portable computer, the computer won't be able to make the connection, since the phone number being used is not registered.

This last problem can be resolved by providing users with a cellular telephone and modem. Using a portable or cellular system, a user can be anywhere the cellular system can receive a signal. Then as long as the portable phone is registered with the system, a call-back unit will be able to locate the user and establish a connection. Several companies, including IBM, make laptop computers that have built-in cellular phones and modems for use by sales and executive personnel. These systems are of course susceptible to the noise and interference that normally affects cellular equipment.

Another problem with the last solution outlined is that transmission over cellular phones is susceptible to interception by unauthorized users with the proper equipment. If company secrets are transmitted in this manner, there is a good possibility that they could be intercepted and used without the company knowing it. When high security is a necessity, then additional devices such as encryption equipment must be employed.

Encryption Equipment

Some data communication networks, such as those employed by the government and military, require very secure communication. For this purpose, encryption equipment is used to scramble the data at the sending location and reconstruct it at the receiving end. Fig. 5-12 depicts this configuration. Encryption is the transformation of data from meaningful code into a meaningless stream of bits. To make this transformation, the data is sent through an encrypting algorithm with the result being the set of meaningless bits. To see the data in its original format, the

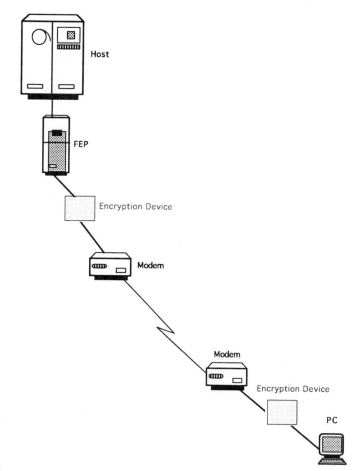

Host

FEP

Encryption Device

Modem

Modem

Encryption Device

PC

Fig. 5-12. Encryting devices in a communication system.

scrambled data is sent back through the algorithm which in essence now works in "reverse," restoring the original message. This is somewhat similar to the scrambling that we experience with cable television premium channels. The signal is scrambled as it leaves the broadcasting studio. In order for us to see the original signal, a descrambler or decoder is necessary to restore the original signal.

Modern encryption devices expect digital information as input, and produce digital information as output. The function of these devices is governed by standards set by the U.S. National Bureau of Standards (NBS). This set of standards is called the Data Encryption Standard (DES), which uses 64 bits to encrypt blocks of 64 bits. Eight of the 64 bits are used for error detection, and a 56-bit pattern is used for the encryption key. This provides 2^{56} possible different key combinations or more than 72 quadrillion possibilities for the key used in encrypting and decrypting the message.

During the transmission of an encrypted message, the same key must be used in the sending and receiving end of the transmission. This means that there must be a mechanism for sending the key to the receiving user. Sometimes the overhead involved during this operation can be costly since expensive and secure lines must be used, or some special courier.

Encryption can be achieved through software or hardware implementation. Hardware encryption is faster but less flexible than software encryption. However, there are many chips that implement the DES algorithm that can simply be plugged into a computer and are ready for use. Software encryption is normally used only when there are small amounts of data to be encrypted; otherwise, hardware encryption is employed.

Miscellaneous Equipment

In addition to all the data communication devices already mentioned, there are other hardware devices that help in the installation and maintenance of data lines. One of the most common is the breakout box, and it is used to configure the proper cable assignments required in data communications. Although used in several forms of communications, the breakout box is most commonly used to configure pin assignments in

RS-232 ports and serial data communications. Although the RS-232 is considered a standard, each manufacturer of computing equipment implements one of several versions of the "RS-232 standard." This creates incompatibilities between devices that use the serial port as the main communication device. Some of these cases are terminals and peripherals attached to computers running the UNIX system. In this system, most terminals connect through the RS-232 or serial port, with many of the printers in the system also connected through the serial port. Unfortunately, an RS-232 pin configuration that works for one type of terminal may not work with another terminal from a different configuration. For these reasons, many system technicians make use of the breakout box.

Breakout Box

A breakout box is a passive device that can be attached to a circuit at any connecting point, but it is normally attached at the location of a serial port on a device or computer. It can be programmable or nonprogrammable, with the latter being the most commonly used. Once the breakout box is installed it can perform the functions below:

1. Monitor data activity on the circuits. Each line circuit has a light-emitting diode (LED) on the breakout box. If there is a signal on the line, the LED lights up.

2. Exchange line connections. One of the major causes of improper communication between devices is crossed lines. Line connections can easily be changed without the need to build a connector for each change.

3. Isolate a circuit. A single line which is suspected of causing the problem can be prevented from transmitting to the receiving device and isolated to see if it is the cause of the errors.

4. Voltage levels can be monitored. Some breakout boxes have voltage meters built in. This allows the user to detect unusual voltages in the circuit.

With the use of a breakout box a user or technician can "quickly" attach a computer to a device and experiment with the pin configuration until the right combination that allows the proper transmission of data without any losses is achieved. Some newer types of breakout boxes claim to be completely automatic. That is, they will automatically detect the right pin configuration for the sending and transmitting devices and adjust themselves to make sure that both devices work properly. Such devices seem to work well in many situations. However, they can't always automatically detect the right configuration. These devices will save a lot of time if they are able to automatically figure out the right cable configuration, but there is a good possibility that you may still have to use a normal breakout box and some trial-and-error techniques before an optimal solution can be found.

Summary

Several types of electronic devices are used in the design and installation of data communication networks. The most commonly used are concentrators, cluster controllers, PBXs, matrix switches, line adapters, and security devices.

A concentrator is a line-sharing device whose primary function is the same as that of a multiplexer. It allows multiple devices to share communication circuits. Unlike multiplexers, concentrators are intelligent devices that sometimes perform data processing functions and provide auxiliary storage.

Cluster controllers are designed to support several terminals and the functions required to manage those terminals. Also, they buffer data being transmitted to or from the terminals, perform error detection and correction, and poll terminals.

Private branch exchanges are electronic switchboards which connect to all the telephone lines of the organization. They can handle data communications in a digital format. Their flexibility in this area, especially when it comes to connecting a terminal or microcomputer to a host system, makes them a popular device used in data communications.

A matrix switch is similar to a private branch exchange and allows terminals and other electronic devices to access multiple host processors without the need to physically move any communication line. They are less sophisticated than private branch exchanges but are also less costly than PBXs.

Several other devices can be used to expand the communication distance between users and the host system. These devices are called line adapters and they come in different varieties, such as line monitors, channel extenders, line splitters, and port-sharing devices.

Securing data transmission lines is an important aspect of data communication today. Several pieces of hardware can assist in protecting data flowing through communication circuits. These devices include call-back units and encryption equipment.

Other devices used in monitoring and improving line channel performance are the breakout box and data compression device. The breakout box is a passive device that can be attached to a circuit at any connecting point. A data compression device can increase the throughput of data over a communication line by compressing the data.

Questions

1. Why do we need devices to communicate more than a few hundred feet from a mainframe?
2. What is the main purpose of a matrix switch?
3. Why do we use breakout boxes?
4. What are concentrators?
5. What is the function of a protocol converter?
6. What is the function of a PBX?
7. What is a cluster controller?
8. Describe four different types of line adapters.
9. How does a line monitor work?
10. Why is hardware encryption used?
11. What device(s) could we use to increase the efficiency of a data communication line?
12. What device(s) could be used to increase the use of a data communication line in terms of the amount of data to be transmitted?

Projects

Creating Interfaces

The projects in this chapter are a continuation of the projects from the last chapter and are intended to familiarize the student with the basic hardware required to connect computers and printers using standard RS-232 ports. The basic equipment required to perform the projects is outlined in project 1 of the previous chapter. As an additional challenge, the instructor may provide unknown or lesser known serial printers and instruct the student to design the interface between the printer and a microcomputer.

Minimum Interface between a Printer and a Microcomputer

To connect a printer to a computer using the serial port, a minimum null modem eliminator can be used in most cases. The minimum null modem eliminator can be used on devices that support the X-On/X-Off protocol. If your computer and printer support this communication protocol, then pins 4 and 5 can be loop shorted on both systems and also pins 6, 8, and 20 can be shorted. However, all the handshaking must be done through software and not through the hardware. In most cases additional software is not required when printing documents using the interface discussed in this section. The sending software program needs to be instructed that it is communicating with the printer serially and that X-On/X-Off should be used in addition to the typical serial parameters.

To construct the minimum null modem eliminator, follow the configuration in Fig. 5-13.

General Interface between a Printer and a Microcomputer

In some situations a minimum null modem eliminator is not sufficient for the printer and the computer to communicate. If the printer seems to "lose" characters or if it prints correctly for a while and then it stops, the configuration in Fig. 5-15 may solve the problem. Some printers require pin 11 (printer ready) to become active by a signal from the union of pins 6 and 8 as in Fig. 5-14.

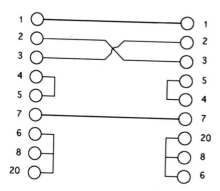

Fig. 5-13. Minimum Interface between a printer and a PC.

Fig. 5-14. General Interface between a printer and a PC.

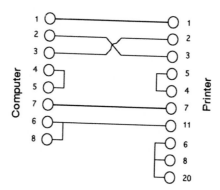

Communication Media

Objectives

After completing this chapter you will:

1. Understand the different types of data communication media available in the market place.

2. Be able to make educated decisions on the proper types of transmission media to solve a data communication problem.

3. Understand the selection criteria for the different types of transmission media.

Key Words

Bandwidth   Cellular Radio

Coaxial Cable   Data Channel

Kilobits per Second   Microwave

Optical Fiber   Satellite

Twisted Pair

Introduction

All data communication equipment needs some type of transmission medium in order for the transmission to take place. Whether this communication medium is some type of conducting metal, water, air, or vacuum is not as important as recognizing the limitations that the medium imposes on current technology.

The educated data communication manager must understand the limitations and capabilities of all transmission mediums available to perform his or her duties as the person responsible for a successful data communication environment.

Each of the data communication media explored in this chapter has advantages and disadvantages that make it appropriate for some companies and inadequate for other data transmission needs. Although many managers make decisions about the transmission medium based on its data volume capacity and speed of transmission, many other factors affect the overall success of the implementation of a data communication system. The right medium is, of course, a key element in a successful operation. However, speed alone should not be the criterion for determining the appropriate medium.

Additionally, the services offered by common carriers should not be overlooked. These companies have been providing data communication services for many years, and their expertise in this area is often unmatchable by company experts. Many companies may benefit from the offerings of such carriers, if for no other reason than the managing of the communication facilities. This is a task that many small and medium-sized companies tend to overlook.

Therefore, the following chapter should be read with an open mind if a broad understanding of all solutions is to be gained. The chapter presents different types of data transmission media, and then explores some selection criteria for choosing one of these media. Also, the telephone central office is explored along with some of the typical services provided by common carriers.

Circuit Media

The data transmission medium is the physical path that the signal must use in order to travel from the sender to the receiver. There are many types of transmission media to choose from, but they can be classified in general terms into two types.

1. Guided transmission media
2. Unguided transmission media

Guided transmission media include several types of cabling systems that guide the data signals along the cable from one location to another. The other type, unguided transmission media, consists of a means for the signals to travel, but nothing to guide them along a specific path. Examples of these types of transmission media are air and water.

Guided transmission media work by attaching the transmitter directly to the medium. The transmitter can be a microcomputer, terminal, peripheral device, or even a cable television station. The signal travels through the cable and, at the other end, the receiver is also attached directly to the cable.

The cables used in guided transmission are basically wire conductors. Conductors can themselves be classified into four major groups: open wire, twisted pair cable, coaxial cable, and optical fiber cable. Each of these has its own capabilities in terms of data carrying capacity and speed of transmission. At the low end we can consider the open wire, and at the high end we have optical fiber. Of course, prices increase as the transmission performance of the cable increases.

Unguided media use antennas for the transmission and reception of the data signals. Among the different types of signals that can be transmitted using this format, we have microwave and satellite signals. Although unguided media such as air don't guide the signals along a specific path, the direction of the signal transmitted can be chosen by employing different configurations and arrangement of antennas. In this fashion, a beam of microwaves can be concentrated along a direction where a receiving antenna is expected to be located. The ability to focus a beam of signals in an unguided medium depends on the frequency of the signals being transmitted. The frequency of a signal is the number of cycles per second that signals go through, meaning the number of times the signal varies between two settings in one second. As the frequency gets higher, it is easier to focus the beam in a specific direction.

Although this chapter doesn't discuss all possible types of media configurations, it will discuss the most common types that are found in the market place. In most, if not all cases, the different data transmission media described below will satisfy the requirements of any data communication system.

Guided Media

Open Wire

Open wire lines have been around since the inception of the data communication industry. An open wire line consists of copper wire tied to glass insulators, with the insulators attached to wooden arms mounted on utility poles. While still in common use throughout the world, they are quickly being replaced by twisted pair cables and other transmission media. Communication on this medium is susceptible to a large degree of interference, since the cable is open in the atmosphere.

Because of the susceptibility of open wire to interference, in current times it is typically wrapped with an insulating plastic coating and twisted together, hence the name twisted pair (see Fig. 6-1). The cables are twisted in pairs because the electrical effect of one current is cancelled by the electrical effect of the other, therefore reducing the amount of interference that the signal is subjected to. In this manner, the signals from one pair of cables are prevented from interfering with the signals of another pair, a type of interference that is sometimes called crosstalk. Twisted pair wiring is a common type of data transmission media found in homes and buildings. Therefore we need to study it further, along with some of its data communication applications.

Fig. 6-1. Twisted pair wire.

Twisted Pair Cables

A twisted pair cable, as mentioned before, is composed of copper conductors insulated by paper or plastic and twisted into pairs. At the location where the pairs enter a building, a terminating block, also called a punchdown block, is normally found. These pairs are bundled into units and the units are bundled to form the finished cable. Fig. 6-2 shows a terminal connector where twisted pair cables are being used. The terminating block serves several purposes. One of the functions of the terminating block is to act as a distribution panel. From the terminating block wires are distributed to offices or to other distribution panels or blocks located throughout the building. Another function of the terminating block is to act as a demarcation point where the responsibility of the common carrier (the public company who owns the cable) ends and the responsibility of the building owner begins. Any cable that is distributed from the terminating block belongs to private owners and they are responsible for its maintenance and upgrade. This same concept applies to home owners. The phone company owns the twisted pair cable that is used to bring the phone signals up to the house. But the house owner is responsible for the twisted pair phone cable installed throughout the house.

Fig. 6-2. Terminal connector for connecting twisted pair cables.

The size of twisted pair cable is measured in gauges, with typical twisted pair cables coming in 26, 24, or 22 gauge. The smaller the gauge number, the bigger the wire. This type of gauge corresponds to thicknesses from 0.0016 to 0.036 inch.

A variation of twisted pair is called the shielded twisted pair or data-grade twisted pair. Shielded twisted pair is twisted cable put inside a thin metallic shielding of aluminum foil or woven-copper shield and then enclosed in an outer plastic casing. The shielding provides further isolation from the interference caused by the signal-carrying wires. Also, it is less susceptible to interference signals produced by electrical wires or nearby electronic equipment. Additionally, shielded twisted pair cables are less likely to cause interference themselves.

Because of this insulation, shielded twisted pair wire is capable of carrying data signals faster than normal twisted pair wire. However, this type of wire is more expensive and difficult to work with than unshielded twisted pair wire and it requires custom installation to have a "clean" connection and avoid interference from poorly attached cable. Additionally, the shielding affects the transmission characteristics of the line and reduces the distance over which a signal can be effectively transmitted.

Twisted pair, whether shielded or unshielded, is used to transmit analog and digital signals. If an analog signal is being transmitted, amplifiers are normally required every three or four miles. If digital signals are being transmitted, some type of repeater is required every one or two miles. It has limited distance carrying capabilities, limited bandwidth, and limited data transmission speed. That is, it is very limited in the total amount of data it can transmit per unit of time and has low transmission speeds. Additionally, transmission frequencies can be high for long distances. In this case, electrical interference in the form of crosstalk between adjacent circuits is a problem for twisted pair cables. Even if shielded twisted pair wire is used, the problems above still apply, although to a lesser degree. However, it is inexpensive and commonly available in most offices and buildings. This makes it a popular data transmission medium in data communication systems. To solve some of the problems with twisted pair wire, coaxial cable is employed.

Coaxial Cable

Coaxial cable consists of two conductors. The inner conductor, normally copper or aluminum, is shielded by placing it inside a plastic case or shield. The second conductor is wrapped around the plastic shield of the first conductor. This further shields the inner conductor. Additionally, the second conductor (shield) is covered with plastic or some other protective and insulating cover (see Fig. 6-3).

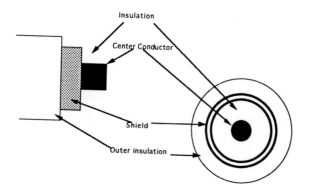

Fig. 6-3. Coaxial cable.

The outer conductor shields the inner conductor from outside electrical signals and reduces the electromagnetic radiations of the inner conductor. The distance between the conductors varies, along with the type of shielding and insulation material used. This difference gives each type of coaxial cable a unique characteristic normally called impedance. The impedance is a measure of the resistance that the conductor has to the flow of electrical signals. Typical diameters of coaxial cables range from 0.4 to 1 inch.

Coaxial cables are sometimes grouped into bundles. Each bundle can carry several thousand voice and/or data transmissions simultaneously. This type of cable has little signal loss, signal distortion, or crosstalk. Therefore, it is a better transmission medium than open wire or twisted pair cables.

It is one of the more versatile transmission mediums and it has wide acceptance in the communication industry. It is used extensively in television distribution (cable television), local area networks, and long distance phone transmission. We have all seen the coaxial cable that cable companies use in distributing their signals from a distribution building to homes. Today, over half of the residential homes in the US have cable television, and most of them are connected through coaxial cable.

Coaxial cable is heavier and more expensive than twisted pair wire. It can carry a greater capacity of data over longer distances and it is stronger than twisted pair. This makes it a common choice of data transmission media in factories and other areas where there is a harsh environment. The typical bandwidth of coaxial cable is between 400 Mhz and 600 Mhz. This large bandwidth is what gives coaxial cable its high data carrying capacity.

It can carry analog and digital signals and, because of its shielded concentric construction, it is less susceptible to interference and crosstalk than twisted pair cable. For transmitting a signal over long distances, repeaters are required every few miles with the number of miles depending on the frequency of the data being transmitted. With higher frequency of data signals, the distance needed between repeaters becomes shorter.

Local area networks have been using coaxial cable as a medium for transmitting data to workstations. Coaxial cable can support large numbers of devices with different data and protocols transmitting over the same cabling system over short and long distances. However, it is important to note that there are many types of coax cable with different electrical characteristics. Not all coaxial cable can be used with a particular networking scheme.

It takes some practice to work properly with coaxial cable since it is bulkier than twisted pair wire. However, the skill of connecting devices using coaxial cable shouldn't be overlooked. One bad connection can render an entire system inoperative. It is wise to invest in good connectors regardless of their price. Additionally, a good crimping tool should be used. Also, invest in good quality coaxial cable. There are many vendors of poor quality coaxial cable that tends to break down after time and corrosion expose the conductors.

Optical Fiber

Optical fiber consists of thin glass fibers that can carry information at frequencies in the visible light spectrum. The data transmission lines made up of optical fibers are joined by connectors that have very little loss of the signal throughout the length of the data line (see Fig. 6-4).

Fig. 6-4. The flexible optical fibers shown in this photograph are approximately the diameter of a human hair. (Courtesy of AT&T Bell Laboratories)

At the sending end of a data circuit, data is encoded from electrical signals into light pulses that travel through the lines at high speeds. At the receiving end, the light is converted back into electrical analog or digital signals that are then passed on to the receiving device.

The typical optical fiber consists of a very narrow strand of glass called the core. Around the core is a concentric layer of glass called the cladding (see Fig. 6-5). After the light is inserted into the core it follows a zig-zag path through the core. The advantage of optical fiber is that it can carry large amounts of information at high speeds in very reduced physical spaces with little loss of signal.

Fig. 6-5. Optical fiber components.

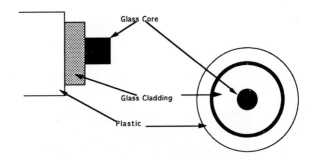

There are three primary types of transmission modes using optical fiber. They are single mode, step index, and graded index (see Fig. 6-6).

Single mode transmission uses fibers with a core radius of 2.5 to 4 microns. Since the radius of the fiber is so small, light travels through the core with little reflection from the cladding. However, it requires very concentrated light sources to get the signal to travel long distances. This type of mode is typically used for trunk line applications. A trunk line is the cable that carries the signal from a central office to a PBX or building where the signal will then be distributed.

Step index fiber consists of a core of fiber surrounded by a cladding with a lower refractive index for the light. The cable has an approximate radius of 30 to 70 microns. The lower refractive index causes the light pulse to bounce downward back toward the core. In this type of transmission, some of the light pulses

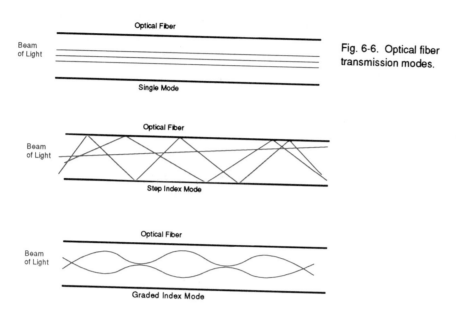

Fig. 6-6. Optical fiber transmission modes.

travel straight down the core while others bounce off the cladding multiple times before reaching their destination. This mode is used for distances of one kilometer or less.

Graded index fiber has a refractive index that changes gradually as the light travels to the outer edge of the fiber. The cable has a radius of 25 to 60 microns. This gradual refractive index bends the light towards the core instead of just reflecting it. This mode is used for long distance communication.

The promise of optical fiber as one of the best mediums of communication comes from its high bandwidth. Optical fiber has a bandwidth range of about 10^{14} to 10^{15} Hz. With a bandwidth much larger than any other type of cable, a single optical fiber can carry the signals of thousands of simultaneous telephone conversations. In addition, optical fiber can carry signals much faster than other cabling schemes without distortion.

In terms of local area networks, the speed of optical fiber is not a good reason to choose it as the data transmission medium. In this situation, fibers carry data at about the same speeds as coaxial cable. However, optical fiber can carry the data longer, more reliably, and more securely than any other type of media. Additionally, fiber has the potential to carry data at higher speeds as the technology develops to take advantage of such a possibility.

Optical fiber can carry digital signals for long distances without the need of repeaters. Additionally, optical fibers don't pick up electrical noise from nearby conductors. On the other hand, copper-based conductors, regardless of the amount of shielding used, always become antennas. The amount of interference in the copper is directly proportional to its length. Since the signal travelling in an optical fiber is not electrical, none of these problems apply.

Optical fiber has additional benefits relating to security. Electrical signals traveling in a coaxial or twisted pair cable can be detected since electromagnetic radiation is emitted. This radiation, with the right equipment, can be used to obtain the original message. Light, on the other hand, doesn't emit electromagnetic radiation. Therefore, it is much more difficult for unauthorized users to pick up the signal in the fiber. Additionally, tapping into an optical fiber, although not impossible, is more difficult than tapping into twisted pair or coaxial cable.

Although more expensive than coaxial cable and twisted pair, optical fiber has the following advantages over them:

1. It has a greater capacity for carrying data due to its large bandwidth.

2. It has the potential for greater speeds of transmission than coaxial or twisted pair cables.

3. It is smaller in size and weight than other conventional cabling systems.

4. It can carry a signal over longer distances than other cabling systems with a smaller attenuation. That is, the signal loss over long distances is less with optical fiber.

5. It is not susceptible to electromagnetic radiation from nearby cables, light fixtures, and motors.

All these features of optical fiber make it a compelling transmission medium. As we move closer to the 21st century, the needs and demands of users are no longer just access to text-based data. Newer technologies such as multimedia are becoming standards in the workplace and in education. Multimedia technology incorporates sound, graphics, animation, and full motion video. Documents that incorporate multimedia techniques are being sent through traditional communication media that can handle the massive amount of data that such documents contain. Just a few seconds of full motion video require millions of bytes of information. If companies and institutions expect to move their data communication needs into the future, they will have to design data communication systems that can handle the large amount of information that a multimedia document may require. Electronic mail with voice and video is now available. However, only optical fiber has the bandwidth and speeds of transmission required to manipulate such massive amounts of data effectively and efficiently. By the beginning of the next century, optical fiber will be the dominant data transmission medium for fixed-location applications.

Unguided Media

Microwave

Microwave, or radio transmission as it is sometimes called, is a high frequency radio signal that is transmitted over a direct line-of-sight path between two points. The concept of line-of-sight is important since the earth has a curvature. This necessitates that microwave stations be no more than 30 miles apart. Fig. 6-7 shows a picture of a microwave tower and transmission station.

From the picture you can see one of the most common types of microwave antennas, the parabolic antenna or "dish." A normal size for this type of antenna is 10 to 12 feet in diameter and it is fixed to some stationary structure. The function of this antenna is to focus the microwave signals into a narrow beam that is transmitted to a receiving antenna that is directly in the line-of-sight of the sending dish. Microwave antennas are located in high places such as the rooftop of a building and on rigid structures that have a substantial height above the ground.

The primary purpose of microwave towers is to connect computers or communication equipment that are located in different geographical areas. For example, a company with several offices distributed throughout a city could use microwave communications to connect all of their data processing equipment. In this case, the company, if it is a private enterprise, is not allowed to lay its own cabling system across the public right-of-ways (streets and highways). Only common carriers such as AT&T have permission from the local and federal government to perform such actions. However, it is possible for the company in the example to lease lines from a common carrier to connect its distributed offices. Depending on the amount of equipment to be connected and the data communication and processing needs of the company, it may be more cost effective to set up a microwave communication system to solve its communication needs. As long as the microwave antennas are within a line-of-sight of each other, the company in question will be able to connect all of its equipment without the need to lease lines from a common carrier.

Fig. 6-7. This microwave tower is located in New Jersey. Both parabolic and horn antennas can be seen. (Courtesy of AT&T Bell Laboratories)

But, what happens if the antennas are not in a line-of-sight? Then, in this case, repeating microwave stations must be employed. The typical line-of-sight is about 25 to 30 miles depending on the type of terrain that the microwave tower is located on. Beyond this distance, relay or repeating stations must be employed, otherwise the signal is lost into space (see Fig. 6-8).

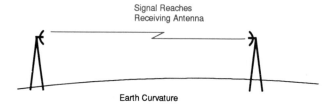

Signal Reaches
Receiving Antenna

Earth Curvature

Fig. 6-8. The curvature of the Earth affects the distance between microwave antennas.

A typical microwave system transmits signals with a frequency in the range of two to forty gigahertz. As the frequency increases, so does the bandwidth and therefore the potential for higher carrying loads. Also, as the frequency increases, the data transmission rate increases, but at high frequencies the attenuation of the signals also increases. Therefore, high frequencies are used only for short transmitting distances. These frequencies are subdivided into several types of transmission areas.

There are three main groups of radio systems used for communications lines. They are broadcast, beam, and satellite. Broadcast radio is limited to a unique frequency within the range of the transmitter. Radio beam transmission needs to be repeated if the signal is to travel farther than 30 miles. Normally, radio beam repeaters are found on top of buildings, mountain tops, and radio antennas. Satellite microwave radio is employed to avoid the limitations imposed by the earth's curvature, and it is described in the next section.

Microwave transmission offers speed, cost effectiveness (since there are no cables), and ease of operation. However, it has the potential for interference with other radio waves. This has become more apparent since the popularity of microwave transmission has increased over the last few years. With many microwave systems in place, especially in large cities, the chance of different transmissions overlapping each other and causing interference has increased. Additionally, commercial transmissions can be intercepted by any person with a receiver in the line of transmission, thus creating security risks. Another problem with microwaves is attenuation due to weather conditions. Microwaves tend to be attenuated by the water droplets from rainfall, especially when the transmission frequency is above 10 gigahertz. But even with these problems, microwave technology is a popular solution to data communication problems and needs.

Satellite Transmission

Satellite transmission is similar to microwave radio transmission. But instead of transmitting to an earth-bound receiving station, it will transmit to a satellite several thousand miles out in space (normally approximately 22,300 miles). Fig. 6-9 shows a picture of a transmitting satellite dish antenna.

Fig. 6-9. These satellite dish antennas are about 5 meters in diameter. Other dish antennas are as small as 1 meter. (Courtesy of Contel ASC)

The basic components of satellite transmission are an earth station, used for sending and receiving data, and the satellite, sometimes called a transponder. The satellite receives the signals from an earth station (uplink), amplifies or repeats the signal, changes the frequency, and retransmits the data to another receiving earth station (downlink). The change in frequency is done so the uplink does not interfere with the downlink (see Fig. 6-10).

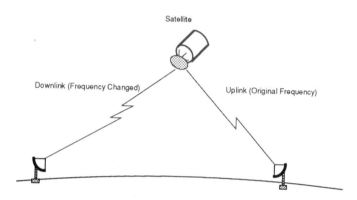

Fig. 6-10. Uplink and downlink satellite transmissions.

In satellite transmission, a delay occurs because the signal needs to travel out into space and back to the earth. Typical delay time is 0.5 second. There is an additional delay due to the time required for the signal to travel through ground stations.

But just as with the earth-bound microwave antennas, a satellite must be within a "line-of-sight" of its earth stations. We use the words line-of-sight to indicate that the earth-based station and the satellite must be in locations that allow for the transmission and reception of a direct beam of microwave signals. Because of this, communication satellites remain stationary with respect to their position over the earth.

Two satellites that use the same frequencies cannot be too close to each other. Otherwise, they will interfere with each other. To avoid this situation, nations that place satellites in orbit around the earth follow a standard that requires them to place satellites with a minimum of 4 degrees of angular spacing as measured from the earth if the satellite transmits in the 4 to 6 gigahertz band. Also, the standard requires a 3 degrees spacing if the satellites transmit in the 12 to 14 gigahertz band. This standard limits the number of satellites that can be placed in orbit.

As stated before, satellites use different frequencies for receiving and transmitting. The frequency ranges are from 4 to 6 gigahertz (GHz), also called the C-band; 12 to 14 GHz, also called the Ku-band; and 20 to 30 GHz. As the value of the frequency decreases, the size of the dish antenna required to receive and transmit the signals needs to increase. The Ku-band is used to transmit television programs between networks and individual television stations. Since signals in the Ku-band have a higher frequency, their wavelength is shortened. This allows receiving and transmitting stations to concentrate the signals and use smaller dish antennas.

One of the most common uses of satellites is in the transmission of television signals. Satellites are being used extensively in the US and throughout the world for this function. For example, to broadcast a show throughout the continental US, a television network sends its signal to a satellite that in turn retransmits the signal to a series of receiving stations on the ground. From this station, through microwave or coaxial cable, the signals are relayed to the sets in people's homes.

Satellites are also used extensively for point-to-point trunks between telephone central offices in public telephone networks. Also, they are used by businesses to connect private networks. A user or business leases one or more channels in the satellite. It then connects data processing and communication equipment in a building with similar equipment in a branch or office located thousands of miles away. But, until recently, such use of a satellite has been expensive. However, recent developments in the very small aperture terminal (VSAT) system provide low cost alternatives to expensive traditional satellite transmissions. Using this scheme, several stations are equipped with low cost antennas. These stations share a satellite transmission capacity for transmission to a central station. The central station exchanges messages with each of the stations and also relays messages between the stations.

Security poses a problem with satellite communications, because it is easy to intercept the transmission as it travels through the air. In some cases, a scrambler is used to distort the signal before it is sent to the satellite, and a descrambler is used in the receiving station to reproduce the original signal. This is the procedure used by several premium cable television channels such as HBO and CINEMAX. A business could employ similar techniques by using some type of software or hardware encryption of the data signal that it needs to transmit.

Cellular Radio

Traditional mobile telephones always had a problem with the availability of channels assigned to communication. It is common to find 20 channels being shared by 2,000 users, making it difficult to obtain a channel to use for communicating with someone else. Cellular radio solves this problem. Cellular radio is a form of high frequency radio transmission where the signals are relayed from antennas that are spaced in strategic locations throughout metropolitan areas.

Each area of service is divided into cells, and each cell has a fixed transmit and receive site. If a person is using a car telephone and moves to the edge of a current cell, the cellular radio system automatically moves the user's communication to another antenna that is closer. In this manner, transmission is not interrupted and the user doesn't have to worry about moving from one cell to another. Additionally, the quality of the transmission is comparable to that found in common hardwired telephone systems.

Cellular radio can be used for voice or computer data communications. A user dials into the cellular system, and the voice or data is transmitted directly from the user's location to the cell antenna. From here it is retransmitted throughout the service area, or in some cases it can be transmitted to a satellite for communications over long distances.

Several laptop and palmtop computers have cellular radio transmission capabilities. This allows a user to be at any location and dial into a central location for the downloading or uploading of data, freeing the sender from locating a telephone outlet and communicating in traditional ways. Many sales personnel, police, or individuals who need access to a central site on demand use cellular radio for their data communication needs.

Circuit Media Selection

With all the different options available for use as a transmission medium, which one is the most efficient and cost effective for a company? The answer to this question may be a single product, but is most likely a combination of products. In any case, many factors influence the decision of choosing a medium for a data communication network. These factors include cost, speed, expandability, security, and distance requirements. Decisions regarding these factors cannot be made independently. Deciding on a cabling scheme depends on the hardware that you have or plan to purchase. Software requirements may indicate a specific cabling system, and the hardware may have to be reconfigured for it.

In addition, data communication system designers will have to contend with two types of designs, one for the communications within the building or campus, and one for the communications to remote locations. Normally, the decisions that apply to communication beyond the immediate premises of the business have broader issues and implications than the decisions required for implementing a data communication system within the immediate business physical environment. This is due to the user not caring about the type of communication medium used by the common carrier providing the transmission media. That is, the user doesn't care that a particular carrier uses one hundred percent optical fiber or coaxial cable. The user is only concerned with the cost and quality of the service that the common carrier provides.

When it comes to providing data communications solutions for in-house needs, many types of issues need to be addressed since the options are wide in terms of cost and the services that they provide. One such crucial decision will involve choosing the right data transmission medium. Although, as mentioned before, these issues should be considered at the same time, for pedagogical reasons each factor will be considered individually.

Cost

The cost of a given communication network will include not only the cost of the medium itself, but also the supporting hardware and software required to manage the network. Installing the cable and supporting hardware and software is just the beginning of the maintenance process. Many managers say the cost of installing the transmission medium is the largest piece of the entire cost of having a data communication system. They are incorrect. The major part of the cost is the personnel required to maintain the system.

The expertise required to maintain a system will increase with the size of the system. At the end of its life cycle, the cost of installing the communication system may be insignificant compared with the cost of personnel required to maintain the system.

In addition, the cost of further expansion must be taken into consideration. For example, a business that is established in Dallas may consider Dallas, Houston, Chicago, and New Orleans as its target cities. To connect its regional offices to its headquarters, this emerging company can use leased lines from a common carrier. However, if it is projected that within five years their contact offices will be in many more cities, a satellite network may be a more cost effective solution than leased lines.

The cost comparisons used in the design and selection of a data communication system must be projected over the expected life of the system and must include at least the following elements:

1. The cost of the transmission medium.
2. The cost of installing the transmission medium and all communication and data processing equipment that will support the system.
3. The cost of personnel to maintain the system.
4. The cost of personnel to train users on how to use the system.
5. The cost of upgrades or additions as the needs of the company and users expand.
6. The cost of the software and software upgrades required to keep the system running.
7. The cost of any leased lines or satellite channels leased from common carriers.

Although there are many more factors that affect the overall cost of a data communication system, the above need to be considered during the feasibility and design phases of the life cycle of the system (see chapter 12).

Speed

The transmission speed of data communication systems ranges from a low of 300 bits per second to several million bits per second. Some media, such as twisted pair cable, are less expensive than optical fiber. However, optical fiber can transmit at much higher speeds than twisted pair cable. The cost of increased speed must be balanced against the needs of the data communication system and its users.

Two factors dictate the speed of the data transmission medium: the response time expected by users and the aggregate data rate. The response time is the time it takes from the moment a terminal sends a request to the time the response from the host gets back to the user. A good response time is two seconds or less. However, longer response times may be tolerated to sustain a lower cost of the medium. Also, it is typically better to have a slow response time that is consistent than a response time that is unpredictable. Most users would get frustrated with the data communication system if one day the response time is one second or less and the next day the response time increases to several minutes for no apparent reason.

The aggregate data rate is the amount of information that can be transmitted per unit of time. A company's users may be satisfied with transmission speeds of 9600 bits per second. But at peak processing times, with large files, the speed requirements may range as high as 19,200 bits per second or more. The same communication medium may not work for both speeds.

The planning phase during which the data communication system is designed must consider peak loads in order to have a predictable response time for users. A twisted pair cabling system may be adequate for most types of transmission, but if, during a peak time, speeds of 10 megabits per second or more are required, a different wiring system should be considered.

Additionally, future requirements of the system must be taken into account. For example, if a network is being implemented in an educational institution to satisfy the initial needs of teaching programming languages, designers may choose to implement twisted pair wires. However, as the sophistication of the users increases and technology advances, the rest of the college may decide to use the system and incorporate multimedia concepts into the network. Then the twisted pair scheme will not work. In this case, it would have been better and more cost effective to spend the additional monies and implement the data communication system using optical fiber.

In order to show some comparison of the speed of data transmission of the circuit media here discussed, the following table provides some common transfer rates.

Private/leased lines	300 to 80,000 bits per second
T1-type media	1.5 megabits per second
Coaxial cable	1 to over 500 megabits per second
Optical fiber	over 2 gigabits per second
Microwave	up to 50 megabits per second
Satellite	up to 50 megabits per second

Don't forget that the complexity and cost of the transmission medium tends to increase as we move down the elements in this list. Also, cost and speed are just two of the factors that should be considered when choosing the transmission medium for a data communication system. Regardless of the speed of the transmission medium, it may not work for a company unless it has expansion capabilities.

Expandability

Eventually, most data communication systems need to be expanded by adding more devices at a location or by adding new locations. Some transmission media offer more cost effective expandability than others. For example, coaxial cable- and satellite-based networks are easier to expand into new locations. If a corporation has headquarters in Dallas, Texas, and opens new offices in London, Great Britain, it may be easier and relatively inexpensive to lease a satellite channel to extend the data communication system from headquarters to the new office. Of course, we say that it may be inexpensive, but the actual costs and savings will depend on the needs and volume of the data transmission requirements imposed on the system.

In many situations, leased telephone lines make expansion into new areas more difficult and costly. The installation of leased lines and the expense of their monthly lease, along with the low data transmission speed, may make using leased lines cost prohibitive. In a situation where high volumes of data must flow constantly between two remote locations, a leased line may not be the best solution. Microwave and other technology should be considered and their costs compared over the life of the systems. This will provide a more accurate picture of the actual costs than just comparing the initial costs of setting up the data communication system.

Future expansions must be considered whenever a data communication network is being designed. For example, a company can install twisted pair cable throughout an entire building. Two or three years after installation it may find that it needs coaxial or optical fiber media. In this case the cost of rewiring the building is larger than it would have been to install it initially. When planning communication systems, both short-range and long-range needs must be considered. This emphasizes the importance of planning when considering a data communication system. Planning must include solutions not only for the immediate needs (short-range goals), but also must include anticipated or future needs that encompass a time length longer than three years (long-range goals). Additionally, the planning process must be done according to some type of life cycle development (see chapter 12). This will ensure that all aspects of the planning process are taken into consideration, as they should be if the project is to be successful.

Security

The lack of security in a data communication network will allow hackers or unauthorized persons to have access to vital data. The data could be used to gain an advantage in the market place, or it could be altered or destroyed, with catastrophic consequences for a business.

Providing a completely sealed network where unauthorized persons can never access the network is impossible. However, some media, such as optical fiber, are more difficult to penetrate than other media, such as coaxial cable or satellite. The most vulnerable medium to the average hacker is switched lines. Once an individual gains access to the switching equipment, this person has good access to the rest of the network. Switching equipment should be protected by using account identification numbers, passwords, and perhaps a call-back unit, as the one described previously.

Another type of security threat is the invasion of the system by a computer virus. A computer virus could be introduced into the data communication system by an employee of the company. Once inside the system, a computer virus could become an irritation to users or it could destroy data in user computers or host systems. To protect communication systems from this type of security threat, anti-virus or virus scan software can be used to check any disk before it is used in any workstation or to check any file that flows through the system. Monitoring software can also be used to alert system operators to any unusual activities that may be the action of a computer virus.

Not only must a system protect itself against unauthorized users and computer viruses, but it must guard against any physical disaster such as a fire. Many systems have redundant lines and backup systems. Then in case of fire or some other catastrophic event, the critical aspects of the data communication system will continue operation by using alternative equipment and transmission media. Many corporations that use microwaves or satellite communications also have leased lines as backups, in case their primary transmission medium fails.

However, no matter how much backup a system has, it needs a good disaster recovery plan. Security on any data communication system is greatly enhanced by having a proven and well-designed disaster recovery plan as is described in chapter 12. A good disaster recovery plan is a sign of good management of a data communication system.

Distance Requirements

The distance between a sender and a receiver can determine the type of medium used for data transmission. For example, if two sites that need to be connected are hundreds of miles apart, it is not possible to lay coaxial cable between them. In this case leased lines, satellite, and microwave transmission need to be explored. Don't forget that only common carriers are allowed by law to lay cable across public right-of-ways such as highways. Therefore, if there is a public right-of-way between two locations, even for a short distance, leased lines or microwave communications must be considered since private cable couldn't be used.

Additionally, distance requirements will have to be measured against the volume of data that needs to be transmitted. If two locations are just a few feet apart, but the volume of data to be transmitted is heavy, such as in the use of multimedia technology, optical fiber may be a better solution than twisted pair wire.

Also, distance affects the number of devices that may be served. For short distances twisted pair, coaxial cable, and optical fiber may be used, but even these cabling schemes have limitations in how far they can transmit data without the need of repeaters. The cost of all these devices must be taken into account when designing the data communication system. And, for long distances, the average business may have to rely on local carrier lines, microwave, or satellite media.

Environment

The environment in which a medium must exist will eliminate some options from consideration. For example, local building codes may prohibit a company or educational institution from laying cables under right-of-ways. In this case, microwave radio transmission may need to be used. Another example is a case where phone lines are sharing conduits with electrical wires. This may cause too much interference with digital data transmission.

During the planning stages of a data communication network, the location of the medium and local constraints must be taken into account to avoid costly modifications during installation. For example, if twisted pair wire is used, care must be taken to locate the cable away from electrical motors, fluorescent lights, and other equipment that may cause interference with the data flowing through the medium. Also, some types of communication strategies may not work on all types of cables. A specific strategy may require coaxial cable and may not work with twisted pair wire. Therefore care must be taken to ensure that the communication strategy adopted is compatible with the transmission medium available.

Maintenance

The type of maintenance required for a communication network must also be considered during the planning stage. If a coaxial line or twisted pair wire is broken or becomes defective, it can be repaired easily by finding the troubled section and replacing it. However, if a satellite malfunctions and needs repair, the time required to place it back into normal operation may be lengthy. This is why many communication companies have multiple media backup networks.

Additionally, the personnel requirements to maintain a microwave data communication system are different than the personnel requirements for a local network using twisted pair wires. Even though a data communication strategy may seem the best solution in terms of its capabilities, the maintenance and cost of personnel required to perform such maintenance may render the system too costly to be effective. These economic comparisons must be performed during the planning stages of the system and must be used to find a solution that not only solves the data communication needs of the company but is affordable.

Leased vs Switched Lines

When using telephone lines for the transmission of digital information, the options are to use a leased line or to use a switched line, both of which must be rented from the phone company. A leased line, also called a dedicated line, is managed differently to carry computer information. The leased line is set up to bypass switching equipment at the phone company and it is dedicated to connect two systems 24 hours per day and seven days per week.

If the line is not leased, a phone call must be made to the computer that will become the host during the communication session. After the connection is made, data is transmitted and routed over any available telephone lines. These types of lines are called switched or dial-up lines because the data transmitted must pass through switching equipment at the phone company so it can be routed to available lines.

If a connection between computers needs to be kept for long periods of time, such as 12 hours per day or more for the entire week, a leased line will be more cost effective than a switched line. However, if the connection between computers is performed during short intervals of time or occasionally, the switched line will be a better alternative.

In the United States, the process of getting a leased line from common carriers became more complex since the Bell Telephone System's divestiture and the Federal Communications Commission's Computer II decision.

If a person wants to lease a single full-period telephone line across state boundaries, the efforts of several vendors may have to be coordinated. These vendors are the long distance carrier, the local carrier that connects the long distance carrier to the customer, and the vendor of the equipment at the customer site.

Also, the type of service required will have to be decided, sometimes called the grade of service. The grade of service is related to the speed of transmission of the leased line. This is because leased lines are specially configured for data transmission in several ranges of data transmission speed.

T1 and T3 Service

The data transmission speed of a leased line ranges from a low 2500 bits per second to over 45 megabits per second. However, there is a basic unit of measurement for this type of data service called the T1 circuit or channel. A T1 channel has the capacity for carrying data at 1.544 megabits per second, and it contains a set of technical characteristics for the signaling and terminating of the circuits.

Although lines using the T1 specification can be used to connect locations that are close together, data communication system designers think of T1 channels as lines connecting locations hundreds or thousands of miles apart.

Leasing a T1 line can be expensive. Common carriers like AT&T charge over $10,000 per month for a T1 channel that covers 1,000 miles. Unfortunately, the costs are not proportional to the distance covered. A T1 line covering 500 miles costs over $7,000 per month.

What if a company needs to transmit at rates faster than 1.544 megabits per second? Then another type of line, called the T3 circuit, can be employed. T3 circuits can transmit at speeds of over 45 megabits per second. However, the cost of leasing a T3 circuit can be over $100,000 per month.

There is a way to reduce the cost of T1 links. It is called the fractional T1 circuit. A fractional T1 circuit is a circuit that adheres to the T1 specifications but transmits at slower speeds with a basic rate of service of 64 kilobits per second. Long distance carriers sell fractional T1 circuits at rates of 384, 512, and 768 kilobits per second.

A leased line may be a good solution for many communication needs. However, in addition to the costs outlined above, data communication system designers must also take into account the cost or fees of the terminating equipment and circuits required to establish the communication link. All of these can make leasing a line a prohibitive solution for many companies. Line leasing is just one of the many services that are available from common carriers and local telephone companies. Other services are explored in the next chapter.

Summary

The data transmission medium is the physical path that the signal must use in order to travel from the sender to the receiver. There are many types of transmission media to choose from, but they can be generally be classified into two types.

1. Guided transmission media
2. Unguided transmission media

Guided transmission media include several types of cabling systems that guide the data signals along the cable from one location to another. Examples of this type of transmission media are open wire, twisted pair wires, coaxial cable, and optical fiber cable.

The other type, unguided transmission media, consists of a means for the signals to travel but nothing to guide them along a specific path. Examples of this type of media are microwave, satellite transmission, and cellular radio.

Open wire line consists of copper wire tied to glass insulators with the insulators attached to wooden arms mounted on utility poles. Open wire was replaced by twisted pair cables and other transmission media. This is due to the large potential for interference from electrical noise and weather as it lies open in the atmosphere.

Twisted pair cable is composed of copper conductors insulated by paper or plastic and twisted into pairs. At the location where the pairs enter a building, a terminating block, also called a punchdown block, is normally found. These pairs are bundled into units and the units are bundled to form the finished cable.

Coaxial cable consists of two conductors. The inner conductor, normally copper or aluminum, is shielded by placing it inside a plastic case or shield. The second conductor is wrapped around the plastic shield of the first conductor. This further shields the inner conductor. Additionally, the second conductor (shield) is covered with plastic or some other protective and insulating cover.

The last type of guided media covered in the chapter is optical fiber. Optical fiber consists of thin glass fibers that can carry information at frequencies in the visible light spectrum. The data transmission lines made up of optical fibers are joined by connectors that have very little loss of the signal throughout the length of the data line.

In the unguided transmission media arena, one common type of transmission mode is microwave transmission. Microwave, or radio transmission as it is sometimes called, is a high frequency radio signal that is transmitted over a direct line-of-sight path between two points. The concept of a line-of-sight is important since the earth has a curvature. This necessitates that microwave stations be no more than 30 miles apart.

Another type of unguided transmission media is satellite communications. Satellite transmission is similar to microwave radio transmission, except that it transmits to a satellite several thousand miles out in space (normally approximately 22,300 miles) rather than to an earth station.

The last type of unguided transmission media discussed in the chapter is cellular radio. Cellular radio is a form of high frequency radio transmission where the signals are relayed from antennas that are spaced in strategic locations throughout metropolitan areas.

There are several criteria that can be used to select the appropriate type of transmission media. These criteria are cost, speed, expandability, security, and distance requirements. Decisions regarding these factors cannot be made independently. Deciding on a cabling scheme depends on the hardware that you have or plan to purchase. But software requirements may indicate a specific cabling system, and the hardware may have to be reconfigured for it.

Questions

1. Describe the advantages of twisted pair over coaxial cable.
2. Describe the advantages of coaxial cable over twisted pair.
3. If computer data and video data were to be distributed over the same medium for multimedia purposes, which cabling scheme would you use? Why?
4. How can cellular radio be of benefit for a company?
5. What is a transponder? How does it work?
6. Describe three selection criteria used in deciding the type of transmission media used in data communication.
7. What types of data transmission can be performed through local telephone lines?
8. What criteria can be used in deciding whether to use leased lines or switched lines?
9. What is a T1 circuit?

Projects

The following are research projects rather than hands-on projects. However, they play an important role in the acquisition and retention of the topics discussed in this chapter. The result of these projects should be a short term paper that follows the criteria established in most technical writing classes. Many students graduate without knowing how to prepare technical documents, and that becomes a handicap in their professional work. These projects will not introduce the student to technical writing topics, but the instructor should emphasize such topics and demand that all work have a professional look and content. For this purpose, the instructor may make available some type of sophisticated word processor with desktop layout capabilities and/or presentation equipment, so the students can begin to have a feel for the need and usage of such technology. For this reason, the projects below serve a dual purpose and they should be performed.

Comparison of Data Communication Media

Using the local library, find out the cost per foot for the installation and/or leasing of the different transmission media discussed in this chapter. Additionally, research the speed and other technical aspects of the media, and produce a report that outlines their strengths and weaknesses. Compare the cost per megabyte of transmission of each of the media and propose situations or scenarios where one type of media may be more suitable than others. Justify your answers with technical facts or cases.

Exploring Solutions to Data Transmission Needs

Find out the data processing capabilities of your institution or choose a specific existing company and perform the same functions. Describe how they implemented the transmission medium and how they are using it. Additionally, find future expansion plans and recommend transmission media solutions to such plans.

Communication Networks and the Central Office

Objectives

After completing this chapter, you will:

1. Understand the concept of data communication.
2. Obtain an overview of the history of data communication.
3. Understand the basic requirements of a communication system.
4. Understand the basic concepts of networking.
5. Have a general understanding of the role of the telephone company central office in a data communication strategy.
6. Understand the basic services of a common carrier.

Key Words

Bulletin Board	Data Communication
Centrex	E-mail
EBBS	Electronic Transfer
FX	Home Banking
Information Service	Interexchange Channel
ISDN	Modem
Network	Public Network
Satellite	SDN
Telecommuting	Teleconferencing
Videotext	X.25 Standard
X.400 Standard	

Introduction

The material covered in this chapter is a prelude to the more technical aspects of data communication networks that will be explored in the rest of the book. Before the student devotes many hours mastering the sophisticated concepts of communications and networking, a general understanding of the capabilities of such networks and communication systems should take place. In addition, the student must have an understanding of the general subdivisions or components of such systems along with some of the historical efforts that were required to create today's complex communication systems.

The chapter begins with an introduction to the concept of data communication and its importance in the business world. It then provides a brief history of the most important developments that have shaped the data communication industry, followed by the most important functions that a data communication system must provide. Then, the major players or providers of public communications are discussed along with general requirements of a data communication system. And finally, the chapter closes with a discussion of some basic services that can be accessed through existing data communication networks.

The last topics in the chapter are sometimes difficult to place in a data communication book. However, the topics discussed which are related to network use are becoming commonplace in the work environment. These items include electronic mail, electronic bulletin boards, and facsimile technology. Even though these subjects were not part of the mainstream of corporate America until recently, they are quickly making an impact on the way we perform electronic transactions with the personal computer. For these reasons, they are included in this chapter which provides a general overview of communications, data communication networks, and services that can be accessed.

Data Communication Systems

Definition

Although the concept of data communication was discussed in previous chapters, a formal definition needs to be formulated. Data communication is the transmission of electronic data over some medium. The medium can be coaxial cable, optical fiber, microwave, or some of the other data carrying media previously discussed. The hardware and software systems that enable the transmission of data make up what are called data communication networks. These networks are an important component of today's information-based society, a society that is dominated by computers and the need to have access to accurate and timely information.

In this age of high speed computers and data communication networks, many companies exist only to manage data and provide information to other corporations. A new type of industry has emerged in recent years that doesn't create any physical products. This industry is called the information service industry. Their main product is information. As such, information is a commodity that can be sold and purchased. In addition, many companies that create products for the consumer market also produce information that can be sold for a profit. One such case is a car manufacturer that sells data stored in its customer database to other companies that may offer products for the car sold. Companies that have large mailing lists sell them to other corporations that are interested in the same types of customers.

Although the legal and moral implications of such transactions can be debated, the fact still remains that information is a commodity and its value depends on the accuracy and the timeliness of such information. The accuracy, of course, depends on how the data was acquired. Both accuracy and timeliness also depend on the accuracy and speed of the data communication network employed. If data transmitted through a network can't be trusted because it takes too long to reach its destination, the data communication system is a failure. Information consumers, such as a stock exchange, couldn't operate if the information in a file took hours to sort and display on monitors, or if portions of the data were lost in the transmission process.

It can be generalized that the value of the communication system depends on the knowledge transmitted by the system and the speed of movement of the knowledge. High-speed data communication networks transmit information that brings the sender and the receiver close together. Therefore, a good communication system is a major component of a successful business organization. The ability to provide information in a timely and accurate fashion is the key to survival in the 1990s and the decades ahead. Because of this, data communication is one of the fastest growing segments of the communication market.

Functions

An effective data communication system has a series of characteristics or functions that are easily recognized. These characteristics are the result of the behavior and functionality of the system as it provides information to its users, as it captures the information, and as it allows its users to communicate with each other. These characteristics can be further categorized by the features associated with them.

First, an effective data communication system must provide information to the right people in a timely manner. Having information at the proper place in a timely fashion can mean the difference between making a profit and sustaining a loss. Today's companies have networked data communication systems that can deliver text, voice, and graphical information at speeds that were thought impossible just a few years ago. By integrating communication and computer technology, a letter or report can be delivered anywhere in the world in seconds or minutes. Sometimes the information is delivered instantaneously as it is being produced, as in the case of video conferencing. This is more prevalent today as cellular data communication is currently making this need a reality for many corporations. A company employee can use a laptop computer, a modem, and a cellular telephone to access data bases at a central location directly from a customer site where a telephone line may not be available.

Second, a data communication system needs to capture business data as it is being produced. Data communication systems are being used more and more as input mechanisms to capture data about the daily business operations of a corporation as the data is generated. On-line computer applications allow a business to enter customer information, produce an invoice to the customer, and provide inventory and shipping information while the customer is performing the transaction. In addition, once the information is entered into the system, it is available to other users instantaneously.

The survival of many businesses depends on having data available on a real-time basis. Imagine, for example, an airline reservation system that cannot provide timely notification of flight information to passengers or a bank that cannot post deposits on a timely basis. Transportation, finance, insurance, and other industries require complex, fast, and accurate data communication systems for their business survival. As a result, companies have developed parallel systems and proper backup systems to ensure that their communication networks have a minimal amount of "downtime" (time when the network is not functioning). The survival of the company depends on the data communication network being accessible at all times.

Third and finally, data communication systems allow people and businesses in different geographical locations to communicate with one another. Data communication systems allow employees of companies separated by large distances to work as if they were in close proximity. Corporations can communicate with manufacturing operations in a geographical location far away from their administrative headquarters. Inventory, personnel, and other company data can be transmitted from one location to another through high-speed data communication networks. In this manner, the corporation can operate as a single entity. Managers can instantly review inventory levels in the manufacturing location. Engineers can deliver new designs in real-time, and managers can share timely and accurate information in order to make strategic decisions.

Data communication systems combined with computer technology are an integral part of today's companies. As a result, a business can become more effective and efficient in the world market than was possible a few years ago.

A Brief History

The first data communication systems were created in 1837 as a result of the invention of the telegraph by Samuel F. B. Morse. Even though the United States government declined to use the telegraph, in 1838 Morse created a private company to exploit his invention. By 1851, over fifty telegraph companies were in operation. Today's Western Union Telegraph was formed in 1856 and became the largest communication company in the United States ten years later.

In 1876, the U.S. patent office issued a patent to Alexander Graham Bell for his invention of the telephone, with the Bell Telephone Company then being formed in 1877. The first telephone system didn't have switching offices or exchanges. If a subscriber wanted to establish a communication with another subscriber, he had to have a pair of telephone wires attached directly to the phone at the location of the receiving call. Therefore, if a business needed communication with fifty other businesses, then it had to install fifty pairs of wires. When a call was made the right wires had to be connected to the telephone. In addition, telephones didn't have bells or ringers. Therefore, both parties had to be on-line at the same time since there was no way for one party to know when the other was making a call.

However, technology progressed rapidly, and by 1878 Bell installed the first telephone exchange with an operator. By using wire jumpers a telephone operator could connect a user to different locations. Therefore, subscribers didn't require a pair of wires for each location that they wanted to reach.

In 1885, American Telephone and Telegraph Company (AT&T) was formed to build and operate long distance lines in order to interconnect the regional phone companies. This allowed the connection of the individual Bell company subsidiaries operating throughout the country to connect all their subscribers.

Technology continued to progress, and by 1892 automatic switching began with the introduction of the first dial exchange in La Porte, Indiana. This system worked by using a series of electromechanical selector switches, called relays, to automatically place the incoming call on the right outgoing line. This process took time to complete and that is the reason the first telephone used round dials. The round dials provided a deliberate waiting period after each digit was dialed, giving the switch time to set up the connections. The electromechanical switch was replaced later by the electronic switch. With this type of device the delay used for the relays was no longer required, and push-button telephones could then be used to make the connection.

The vacuum tube was invented in 1913, and in 1941 came the integration of computer and communication technology. This was an important step in the evolution of communication systems. The computer enabled the creation and management of faster and more sophisticated systems. With this integration, the usage and development of new systems accelerated, lowering the cost of communication and increasing quality and efficiency.

In 1943, submersible amplifiers and repeaters were developed, facilitating communication across large distances and among international customers. But it was the invention of the transistor in 1947 that revolutionized the telecommunication industry. The transistor allowed for the development of smaller and faster computers that, through mass production, became relatively inexpensive and within the reach of many companies and users. The integration of communication systems and computers would not be what it is today without the invention of the transistor and subsequent developments in integrated circuitry. This technology led to the development of satellites with the first satellite being launched in 1957, expanding the opportunity for worldwide data communications.

In 1968, an important decision, known as the Carterfone Decision, was made by the Federal Communication Commission (FCC). The FCC decided that a small Dallas based company (Carter Electronics Corporation) could attach its Carterfone product to the public telephone network. The Carterfone allowed the connection of private radio systems to the phone network. When AT&T refused to allow Carter Electronics to attach its product to the phone system, Carter Electronics sued and won. This decision opened the door for the attachment of non-AT&T equipment to the public phone system and spawned a new era in the communication industry. It also help in breaking the monopoly that AT&T and the Bell companies had over the phone system.

Other antitrust suits against AT&T from the period of 1974 to 1982 ended in 1984, in the divestiture of AT&T from its 22 Bell companies. This allowed many other companies to provide phone services to individuals and corporations, ultimately increasing the quality, sophistication, and types of offerings that a communications company could provide. It also helped in reducing the cost of using data communication systems. Table 7-1 shows a summary of the history of data communication.

Table 7-1.

	Summary of Data Communication History
1837	Invention of the telegraph
1856	Western Union was created
1877	The Bell company was formed
1885	AT&T was created
1913	Invention of the vacuum tube
1941	Integration of computing and communication technology
1947	Invention of the transistor
1957	First satellite was launched
1968	Carterfone decision
1984	Divestiture of Bell company

Today, the network of available telephone lines, microwave stations, and satellite stations continues to expand. Computer technology continues to become faster and more economical. Data communication has become a worldwide enterprise. These systems, although complex, have three common characteristics that are used to subdivide them. These characteristics are what are called the data communication system basic components.

Basic Components

Data communication systems can be divided into three major components:

1. The source of communication. This is the originator of the message to be sent. This source can be a simple telephone used by a human or it can be a computer that calls another computer for the purpose of exchanging data.

2. The medium of communication. This is the physical path through which the message has to travel. It can consist of twisted pair wires, coaxial cable, optical fiber, microwave, or some other type of data carrying media.

3. The receiver (sometimes called the sink or host) of the communication. This is the receiver of the message. The receiver can be a telephone that is answered by a person or it can be a host computer answering the call from a calling computer or terminal.

The Sender

Although the communication established between two people through the use of the telephone is of importance, in this book we are more concerned with the communication requirements when two or more computers want to establish a communication link. This is because in many situations a computer is both the sender and receiver. If two computers have a communication link established and data is flowing from one machine to the other, one of the machines is transmitting data at times and at other times may be receiving data.

The Communication Medium

The medium can be a leased line from the telephone company (also called a common carrier), a proprietary coaxial line, optical fiber, microwave, satellite, or other facilities. Fig. 7-1 depicts a basic data communication system. This system includes computers or terminals that act as senders, modems, connector cables, telephone switching equipment, interexchange channel facilities, a receiver, and a host computer. The items in Fig. 7-1 will be explained in more detail in further chapters, but a general description follows.

Fig. 7-1. A basic data communication system.

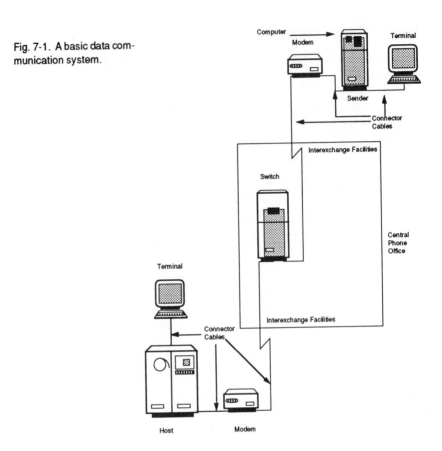

The computer and terminal are used to enter information. This device can be a terminal attached to a minicomputer or mainframe, or a microcomputer with a keyboard and a printer, or it can be a FAX machine, or any other input device.

The connector cables in Fig. 7-1 connect the sender to a modem. The modem is an electronic device that converts digital signals originating from a computer or FAX machine into analog signals that the telephone equipment can transmit. The signals go from the modem to a local telephone switch that connects the home or office to the telephone company central office or some other carrier. Then, at the central office, switching equipment connects the sender's equipment to a line that terminates at the receiver's location and equipment.

The Central Office

The central office (sometimes called the exchange office) contains switching and control facilities operated by the phone company (see topic later in this chapter). All calls and data exchanges have to flow through these facilities unless there is a leased line. If there is a leased line, the phone company wires the line around the switching equipment in order to provide an unbroken path. An example of a commonly used lease line is the T1 line previously discussed.

The Interexchange Facilities

Interexchange channels (IXCs) are circuit lines that connect one central exchange office with another. These circuit lines can be microwave, satellite, coaxial cable, or other physical media. They simply relay communication data from one geographical location to another for the purpose of routing the call.

The Host

Finally, the receiving end has another modem to convert the analog signals from the telephone company back to digital format. These signals are then transferred to a host computer that processes the received message and takes appropriate action.

There are many other components that can be incorporated into the data communication system depicted in Fig. 7-1. Later chapters provide further details of these components, as well as an in-depth discussion of communication networks that incorporate computer technology. However, one component of the data communication system, the communication network, is worth discussing at this point.

The Data Communication Network

A network is a series of points that are connected by some type of communication channel. Each point (sometimes called a node) is typically a computer, although it can consist of switching equipment, printers, FAX machines, or other devices. A data communication network is a collection of data communication circuits managed as a single entity. Then what is the difference between a data communication system and a data communication network? The collection of data communication networks and the people that enter data, receive the data, and manage and control the networks make up the communication system. Fig. 7-2 shows examples of multiple networks which are part of a data communication system.

Fig. 7-2. Multiple networks in a data communication system.

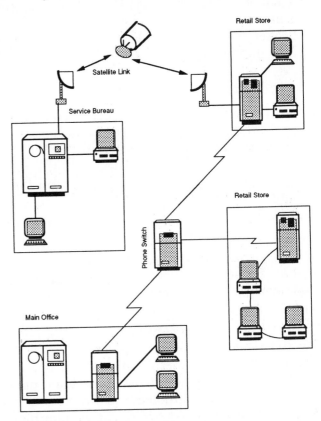

Even though almost anyone can establish a data communication network, successful network implementations have a common set of characteristics. These characteristics, sometimes called requirements, of a data communication network must be observed if the network is to be efficient and effective in its role. To create a successful implementation, a network designer must be aware of all the different configurations and possibilities that are at his or her disposal in designing the network. The network designer must be well schooled in design techniques as well as have an excellent understanding of the data communication field. This last point may seem trivial, but many companies leave network designing, especially local area network designing, to individuals without the proper background and training. The end result is a poorly configured system that is blamed for the difficulties and problems in communicating data within the company and a lack of user confidence in technology.

Requirements of a Data Communication Network

As discussed above, there is a set of major criteria that a successful data communication network must meet. These are performance, consistency, reliability, recovery, and security criteria.

Performance

A data communication network must deliver data in a timely manner. Performance is typically measured by the network response time. Response time is normally considered the elapsed time between the end of an inquiry to the network and the beginning of the response from the network or system. The response time of a communications network must meet the expectations of the users.

Many factors affect the response time of a network. Some of these factors are the number of users on the system, transmission speed, type of transmission medium, and the type of hardware and software being employed. For example, assume that a network was designed to handle the data communication needs of 20 individuals and their associated equipment. If the company that houses them has a growth period during which the number of users is doubled, then most likely the response time of the communication system will typically increase, in some cases by several orders of magnitude.

In addition, twenty users communicating through a medium at 10 megabits per second will get a different response time than the same number of users with a 2.1 megabit per second medium. Also, the type of data transmitted makes a difference in the response time of the network. If text files are transmitted through a 2.1 megabit transmission path, then the response time will be less than the same network transmitting large graphics files and text files at the same time.

Although there is a tendency to relate the performance of a data communication network to its hardware, another big factor that will affect response time is the type of software running the system. The network operating system and the different protocols that must be handled by the network will have a large impact on the performance of the network. It is true that, if a network is slow, introducing faster hardware and a faster communication medium will decrease the response time. But, in many cases, the increase in speed of transmission gained by using this method is small compared to the gain obtained by using an efficient operating system and network operating system that are specifically designed to handle data communications between users. And just as important as the response time itself is the consistency of the response time across the network.

Consistency

Predictability of response time, accuracy of the data transmitted, and mean time between failures (MTBF) are important factors to consider when choosing a network. Inconsistency of response time is annoying to users, and sometimes it is worse than a slow but consistent response time. Users typically prefer having a consistent response time of three seconds that they can depend on to having, for example, a one-second response time that, on occasion, varies to 15 seconds. Unpredictable performance may motivate some users to rely on other means of acquiring and transmitting their data, making the data communication network inadequate as a data communication solution for the company.

Accuracy of data is important if the network is to be deemed reliable. If a system loses data, then the users will not have confidence in the information generated by the system. An unreliable system is often not used, and, if it is used, users tend to duplicate the data entered into the network by using manual systems. The end result is that users spend additional time manually duplicating everything they send through the network, thus increasing the amount of time they spend on a function. This decreases their productivity, increases the cost to the company, and tends to demoralize the users of the system.

Reliability

In addition to the accuracy of the data transmitted, another factor that contributes to network reliability is how often the network is unusable. This is often called network failure, and it is measured by the mean time between failures.

Network failure is any event that prohibits the users from processing transactions. Network failure can include a breakdown in hardware, the data carrying medium, and/or the network controlling software (network operating system). With today's data communication networks as complex as they are, the number of components that can fail during the operation of the network is continually increasing. But modern equipment has a failure rate that is less than similar but older equipment. In addition, new monitoring techniques and redundancy in the network contribute to increasing the time during which the system is operational.

As mentioned above, the failure rate of the network and its equipment is measured by the mean time between failures. The MTBF is a measure of the average time a component is expected to operate between failures. This time is normally established by the manufacturer of the equipment, and users normally trust the numbers provided by the maker of the equipment. However, many user groups and trade publications have their own statistics, and users are advised to compare these numbers with those provided by equipment manufacturers. In addition, these statistics provide some indication of the time of recovery after a failure. This refers to the length of time for the equipment or the network to become operational after a failure.

Recovery

All networks are subject to failure. After a failure, the network must be able to recover to a prescribed level of operation. This prescribed level is a point in the network operation where the amount of lost data is nonexistent or a minimum. Recovery procedures and the extent of recovery will depend on the type of hardware and software that control the network.

Some networks use log files that are saved continually to a hard disc. These log files contain all transactions performed since the system was turned on or since a predetermined date. If the network fails, then many network operating systems are capable of using the log file to rebuild transactions that were lost when the system went down. Less sophisticated systems rely on a network operator to rebuild the system based on the log file. In addition, many networks employ what is commonly known as mirror techniques with their hard drives. Using this technique data is saved to two different hard disks at the same time. In this manner, if a hard disk failure occurs, the other hard disk is brought on line and the system can stay operational. Mirror techniques enhance the reliability of the network, but they also enhance another critical aspect of the network, its security.

Security

Network security is another important component in communication networks, especially when computer data is involved. A business's data must be protected from unauthorized access and from being destroyed in a catastrophic event such as fire. Therefore, companies are placing more stringent security measures on networks in order to safeguard their data. When a communication network is being designed, security must be carefully considered and incorporated into the final design.

A network's security is enhanced by the use of identification numbers and passwords for all of its users. In addition, call-back units can be used to reduce the number of unauthorized callers. These units assure that the caller or user of the network is in an authorized location and/or terminal. However, even these measures are not enough in safeguarding the data transmitted through and stored in the network.

Another technique employed when security is a high priority is encryption. With this method, data that needs to be transmitted is encoded with a special security key. The result is that, to unauthorized users, the data looks like garbage. At the receiving end, the same key is used to decode the data and convert it to its original format. Security keys and encrypting are commonly used in the defense industry.

Data on a network is also threatened by computer viruses. A computer virus is a program that invades programs inside computers in the network and then performs unwanted functions on the programs themselves and the data stored on disks. These functions can be from simply displaying annoying characters on the screens of network users, to destroying the data stored on the user hard disks and network servers. Several programs and monitoring software can be used to alert network administrators to the presence of such viruses. For a further study of this topic see chapter 12.

Applications of Communication Networks

During the 1990s, data communication networks will be a faster growing industry than computer processing itself. Even though both industries are now integrated, we are moving from the computer era to the data communication era. A recent survey indicates that, during this decade, the majority of new career opportunities will be related to the communication field, especially in local area networks and their connectivity to other systems. Data communication networks are appearing in all places where one computer needs to exchange data with another computer. Teaching institutions are connecting their students and administrative workstations. Companies connect each department with a local area network and then connect individual local area networks into a single network, and corporations that cover the world connect their regional networks into wider area networks through the use of satellites.

Also, many business systems currently use data communication networks as the "backbone" for carrying out their daily business activities. Data communication networks can be found in every segment of industry. On-line passenger systems, such as American Airlines' SABRE, have changed the way people travel. In addition, an airline's computer is normally connected to all other airlines via telecommunications. In this manner, reservation agents from United Airlines can make reservations for flights on American Airlines. Car rental companies, such as Avis, and hotel chains, such as Holiday Inn, could not function effectively without their reservation systems. The type and scope of communication networks are wide and extensive. But a few applications of data communication networks are commonly found in many modern companies. These types of applications are discussed below and include videotext, satellite, public networks, teleconferencing, and telecommuting.

Videotext

Videotext is the capability of having a two-way transmission between a television or computer in the home and organizations outside the home. It allows people to take college courses at home, conduct teleconferences from the home, play video games with players in other locations, utilize electronic mail, connect with the bank and grocery stores, do on-line mail shopping, utilize voice store and messaging systems, and carry out many other functions.

Fig. 7-3 shows a screen display of a bulletin board that is used for discussing expert advice on computer topics. The conferencing system can be accessed from a home by using a microcomputer and special hardware to call a host computer and use it to "talk" to other people on the system. This is a common process used on many public and commercial bulletin boards (see topic below). With it, an electronic public forum or a question and answer session that involves dozens of people simultaneously can be conducted. In addition, it is a quick way to have on-line training between a customer and a service company.

Fig. 7-3. Bulletin board screen with expert advice.

Satellite

By using a home satellite TV receiver and transmitter, people will be able to communicate with others via a satellite dish located on their property. This antenna can receive and transmit voice or data to any other part of the world by relaying it to other satellites orbiting the earth.

Many steps have been taken to reduce the cost of transmitting data using this method. Today the cost of receiving data using a home satellite dish is relatively low. One use of this technology has been tested by politicians when they conduct electronic town meetings. When one of these "meetings" takes place, the satellite and frequency of transmission are normally available to the public. A person with the right equipment and information can tune into the satellite channel and receive the transmission without the interruption of commentators normally found in commercial television.

In addition to home satellite systems, many computer users have data communication through ham radio. With the appropriate equipment, a ham radio operator can transmit computer data through the radio waves without having to pay the fees normally associated with satellite transmission. Of course, the speed and clarity of the transmission is lower when using this method.

Public Communication Networks

Public communication networks have standard interfaces that allow almost any type of computer or terminal to connect to other computers or terminals. Many companies already have their own private telephone branch exchange (PBX). These systems can connect terminals and computers in the company to other systems anywhere in the world by using satellite, radio, and microwave transmission.

Using public networks an individual can use a terminal or computer and a modem from his or her home and connect to other computers and networks located in a different geographical location. This capability is used by many progressive companies to allow their employees to work from their homes. This has increased the efficiency of many employees since they can now spend the time required to travel back and forth from the office performing their jobs. Additionally, companies are now able to keep valuable employees that they could otherwise lose, such as new parents who want to stay home with their children. By using a personal computer, a modem, and a public network, these employees can now minimize the amount of time spent at the office.

In addition to traditional transmission media offered by public networks, cellular radio loops can be used to replace copper wire as the communication medium for computers. This increases the ability of an employee to be at a required location and still be in touch with the main office's network and host systems.

Teleconferencing

Video teleconferencing allows people located in different geographical regions to "attend" meetings in both voice and picture format. A video teleconference is accomplished by using a television camera and associated equipment to transmit voice and video signals through satellite networks. Many teleconferences have the same type of equipment at both sites, allowing all attendees to talk to and see each other, including selected computer displays. Other teleconferences have the projection equipment at a single location, and participants at remote locations can communicate back to the central transmitting site by using telephone communications.

Documents can also be made available to all people attending the teleconference almost instantaneously. This can be performed with the use of facsimile machines or by using a scanner and then transmitting the scanned image. However, if the required document exists in digital form, the data can simply be transmitted with the use of a modem and a receiving modem and computer system.

Telecommuting

This application, as explained before, allows employees to perform office work at home. Through the use of a terminal or a personal computer and a modem, an employee can be in constant communication with the company and perform his or her work more efficiently and without wasting the time required to travel to and from the office. This allows employees to have greater time flexibility, less stress, optimized scheduling, and many other benefits. The employee is then free to schedule his or her work to allow for maximizing use of the available time. In most of these cases, the employee visits the office once or twice per week for meetings or other duties, but this time is minimal when compared to the weekly schedule.

Electronic Mail

Electronic mail (e-mail) provides the ability to transmit written messages over short or long distances instantaneously through the use of a microcomputer or terminal attached to a communication network. The people communicating through electronic mail do not have to be on-line at the same time. Each can leave messages to the other and retrieve the replies at later times. Fig. 7-4 shows a screen that is typical of many electronic mail systems.

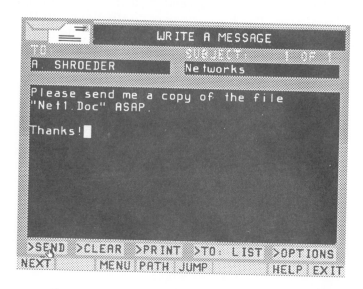

Fig. 7-4. Screen from an electronic mail system.

Electronic mail has the ability to forward messages to different locations, send word processed or spreadsheet documents to any user of the network, and transmit the same message to more than one user by using a mail list. A mail list contains the names and electronic mailbox addresses of people that the message must be sent to. The electronic mail system reads the names and addresses from the list and sends the message to all users on the mail list. Electronic mail significantly improves corporate and individual communications. Additional information on electronic mail is presented later in this chapter.

Home Banking

Computers can handle the traditional methods of making payments through home banking. A user with a terminal or microcomputer can connect to his or her bank's computer network through electronic mail and pay bills electronically, instead of writing paper checks. The user can indicate the amount of a payment and the receiver of the payment electronically, and the bank processes the transfer of funds. Additionally, new home banking systems offer many other services besides personal fund transfers. Some of these services are providing checking account balances, ticket purchasing, and stock information services. Fig. 7-5 shows a screen of a home banking service software program. The banking service displayed in the figure has services for bill paying, credit card acquisition, money markets, IRAs, loans, and mortgages.

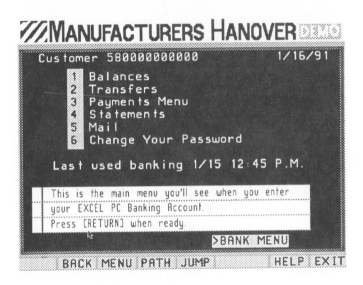

Fig. 7-5. Home banking service offering.

Also, many electronic home banking services are being connected to other consumer services such as grocery stores. With this service, an individual can use a personal computer and modem to dial a database of products belonging to a grocery company or store. The user selects the type and quantity of the products needed and then instructs the system to produce a balance. The balance is then forwarded to the electronic home banking system which transfers the balance to the grocer's account, and the bag of groceries can be picked up by the customer. Or, for a small fee, it can be delivered to the customer's address.

Electronic Funds Transfer

The ability to transfer funds electronically from one financial institution to another has become a necessity in today's banking world. Commercial banks transfer millions of dollars daily through their electronic fund transfer (EFT) system. The large number of transactions that are made every day by banks requires the use of computers and communication networks to increase speed and cost efficiency.

Imagine the amount of time that it would take to manually handle all funds transfer transactions that take place in a single day at the New York Stock Exchange. Although some people think that the use of technology in such settings is more harmful than good, today's financial transactions couldn't be accomplished without the use of effective data communication networks. The modern western world couldn't exist as we know it without such communication systems.

Information Utility Services

Information utility services offer general and specialized information that is organized and cross-referenced, much like subjects are in libraries. Items are organized into databases and each database contains several categories of services, such as access to news, legal libraries, stock prices, electronic mail services, conferencing, and games.

The desired information is located by signing onto the information service and then selecting the topic of interest from a menu. Once the topic is selected, search criteria can be entered and the system will display the information on the screen. This information can then be captured (downloaded) onto the hard disk of the user's microcomputer for further examination. More information on this topic is presented later in this chapter.

Electronic Bulletin Boards

The electronic bulletin board system (BBS or EBBS) consists of a computer or microcomputer that is used to store, retrieve, and catalog messages sent in by the general public through their modems. The telephone company provides the link between the person using the BBS and the host computer of the BBS. The primary purpose of BBSs is for people to leave notes to others.

Additionally, some BBSs are now being used for group conferencing. They offer a variety of messages and services to their users. Some of these services are electronic "chats" with other users, making airline reservations, playing games, and sending and receiving messages. Fig. 7-6 displays some of the services offered by a privately owned information utility service.

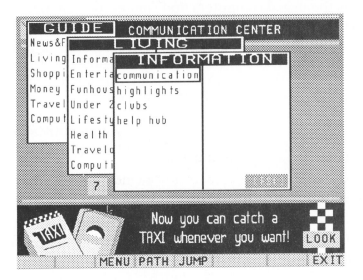

Fig. 7-6. Information utility service.

Value Added Networks

Value added networks (VANs) are alternative data carriers to the traditional public data carriers such as AT&T. VANs are now considered common carriers and are subject to all government regulations. They can be divided into public and private VANs.

Private VANs own and operate their networks and are not accessible to the public. One example of a private carrier is the SABRE system used by travel agents to make reservations and check prices. Public VANs offer a wide variety of communication services to the general public. These services include access to databases and electronic mail routing. An example of a public VAN is Telenet.

The Telephone Company's Central Office

Telephone companies use a location, called the central office, to terminate all the phone lines from customer sites and connect them to equipment that makes the service possible. In addition, each central office is connected to another central office whether or not it belongs to the same company. This allows customers to choose any service company and establish a communication link with other sites regardless of which company services the receiving location.

Modern central offices are basically switching stations that enable them to connect thousands of customer calls to their required destinations. The switching equipment in these offices is programmable computers that have a high redundancy in their communication distribution so a failure of any portion of the equipment can be circumvented.

Since the central office is composed of modern computers, they require fewer workers to maintain the communication system than older central offices. However, the technological skill of the personnel required to maintain current systems is high. Ability to diagnose a problem that occurs in the system requires excellent knowledge of highly sophisticated equipment.

The line connecting each central office is called a trunk. A trunk can be defined as a circuit connecting telephone switching computers or switching locations. Typical transmission media for trunk lines are coaxial cable, optical fiber, or microwave radio.

Since the divestiture of the Bell companies, telephone companies started to provide a variety of services to solve data communication problems. Among these offerings are the following:

1. Discounted calling
2. WATS services
3. Software defined network
4. Centrex
5. Foreign exchange lines
6. Voice messaging
7. Audio teleconferencing
8. Marine and aeronautical telephone service
9. Cellular telephone service
10. Integrated Services Digital Network

Although the above list doesn't include all possible offerings, it has the most commonly used services.

Services Provided

Discounted Calling

Customers with a large volume of long distance telephone calls are normally eligible for special discounts from the normal fares for communication. Discounting is performed based on the volume and total cost of the calls made per month by an individual or company. The amount of the discount varies. It is normal to find discounts of 10% for customers that make calls totaling $100 per month, up to 35% for customers that have a volume of $2,500 per month. For customers that incur costs of $10,000 or more there are discounts of 45% or more.

Wide Area Telecommunication Service (WATS)

Wide area telecommunication service (WATS) offers large discounts to a company that has a high volume of telephone calls. A WATS line works in the same manner as a normal telephone line. Only one call can be made or received at any given time. Customers pay a fee to have the WATS service and then pay another fee for each minute that they use the line. Although it seems like a double take from the phone company, the discounts offered by this type of service when the volume of calls is large is substantial.

The WATS service is classified according to the geographical area that it covers, the coverage of the band used, and the direction of the call. The geographical area can be intrastate, interstate, or international. The intrastate option offers discounts for calls received or made within the state of the customer with the WATS service. The interstate is provided to customers who need to have telephone communication outside the state where they are located. And international is a service provided to those customers that have a large volume of international calls.

The band coverage is a format used by the phone companies to provide phone services and discounts throughout the United States, based on the distance between the caller and the receiving location. In this format, the continental United States is divided into five concentric bands, with the home state at the center of the bands. Each of the bands contains approximately 20 percent of the telephones in the country. Therefore, if a customer places a call to any state that is within the first band, a special discount applies to that call. If, after that call, the same customer places a call to another state that is in a different band, then a different tariff will apply to the call, and so on with the rest of the locations in the other bands.

The direction of the call can be in-WATS or out-WATS. In-WATS is what is commonly known as an 800 telephone service. A customer dials the WATS line of a company and the company pays for the connection. The company receiving the call gets a special rate for the cost of the connection and therefore provides a service to its customers. The out-WATS is basically the opposite of the in-WATS. Individuals at a company get special rates for any phone communications that they perform when they dial out to a remote location.

The WATS concept provides a form of bulk telephone pricing that is profitable for the carrier and customer alike. In addition, it allows companies to provide special services to customers without them having to pay for the cost of the service directly. Many companies have in-WATS lines for their customers and sales personnel so they can access a central host computer for pricing of goods, or some other needs.

Software Defined Network (SDN)

Software defined network (SDN) is another bulk pricing or discount pricing offered by AT&T that is designed to benefit large companies. A company can access SDN through switched or leased lines. Once in the system, the company receives several services, including discounted prices for the calls made, seven digit dialing to all locations belonging to the company, special billing, and special authorization codes for company employees who need access to specialized telephone calls.

Software defined networks are virtual leased line services. This means that instead of leasing a direct line from point A to point B, an SDN leased line utilizes public switched networks. This type of network enables customers to use dial-up facilties for extending private networklike functions to areas that otherwise couldn't afford the cost of fixed-wire leased lines. This is because an SDN leased line is less expensive than a physical voice grade direct line that is leased to connect two points.

Centrex

Centrex is a service provided by telephone companies that is similar to the offerings of private branch exchange or PBX. Basically, the main difference between a PBX system and a Centrex system is that, in the latter, the equipment is located at the central office of the telephone company instead of being located at the customer site.

The Centrex service uses the same equipment that the telephone company uses for switching lines in its normal operation. All the functions that were mentioned previously in the description of the PBX also apply to the Centrex service. Then why would a company choose to have a Centrex service instead of a PBX? The answer to this question will depend on the amount of control that the company wants over its phone and data communication services.

If a company acquires a PBX, it owns the local switching equipment and it must have personnel to maintain and program the PBX as necessary. If the company chooses the Centrex approach, it doesn't have to make the capital purchase required for the switching equipment, and all maintenance and upgrading are performed by personnel at the central office. In this case, the company pays a monthly fee for using the system.

Foreign Exchange Lines (FX)

If a company makes or receives a large volume of calls from one distant location, it can request a foreign exchange line (FX line). This FX line connects the customer to a remote central office so the calls appear to be made from the remote central office. For example, if a company resides in Dallas, but needs to access Kansas City, it could request an FX line for Kansas City. In this manner, if an employee of the company in Dallas makes a call to Kansas City, the call is made at the local telephone rate in Kansas City. Customers of the company located in Kansas City can access the company by using a local telephone call, but the phone will ring in Dallas.

Voice Messaging

Some telephone companies are now providing voice messaging for companies and even individual users. Voice messaging systems provide an electronic mailbox where callers can leave messages for other people. It is similar to electronic mail, except that it uses a digitally recorded voice instead of text typed from a terminal or computer.

Since voice messaging uses a digitally recorded voice, it can have the same functionality as that found in many electronic mail systems such as mail forwarding, storing messages permanently, and sending messages to other individuals or group of individuals.

Although, the public phone companies are not the main providers of this type of service (private voice networks are the main providers), they are slowly beginning to branch out into this type of service with relatively good success. This service can also be made available to individual users, but the price is high when compared to voice systems provided from private companies.

Audio Teleconferencing

Audio teleconferencing is a service provided by telephone companies that uses a room specially equipped with an omnidirectional microphone and a speaker at the center of a table or room where the conference will take place. Both of these devices are connected through the telephone lines to a similarly equipped room at a remote location.

At one of the conference rooms, one of the participants makes a call to the other room and the meeting begins when the call is answered. Through the speaker, all the participants in one room can hear the voices of the participants in the remote conference room. And through the use of the omnidirectional microphone, any participant's voice can be received by the microphone and transmitted to the remote location where it is broadcast through the connected speaker.

Audio teleconferencing is useful for allowing a group of people to converse with specialists or experts at remote locations or for conducting meetings between central offices and branch offices. Many audio conferences are also connected by a facsimile machine that provides an almost instant feedback on any type of visual that can be placed on paper.

Marine and Aeronautical Telephone Service

Marine and aeronautical telephone service is provided by using radio communication. In this case a transmission is established between a transceiver in a boat or airplane and a receiver that is connected to a common carrier. The equipment based on land and belonging to the public carrier is normally voice activated. This means that it switches between being a receiver and a transceiver when one of the participants in the communication stops talking.

Commercial airlines use this type of communication extensively on their commercial flights. Telephones are available on one of the seats in front of the passengers or in the cabin of the airplane. A passenger uses a credit card to unlock the telephone and then dials the number that he or she needs to contact. The call is transmitted to the closest ground receiving station, then routed over normal telephone circuits to the destination address. Once the call is completed, the passenger returns the phone back to its handset, and the customer's credit card is billed for the call using a flat rate plus a per-minute fee.

Cellular Telephone Service

Although many private companies are offering cellular services to customers, public carriers offer the same type of service. Cellular radio, as described before in this chapter, is a form of high frequency radio communication that uses antennas for retransmitting the calls placed from a home or automobile. These antennas are located strategically throughout a city. The city itself is divided into cells, with each cell containing its own antenna.

Many companies use cellular radio as a means for transmitting data from a portable computer to a central computer. However, it is important to note that cellular radio calls can be picked up by any individual with the proper receiver. Therefore, this is not a good means of transmitting data that needs to be secured from unauthorized users or individuals.

Integrated Services Digital Network (ISDN)

The Integrated Services Digital Network (ISDN) is one of the broadest programs undertaken by the telecommunication industry. The goal of ISDN is to connect every home and organizational desktop with a high-speed digital service using copper wiring or optical fiber. Although the original specifications of ISDN use copper wiring as the main communication link, some companies providing ISDN services use optical fiber in some of the transmission links.

Many common carriers in the United States already provide ISDN services, but they do it primarily in the cities. As the demand for this type of service grows, so will the number of installations. The primary problem in providing ISDN services to everyone is that current switches in central offices need to be equipped with new hardware and software in order to allow the ISDN calls to pass through. In addition, the line from the telephone central office to the average household is equipped to carry analog signals instead of digital signals. To provide ISDN services to homes, these lines, or local loops as they are called, will have to be converted to carry the new digital ISDN signals.

The designers of ISDN developed a set of technology standards that divide the available bandwidth into channels of two types. One is called the "B-channel," and it carries a digital signal at speeds of 64 kilobits per second. The other channel, called the "D-channel," carries digital data at speeds of 16 kilobits per second. This channel is used for signaling. It sends requests to the ISDN switch while moving data from applications.

The service provided by ISDN can be divided into the basic and primary services. The basic service, also called the 2B+D, uses two 64 kilobits per second B-channels and one 16 kilobits per second D-channel. This basic service is expected to be provided to all home customers and small companies. The other type of service, the primary service, is called the 23B+D. It provides 23 B-channels for data transmission and one D-channel for signaling.

ISDN circuits have a large bandwidth that enables transmission of digitized voice and data simultaneously. Using the basic service, an individual can have a telephone conversation and transmit data at 64 kilobits per second at the same time. In addition, incoming calls can be identified by their telephone number and even more data can be transmitted to the receiver before the call is actually established. This capability has raised some questions about the privacy rights of the calling party.

Computers can use the basic service as an open line for the transfer of data at nearly 150 kilobits per second. This may seem slow when compared to the 10 and 16 megabit per second transmissions of current local area networks. However, as we will see in later chapters, local area networks use media-access protocols to control access to the cable. In addition, nodes in the system must wait, retry, repeat, and perform many other functions that are required to have a successful operation. This overhead slows the actual throughput of the local area network to just several hundred kilobits per second. When compared to this, the ISDN transmission speed is not bad, since an ISDN circuit doesn't have to be shared with any other nodes in the circuit.

Additionally, companies can subdivide the bandwidth of the primary ISDN service in any way that they choose. Half of the capacity, 772 kilobits per second, could be used to transmit television signals, and the other half could be used to transmit voice and computer data simultaneously.

The benefits of ISDN are numerous, but the major benefit is that ISDN can provide alternative links to personal computers, mainframes, and existing local area networks across thousands of miles using a fast digital service. In the near future, ISDN may replace and displace today's traditional networks at many locations.

Some additional benefits of ISDN are as follows:

1. It provides efficient access to public networks.
2. It can handle digitized voice and data simultaneously.
3. It has a good signaling channel, the D-channel, which is a requirement for networking.
4. It provides a standard interface that is internationally recognized.

Although the progress toward a complete ISDN service in all public networks has not been as fast as many expected, the progress has been steady. Full ISDN implementations throughout the United States can be expected in just a few years.

Local Line Capabilities

The local telephone lines can carry voice data using an analog format, and with some special equipment can carry data produced with a computer. Although modern telephone systems are more digital in nature, the communication system from the central office to homes and offices is designed for analog communication.

The central office has special equipment that translates the analog signals coming from the home or office phone line into a digital signal that modern switching equipment requires. It is because of this analog nature of the local loop that a modem must be used to communicate over telephone lines. The digital signal of the computers is converted into analog form by the modem, then it is converted back into digital form at the central office. It is converted back into analog form before being retransmitted to the receiving stations, and converted again from analog into digital form by another modem at the receiving site.

The data transmission speed capability of these local lines depends to some extent on the equipment being used to perform the communication. Normally a computer can transmit with speeds of 300 up to 9,600 bits per seconds. However, some newer transmission equipment is capable of increasing this speed to 32 kilobits per second and higher using normal local lines. Additionally, some smart modems, although not transmitting at speeds over 9,600 bits per second, have compression ability and correction capabilities that enable them to increase the throughput by several factors. In this fashion, a modem transmitting at 2,400 bits per second can have a higher data transmission rate than a modem transmitting at 9,600 bits per second, but without the sophistication of the first type of modem.

Common Carriers

Throughout this chapter we used the words "common carrier" whenever a reference was made to one of the Bell companies or some other providers of telecommunication service. A common carrier is a company that has been authorized by the federal government to sell and lease services to the public. These companies are regulated by the Federal Communications Commission (FCC) to provide communication services throughout the United States. The regulation is a method to ensure that the service and equipment that these companies provide will work with those provided by every other company in the same type of business.

Although the word "regulated" is used, these companies are profit companies. The regulation is mostly in the price that they can charge for their communication services. However, companies such as US Sprint and MCI are deregulated in terms of the types of services they are allowed to provide. Each company is free to choose other types of businesses to enter besides the telecommunications market.

There are hundreds of common carriers in the United States. Some of the biggest names are AT&T, US Sprint, MCI Communications, General Telephone and Electronics (GTE), and the seven Bell Operating Companies (BOCs). The rest of the carriers tend to be small, with subscriber numbers ranging between 100 and 200 members.

The Bell Companies

Although there are hundreds of companies that can provide communication services in the United States, AT&T and its previous companies, the Bell Operating Companies, used to have the great majority of the communication business in the US.

During the later years of deregulation, the 22 original companies owned by AT&T were consolidated into seven Bell Operating Companies (BOCs). These companies are responsible for providing the telephone service to most homes and businesses. In addition, they also supply the local loop connections between the home and office and the central offices, making voice and data communication possible.

The service areas of the seven Bell Operating companies are broken into smaller service areas called local access transport areas or LATAs. The LATA provides a geographical boundary within which the local Bell Operating Company can provide services. Outside this boundary, the local Bell Operating Company must turn the service over to another carrier such as AT&T or MCI. The geographical areas covered by the LATAs in most cases conform to state boundaries and community interests with most states having multiple LATAs. In some sparsely populated areas a single LATA is the main provider of communication services.

Although prohibited from offering any other services besides communications in the beginning of their existence, deregulation has allowed these companies to venture into new services and product offerings. Each of the Bell Operating Companies is allowed to market products from other manufacturers that include, but are not limited to, office automation equipment, PBX, cellular radios, and modems. Now some of these companies are being allowed to manufacture and market their own equipment, placing them in direct competition with traditional office and network providers such as IBM.

American Telephone and Telegraph (AT&T)

After the divestiture of the original AT&T, a new company called AT&T Communications was formed. The main business of this company is to provide long distance communication services to the public. In addition to this mission, AT&T also kept the Bell research laboratories and its manufacturing division, Western Electric, from the divestiture of the original company. This provided AT&T with the ongoing expertise and access to equipment required to continue the traditional role of data and voice communication provider over large geographical areas.

After the divestiture, AT&T was left as an independent company from the Bell Operating Companies. However, many other companies have jumped into the long distance communication market placing them in direct competition with AT&T. Some of its biggest competitors are MCI, GTE, and US Sprint, and they also provide the services required to interconnect the different LATA service companies.

Services Offered Through Communication Networks

Whether a person uses a public data communication network, a private network, or a value added data communication network, he or she can access a wide range of services. The options continue to grow in terms of the number of users and the sophistication of the services offered to customers. Many of these services were, at one time, available only to employees of large corporations such as IBM. With increased competition and the cost of computer electronics dropping every year, these services are now available to the average consumer. The services most commonly available through data communication networks are:

1. Electronic mail and transfer of documents in digital format
2. Transfer of documents through facsimile technology
3. Information services
4. Commercial electronic bulletin boards

Electronic Data Interchange

Electronic data interchange (EDI) is computer-to-computer communications among different enterprises for the purposes of performing daily business operations. Using EDI, corporations send inventory information to suppliers, invoices to customers, and checks to banks, to name but a few uses. Before the advent of computer networks, all transactions were performed by using paper and postal delivery. With electronic data interchange, all of these business transactions can be performed electronically and almost instantaneously.

Some systems initiate the exchange of information automatically without human intervention. Many inventory systems are programmed to call company suppliers when the inventory of a product falls below a predetermined number. Other systems automatically initiate electronic invoicing when a given date is reached. Also some purchasing systems automatically call possible vendors to obtain a bid when purchase orders are entered into the system.

Electronic Funds Transfer

The ability to transfer funds electronically from one financial institution to another has become a necessity in today's banking world. Commercial banks transfer millions of dollars daily through their electronic funds transfer (EFT) system. The large number of transactions that are made every day by banks requires the use of computers and communication networks to increase the speed and cost efficiency of doing business.

Electronic Mail

Computer networks provide the necessary tools for a new type of industry, electronic mail service. The main function of electronic mail services is to serve as a centralized clearing house for electronic messages. These messages can be grouped according to the purpose for which they are intended. Some of these are:

1. E-mail
2. Electronic data interchange
3. Electronic funds transfer

E-mail

Electronic mail (e-mail) provides the ability to transmit written messages over short or long distances instantaneously through the use of a microcomputer or terminal attached to a communication network. The people communicating through electronic mail do not have to be on-line at the same time. Each can leave messages to the other and retrieve the replies at later times.

Electronic mail has the ability to forward messages to different locations, send word processor or spreadsheet documents to any user of the network, and transmit the same message to more than one user by using an electronic mail list. An electronic mail list contains the names and electronic mailbox addresses of people that the message is sent to. The electronic mail system reads the names and addresses from the list and sends the message to all users on the mail list.

Electronic mail services improve corporate and individual communications significantly. Users can send documents or messages and they don't have to wait for several days for the message to be delivered. In addition, an employee who is on a business trip can use a laptop computer to check any messages that may be in his or her electronic mailbox.

A variation of e-mail is voice mail. Voice mail systems use a computer to record voice messages and store them in an electronic database that can then be scanned by each voice mail user to play the audio message back. Voice mail systems have similar capabilities to those found in e-mail systems. The main difference between the two is in the equipment used to deliver and repeat the message. In a voice mail system, the telephone is used as the main interface between the user or customer and the system itself. In e-mail, a terminal or computer is used as the means for sending and reading the message.

Types of E-mail Systems

E-mail systems can be categorized into:

1. Public and private commercial e-mail carriers
2. Closed e-mail systems
3. Personal computer-based e-mail systems

Public and Private Carrier

Private commercial e-mail carriers are specialized carriers that lease telephone lines from public carriers such as AT&T or set up their own networks. They support selected users who perform business directly with the network company and often provide customized enhancements applicable to the needs of their users. One example of a private carrier is IBM, with its extensive network system that connects all of the IBM branches and offices throughout the world.

Public carriers, on the other hand, take calls from any user who needs or wants to access the network. When the word "public" is used in this context, it means that the network is accessible to the general public and not necessarily that it is owned by the government. Some examples of public carriers are GTE's Telenet and Tymeshare's Tymenet.

Closed E-Mail

A closed e-mail system allows individuals within a company to exchange messages. It is called a closed system because the documents and messages sent throughout the system are available only to the employees of the company. In many cases, a minicomputer or mainframe acts as the e-mail server and router. Any terminal or microcomputer attached to the server can access the e-mail system and send or receive messages.

PC-Based E-Mail

Personal computer-based e-mail systems use a personal or microcomputer as the electronic post office. Normally, this type of e-mail system is part of a PC-based local area network. A workstation on the network can send any type of electronic message to another workstation by "attaching" the message to the address of the receiving microcomputer. The address in most instances is nothing more than the network name of the user who is to receive the message.

Communication Standards

With the data communication field growing at a very fast rate, the number of options and companies providing services increases continually, making it difficult for consumers and network designers to choose the right option for them. In addition, each equipment manufacturer has its own way of transferring the data and adding proprietary options to its systems. In order to bring some organization to this field and to ensure that equipment from one manufacturer is capable of co-existing with equipment from another manufacturer, some companies have created standards. In the electronic mail and document transfer arena two standards are widely implemented. One is the X.400 standard and the other is the X.25 standard. This doesn't mean that they are the only standards in use today. On the contrary, many other good "standards" are in use throughout the market. But these two standards have been widely accepted by most of the major players in the communication industry.

The X.400 Standard

As the makers of e-mail systems proliferate, several international associations have created standards that allow different e-mail systems to communicate with each other. One of the fastest emerging and most important standards is called X.400. It was established by the Comite Consultatif Internationale de Telegraphique et Telephonique (CCITT). Many vendors, including IBM, Telenet, and DEC have announced support for this standard. It is used extensively in the international community.

The X.400 standard specifies data transmission in the form of messages and the information that accompanies the message. Using this communication standard, network nodes can send and receive information from one another without the need for a central host computer. In addition, the X.400 standard also allows for the transmission of multimedia messages such as voice, graphics, and FAX messages.

Some of the services provided by the X.400 standard are:

1. Message identification
2. Time of submission
3. Indication of the type of content
4. Access management
5. Delivery notification
6. Nondelivery notification
7. Multiple destination delivery
8. Importance indication
9. Primary and copy receivers indication
10. Reply requested indication
11. Encryption indication

The X.25 Standard

The CCITT has also published a wide area network standard called the X.25. The X.25 standard is used throughout much of the public bulletin board industry and is used extensively in the United States by most public data networks, such as Tymenet and Telenet.

A network using X.25 is a packet switching network. A packet switching network breaks the data into packets before transmission across the WAN. These packets are sent out after they are built in a packet assembly/disassembly facility called PAD. In many cases a PAD is a card that fits in one of the expansion bays inside a computer. For further study of packet switching networks, see chapter 9.

In addition to the benefits outlined above, the X.25 protocol is "transparent." As long as the receiving computer understands the data sent by the sending computer, the communication takes place. This transparency allows X.25 packets to be encapsulated in other protocols such as IBM's SNA. This allows diverse systems to use the same wide area network system.

Also, a LAN may access public and private WANs through the use of an X.25 gateway. Most X.25 gateways for a PC-based LAN consist of a PC, a wide area communications board, communications software, and a synchronous modem.

Functions of an E-mail Package

All e-mail systems provide a basic set of features that are composed of creating, sending, receiving, reading, and printing documents. In addition to these functions, most e-mail systems have enhanced capabilities that vary according to the maker of the product. Also, many new systems have a help feature that provides a list and explanation of all features available.

Although the following list does not contain all features available in sophisticated systems, it describes some of the commonly available services that most modern e-mail programs offer.

1. Create a message. Messages need to be created before they can be sent. Although large documents will probably be created using an independent word processor, e-mail packages have text editing capabilities that allow for the creation of small documents or messages that can then be sent electronically to other users.

2. Send a message. Messages and documents can be sent through e-mail systems with different levels of priority. Most systems support first class, registered, and regular mail. A document sent with the registered mark on it may require an acknowledgment of the recipient in the form of a message back to the sender. In this manner, the sender will know the time and date the receiver read the message.

    In addition, mail can be sent regular, express, or immediately. Immediate mail is delivered within seconds of being sent. Express mail is collected electronically at various points and forwarded to its destination at regular intervals throughout the day or when the activity on the network has declined. Regular mail is collected electronically and sent to its destination when the charges are the lowest or the activity of the network is low.

3. Receive a message. Documents sent electronically are placed in the receiver's "electronic mailbox." In some systems, this mailbox is called a "basket." There could be incoming baskets and outgoing baskets. Mail can be read from the incoming basket and sent from the outgoing basket. Notification of new mail in the in-

coming basket is done automatically on most systems by displaying a message on the screen when the user logs in.

4. Read the message. Messages can be read by the recipient in the order that they reach the incoming basket or in some prioritized order. Also, messages can be deleted or stored for further reading.

5. Print the message. Messages can be printed, provided that a network printer is available or that a printer is attached to the terminal or microcomputer that is being used for communications.

Modern e-mail systems contain additional features. Some of these are:

1. Time of submission
2. Indication of the type of content
3. Delivery notification
4. Nondelivery notification
5. Multiple destination delivery
6. Importance indication
7. Primary and copy receivers indication
8. Reply requested indication

Choosing an E-mail System

Although different types of e-mail systems are available, some basic questions should be answered before an organization purchases or leases e-mail services. Even though the type of questions that a service provider must answer are complex and extensive, the following list provides a general framework by which a decision can be made.

1. What mail system will you need to communicate to?
2. Can mail be prioritized?
3. What tools are available for finding a message?
4. What security measures are available to keep the communications private?
5. What word processors does the system support?
6. What other software programs does it support (e.g., Lotus 1-2-3, graphics programs, etc.)?
7. What are the workstation requirements?

8. Does it support office functions such as electronic calendars, automatic forwarding, and alerts and alarms.
9. What is the speed of transmission?
10. What is the monthly fee?
11. Are there any surcharges?
12. What "user-friendly" features does it have?
13. Can users check their mail from remote locations?
14. What backup options are available?

Beyond E-mail?

Although electronic mail systems can be used to deliver documents without the need of the US post office, the documents sent through the data communication networks to the e-mail system must first be generated. In many cases, the documents are generated by software programs and they already reside in electronic format. But many documents are in paper form and they need to be converted into digital form. The device that can accomplish this task is the scanner. A scanner takes text or images from a document and converts it into a graphical image that can be stored as such or read by optical recognition software in order to "extract" the text out of the image and perhaps store it as an ASCII file.

Additionally, a figure or text scanned into an electronic document can be sent as a FAX document using a computer equipped with a FAX board. A FAX board allows a PC to act as a FAX machine. That is, it can send and receive documents, unattended, through the telephone lines. The main difference between a stand-alone FAX machine and a computer equipped with a FAX board is how the document is placed in the FAX machine for sending. A stand-alone FAX machine can receive documents that are on any type of paper. To send a FAX using a FAX board and a computer, the document must first be converted into electronic format.

Facsimile Technology and the Personal Computer

A facsimile (FAX) terminal is able to transmit an exact picture of a hard copy document over telephone lines anywhere in the world (see Fig. 7-7). It is a quick and inexpensive way to send documents any place where there is a telephone line and another FAX machine. In the earlier days of FAX machines, the speed of transmission was slow, documents were fed into the machine manually, and the quality of the output was poor. In newer facsimile machines, all of these problems have been corrected or reduced.

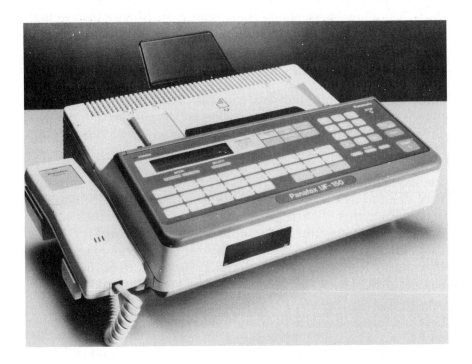

Fig. 7-7. The Panafax UF-150 facsimile is small and lightweight. It can also be used as a copying machine. (Courtesy of Panasonic Corporation)

FAX machines are divided into four major groups, according to their technology and speed.

1. Group 1 is the oldest of the FAX machines. It required manual document feed and manual communication links. Also, it required between four and six minutes to send a document and the output quality was very poor.

2. Group 2 FAX machines were developed in the 1970s. The FAX machines belonging to this group showed speed transmission improvements over group 1 machines. This type of facsimile could transmit a document in one to three minutes.

3. Group 3 FAX machines are high-speed terminals. These types of machines are capable of transmitting a document in less than a minute. Also, most of them have automatic document feeders, automatic dialing, automatic connection, laser quality output, and other advanced features.

4. Group 4 FAX machines are the latest generation of facsimile devices. They use digital telephone networks to increase the speed of transmission and the options available. New facsimile machines that are appearing in the market use ISDN and other new technologies to increase the speed and quality of the transmitted document.

Most newer FAX machines are group 3 or 4. The group 3 machines can transmit a page in approximately one minute or less. Group 4 machines can transmit an 8 1/2 by 11-inch page in approximately 20 seconds. Additionally, group 4 FAX machines have a higher image transmission quality.

Since the signals produced by a facsimile machine are digital in nature, they can be read into a computer and stored as bits. This has led to the development of FAX boards that can be added to microcomputers. With these boards, any document created on a personal computer can be transmitted to any FAX machine through phone lines. Messages sent by FAX machines can also be received by the FAX boards inside microcomputers, and a picture of the document can be stored on a disk or sent to an attached printer.

If a FAX board is used, documents that need to be sent must be scanned using a desktop scanner or produced using a software product. In the case of the scanner, it will produce a graphical image and store it on the hard disk of the computer that contains the FAX board. Using software, the phone number of a receiving FAX machine or computer with a FAX board is dialed. After the receiving machine answers the phone call, the document is sent and printed on the FAX machine or stored on the local disk of the receiving computer. The received document can be displayed in graphical format, or an optical character recognition (OCR) product can be applied to it. The OCR program can extract the text characters in the document and store them in a text file or place them inside a word processor or some other software product.

If a document is produced with a software package that can create documents that are readable by the computer with the FAX board, the scanner is not required. For example, a document can be created with a word processor or spreadsheet, using a computer with a FAX board. After the document is created and saved, it can be transmitted directly from the hard disk of the computer to a receiving FAX machine or computer equipped with a FAX board.

The Facsimile Transmission Process

To use a facsimile device the following equipment is required:

1. Two compatible units, one unit at the sending location and the other at the receiving location.
2. Two phone ports, one at the sending location and the other at the receiving location.
3. If the machines are not equipped with dialing and phone receiving capability, then two telephones will be required, one at the sending location and the other at the receiving location.
4. Paper for the sending and receiving documents. In some cases plain paper can be used; in others, a special type of paper needs to be used. It depends on the machines.

Transmitting a FAX Document

To transmit a document using facsimile equipment, the following steps can be taken:

1. Make sure that both units are powered and supplied with paper.
2. Place the document to be sent in the transmitting or sending machine.
3. Using the phone capabilities of the FAX machine or a telephone attached to it, dial the phone number of the receiving FAX machine.

4. After a dial tone is received, press the Send button on the machine.

5. After the message has been received, hang up the telephone.

If a computer with a FAX board is used, the process is as follows:

1. Create the document and store it on the hard disk of the computer containing the FAX board.

2. Run the FAX communication software that comes with the FAX board.

3. Using the dialing utilities of the software, dial the phone of the receiving station. It doesn't matter whether the receiving station is a FAX machine or a computer equipped with a FAX board.

4. Use the command in the software to send the document.

The document will be read from the disk and sent through the phone lines to the receiving station.

Bulletin Boards

The electronic bulletin board system (BBS or EBBS) consists of a computer system that is used to store, retrieve, and catalog messages sent in by the general public with the use of a terminal or microcomputer and a modem. The telephone company provides the link between the person using the BBS and the computer that is the host of the BBS.

The main reason for the existence of electronic bulletin boards is for people to leave messages to others. Also, some BBSs are being used for group conferencing. They offer a variety of messages and services to their users. Some of these services are electronic "chat" with other users, making airline reservations, playing games, and sending and receiving messages.

Types of Bulletin Boards

Computerized bulletin boards offer a wide variety of services and physical setups. However, they can be categorized into three major areas.

1. Commercial bulletin boards
2. Local public bulletin boards
3. Specialized bulletin boards

Commercial Bulletin Boards

Sometimes called an information utility service, this type of bulletin board offers both general and specialized information that is organized and cross-referenced, much like subjects in libraries are organized into databases. These BBS offer several categories of services such as access to news, legal libraries, stock prices, electronic mail services, conferencing, and games.

Many commercial systems of this type have emerged in the past few years, with services and prices ranging from a low $10 to $15 flat fee per month to $10 to $15 per minute of use. The price of the usage depends on the type of information required. Research information services such as Dialog are more expensive than home oriented services such as Prodigy.

It is important to note that if a user lives within the borders of a large metropolitan area, the connection fee to access the bulletin board is nonexistent, except for the usage fee of the system. However, if a user lives outside the local phone area of the network that provides access to the bulletin board, then a long distance connection fee to the network is also assessed by the phone company. In this case, a single connection to one of these system can become expensive.

Local Public Bulletin Boards

This type of bulletin board is a dial-up system that serves a limited geographical area. They are operated out of individual homes and by local computer clubs. They act as message clearing houses for individuals with common interests. Typically there are no fees for the use of this type of bulletin board, and, if a fee is charged, it is nominal.

In addition, many of these bulletin boards are also storage locations for much of the public domain and shareware software products on the market. With the proper software, a computer, and a modem, a user can download any available software products residing on the bulletin board's file server.

Specialized Bulletin Boards

This type of bulletin board is set up by corporations to serve a particular need of the company employees. For example, a company may set up a BBS so its sales agents can obtain instant communication with other personnel. Or it may use it to conduct electronic forums of certain topics or products several times per month. Also, many companies use it to answer questions of personnel that are located in different geographical locations than the technical staff responsible for their system.

Components of an Electronic Bulletin Board

All electronic bulletin boards have several elements in common. These elements include:

1. Modem. A modem (or several modems) is necessary to allow users to connect to the EBBS. The caller will also be required to have a modem connected to his or her computer to perform the connection. The modem receives the analog signals coming from the phone lines and transforms them into a digital format that the host computer can understand.

2. Telephone lines. Commercial EBBS may have hundreds of modems, while local or PC-based EBBSs may have only one or two phone lines. The phone lines become the transmission medium for the connection between modems. Although some EBBSs are attached to networks and don't use the public phone carriers as the physical connecting medium, most EBBSs use the phone lines as their transmission medium.

3. High-capacity computer. The EBBS would not be possible without the use of a computer. The size of storage that the computer possesses is important for the electronic bulletin board service. Larger disk space allows for more and longer messages to be stored.

4. EBBS software. All the hardware needs to be controlled by software. The EBBS software not only controls communications, but facilitates the management of the entire operation. Good bulletin board software contains a series of utilities that facilitate the maintenance, operation, backup, and security of the system.

5. System operator. The system operator (sysop) is responsible for installing software, setting up the EBBS menu, answering questions, solving problems, and monitoring the activity of the bulletin board.

Services Provided

The services provided by an electronic bulletin board differ according to the type of company that provides the service. However, commercial bulletin board services provide most of the services listed below.

1. Message centers
2. News services
3. Shopping services
4. Specialized clubs
5. Entertainment services (games, etc.)
6. Electronic mail
7. Banking services
8. Travel services
9. Various professional services
10. Conferencing
11. Electronic libraries

Popular Electronic Bulletin Board Systems

Quite a few commercial and public EBBSs are in operation across the USA. Some offer a large variety of services and are also called information services. Some of the best known are:

1. Dow Jones News/Retrieval Services
2. CompuServe
3. GEnie
4. DIALOG
5. Prodigy

Summary

Data communication is the transmission of electronic data over some medium. The systems that enable the transmission of data are often called data communication networks. For a data communication system to be effective, it must provide information to the right people in a timely manner, capture business data as it is being produced, and allow people and businesses in different geographical locations to communicate with one another.

The basic components of a data communication system are the source of communication, the medium of communication, and the receiver of the communication. All data communication systems must meet a minimum set of requirements which include performance, consistency, reliability, recovery, and security requirements.

Data communication systems are composed of data communication networks. A network is a series of points that are connected by some type of communication channel. Each point is typically a computer, although it can consist of many other electronic devices. A communication system is a collection of communication networks and the people using and managing the networks.

One source of data communication solutions may be the telephone company. Telephone companies use a location, called the central office, to terminate all the phone lines from customer sites and connect them to equipment that makes the service possible. In addition, each central office is connected to another central office whether or not it belongs to the same company. This allows any customer to choose any service company and establish a communication link with any other site, regardless of which company services the receiving location.

With the divestiture of the Bell companies, telephone companies started to provide a variety of services that solve data communication problems. Among these offerings are the following:

1. Discounted calling
2. WATS services
3. Software defined network
4. Centrex
5. Foreign exchange lines
6. Voice messaging
7. Audio teleconferencing
8. Marine and aeronautical telephone service
9. Cellular telephone service
10. Integrated Services Digital Network

Of these, the Integrated Services Digital Network (ISDN) offers some of the greatest possibilities. ISDN is one of the broadest reaching programs undertaken by major telecommunication companies in the industry. The goal of ISDN is to connect every home and organizational desktop with a high-speed digital service using copper wiring or optical fiber. The benefits of ISDN are numerous, but the major benefit is that ISDN can provide alternative links to personal computers, mainframes, and existing local area networks across thousands of miles using a fast digital service. In the near future ISDN may replace today's traditional networks at many locations.

Data communication networks provide access to many popular services that individuals and businesses are using in their daily activities. These services, available through data communication networks, include the use of electronic mail, bulletin boards, media conversion, and facsimile technology.

The main function of electronic mail services is to be a centralized clearing house for electronic messages. These messages can be grouped according to the purposes for which they are intended. These purposes are:

1. E-mail
2. Electronic data interchange
3. Electronic funds transfer

Electronic mail (e-mail) provides the ability to transmit written messages over short or long distances instantaneously through the use of a microcomputer or terminal attached to a communication network. Electronic data interchange is computer-to-computer communications among different enterprises for the purposes of performing daily business operations. Electronic funds transfer is the ability of computer networks to perform financial transactions without the need to perform actual currency exchanges.

Enhancing the flexibility of electronic mail, a facsimile (FAX) terminal is able to transmit an exact picture of a hard copy document over telephone lines anywhere in the world. It is a quick and inexpensive way to send documents any place where there is a telephone line and another FAX machine. The speed, quality, and convenience have greatly improved since the early days of FAX machines.

The electronic bulletin board system (BBS or EBBS) consists of a computer or microcomputer that is used to store, retrieve, and catalog messages sent in by the general public through their modems. The telephone company provides the link between the person using the BBS and the host computer of the BBS. The main reason BBSs exist is for people to leave messages for others. Also, some BBSs are now being used for group conferencing. They offer a variety of services to their users.

Questions

1. Briefly describe the concept of data communication.
2. Name some of the possible data transmission media.
3. What are the functions of data communication systems?
4. Briefly name the most important historical events that shaped the communication industry up to the 1990s.
5. Describe the basic components of a data communication network.
6. What is a communication network?
7. What is the difference between a communication network and a communication system?
8. What are the major requirements that a data communication network must possess?
9. What is meant by mean time between failures (MTBF)?
10. Discuss three applications of a data communication network.
11. What is e-mail?
12. What types of electronic mail are available to corporations?
13. What features can be found on most e-mail systems?
14. What is a bulletin board system?
15. What is an information service?
16. What functions are provided by commercial bulletin board systems?
17. Name four commercial information services.

18. What is the X.400 standard? Why is it important?

19. What is the purpose of a FAX machine?

20. Briefly describe the different generations of FAX technology.

21. What is ISDN?

22. How can ISDN be beneficial for the average computer user?

23. What services, besides ISDN, can a telephone company provide?

Projects

Understanding an Existing Computer Communication System

This project will make the student familiar with a currently implemented data communication system. It provides a way to visualize the concepts and hardware discussed in the chapter. In addition, it allows the student to acquire a "feel" of how people use the components of data communication systems and to observe some of the equipment and processes that will be explained in more detail in subsequent chapters.

Visit the data center at your institution and find what types of network and data communication facilities are available for the private use of the institution and which facilities are available for general public access. Try to answer all the questions below by asking data center personnel or by observing the daily operations and hardware present at the center.

a. What types of mainframes or minicomputers (hosts) are available?

b. What types of personal computers are available?

o Laptops

o Macintosh Classic/SE

o Macintosh II family

o IBM PC/AT

o IBM PS/2

o IBM-compatible clone

o Other

    c. Are the hosts networked?

    d. Are the personal computers networked?

    e. How are the personal computers connected to the host?

    f. Is electronic mail available?

    g. How is the electronic mail accessed?

    h. What databases are available in the institution library?

    i. How often do they experience downtime?

    j. Find out how the staff conducts business when their computer or terminal is down.

    k. How is the data protected from unauthorized access and accidents?

Also, find out how many telephones they are using including outside lines. Find out whether they have their own PBX or if they lease a Centrex system. Find the limitations of their current system and suggest solutions. If they have a PBX, what features does it have? How is it maintained? What is the cost of the system, and does it compare with the cost of having a Centrex system performing the same functions? Always justify your answers with technical facts or cases.

Understanding an Elementary Computer Network

Contact your local bank and write a report that describes how the bank personnel perform their daily routines. Use the outline below as a guide for your report.

    a. Computer systems in use at headquarters and at the branches:

        o Mainframes

        o Minicomputers

        o Personal computers

        o Terminals

    b. Networks used at each branch and between branch and headquarters:

    c. How is electronic funds transfer handled?

  d. What types of value added networks and public networks are used to perform e-mail and electronic funds transfer?

  e. Are there any facilities available for home banking?

  f. What types of disaster recovery plans do they have?

  g. How do the managers at different branches communicate with each other?

Exploring a Communication System

Pick a system to produce a report on:

  a. a cellular system

  b. a voice messaging system

  c. a teleconferencing system

  d. a marine communication system

Produce a two- or three-page report on the capabilities and potential of the system in the data communication field. Always justify any conclusion with technical facts.

Part Three

The Microcomputer and Local Area Network Environment

Microcomputer Connectivity

Objectives

After completing this chapter you will:

1. Obtain a general understanding of the types of communication software available to connect microcomputers to microcomputers and microcomputers to mainframes.

2. Gain knowledge about async data communications.

3. Gain knowledge about sync data communications.

4. Understand the need for protocols in data communications

5. Have a general overview of some of the most commonly used protocols in micro-to-mainframe and micro-to-micro communications.

6. Understand problems associated with noise and interference created by power sources.

7. Understand the different devices available to solve interference problems.

Key Words

Asynchronous	GUI
Kermit	Modem
MS-DOS	Power Sag
Power Surge	Protocol
Synchronous	RS-232
UPS	X-On/X-Off
Xmodem	Ymodem
Zmodem	

Introduction

Since the introduction of the transistor by AT&T's Bell Laboratories, the fields of electronics and communications have undergone a transformation that has been unprecedented in the history of the world. Through innovative techniques, electronics manufacturers have reduced the size of circuitry required to perform many different tasks and introduced the personal computer or microcomputer into the business and home markets.

Companies like Intel and Motorola have been the dominant microprocessor manufacturers for personal computers, and the power of these systems has increased significantly since their introduction in the early 1980s. At the same time, the price of complete systems has decreased as new offerings came on the market and as the competition intensified. The end result is a bonanza for consumers. With many powerful systems priced under $1,000, the capabilities and potential of the computer are accessible to almost everyone.

Today, businesses use microcomputers in almost every facet of daily activities. Personal computers can be found in the automated office, in local area networks, as replacements for terminals for micro-to-mainframe connections, as servers, or simply as stand-alone processing units. In the home, computers are being used for entertainment, as an extension of the office, to keep track of home budgets, to help with homework, and as communication devices that can link the home user to any other system in the world for the exchange of information and ideas.

This widespread use of microcomputers transcends the fields of data communications and computer science. As some of the more recent world conflicts testify, microcomputers and facsimile machines have been the vehicle by which a society disseminated information about an event when the normal journalistic media were unable to provide news of ongoing events. The result was that other people in the same country and in other nations aware of the situation as it was unfolding were able to help this society in shaping the course of history. The microcomputer, with its data communication capabilities, was a key component in bringing these changes about.

However, this widespread use of the microcomputer has alerted organizations about the need to have adequate communication facilities throughout the entire organization and from the organization to the outside world. Although many companies are providing connectivity through the use of local area networks, the home market and much of the business world still use the more traditional terminal emulation capabilities of software and hardware for their communication needs.

In a decade of networks and sophisticated connectivity between computer systems, it is important to understand standard async and sync communications since many connectivity solutions employ these two methods. It is true that the network will eventually be the mainstay of connectivity solutions in the business market, and the ISDN has the same promise for the home user. However, async and sync terminal emulation techniques will always play a role in communication between computers, primarily because they are understood, they are simple when compared to networks, and in most cases they are cheaper. Also, for many communication needs, the slower speed transmissions employed when communicating in one of these modes is more than sufficient to satisfy the user's needs.

The Need for Protocols

As mentioned in chapter 4, the computer industry uses protocols in order for one type of computer to communicate effectively with a computer manufactured by another company. The protocol is a set of conventions or rules that the communicating computer follows in order to complete a data communication task. The idea of protocols is not new. They exist not just in the data communication industry, but in society in general. When a person meets another individual, a salute or introduction is normal before a conversation is established. This in essence is a protocol.

Although the number and types of protocols in data communications are many, personal computers normally follow a few standards. Two of these standards are the asynchronous and the synchronous protocols. As explained in chapter 4, asynchronous communication is characterized by the use of a start bit preceding each character transmitted. In addition, there are one or more stop bits which follow each character. In asynchronous transmission (sometimes called async), data comes in irregular bursts, not in steady streams. The start and stop bits form what is called a character frame. Every character must be enclosed in a frame. The receiver counts the start bit and the appropriate number of data bits. If it does not sense the end of a frame, then a framing error has occurred and an invalid character was received. When this happens, smart systems ask that the sender retransmit the last group of bits.

Because of its relative simplicity and inexpensive implementation costs, asynchronous transmission is very popular in the home and business data communication markets. Most, if not all, personal computers are capable of transmitting data using this method. Additionally, minicomputer and mainframe manufacturers, except IBM, use this protocol on a routine basis to connect their system with the user's terminals.

However, async communications have a low transmission efficiency since at least two extra bits must be added to each character transmitted. Also, asynchronous communication normally takes place at low speeds, ranging from 300 to 19,200 baud.

The alternate method of serial communication is called synchronous serial communication. With synchronous transmission, data characters are sent in large groups called blocks. These blocks contain synchronization characters that have a unique bit pattern. They are placed at the beginning and middle of each block with the synchronization characters ranging in number from one to four. When the receiver detects one of these special characters, it knows that the following bit is the beginning of a character, thus maintaining synchronization.

Synchronous transmission is more efficient than asynchronous communication. It is the preferred method of communications between IBM minicomputers such as the AS-400 and IBM mainframes with the 3270 series of terminals located at users' desks. However, the actual efficiency of the transmission will also depend on many factors, such as how many times bits must be retransmitted. Because of the popularity of these two protocols, the rest of this chapter will be dedicated to studying the transmission process and steps required to connect two computers or a computer and a minicomputer or mainframe using async and sync transmission. Other protocols are discussed in later chapters.

Protocol Functions

The implementation of most of the useful protocols in the market includes rules and processes to handle many situations that arise during the data communication process. Some of these events are outlined below:

1. Starting the communication. The protocols must establish rules for determining how the communication is to be initiated. This includes which stations are the "host" and which are the "slave," whether the communication starts automatically, and which station is allowed to communicate.

2. Character identification. The receiving station must have a way to identify the different frames that contain the characters that make up the message being transmitted, and, of course, there must be rules to identify the characters within the frames.

3. Message control. The receiving stations may receive the frames of several messages in a random order. Therefore, there must be some rules that identify the frames or characters of the different messages so the message can be assembled and provided to the user.

4. Error control. The protocol must have rules for understanding the electrical signals on the lines of the transmission media. Then these rules need to identify the outgoing lines so the sending device can be notified that the message was received. Additionally,

the protocol must have rules for using these lines to identify errors and for notifying the sending device so a retry or some other action can be taken.

5. Ending the communication. The protocol also needs to establish rules for terminating the communication whether this termination is under normal or abnormal circumstances.

All of these rules specify how the different situations arising in the data communication environment will be handled. It is obvious that if a successful communication link between two computers is required, then both machines must be running the same communications protocol. Otherwise, if the rules are not the same, data will be lost in the exchange, much in the same manner as in social occasions where different protocols are observed. In this case, misinterpretation of signals will most likely end in chaos.

Communication Software and Protocols

Asynchronous Communication

Using DOS

MS-DOS or PC-DOS contains a program utility named MODE. This utility can be used to control data transfer between two computers or between a computer and some types of peripherals. To use the MODE utility for communications between two computers, the serial port is used as the input and output port of the personal computer. The MODE utility is used to set up several of the transmission parameters, such as the speed. The sending computer serial port configuration must be the same as that of the serial port of the receiving computer. Before the communication port can be used for data transmission the parameters that affect how the serial port works must be set up. These parameters are as follows.

1. Baud rate. This is the rate of transmission of data, and it is a measure of how many bits per second are sent or received by the serial port of the computer. Typical settings are 300, 1200, 2400, 4800, and 9600.

As the baud rate increases, the rate of transmission also increases, and the time you have to spend waiting for information to appear on the screen decreases.

2. Data bits. This is the number of bits that make up a character. Most microcomputers use seven bits.

3. Stop bits. This is the number of bits used to indicate the end of a character. In most cases, one stop bit marks the end of the character.

4. Parity. This is a method of checking for errors in data communication. If the number of data bits is eight, then normally there is no parity; otherwise, the parity can be odd or even.

These parameters must be the same in the sending and host computers. Once the users determine what the parameters should be, the serial port needs to be initialized. The initialization of the serial port is accomplished by invoking the MODE utility in the following manner.

MODE [port] [baud], [parity], [databits], [stopbits]

where each of the settings can have the following parameters.

Port. It can be COM1:, COM2:, COM3:, or COM4:.

Baud. It can be 300, 600, 1200, 2400, 4800, 9600, or some higher number if the machine can handle it.

Parity. It can be n,o, or e. These stand for no parity, odd parity, or even parity.

Databits. It can be 7 or 8.

Stopbits. It can be 1 or 2.

Therefore, as seen in Fig. 8-1, a typical command may be

MODE COM1: 1200,e,7,1

This will set the serial port to operate at 1200 baud, even parity, 7 bits, and 1 stop bit. After the MODE utility is invoked, data can be sent to the designated serial port and through a serial cable to the destination serial port and computer using DOS redirecting operators.

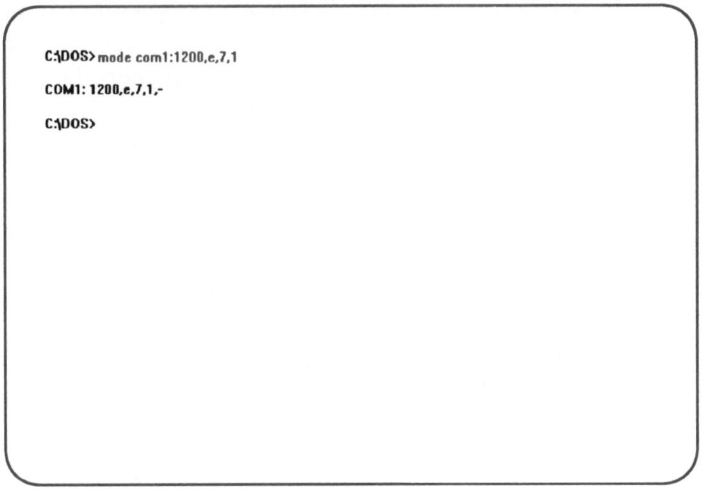

```
C:\DOS> mode com1:1200,e,7,1

COM1: 1200,e,7,1,-

C:\DOS>
```

Fig. 8-1. The MODE command.

Communication Software

Although data communications can be established using the procedure outlined above, for most people this is not convenient. Most async data communications are performed through a data communication program such as CROSSTALK, PROCOMM, MS Windows Terminal, or some other communication program. Many integrated software programs such as Microsoft Works have terminal or communication programs built in so a user doesn't require a separate package

Most data communication programs operate in a similar fashion. the basic operation of these programs is based on setting different options in the software and then establishing a connection. Since the parameters of the data transmission are the same regardless of the software driving it, they all have a way to set the baud rate, parity, stops bits, and other parameters. The main difference between these programs is the addition of a macro language or some other method to automate the communication process.

Many of the more expensive and comprehensive programs have a facility that can be used to create macros or programs that can automatically dial numbers, redial the numbers when they are busy, keep track of the amount of time used during transmission, and automatically upload or download files to and from the host. Some programs, such as the one provided with MS Windows, don't have a macro facility of their own, but use the macro recorder provided with Windows. Additionally, the pull down menus, and their availability when a copy of Windows is installed in a computer system, make the program called Terminal a popular package for beginners and advanced users alike (see Fig. 8-2). At the end of this chapter you will find a project that allows you to explore how some of these packages work by using the Terminal program in Windows.

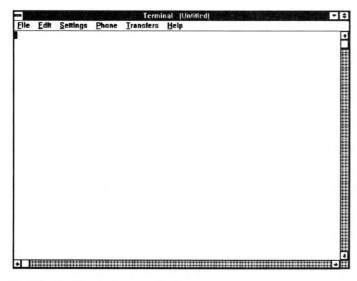

Fig. 8-2. The Terminal communication program.

One of the features of data communication programs is the ability to take software residing on the disks located on the host computer and transfer the information to the user's computer. This process is called downloading. The process in reverse-- taking software from the user's computer and sending it to the host system for storage on one of its disks--is called uploading. For this process to be effective, not only must both computers be using the same communication parameters, but during the transmission process they must also use the same error correction method, which is handled by the protocol.

Protocols

As mentioned before, regardless of the data communication software used for data transmission between two computers, both machines must be using the same communication protocol. There are several protocols that are common to computers running bulletin boards and other microcomputers. Some of these are X-On/X-Off, Xmodem, WXmodem, Ymodem, Zmodem, X.PC, and Kermit.

X-On/X-Off

X-On/X-Off is one of the oldest protocols in the async communication field. Therefore, it doesn't incorporate some of the more sophisticated error checking procedures of newer protocols. For this reason, it is used for the transmission of text only, but it can't be used to transmit binary files or some of the more complex graphical formats currently on the market.

X-On/X-Off works by having one computer send data to another computer and the receiving machine send back an acknowledgment or X-On signal if it is free to receive. If the receiving computer is busy because it needs to save data stored in RAM to a disk, it sends an X-Off signal to the sending computer. This machine then halts transmission until the second computer is free again and sends back an X-On signal. At this time, the transmission continues.

The X-On character sent from one computer to another is a CTRL-S or ASCII character DC3. The X-Off character is CTRL-Q or DC1. Although effective in many data transmission sessions, one of the characters (DC1 or DC3) could be lost due to noise in the line. When this happens the entire communication process can become nullified or unreliable since synchronization of the data is lost.

Xmodem

The Xmodem protocol is one of the most widely used asynchronous protocols developed for use in the microcomputer data communication arena. One of the computers using this protocol is designated as the sender and the other is designated as the receiver. The receiver indicates to the sender that it is ready to receive by sending an ASCII NAK character every ten seconds. When the sender acknowledges this character, it begins sending the file or message.

The data being transmitted is divided into blocks of 128 characters, with each block surrounded by a header and trailer. The header and trailer are used for error correction during the transmission process. The header consists of a start character (ASCII SOH), followed by a character that describes the block number, followed by the data of the same block number with every bit inverted. The trailer consists of a one-byte checksum character that is the sum of all the characters in the block divided by 255, retaining the remainder. The checksum is sent to the other end of the data transmission.

After the block is received, the receiving computer calculates its own checksum character and compares it with the checksum sent by the sending computer. If the two characters are equal, then an ASCII ACK or acknowledgment character is sent back from the host to the first computer so a new block can be transmitted. If the checksums don't agree, then an ASCII NAK character is sent back and the block is retransmitted.

Using this process, the entire message or file is sent block by block. At the end of the transmission, the transmitting computer sends an EOT or end of transmission character and waits for an ACK before it terminates the session.

The Xmodem protocol is used not only for data transmission between microcomputers, but in micro-to-mainframe connections. However, its error checking is not very sophisticated, making the reliability of this process about 95 percent. It means that, in any given transmission, 5 percent of the errors get through. With larger files, the possibility of errors getting through is greater, and this increases the likelihood that the data is unusable.

Also, Xmodem is considered to be a half-duplex protocol because the sender waits for an acknowledgment (stop and wait automatic request or ARQ) of each block before the next block is sent. This half-duplex mode makes the Xmodem protocol inefficient when large amounts of data must be transmitted in a relatively short period of time.

Xmodem-CRC
Xmodem-CRC improves the accuracy of the Xmodem protocol. This protocol adds the decimal value of each character transmitted with a more comprehensive cyclical redundancy check or

CRC by dividing each integer by its prime number. This system improves efficiency to about 99.97 percent. Therefore only about .03 percent of the errors get through.

Xmodem-1K

The Xmodem-1K has about the same accuracy of the Xmodem-CRC, but improves the efficiency of the transmission to over 85 percent when compared to the original Xmodem protocol. The increase in throughput efficiency is a result of dividing the file or message to be sent into 1-kilobyte blocks (1,024 bytes) instead of the original 128 bytes.

WXmodem

WXmodem, also called window Xmodem, improves the transmission efficiency of previous protocols by transmitting data at full-duplex instead of half-duplex. That is, this protocol sends data continuously without waiting for an ACK or acknowledgment character being sent back from the receiver. This protocol divides the message or file into packets that have a unique number. By using this number the receiving system can assemble the original message from the packets.

Ymodem

Ymodem is also a cyclical redundancy check type of protocol, but it uses 16 bits instead of 8 bits. By using two bytes instead of one, the Ymodem protocol can increase the accuracy of transmission to 99.99 percent and it also has the ability to transmit larger files than the original Xmodem protocol. The Ymodem protocol also differs from Xmodem in that it uses 1-kilobyte blocks instead of the original block of 128 bytes.

Zmodem

Zmodem is a newer protocol that doesn't derive from the original Xmodem protocol. It was created to send files and messages over packet switching networks such as Tymnet. It also uses a CRC method for error checking, but it is more powerful than the other protocols mentioned before. Like the WXmodem protocol, it is a full-duplex protocol that uses continuous ARQ.

Kermit

The Kermit protocol is one of the most widely used protocols in the United States for data communication. Created and copyrighted by Columbia University, it has existed in the public domain for a long time as a free communication program. There are many versions of Kermit available, and they can be found on most bulletin boards.

Kermit uses the RS-232 port as its main communications port, and it works on many different types of microcomputers and some mainframes. It provides error checking for the transfer of text and binary files using 7- and 8-bit codes.

Although Kermit includes terminal emulation and other features often found in communication software, Kermit was designed as a protocol for file exchange over data communications and not as a substitute for a sophisticated communications package. However, it is suited for and used extensively in connecting microcomputers with IBM mainframes. With Kermit running on both systems, the ASCII-EBCDIC conversions and error checking required in this scenario are performed exclusively on the mainframe. The Kermit program running on the mainframe converts the EBCDIC characters into ASCII and vice versa, and adds or removes the error checking characters.

X.PC

X.PC is a protocol developed by Tymnet to connect asynchronous devices to packet switching networks. This protocol assembles the transmitted file or message into packets before being sent to a network device for the purpose of converting to the X.25 standard format. A packet is a series of binary digits that includes all data and control signals. These digits are then sent through the network and switched as a composite whole. At their destination address, the packets that make up the file or message are disassembled to reconstruct the original file.

Tymnet developed this protocol to connect async devices throughout the country to different networks and commercial information services. This protocol is also used as a file transfer protocol, because it allows several different sessions to take place through a single modem and a telephone circuit and still uses error checking capabilities. This allows a single microcomputer to access several host minicomputers or mainframes.

As mentioned before, asynchronous protocols are used extensively because async transmission is easy and inexpensive to implement. Therefore, most microcomputers come with the capability to perform this type of data communication without the need to have complex equipment or software. However, although async transmission is simple, it is not as efficient as synchronous transmission.

Synchronous Transmission

Synchronous transmission normally works by transmitting blocks of data instead of individual characters. This type of transmission can be divided according to how the computer determines that a message has been received and that all the data is correct. The different types of sync protocols are character-type, byte-count-type, and bit-type.

Protocols

Character-Type

A character-type protocol makes use of special characters that indicate the start and the end of the message being transmitted. The most common of these protocols is the Binary Synchronous Communication protocol, or BISYNC, which operates in half-duplex mode.

Messages are synchronized in BISYNC by using the SOH, STX, ETB, and EOT characters. These characters indicate the start and end of the message itself. The characters that make up the message are synchronized by sending special characters (SYN) at the beginning, middle, and end of each message transmitted. The number of characters sent depends on the hardware, but normally at least two characters are sent (see Fig. 8-3).

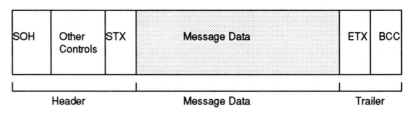

Fig. 8-3. Message components for a character-type protocol.

Byte-Count-Type

Byte-count-type protocols use a special character to indicate the beginning of the message header. This header is then followed by a series of bytes that indicate the number of characters that make up the data to be transmitted. Following the header, the actual data is sent, and then a byte or sets of bytes that contain the block check (see Fig. 8-4).

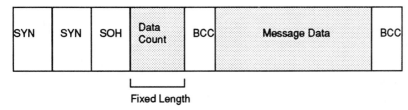

Fig. 8-4. Message components for a byte-count-type protocol.

Of these types of protocols, one of the best known is the Digital Data Communications Message protocol or DDCMP. In this case, the header contains at least two SYN characters, followed by the SOH character, followed by a set number of bytes that contain the number of characters in the data portion of the message, followed by control or block check characters, followed by the data, and terminated by more control or block check characters.

The main advantage of DDCMP over BISYNC is that DDCMP operates in full-duplex or half-duplex mode. This is in contrast to BISYNC which operates only in half-duplex mode. The end result is that DDCMP tends to be more efficient than BISYNC, especially for long messages.

Bit-Type

Bit-type protocols make use of a single character to indicate the start and end of a message. This character is called the flag character. The message is composed of the header which has a set length and contains the flag character, and it is followed by the data field which also has a set length (see Fig. 8-5). The same flag character is used to mark the end of the message.

Fig. 8-5. Message components for a bit-count-type protocol.

The most common of these types of protocols is the Synchronous Data Link Control protocol or SDLC. The SDLC protocol uses a flag that is unique, and its pattern is 01111110. The uniqueness of this character is preserved in the message, which requires that no other bit pattern may have six consecutive 1 bits in the data field. This check is performed by the hardware, which uses a technique called bit stuffing to place a 0 bit after all series of five consecutive 1 bits located in the header or data field section of the message. When the message is received, the extra 0 bit is removed by the receiving computer.

SDLC is capable of operating in full- and half-duplex modes but switched lines are supported only in half-duplex mode. In full-duplex mode, SDLC uses a continuous ARQ. This means that data is continuously sent until an error occurs. This is in contrast to the BISYNC protocol that needs to wait for the ACK of the receiving computer after each block is received.

Synchronous Software

Since IBM has popularized the use of sync transmission with its mainframe and minicomputer offerings, and since much of the sync data communication is to or from IBM hardware, we will discuss several products that are available to establish connections between personal computers and IBM mainframes. Although much of the earlier connectivity between users and IBM mainframes was performed through terminals, today's preferred communication device is the microcomputer.

With a personal computer, users from system programmers to administrative assistant personnel link to the mainframe and execute multiple sessions. Some use one session to monitor mail systems, while on another session they may be using a scheduling system. However, most if not all, users don't want to have a terminal on their desk to perform the functions mentioned above, since a microcomputer performs those functions more effectively.

The solution is to use a personal computer to act as one of the IBM terminals to link to the mainframe, and then switch back to the personal computer to perform whatever tasks are required from it. One of the most popular connectivity software programs is IRMA, DCA's terminal emulation package. By using a combination of software and hardware, this product allows the personal computer to act as a native terminal to the mainframe.

However, communicating with an IBM mainframe from a personal computer is more complicated than connecting to another microcomputer, because of the different communication protocols used by both systems. The IBM mainframe uses the Extended Binary Coded Decimal Interchange Code or EBCDIC, and likes to establish communications synchronously. The microcomputer, on the other hand, uses the ASCII code and prefers to establish communication links asynchronously.

Additionally, the keyboard used by native IBM mainframe terminals, called the 3270 family of terminals, is different from the keyboard used on the microcomputer. And some of the keys found on an IBM 3270 type of terminal are not available on the standard keyboard found on personal computers. Therefore, not only does the terminal emulation software have to resolve the difference in the mode of transmission, but the keyboard of the personal computer needs to be remapped so all the key combinations found on the 3270 type of terminal can be duplicated by users on the microcomputer's keyboard. Therefore, any connectivity solution must take into account these factors.

The solutions available in the market place can be divided into three areas. One solution is provided by adding an expansion card and software that make the personal computer act like a 3270 type of terminal when it is attached to a cluster controller. This is popular because of its simplicity, and it doesn't impose a burden on the mainframe itself.

The second type of solution is to use a protocol converter that acts as an interface between the personal computer and the mainframe. In some cases, the front end processor is itself a protocol converter and the burden of communication is placed on it. However, although still used in many situations, this type of solution is expensive when compared to the cost of microcomputers and some of the other communication solutions on the market.

The third type of solution is one that is gaining momentum very quickly. This solution provides personal computers access to IBM mainframes through a local area network. This is becoming popular as the number and sophistication of local area networks increases. However, a protocol conversion is still required. But due to the increased power of the personal computer, this task is quickly being placed on the microcomputer itself.

Terminal Emulation in the IBM World

Although all communication software programs that connect a personal computer to an IBM mainframe provide terminal emulation, some have much more functionality than others. Also, some of these programs give the user the capability to display graphics created with the mainframe and change the color of the text and screens displayed by the system.

Another differentiating factor between these programs is the ability to display one or more sessions at a given time. If a program makes the personal computer work as a Control Unit Terminal or CUT, only one session can be established between the mainframe and the microcomputer. If the program allows the microcomputer to operate in Distribute Function Terminal or DFT mode, then multiple concurrent sessions can be established.

Additionally, IBM has created several Application Program Interfaces, or APIs, that aid in creating communication sessions between their personal computers and their mainframes. When one of these APIs is available, system programs that create the communication application can use simple commands that move data through the network to interact with the mainframe. The API is responsible for converting the commands, provided by the application creator, into the actions required to perform the requested events. These commands can be provided to the system in one of several popular programming languages such as C or COBOL, or some script language provided by a company that supports the API.

Some of the most popular of these APIs are the High Level Language Application Interface or HLLAPI (an enhanced version of this is called the EHLLAPI), the 3270-PC API, and the Advanced Program-to-Program Communications or APPC. The first two run only on the microcomputer and the last requires software on the mainframe and microcomputer sides. Of these, the HLLAPI or EHLLAPI as it is also known, is quickly becoming the most widely used API for local area networks.

GUIs and the IBM Mainframe

With the advent of Microsoft Windows 3.1 and OS/2, the world of communications between microcomputers and IBM mainframes was transformed from a character-based environment to one of graphics and highly flexible communication products. Under the standard DOS environment, communication products use character-based screens that, although functional, don't take advantage of the processing capabilities of the micro-computer. Additionally, few of the DOS-based products can display multiple windows on the screen that show multiple sessions. In order to go from one session to another, users must switch or "page" between the different sessions. One exception is the Extra! 3270 type emulator created by Attachmate. This program can display multiple windows on the screen but the windows don't show a complete screen.

Under the control of Microsoft Windows or OS/2, 3270 type emulators, users can display multiple screens showing multiple sessions simultaneously without much effort. Also, each window can be resized and the aspect ratio of the screen is automatically adjusted to display the entire session. This allows users to display and monitor as many sessions as memory allows and still be able to work on any other applications that can run under the environment.

One popular product that runs under the Microsoft Windows and OS/2 environments and uses the EHLLAPI interface for communicating with IBM mainframes and minicomputers is Wall Data's Rumba program. Using Rumba, a user can commu-nicate with any IBM mainframe or AS-400 minicomputer in a manner that allows each user to view and use the communica-tion session the same as any other Windows or OS/2 applica-tion.

With this type of program users can customize the screen colors and the keyboard to suit their needs. With the use of "hotspots," the mouse can be utilized to click on certain words or locations on the screen to initiate an event or execute a command on the mainframe. In addition, menus, dialog boxes, and on-line help guide users through the application, reducing the time and effort required to learn and use the mainframe program. Other prod-ucts such as LinkUP 3270 for Microsoft Windows from Chi Corporation and IBM's Windows Connection are also viable products that enhance the capabilities of DOS-based 3270 type emulators.

Perhaps the feature that truly distinguishes these products from their DOS counterparts is the ability to interface with other applications through dynamic links. In the Windows environ-ment, the products mentioned above can be linked to spread-sheets, databases, and other programs through Dynamic Link

Libraries, or DLLs, and new embedding techniques such as Object Linking and Embedding or OLE. DLLs are program elements shared by all Windows programs, allowing for a more efficient use of main memory. By placing calls to these DLLs, programmers can avoid the re-creation of routines that can be performed by the DLL in use. This reduces the time required to create an application, and therefore increases the productivity of the application designer.

Through DLLs or some of the other linking techniques, a personal computer can be instructed to use the connectivity programs mentioned before to connect to a mainframe and query one of its databases. When the data is found, the emulation program retrieves the data and copies it to another application, such as a spreadsheet, running on the personal computer. The user can then view or change the data in the spreadsheet and make any required changes. These changes can then be automatically reflected in the mainframe database by sending the data from the spreadsheet to the emulation program and to the mainframe, without the user needing to perform any additional actions.

Another use of DLLs and other linking technologies is the creation of interfaces that are easier for people to use and understand. Through programs like Visual Basic, Toolbook, and Hypercard, application designers can use linking technology such as DLLs to create an interface that uses the terminal emulator to provide the data to the user in a different format than the one shown by the mainframe (see Fig. 8-6). Using these interfaces, users can see and understand the information more easily than using the character format of the mainframe. The user can then make any changes to the actual data by making the changes to the information displayed in the interface program.

This sharing and visualization of data in a manner that is transparent to the user has vast implications. These technologies increase the effectiveness and efficiency of computer users by relieving them from having to learn several operating environments. They allow users to concentrate on the job to be performed and not on how to establish the communication process. Additionally, they relieve the mainframe from tasks that are performed more easily on microcomputers, and provide true seamless integration of the personal computer and the mainframe. The end result is an increase in the productivity of users and the computer.

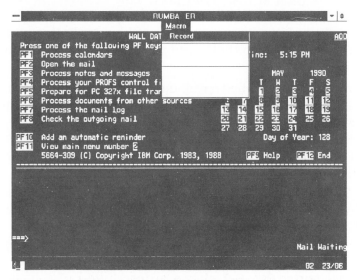

Fig. 8-6. Mainframe data can be displayed inside windows providing a different "look and feel" for the user.

Communication Hardware

The simpler method of communication from one computer to another is through the use of computer disks, or diskettes as they are called. Although it seems like a trivial topic, data communication using disks can at times be the best method of transferring data if the files to be transferred are small and the transfer is done only occasionally. The next step in data communication between two microcomputers is through an RS-232 or serial cable connected to the serial I/O port of the computer.

Most personal computers have at least one serial port located at the back of the machine. This port is capable of transmitting data from a low 300 bits per second to several thousand bits per second. This is the preferred method of communication to connect a microcomputer to other hosts through the telephone lines. Also, several low end networking programs use the serial port to transfer files between the computers in the network.

The RS-232 Cable and Null Modems

In order to connect two computers through their serial ports a null modem cable is required. A null modem is a cable that crosses some of the pins of the serial port. This crossing is required because the sending line of one computer must be connected to the receiving line of the other computer. Otherwise both computers would be connected to their sending lines and no one would be listening.

This type of cable is called a null modem because it performs the job that normally is performed by modems when two computers communicate over telephone lines. However, in this case, since all the signals traveling through the cable are in digital form, an actual modem is not necessary to convert the signals to a different format.

There are two serial port configurations found at the back of most computers. One is a serial port that uses a nine-pin format and the other uses twenty-five pins or lines. In the latter case, not all lines are needed to establish a successful communication link between two computers and the same is true for the nine-pin serial ports. Fig. 8-7 shows a description of a basic null modem configuration that can be easily constructed and works in most micro-to-micro communications.

Fig. 8-7. Null modem pin configuration.

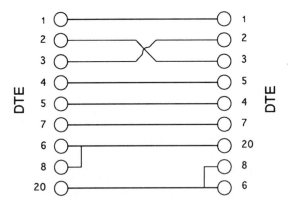

Notice that in Fig. 8-7 pins 2 and 3 are reversed in the null modem cable. This is because pin 2 is the data sending line and pin 3 is the receiving line (see chapter 4). Connecting the sending line of one computer to the receiving line of the other computer allows one to send data and the other to properly receive it. The same situation is performed on the second computer and its sending line. In this manner, one computer sends data and the second receives it, and, when an ACK signal is transmitted, the second computer uses its sending line to commence data transmission again.

Micro-to-Micro Connections

Communication Between PCs

Using a null modem, microcomputers can communicate at speeds ranging from 300 bits per second to 57,600 bits per second and higher speeds depending on the controlling software. However, most communications are performed at speeds of 9,600 bits per second or lower.

A null modem cable is relatively easy to construct. The materials required are as follows:

1. A cable with enough wires for all required connections. Although the null modem configuration described in Fig. 8-7 will work with many types of microcomputers, the actual number of wires and their pin connections vary among equipment manufacturers. With some computers a null modem can be created by using only pins 2 and 3. Others require pins 4, 5, 6, 8, and 20 before the computer can communicate properly. In most cases, the manual that came with the computer will outline the special pin requirements necessary to create a null modem.

2. Soldering iron and connectors with the proper genders. It seems strange to talk about the gender of a connector. But some of the terminology used in data communication uses the words "male" and "female" to describe the physical appearance of a connector. Some serial ports have a "male" connector while others use a "female" connector (see Fig. 8-8).

After the wires are connected to proper pins, the soldering iron can be used to make permanent connections. Some RS-232 connectors use "punched" wiring to perform the connections. In this case, the soldering is not required. The wires are pushed or "punched" into receptacles in the connector and a secured connection is made.

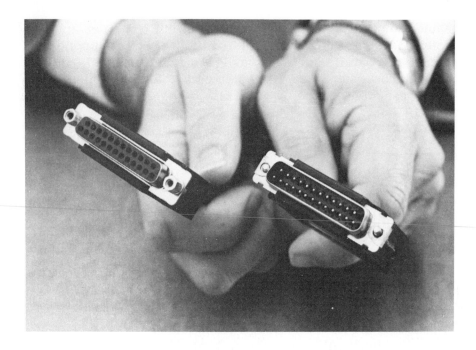

Fig. 8-8. These male and female 25-pin connectors meet the RS-232-C interface standards.

Not all null modems will have to be created by the user. Some companies offer "smart" RS-232 connectors. These connectors require a straight cable to connect them to the serial port of the computer. Then, when power is turned on, these "smart" connectors use built-in circuitry to determine which lines need to be connected and perform the connections automatically inside the connector. It is important to notice that although these types of connectors work in many cases, they are not always able to make the proper connection.

Another type of "null modem package" comes from several companies that bundle a generic null modem cable with communication software. Using this product two computers are connected through their serial port and the same software is used on both machines. The software takes over the communication process and files can easily be transferred from one computer to the other. This is an important point since the null modem is of little use without the controlling software.

Not all data communications between microcomputers are performed through the serial port. Some products use the parallel port to connect the computers. The parallel port offers a greater transmission speed but the distance between the machines is less than the distance that exists between the computers when a serial cable is used.

The techniques outlined above are popular among users of laptop computers. When large amounts of data need to be transferred from a laptop computer to a desktop computer, products such as LapLink from Traveling Software are used instead of the more traditional method of file transfer through diskettes.

To use a product like LapLink, the computers are linked through the serial or parallel ports and the LapLink software is loaded into the two computers. The transferring of data can be controlled from either computer. LapLink is capable of transferring files at speeds of up to 115,200 bits per second through the serial port and up to 200,000 bits per second through the parallel port. This type of software also performs error checking during the transfer to ensure that none of the transmitted data is corrupted.

It is important to notice that the above products don't have to be used if you already have a null modem and some type of communication software. Products such as Microsoft Windows already have a communication package that can be used to transfer data between two computers. See the project at the end of this chapter for a practical use of this technology.

Macintosh-PC Communications

During recent years, the Apple Macintosh has slowly moved into the business world. More and more companies find that they need to support both the IBM PC environment and the Apple Macintosh environment. Since both computers use a different operating system and a different disk structure, data transfer between them requires additional steps in some cases.

There are three different ways to transfer data between an IBM PC or clone and an Apple Macintosh. One way is to transfer data using the Apple File Exchanger and a Mac Superdrive. The superdrive is a drive that is now standard on all Macintosh models. This drive is capable of reading and writing to diskettes formatted on IBM PCs and clones. The Apple File Exchanger is a software utility that is available on all Macintosh computers.

It normally has the ability to transfer text files from a Macintosh folder onto the IBM PC disk in the superdrive. Also, a few other file formats besides text files are supported. With the use of third party software the types of formats that the Apple File Exchanger can handle are increased. However, this data transfer process is slow and tends to introduce errors when transferring some types of graphical and binary files.

The second option for transferring data between IBM PCs and Macintosh computers involves the use of a serial cable and software. A serial cable between the Mac and the PC can be created by connecting the pins as in Fig. 8-9. Then, using some type of communication software such as the communications program in Windows and Microsoft Works on the Mac, the link can be established.

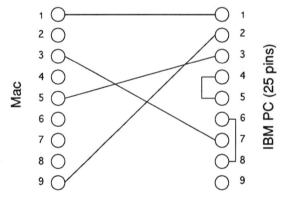

Fig. 8-9. Mac-to-PC cable configuration.

Third party software and hardware can also be used to establish the communication link. One of the most popular products in this category is MacLink Plus. This package comes with all the cables and software required for data communication between the IBM PC and Macintosh computers. Using one of the connectors the serial cable is used to link the Macintosh (through one of its two serial ports) and the PC (through an available serial port). Once the hardware is installed, the software is installed on both computers. After software installation, the communication settings on both machines are made equal (see Fig. 8-10) and communication begins.

Through MacLink Plus one of the computers controls the other through the user interface of the master computer. On the Macintosh side, two windows appear on the MultiFinder. One of the windows displays the contents of the Macintosh hard disk

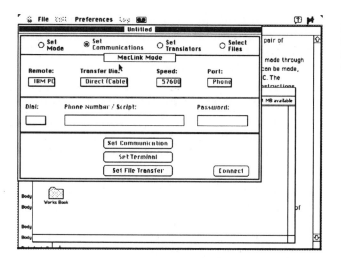

Fig. 8-10. Communication settings to connect a Macintosh and an IBM PC.

and the other displays the contents of the IBM PC as in Fig. 8-11. By using familiar mouse movements, the proper files are highlighted and file transfer begins, with the program taking care of all error corrections that may be required. Through this process, large numbers of files can be transmitted at speeds of over 56,000 bits per second. Although the speed is not as fast as in other communication strategies, such as local area networks, this is an inexpensive and effective method for transferring files between the Macintosh and IBM PC computers. If a more sophisticated means of communication is required, such as e-mail, then the next solution may be better.

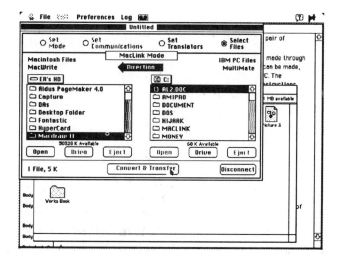

Fig. 8-11. Screen showing the disk contents of the Macintosh and IBM PC.

The third way of connecting a Macintosh and an IBM PC is through some type of network. Most of the popular networking platforms, especially in the field of local area networks, provide for Macintosh connectivity. Some network operating systems, such as Novell NetWare, allow Macintosh computers to share hard disk space on file servers along with IBM PCs. In addition, the connectivity provided by these networks is almost seamless. This means that Mac users can access network equipment and share files with other users in the same manner that they perform these functions from a stand-alone machine.

Additionally, all Macintosh computers are already equipped with networking capability through Apple's own communication network, Apple Share. Using this scheme, several networks can be connected, and through some type of gateway (see chapter 9) they can access data and files on PC networks. A gateway is a device that connects two networks in a manner that is transparent to the network users.

Connecting the Macintosh and the IBM PC through a local area network is probably the most efficient way to provide file transfer and complex communication functions to both platforms. However, when compared to the other two options mentioned before, this last option is expensive and much more complex. When the need of the user is occasional file transfer between the two machines, the serial port connection is probably the recommended method.

Micro-to-Mainframe Connections

As in the case of micro-to-micro connection, there are several methods for connecting microcomputers--whether IBM, IBM clones, or Apple computers--to mainframes. The different types of connections depend on the equipment available and the communication philosophy of the company. These methods are as follows:

1. Connections from a remote location through the use of modems

2. Connection through direct cable

3. Connection through a network

Although communication and connectivity solutions between microcomputers and IBM mainframes were discussed previously in this chapter, the process to connect to non-IBM main-

frames is somewhat similar. The difference depends o
timing used for the connection. Also fewer pieces of equip
are required for the linkage if the mainframe or minicompt
an ASCII-based machine. Therefore, we will concentrate
next section on discussing connectivity strategies for nor
mainframes and minicomputers.

Connecting through Modems

Regardless of the type of connection used to communicate with
the mainframe, some type of emulation program will be required.
With most ASCII-based machines, three commonly used emula-
tions are available. These are TTY, VT-52, and VT-100 emulation. Many mainframes allow this type of terminal emulation.
Otherwise, the user will have to purchase an emulation package
that allows the microcomputer to emulate the native terminal of
the mainframe.

Once the emulation program is acquired, the rest of the equipment needed for the microcomputer side is a modem, a serial
cable, and a telephone outlet. The modem (see chapter 4)
connects to the RS-232 or serial port of the computer via a serial
cable, if it is external, or it is inserted into an expansion slot or
bay if it is an internal modem. Finally, a telephone cable
connects the modem to the phone outlet.

After the hardware is connected, the software needs to be
installed in the microcomputer. Depending on the type of host
that will be accessed, the communication software may be a
specialized emulation program or a generic TTY or VT-100
emulation package. After installation of the software on a hard
disk, the parameters that will control the communication process need to be set up. These parameters will control the modem,
the speed of transmission, and the protocol used for data
transfer.

Although each communication program has its own manner of
how the parameters are set, all of them share the same options.
Fig. 8-12 displays a screen that is used by the Windows
communication program in order to set up the parameters
required to establish a successful communication link. These
parameters include the basic speed of transmission or baud
rate, stop bits, parity, and data bits. Additionally, the screen also
has an option to establish the basic communication protocol. In
the figure, X-On/X-Off is selected to indicate that the protocol is

established by the software, and it is not provided through hardware implementation. The screen in Fig. 8-12 has check boxes for turning on additional error correction measures by selecting parity check. Also, the same screen provides an option for choosing the serial port that will be used in the transmission. In this case, the first serial port or COM1 will be used.

Fig. 8-12. Communication settings for the Terminal communication program.

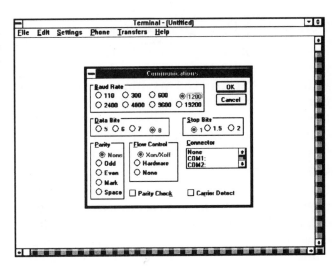

A different menu option in this program provides for the type of protocol that will be used for transferring binary files. Recall that there were many protocols that could be used for this purpose, with Xmodem and Kermit two of the most popular. By selecting the Binary Transfer options in the Setting menu, the screen shown in Fig. 8-13 is displayed. This screen provides an option for choosing between Xmodem-CRC and Kermit for the protocol and error correction mechanism to transfer binary files. Although the Microsoft Windows communication program was used in this example, the process to establish a communication session with most other communication programs is basically the same. The number of menus varies, but the same options are available.

Once the settings required by the host system are matched or implemented by the user on the calling microcomputer, the user instructs the communication software to dial the modem of the host system. This is done by selecting a dialing option in the communication software program, and then typing the complete telephone number of the host location. After the microcomputer

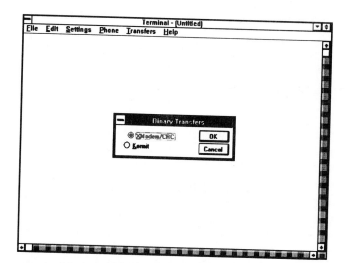

Fig. 8-13. Options for transfer protocol.

modem calls, the host's modem answers and sends a signal back to the originating computer to indicate that communication can begin. Once this signal is received and acknowledged, the actual data transmission begins. Many of the tasks outlined here can be automated with the use of macros or a scripting language that some communications programs provide.

Once the communication link is established and data is being transmitted to and from the microcomputer, files can be uploaded or downloaded. A file is uploaded if it resides on the microcomputer, and it is sent for storage on the hosting mainframe or minicomputer. In the same manner, a file is downloaded if it is retrieved from the host computer and stored on the microcomputer. For this process to take place, both machines must use the same file transfer protocol. Otherwise, the proper error correction mechanism will not be established and data may be lost in the transmission process.

After the connection is terminated, the user logs out of the host and instructs the communication software to hang up the phone. This terminates the telephone link through the central office, and the modem on the host is free to receive a new call. Also, this process terminates the communication on the microcomputer side and returns the telephone line to its original state under telephone control.

Direct Connection

Although a modem connection is easy to set up and use, it is, in the best of circumstances, a slow connection. If the microcomputer and the mainframe or minicomputer are in close proximity to each other, a direct connection through the RS-232 or serial port is possible.

With this technique, a null modem, or a cable configured according to specifications established by the host manufacturer, is directly attached to the serial port of the microcomputer. Once this connection is made, the software that will be used to control the communication session is loaded into memory. Since there is no modem involved, the user selects the port that will be used for the connection on the microcomputer side and sets the parameters as in the process above. Once again, the same parameters must be used on both the host and microcomputer sides.

Once the parameters are established, a telephone number is not required. In reality, at this point the communication is established and all that is required is for the microcomputer to signal the host that it is ready to commence transmission. This is done by sending an interrupt signal to the host computer. This interrupt can be the ESC or ENTER key pressed a couple of times. Once the host receives this interrupt, it becomes aware of the microcomputer, and data transmission can commence.

After the data transmission starts, the communication session is managed in the same manner as if a modem were present. The only difference is in the speed of the transmission. Through direct cabling connection, transmission of 19,200 bits per second and higher can be achieved. To terminate the communication, the user logs out of the host and quits the communication program. Since a modem is not involved, there is no need to hang up and disconnect the transmission.

Network Connection

Although for many types of communication needs the two solutions outlined above are more than sufficient, many companies are opting for connecting their microcomputers to mainframes and minicomputers through networks, and especially through local area networks.

Connectivity through networking has many advantages that are discussed in chapter 9. But through a network, the user's microcomputer still has to use some type of emulation or communication program. In this case, the user loads the communication program. It is already aware of the commands and links required to connect to the host. After the program is in memory, the user sends an interrupt signal to the host by pressing the ESC or ENTER key a few times. This signal makes the host aware of the connection to the microcomputer and respond by establishing an active communication link.

This type of methodology for providing communications from microcomputer to mainframe is fast, efficient, and effective. Users don't have to worry about the different parameters, or how the connection is made. The software resides in most cases on the network server, and it is invoked through a command or by clicking on an icon. The burden of establishing and maintaining the link is placed on the network and software and not on the user. This simplifies the communication process for the user, but adds a level of complexity for those individuals who are responsible for the communication system.

The type of communication methodology implemented at a company is the result of a combination of factors. Some of these factors are available economic resources, the number of microcomputers and mainframe that need to be connected, and the philosophy and politics of the individual responsible for the communication system. Each available solution has advantages and disadvantages in terms of cost, speed of transmission, complexity of the system, and connectivity flexibility. All four factors increase as we move from modem connection to direct connection, then to network connection. Many installations have a combination of the three since the needs of the individuals within the company vary according to the function that they perform.

It is important to notice that, although the discussion above mentions the PC in many places, the connectivity solution for the Macintosh or any other personal computer is the same as the one outlined above. All microcomputers, whether IBM, IBM clone, or Macintosh, are ASCII-based machines with standard parallel and serial ports. Additionally, the same communication products that are available for one system are also available for the other. Therefore, when discussing connectivity options, we refer to all types of microcomputers unless otherwise specified.

The Kermit Protocol

As mentioned before, Kermit is a file transfer protocol developed at Columbia University in 1981. It has been available for the microcomputer since its inception and became popular with the IBM PC as a result of the work performed by Jan van der Eijk, whose version of the Kermit protocol for the IBM PC is included in many packages of popular communication programs.

Kermit is a good protocol for transfering files between dissimilar computers, for high-speed data transfer, for file transfer over long distances, and for transferring groups of files. It has many features including full packets with error checking for both data and ACK/NAK communication. Kermit has a "feature of negotiation" that is performed every time a file is transferred. This process uses an exchange of "send-initiate" packets between communicating computers. The originating or sending computer sends a send-initiate packet to the receiving computer. Once the receiving computer acknowledges the receipt of the packet, it sends its own send-initiate packet to the originating computer along with the acknowledgement. Then the two systems compare the packets and select the operating features required and supported by both systems in order to send the files. This negotiating allows any computer using the Kermit protocol to exchange files with any other computer that also uses the Kermit protocol. Also, it allows operators to modify or alter the communication parameters in order to optimize the transmission of data.

One of the negotiating features employed by Kermit is the packet error checking. Kermit supports 6-bit checksum, 12-bit checksum, and CRC-16. The overhead used in the transmission increases along with the degree of sophistication used in the error checking algorithm. The CRC-16 provides the best error checking with almost 100 percent error detection and it is used sometimes during financial transactions.

In addition to the error checking mechanism employed by Kermit, it can also communicate through both 7-bit and 8-bit data ports regardless of the communication hardware used by the systems. Also, Kermit can transfer groups of files without interruption whether they are text or binary files. However, it converts all data into text during file transfer.

During the negotiating process, Kermit can also agree to perform special file transfer functions. Two of these functions are "file attribute transfers" and "sliding windows." File attribute transfers allow the transmission of up to 94 file characteristics along with the file. Some of these characteristics are file size, file modification time, and file modification date. Sliding windows allow the communication session to take advantage of full-duplex satellite and PDN communications. This allows Kermit to perform data compression on the data being transfered which results in an improved throughput over half-duplex protocols such as Xmodem and Ymodem.

Additionally, Kermit has many other features that allow it to perform in almost any type of working environment. As new releases appear in the market, Kermit increases its functionality to users and gets closer to providing low cost communication between any two types of computers.

Protecting the Hardware

All electronic devices are subject to damage or malfunction due to the influence of external energy sources such as electrical storms and the electromagnetic radiation that electricity-carrying wires produce. A computer is susceptible to many of these types of interferences, and so is the data transmission medium used for transmitting data. There are several devices that can be used to protect against interference from unwanted sources, but the type of equipment used depends on the nature of the interference.

The different types of interferences can be grouped into several categories described as follows:

1. Power surges
2. Power sags and unreliable power sources
3. Electrical interference
4. Static electricity

There are several devices that can be used to protect computers against the problems outlined above. These are power surge protectors, power line conditioners (PLCs), and uninterruptible power supplies (UPSs). The type of device used depends on the equipment to protect, the importance of the data stored on the equipment, and economics.

Power Surges

A power surge is a sudden increase in power, which is capable of destroying the microchips that make up the computer circuitry. The source of the surge can be an electrical storm or an engine that is suddenly turned on near the location of the computer. The surge travels through the electrical lines and reaches the power supply of the computer. If the voltage levels are high enough, the excess energy may go beyond the power supply and reach the communication circuits, which have low tolerance to voltage spikes. The end result can be a "burnout" of the circuitry on a card or the motherboard itself.

Power surges can also travel through the communication circuits, through the modem, and into the computer. This is because most telephone lines operate at between 48 and 96 volts with the voltage sometimes reaching a few hundred volts. Since modern microprocessors contain a larger number of components than their predecessors, they are more vulnerable to surges than previous generations of microprocessors. Therefore it is important to protect the computer from these surges through telephone lines by attaching a line conditioner to the phone line itself.

To protect hardware from surges, a surge protector can be used. A surge protector is a device that responds to a surge after a certain amount of time, such as two nanoseconds, and "clamps" the voltage surge at a specified level. The device redirects the additional energy to the ground, creating a short circuit where the additional power can flow safely when the surge reaches a preconfigured level. Good surge protectors have reaction times of two nanoseconds or less and clamp the voltage surge at levels no higher than ten or fifteen percent above the normal voltage of the power supply. If the surge is very high, then, in most cases, the surge protector tends to burn out before the surge reaches the computer. And of course, no surge protector will protect against a direct electrical strike.

Power surge protectors are the least expensive of all protecting devices. They range in price from a few dollars to approximately $150. They protect equipment from short duration electrical surges (called transients) and voltage spikes. Their price depends on the type of material used to make up the device and how fast these components react to a power surge. Faster reaction time will reflect a more expensive item. Whenever possible, the protector with the fastest reaction time should be purchased. Power surge protectors are normally found at the users' workstations.

Power Sags

A power sag is a sudden and short loss of electrical power. This sudden loss of power can force a computer reset or a network shutdown, losing any information stored in RAM prior to the power loss. In the case of networks, the problem can be more serious. If the network goes down without a proper shutdown, then it may not be able to automatically rebuild itself so it can continue operating. The transactions that were being performed prior to the power sag may be lost.

Power sags are the result of utility companies switching power lines or an engine or motor going on line. In the last case, when a large motor goes on line--that is, is turned on--it requires more energy during the initial stages than when it is operating normally. This initial requirement of energy comes at the cost of the energy that is being supplied to any other equipment on the same power line. Unfortunately, after a motor drains energy for it to start, the power sag is followed by a power surge when the motor reaches a normal operating mode. Other sources of power sags are what utility companies call "brownouts." A brownout is a loss in power due to the utility company lowering the voltage intentionally during peak periods of use.

To adequately protect against sags, a more sophisticated device than the power surge protector is needed. Although some expensive power surge protectors provide some electrical line conditioning and help offset power sags, they are not designed to deal with power losses. The best device to protect against power sags is an uninterruptible power supply or UPS.

Uninterruptible power supplies allow a system to continue functioning for several minutes, even when there is a total loss of power. This additional running time provided by the UPS is enough to safely shut the system or network down. On many occasions, the time is long enough that power is restored without having to shut the system down.

A UPS not only protects against power losses, but it protects against surges and interference from noise that may travel through the electrical lines. The UPS works by switching automatically from externally provided electrical power to power provided by its own internal batteries. This switching takes time and it is important that this time be as short as possible. If the switching time is too long, the system may still go down, and even be damaged by the power supplied by the UPS when it goes on line. Typical switching times are less than 5 milliseconds.

Some expensive UPS systems don't have a switching time because they operate on batteries generating true alternating current at all times. This type of UPS is better, since the one described above generates square wave power instead of sine wave power. Square wave power can damage the delicate electronic circuitry of the computer.

UPS systems are rated according to the amount of watts or volts they can provide in the case of a power loss. They range from 200 watts or 224 watts to several thousand watts depending on the needs of the computer or network. Higher ratings mean more expensive UPSs. To determine the size of the UPS required, the total power needs of all equipment that will be supplied by the UPS are added. For example, assume that a user has a computer, a modem, and a monitor that he or she wants to keep operational in case of a power loss. The power needs of each device may be as follows:

Modem	125 watts
Monitor	125 watts
Computer	224 watts
Total UPS requirements	474 watts

The amount of volts can be converted to watts by using the following formula:

```
Watts = Volts Required x Amperage or Current x Power Factor
```

The volts is the voltage or potential difference of the current that will have to be supplied. The amperage is a measure of the amount of current that will be flowing through the circuit. The power factor is the cosine of the phase angle between the voltage and the current waveform.

Uninterruptible power supplies should be used by all network servers to protect users' data and the network from a sudden and unexpected loss of power. Additionally, the UPS will protect the server against power surges and electrical noise. Whenever possible, a UPS that outputs true sine power should be used instead of the less expensive system that produces square power that could damage the computer system.

Electrical Noise

Electrical noise is interference from other types of electrical devices such as air conditioners, transformers, lights, and other electrical equipment. This noise affects computer users by distorting computer screens and creating "snow" effects on them. This problem is easily corrected by placing the computer or monitor further away from the source of the interference.

A bigger problem occurs when the noise is introduced into the data transmission medium. A type of data carrying media that is succeptible to this type of interference is twisted pair wire. If telephone lines or the data carrying wires of a network are made up of normal twisted pair wire, they should be placed away from fluorescent lights, electrical motors, and electricity-carrying lines.

The electrical interference that is caused by the above devices can introduce errors in the data stream, causing loss of data. In the worst cases, it may render the communication line or network unoperational.

The first line of defense against electrical noise is placing computers and data carrying lines away from possible sources of interference. Additionally, whenever possible, the data carrying medium should be insulated, as it is in the case of coaxial cable. However, even if a company takes all of the above precautions, there is not much that it can do when the interference is coming from lines belonging to common carriers and public utility companies. In this case a power line conditioner or PLC may be employed.

Power line conditioners are devices that guard against electrical noise and interference from other equipment. Most PLCs also protect against surges and sags in electrical power. They tend to filter out electrical noise while maintaining power within acceptable levels for the computer to operate.

PLCs not only regulate the quantity of power flowing into the computer, but also regulate the quality of the power. They use transformers to isolate noise and regulate the voltage. Many user workstations and servers use PLCs to guard against temporary power sags and very short duration power spikes. These devices are also incorporated into all good UPS systems.

Static Electricity

Another form of danger to data and transmission equipment comes in the form of static electricity. Static electricity is generated by walking across a carpeted floor or by rubbing our hands against certain elements. This static electricity accumulates in our bodies until there is an adequate path for the charges to flow to some other object element, which in most cases is the ground.

By walking across a floor, a person can generate charges as high as 15,000 volts. If a person then touches a circuit board or a diskette, this charge is transferred to the touched device. In the case of the circuit board, there is a good possibility that several of the microchips on the board will be destroyed. In the case of the data disk, some of the data stored may be erased. To avoid these problems, users should always "ground" themselves before handling disks or circuit boards. Grounding is accomplished by touching any piece of metal that is grounded properly before handling sensitive equipment.

Also, many computer users experience intermittent problems such as occasional data losses and keyboards that at times are unresponsive. The cause may be an operator that has high levels of static electricity. The solution is to provide this operator with an antistatic mat that can be placed under his or her chair during computer operation. Also, many antistatic sprays are available on the market. Such sprays should not be used on the computer, but rather on the operators of the equipment. Although not as effective as the antistatic mat, they help in controlling static electricity and the problems associated with its presence. Additionally, make sure that all computing equipment is connected to adequately grounded plugs.

Summary

Protocols are used in order for one type of computer to communicate effectively with a computer manufactured by another company. The protocol is a set of conventions or rules that the communicating computer follows in order to complete a data communication task. Although the number and types of protocols in data communications are many, personal computers normally follow a few standards. Two of these standards are the asynchronous and the synchronous protocols.

Because of its relative simplicity and inexpensive implementation costs, asynchronous transmission is very popular in the home and business data communication market. Most, if not all, personal computers are capable of transmitting data using this method. However, async communication has a low transmission efficiency since at least two extra bits must be added to each character transmitted.

With synchronous transmission, data characters are sent in large groups called blocks. These blocks contain synchronization characters that have a unique bit pattern. They are placed at the beginning and middle of each block with the synchronization characters ranging in number from one to four. When the receiver detects one of these special characters, it knows that the following bit is the beginning of a character, thereby maintaining synchronization. Synchronous transmission is more efficient than asynchronous communication. It is the preferred method of communication between IBM minicomputers such as the AS-400 and IBM mainframes, with the 3270 series of terminals located at users' desks.

The implementation of the async and sync protocols as well as any other useful protocol in the market includes rules and processes to handle many situations that arise during data communication. Some of these events are outlined below:

1. Starting the communication
2. Character identification
3. Message control

4. Error control

5. Ending the communication

All of these rules specify how the different situations arising in the data communication environment will be handled.

There are several protocols that are common to computers running bulletin boards and other microcomputers that have a need for data communications. Some of these are X-On/X-Off, Xmodem, WXmodem, Ymodem, Zmodem, X.PC, and Kermit. IBM mainframes and computers using synchronous data transmission use different types of protocols that can be divided according to whether they are character-type, byte-count-type, or bit-type protocols.

A character-type protocol makes use of special characters that indicate the start and the end of the message being transmitted. The most common of these protocols is the Binary Synchronous Communication protocol or BISYNC, which operates in half-duplex mode. Byte-count-type protocols use a special character to indicate the beginning of the message header. Of these types of protocols, one of the best known is the Digital Data Communications Message protocol or DDCMP. Bit-type protocols make use of a single character to indicate the start and end of a message. The most common of these types of protocols is the Synchronous Data Link Control protocol or SDLC.

Microcomputers can acess mainframe computers by using one of three alternatives. One method is by adding an expansion card and software that make the personal computer function like the native terminal of the mainframe. The second method is to use a protocol converter that acts as an interface between the personal computer and the mainframe. The third method provides personal computers access to mainframes through a local area network. This is becoming popular as the number and sophistication of local area networks increases.

There are several methods for connecting microcomputers, whether IBM, IBM clones, or Apple computers, to mainframes. The different types of connections depend on the equipment available and the communication philosophy of the company. These methods are as follows:

1. Connections from a remote location through the use of modems

2. Connection through direct cables

3. Connection through a network

Computers are subject to damage or malfunction due to the influence of external energy sources. Examples are electrical storms and the electromagnetic radiation that electricity-carrying wires produce. A computer is susceptible to many of these types of interference, and so is the data transmission medium used for transmitting data. There are several devices that can be used to protect against interference from unwanted sources, but the type of equipment used depends on the nature of the interference.

The different types of interference can be grouped into several categories, described as follows:

1. Power surges
2. Power sags and unreliable power sources
3. Electrical interference
4. Static electricity

There are several devices that can be used to protect computers against the problems outlined above. These are power surge protectors, power line conditioners (PLCs), and uninterruptible power supplies (UPSs). The type of device used depends on the equipment to protect, the importance of the data stored on the equipment, and economics.

Questions

1. What is the purpose of protocols in data communications?
2. Why are sync transmissions more efficient than async transmissions?
3. What factors must a protocol keep track of as it handles data communications between two computers?
4. What is a null modem?
5. If you were given a choice of an async protocol to use for file transfers, which one would you use? Why?
6. What is an API?
7. What are the connectivity solutions available to connect a microcomputer to an IBM mainframe?

8. What is the importance of GUIs in data communications?

9. What are the different types of interference that can affect data communications?

10. What is the purpose of a PLC?

11. What is the best type of UPS for a network server? Why?

12. What is X-On/X-Off? When can it be used and when should it not be used?

Project

File Transfer between an IBM PC and a Macintosh Using MacLink Plus/PC

The MacLink Plus/PC package contains all the materials required to perform file transfers between an IBM PC or compatible and a Macintosh computer. The connection to transfer the document can be either directly through a cable that connects both machines using their respective serial ports or through telephone lines and a pair of modems.

For this exercise, we will assume that the connection is made through the serial cables of both computers. Before the transfer can be made, the software must be installed on the Macintosh and the PC. The installation is accomplished through the following instructions.

1. Copy the Mac disk to the Apple File Exchange folder that is contained in the System Additions folder.

2. Copy the IBM PC disk to a subdirectory in the PC.

After the software is copied, the machines need to be linked together.

3. Using the serial cable provided, attach one end to the modem or printer port located on the back of the Macintosh.

4. Attach the other end to the serial port of the IBM PC.

Now you are ready to execute the programs that will allow you to transfer the files.

5. Access the folder that contains the MacLink Plus/PC files.

You will get a screen that contains a window showing the contents of the Apple File Exchange folder. Your screen will look like Fig. 8-14.

6. Double click on the program icon MacLink Plus/PC.

7. The initial MacLink Plus/PC screen will appear.

8. Run the MacLink program on the PC by typing ML and pressing the ENTER key in the subdirectory containing the program.

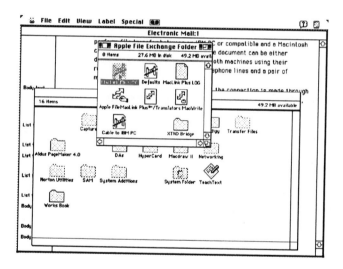

Fig. 8-14. Apple Exchange Folder.

The PC and the Mac need to have the same communication settings for them to work together. The Mac screen should look like Fig. 8-15. The modes of communication are MacLink Mode, Desktop Mode, Terminal Mode, and MacLink Answer Mode. For this exercise the MacLink Mode is the one you want. In this mode, files can be transferred and translated between your Mac and a remote computer running MacLink Plus software.

The Desktop Mode allows the translation of files using the Macintosh super drive. The Terminal Mode operates similarly to the MaLlink Mode, except that it allows the connection of two

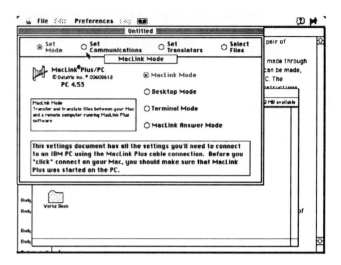

Fig. 8-15. Entry screen for MacLink Plus.

computers using the telephone lines. The Answer Mode allows MacLink Plus running on the Mac to answer the call of another computer using MacLink Plus.

9. Select Set Communications by clicking the mouse on this choice.

10. Make sure that the PC and the Mac have the same settings as in Fig. 8-16.

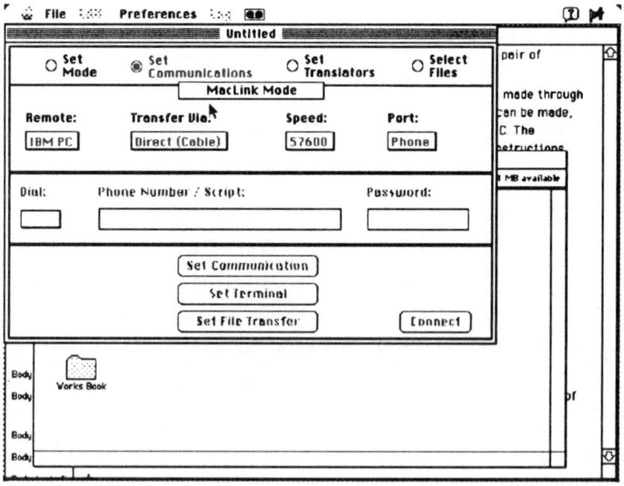

Fig. 8-16. Setup screen for MacLink Plus.

11. Next click the mouse on Select Files.

You will see a screen as in Fig. 8-17.

12. Click the mouse on Connect.

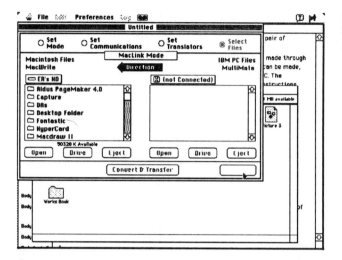

Fig. 8-17. Connecting options for Mac-Link Plus.

The next screen should look similar to Fig. 8-18. In the figure, the left side shows the hard disk and folders on the Macintosh. The right side displays the files on the PC's hard disk.

13. Select the file on the PC that you want to transfer to the Mac by clicking the mouse on it.

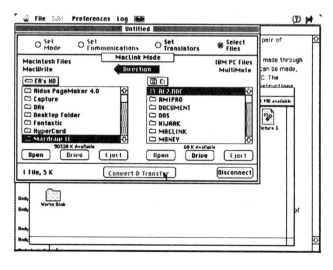

Fig. 8-18. Screen showing the contents of the Macintosh and IBM PC hard disks.

14. Select the folder on the Mac where the file will be placed by clicking the mouse on the folder's name.

15. Click the mouse on Convert & Transfer.

The file will be transferred from the PC to the Mac. To transfer from the Mac to the PC the process can be reversed by instructing the software on the Mac to answer the call of the PC. This is done by clicking the mouse on MacLink Answer Mode on the Mac and selecting Connect from the PC console.

Network Basics

Objectives

After completing this chapter you will:

1. Understand the benefits of networking
2. Understand the difference between local area networks and wide area networks.
3. Learn the standards that are used in designing networking technology.
4. Know the different types of network topologies.
5. Understand the different devices used for interconnecting networks.
6. Obtain a general overview of design considerations for hybrid networks.

Key Words

Bridge

Bus Network

Local Area Network

Network

Ring Network

Software

Wide Area Network

Brouter

Gateway

Metropolitan Area Network

PDN

Router

Star Network

Introduction

The concepts explored in previous chapters become the foundation for understanding the importance and functionality of networks. These networks are the basic building blocks of the information age of the 1990s and beyond. The information system industry is being shaped by the use of networks for interconnecting workstations, peripherals, mainframes, and minicomputers. Students in all areas of business need to understand network connectivity issues and the advantages and disadvantages of the different configurations.

This chapter discusses the benefits of having a networked environment and the basics of understanding networks. The difference between wide area networks and local area networks is explained, along with the different types of network topologies that are found in the workplace. Finally, the technologies required to connect dissimilar networks are discussed, along with related design concepts.

The student should read the material in this chapter thoroughly before reading any of the following chapters. Those chapters assume knowledge and understanding of the general networking concepts explored in this chapter. These concepts are crucial in obtaining an educated view of the benefits and problems of designing and interconnecting data communication networks.

Benefits of Networking

The microcomputer, with all of its benefits and usefulness, has serious shortcomings. Initially, microcomputers were designed with a single user in mind. Multiuser systems were delegated to mainframes and minicomputers. This is generally the way it is today, even though many microcomputers have more processing capacity and memory than a large number of the minicomputers in the business market.

Another problem with the microcomputer is that it was not designed to share its resources among other computers. If a printout is required, the personal computer must have its own printer. If a file must be stored on a hard disk, the personal computer must have its own hard disk. To a lesser extent, mainframes and minicomputers have the same problems. Even though a mainframe has many terminals that share disk space and printer usage, users of other computers within the same corporation may have a need to share resources in an efficient manner.

For example, assume that a corporation has an IBM AS-400 minicomputer, a Digital Equipment Corporation VAX minicomputer, and many personal computers and terminals. On many occasions the data stored on the AS-400 may be required by users of the VAX minicomputer and vice versa. In addition, some data processed in microcomputers and the resulting information must be shared by users of both minicomputer systems. This scenario creates many different types of information needs that must be resolved in an efficient and cost effective manner. Users should not be expected to duplicate data entry procedures or to master the use of multiple diverse and difficult-to-use systems.

How does a system manager resolve the diverse information needs of users? One solution is to provide two terminals for each user, one for the AS-400, one for the VAX, and a microcomputer for those individuals who need access to software that runs on personal computers. Although this will address the different needs of each user, this solution does not solve the problem of sharing data among the minicomputers.

Another solution is to provide every user a personal computer. Through the microcomputer and with the aid of communication software, each user can access one minicomputer, download the data to a personal computer using the communications program, modify the data locally, and, using a different emulation-communication program, upload the data to the second minicomputer. This solution may eventually work, but it assumes that every user is proficient with both minicomputer systems and the personal computer. In addition, to perform the entire transaction properly, the user must have a good knowledge of microcomputers and communication software. These assumptions typically cannot be made. Statistics show that the majority of users in corporations cannot perform all of the above functions without technical help. Finally, even though a user may accomplish the entire transaction without errors, the method employed is not very efficient.

The isolation of computers described in the example results in duplication of hardware, software, and human resources. Each user must perform duplicate functions in order to get the data from one processor to another. These additional functions use time and personnel that could be applied to improve the balance sheet of the corporation.

Another example of the inefficiencies of this approach in a large company would be the implementation of a large number of microcomputers as stand-alone units. If a company has 100 microcomputers and all users need to run a specific package, the company must purchase 100 individual programs if it wishes to remain within the limits of the law. Similarly, each user must be provided with a printer and any other peripherals required to use the software. This duplication of resources is expensive from the installation and maintenance point of view, and space is needed for all the equipment, its containers, and manuals that need to be kept by the company.

Even small companies will find that using computers in an isolated form is inefficient. As an example, imagine a small company that purchases a microcomputer to keep track of inventory. In this scenario, one person keeps the inventory updated, and others occasionally use the microcomputer to check the inventory level and monitor availability of a product. As users find the application beneficial, the demand to use the inventory database increases. The company also grows and expands its product line, adding more inventory items to the database. As the database is used on a continuous basis and the inventory grows, it becomes increasingly difficult to keep the inventory updated, since users monopolize the time during which the computer is accessible. One obvious solution is to purchase more computers and place the database on each of the machines. However, if more computers are purchased to handle the demand, then the complication arises of keeping the database current on all machines.

The current solution to the above problems is to connect all the computers in a network. A computer network can change a group of isolated computers into a coordinated multiuser computer system. A network user can legally share copies of the software with other users, if network versions of the software are purchased. Data can be stored in centralized locations or in different locations that are accessible to all users. Also, printers, scanners, and other peripherals connected to the network are available to all users.

If the inventory system described above was placed on a network with several other computers, the system could be kept updated and could be accessed by many users simultaneously. This is because one of the computers can act as a centralized repository of all software. This computer, normally called a server, will be the only machine that keeps a copy of the database and provides the software to workstations that request it. Since only one copy of the software and data is kept, any user who accesses the database will always have the latest or most current version of the programs and data. Additionally, having this type of centralized system eliminates the need for additional hardware and software, thus lowering the overall cost to the compnay.

The above theme has been at the core of companies or departments that have long used minicomputers and mainframes. It is a centralized system that minimizes the expense of purchasing hardware and software, yet it provides shared resources to all users. The network provides all of that, but goes a step beyond in that it provides all the functionality of the centralized system to users who have a computer on their desk. In addition, the network provides all the advantages mentioned above, regardless of the maker of the computer. In this fashion, minicomputers, mainframes, and microcomputers can all be connected together to share resources, even though some may be IBM computers, some Apple computers, and others may be made by Digital Corporation.

Hardware Sharing

A network allows users to share different types of hardware devices. The most commonly shared items are hard disks, printers, CDs, and communication devices.

Sharing Hard Disks

Today's sophisticated software applications require large amounts of disk space. Software environments such as Microsoft Windows with a word processing package consume in excess of 15 Mbytes of space before any data is saved onto the hard disk. Additionally, as companies require more information about their operation, larger disks are required. A microcomputer database management system such as Paradox or DBase IV managing a corporate database may utilize an additional 20 or 30 Mbytes of storage. And if the above software needs to share disk space with some other operating environment such as SCO UNIX, then the storage requirements for a single computer can be in the hundreds of megabytes. Also, if the base machine is not a microcomputer but a minicomputer or mainframe, the disk storage needs are even greater.

Although the price of disk technology has dropped dramatically in recent years, disks with a capacity to store hundreds or billions of bytes are still relatively expensive. In addition, it is not uncommon for microcomputer users to require hard disk capacities of hundreds of megabytes. It would be too expensive to purchase large disk space for all users or all possible situations that may arise within a corporation.

The cost of storage media is just one factor to consider. In addition, the security and backup of storage devices become more difficult to manage when the devices are isolated. If there are many computers in an isolated format, it is difficult to ensure that all important data is properly backed up and safeguarded against possible loss. In addition, the time to perform all the procedures required to safeguard the data is extensive. This requires full-time personnel to perform just those functions. Another problem that arises is making sure that everyone has the most current version of a program on their hard disks. Since there can be many computers, each with the same copy of the program, it becomes difficult to ensure that everyone has the most up-to-date version of a data file or a program.

All of these problems are greatly reduced, and in most cases solved, by using a network that connects all the individual computers. The network backs up files, and software is stored on the hard disks of one or a few central computers. Additionally, since all the software is maintained in one location, everyone is assured of the latest version of data files and software programs.

Today's networks are based on the concept of sharing access to disk storage devices. These disks are typically installed on special devices called file servers, which will be discussed in the next chapter. A file server is a computer on a network that provides files and programs to those workstations that request them. As outlined above, sharing disk space has several benefits. The most obvious are costs, integrity of the data, and security.

Costs are reduced by purchasing hard disks to be shared among all users, rather than purchasing one for each user or location. Instead of purchasing a 100-Mbyte hard disk for 100 users, the company can provide smaller hard disks for the users and store the programs required by users on a large centralized hard disk with a server. In addition, if the server's hard disk is large enough, it can also be used to save files that a user may want to keep in a location other than his or her workstation. This method of storing data provides users with a "larger" hard disk that has common access. The word "larger" is used in quotations because the user's computer doesn't have the extra hard disk space, but the user does have access to additional storage.

Safety of the data is improved over having it on isolated disks, since a network administrator can make constant backups of all files on the device. This is important when the data manipulated and transmitted through the network is critical to the operation of the company. Remember that it is easier to replace damaged equipment, but some data can't be replaced if it is lost or damaged. Frequent and consistent backups is one the best ways to ensure that all important data will be available if the main hard disk is damaged and the data is lost. Additionally, having the data in a centralized location on the network safeguards this data from being lost by a user misplacing or damaging floppy disks.

Security of the data is enforced by using the network's built-in security systems. Data on isolated disks is an easy target for anyone who wants to damage it. Network management software can prevent unauthorized users from gaining access to important data and deleting or destroying it. Also, many of the network management programs available have computer virus detection capabilities that can prevent these viruses from infecting users' workstations or network servers. Hard disk sharing is only one of the many advantages of networking. Another important device that can be shared through networks is the printer.

Sharing Printers

Printer sharing is common on networks. Printers can be attached to a file server, or connected to the network independently of the file server (see Fig. 9-1). Users in the network depicted in Fig. 9-1 can use any of the printers on the system. Instead of each user having a low-cost printer attached to a terminal or microcomputer, a few high-speed, high-quality printers can be purchased and connected to the network. Any user needing a fast printout can send the output to the printer nearest to his or her station. This ability to share output devices

Fig. 9-1. Network showing user stations and file server.

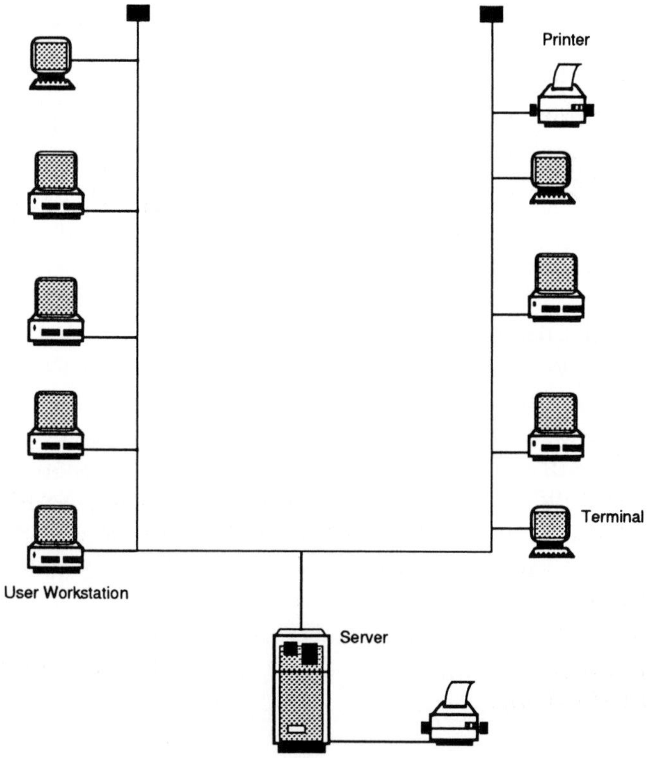

reduces the cost of the overall system to the company, and at the same time provides the capability for users to have access to better-quality output devices than would otherwise be possible.

Printers are not the only devices that can be shared on a network. Input equipment can be shared along with output devices. Some of these additional devices include facsimile machines, scanners, and plotters. Scanners and facsimile machines have been around the computer industry for a long time. However, they have become popular only during the last few years as their prices dropped and their quality improved.

A facsimile machine can be shared as both an input and output device. If the facsimile is an independent machine, it can be attached directly to the network. Then output can be directed to it through the use of specialized software. In the same manner, if the facsimile device and its software are smart enough, any input received can be transmitted and routed to the intended receiver. A facsimile machine can also be shared by attaching it to a workstation and making the workstation act as a gateway or printer server. Also, new facsimile boards that fit inside the computer provide a closer integration of this technology into modern networks and connectivity strategies.

Plotters and other output devices can be shared the same way a typical printer is shared. To the network, a plotter or a printer is simply a logical output device, and they are treated relatively the same. Also, scanners can be shared by attaching the scanner to a workstation and using the workstation to distribute scanned images through the network. Some modern scanners have expansion slots that can be fitted with a network card that provides the scanner with its own identity to the network. This allows the scanner to function on the network without the need of being attached to a specific computer.

Sharing Communication Devices

Personal computer users on a network often need to access remote systems or networks. One possible solution is to provide them with modems and terminal emulation software to access other systems from their individual workstations. This solution is expensive and places a burden on the users who must know all the parameters and communication settings for their particular hardware.

A better solution is to provide users on a network with access to shared modems, gateways, bridges (these devices are more fully discussed in this chapter), and other network and data communication devices without the need to purchase one for each user (see Fig. 9-2). Many companies set up what is called a "modem

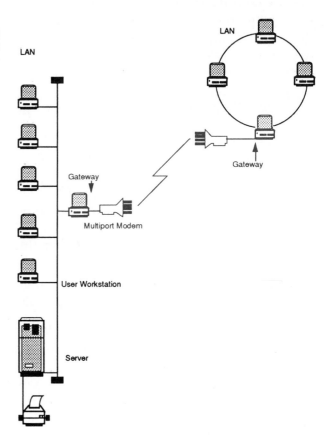

Fig. 9-2. Connecting networks located in different geographical areas.

pool." This is a group of modems that are located in a single place and connected to several communication lines. The modems in the pool are available to users on a "first come, first served" basis. The modems are controlled, in most cases, by a gateway server computer. When a user needs to access another computer at a remote location, the user instructs his or her workstation to connect it to an available modem in the "pool." If a modem is available, the modem is logically given to the workstation for the duration of the communication session. From this point on, the user's workstation utilizes the modem as if it were attached directly to the workstation. After the communication session is over, the modem is returned to the pool, and it is made available to another user who may request it.

In summary, the benefits of sharing hardware on a network are clear. Costs can be reduced by avoiding duplicate hardware, and at the same time users can have access to a variety of devices. Also, data security and safety are improved by having up-to-date backups and enforcing the security measures that are available with each network.

Software Sharing

Networks also provide benefits in software sharing. Instead of purchasing an individual application program for every user in a company, a network version of the program can be obtained. The software program can be stored on one of the network servers, making the program available to any network authorized user. Also, software designed for networks allows multiple use of the software simultaneously, making a network of personal computers a multiuser system. In this case, users can share the data produced and used by the package at any given time, even though parts of the data files may be in use by another computer.

There are many advantages of sharing software. The most important are cost reduction, legality of the product, sharing data, and having current upgrades. Cost reduction has been explained before. As a further example, imagine the need to purchase 100 copies of a spreadsheet. Even with group discounts, the price of acquiring all of those packages can be as high as $50,000. Purchasing a network version of the same package for an unlimited number of users will result in much lower cost. In addition, when an upgrade is available, there is a single cost that is a fraction of the cost of the upgrades for 100 separate copies. Also, software designed for networking places data files in centralized locations that all authorized users can access.

Through the network managing utilities, administrators can enforce security and the legality of all copies used, leaving the user to concentrate on generating and analyzing the data. If a company purchases a license to use 10 copies of a spreadsheet, the number of users that can concurrently access the program can be controlled by the network management system. If all 10 copies of the spreadsheet are being used and another user tries to load a copy of the program, the network management system informs the user that all legal copies are being used and that a current running copy must be closed before a new copy can be loaded into the user's workstation.

As stated previously, backups are also easier to enforce and maintain if all the software resides on one or a few servers. Additionally, some types of networks allow a technician to back up not only the server's hard disks, but also the hard disk of user workstations. Although a network administrator wouldn't want to get into the practice of backing up all users' workstations, the ability to perform centralized and automatic backups enhances the security of the data in case of a disaster.

Networking multiple computers also has an added advantage. The productivity of users can be enhanced by taking advantage of "groupware." Groupware is software that includes electronic mail (e-mail), calendar, appointment, word processing, alarm clock, and other time management software. It allows a user to manage his or her time electronically and communicate this information to other users on the network. It is intended to eliminate much of the interoffice paperwork, making information available to all users faster.

Using groupware, a user can create a memo, mail a copy of it to many other users, check their calendars for an opportune time for a meeting, and schedule the meeting automatically for the people in a given office or department. In addition, electronic alarms can be attached to the calendar to alert users of important events. These and other time management groupware products allow the system to perform the daily operations of the company and keep its employees in contact with each other.

However, even with all the advantages mentioned above, they are expensive and they are not problem-free from an administrative and technical point of view. Many companies don't look closely at these problems until it is too late to reverse costly and time-consuming events that are put in motion when a network is implemented. These problems or challenges are explained in the next section.

Challenges of Networking

Although the implementation of a network carries many benefits, as outlined in the beginning of this chapter, its introduction into the work environment presents new challenges and costs that are sometimes not anticipated. These challenges can be summarized as the cost of networking.

The cost of networking includes, but it is not limited to, these factors:

1. The cost of acquiring and installing cables and associated equipment for the transmission of data. Different types of transmission media come with advantages and disadvantages that vary greatly. The cost of the media varies according to the data transmission capacity and speeds of movement through the cable. In addition, it is easier, and therefore cheaper, to install twisted pair wire than it is to install optical fiber. The purchase of transmitting media is just one aspect of this cost.

   Specialized personnel may be required to lay the cable. The cost of contracting a company to perform the "pulling" or layout of the cable will also depend on the number of difficulties that the installers have to overcome as they perform their job. It is cheaper to install cable when a building is being constructed than to have to drill through several feet of concrete after it is built. Also, if the distances are large, additional equipment such as line adapters may be required. The cost of these adapters tends to increase as the sophistication of the media increases.

2. The cost of purchasing the network operating system, and network versions of individual software packages. Depending on the type of network being implemented and the number of users, the cost of the software to run the network, the network operating system or NOS, can be several thousand dollars. Even companies with small networks can expect to pay a few thousand dollars for the NOS. Additional modules to the NOS such as network monitoring software and virus protection are not normally included in the basic network operating system package. Depending on the type of network

being installed and the number of users, the complete set of software to operate the network can be more expensive than most of the hardware pieces. And, of course, the network operating system alone is not sufficient. Application software must also be acquired.

Software applications that were running on an individual basis may need to be upgraded in order to obtain network licenses. Additionally, many software programs designed for an individual computer will not execute on a network without modification of the source code. If a company has a heavy investment in software that is not able to run on the network, then the cost of acquiring new software to replace the old can run the cost of the network beyond the fiscal possibilities of the company. And, if the network contains many users and sophisticated applications, someone must maintain the servers and the physical layout of the network itself as people and workstations are relocated.

3. The cost of personnel to manage software installation, expand and reconfigure the network, provide backup, maintenance of hardware and software, and maintenance of the network/user interface. As users become confortable with the network, their use of it will increase and with this increase come demands for additional network services. Also, people may need to be relocated within an office or building. Someone has to ensure that the network services for these users are not interrupted.

In some cases, the number of users or programs used through the system may exceed system resources. Technical personnel will be needed to "tune" and enhance the network to make sure that it works efficiently and effectively. Periodically, passwords may need to be reassigned, backups need to be perfomed, hard disks need to be defragmented, and old accounts need to be erased to make room for new accounts. All of these functions require personnel trained and educated in the operation of networks. This is an important point that was mentioned before. Many companies delegate the operation of networks to individuals who don't have any formal training in system design and network operations. These individuals learn as much as possible as they perform their duties, but by the time they learn enough about the network, it may have deteriorated to the point of needing a major and costly overhaul. Technical and network operating personnel must have the formal training that today's sophisticated systems require in order to perform efficiently and effectively.

Finally, as users are added to the network, the security and safekeeping of data become critical. Personnel will be required to maintain the network on a full-time basis and to ensure that proper backups are made in a consistent and timely fashion. The network interface will need modification as types and quantities of users change. In most cases, companies should expect that to install a network that serves many users, additional trained personnel need to be hired in conjunction with the purchase of the network itself. A lack of proper personnel is one of the most common factors contributing to a poorly designed system and to the failure of networks.

4. The cost of bridges and gateways to other networks, and the software and other equipment required to implement the connection. After the network is implemented, there may be a need to connect it to other communication systems. The equipment used in the networking field to provide connectivity among different network platforms comes in the shape of gateways, routers, brouters, and bridges.

   The technical staff in charge of the network needs to be aware of the differences, capabilities, and cost of these devices. Each was designed for a specific purpose, and using them in the wrong situation or place could disrupt the operation of the network. The cost and challenge of performing this connection are an additional burden to network managers, and additional personnel and training may be required.

5. The cost of training users of the network and the personnel required to manage the network. This is an ongoing and hidden cost due to the turnover of personnel.

Many companies don't consider this cost in their design stage. Although the cost of training a network administrator and technical operation staff is in many cases accounted for, the cost of training users is many times ignored. If a user is being trained on how to use the network, the hours spent in training are lost production to the company. Also, if the training is performed off-site, then a replacement may have to be hired during the training period.

Many administrators claim that the above cost is offset by the saving introduced by the employee after the training is completed. Even though an employee may perform his or her duties more efficiently after learning how to use the network, there is a cost associated with training users, and outside consultants or training personel need to be included in the cost. If the company has a high turnover ratio, this cost will be large.

6. The cost of maintenance, including installation of future software upgrades, correcting incompatibilities between the network operating system and new software upgrades, and correcting hardware problems. As new versions of the network operating system become available, old software programs may not be able to co-exist with the new operating system. In such cases, new versions of application software must be secured. (Of course, if the number of users is large, having a network license can provide substantial savings over purchasing many individual copies of the same program.) The number and frequency of upgrades is a cost that must be scheduled into the system life cycle (see chapter 12).

7. The cost of hiring a network administrator or specialist to manage the system or to solve problems as they occur. Although many companies use existing personnel to manage new networks, these people will have to give up a minimum of approximately 10 to 20 hours per week to manage and back up the network. Their absence from a task for which they were originally hired will eventually have to be compensated for by hiring assistants or by increasing the salary of such personnel.

8. The cost of network versions of software. Software designed to work on a network is normally more expensive than individual copies of the application. For a network that contains large numbers of users working with a software application, there are cost savings in purchasing a single network version of the program. But for a network with a small number of users, such cost savings may not be realized.

In small companies the task of implementing and managing the network can be performed by one or two persons. However, in large companies, there will be a need for several full-time employees to perform network management duties. These costs will become a sizable portion of the operational budget of the company. It is important that any implementation of a network follows the rules for system design. Only in such a case will the company be assured that all possible problems and obstacles in the success of the network implementation have been properly addressed and anticipated (see chapter 12).

Types of Networks

The geographical area covered by a network determines whether the network is called a wide area network (WAN—see Fig. 9-3), metropolitan area network (MAN), or a local area network (LAN). Wide area networks link systems that are too far apart to be included in a small in-house network. Metropolitan area networks connect across distances greater than a few kilometers but no more than 50 kilometers (approximately 30 miles). Local area networks usually connect users in the same office or building. In some cases, adjacent buildings of a corporation or educational institution are connected with the use of LANs. However, the boundaries of a type of network are not as clearly defined in real life as they are in this book. Many companies have networks that encompass hundreds of miles, yet they are still called local area networks. This book will try to differentiate among the three types according to the distance they cover, but keep in mind that their definitions are sometimes altered by the people who implement and manage them.

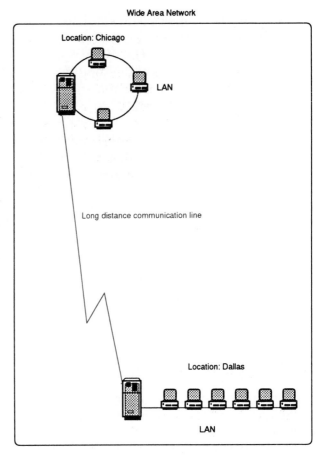

Fig. 9-3. A wide area network.

Wide Area Network (WAN)

Wide area networks cross public right-of-ways such as highways and streets, and must use common carrier circuits for their transmitting medium. They use a combination of the hardware discussed in chapters 4 and 5. Wide area networks use a broad range of communication media for interconnection that includes switched and leased lines, private microwave circuits, optical fiber, coaxial cable, and satellite circuits. Basically, a wide area network is any communication network that permits message, voice, image signals, or computer data to be transmitted over a widely dispersed geographical area.

Metropolitan Area Network (MAN)

Metropolitan area networks connect locations that are geographically located from 5 to 50 kilometers apart. They include the transmission of data, voice, and television signals through the use of coaxial cable or optical fiber cable as their primary medium of transmission, although many metropolitan area networks are implemented through the use of microwave technology.

Customers of metropolitan area networks are primarily large companies that need to communicate within a metropolitan area at high speeds. MAN providers normally offer lower prices than the phone companies and faster installation over a diverse routing, and include backup lines in emergency situations.

Local Area Network (LAN)

LANs connect devices within a small area, usually within a building or adjacent buildings. LAN transmission media usually do not cross roads or other public thoroughfares. They are privately controlled and owned with respect to data processing equipment, such as processors and terminals, and with respect to data communication equipment such as media and extenders. Local area networks are covered in detail in the next chapter.

Many local area networks are used to interconnect the computers and peripherals within an office or department. Through specialized hardware and software, each department's LAN is connected to a larger local area network within the company's building. Then this larger LAN is connected to a metropolitan area network that may interconnect different offices or branches throughout a large city. And finally, the company's MANs may be connected to a wider area network that interconnects the company's regional or international offices.

Each of the types of networks mentioned above has a set of standards that most manufacturers adhere to in order for their equipment to work with equipment manufactured by other companies. This set of standards is a necessity in a computing field that sees equipment manufacturers trying to impose their own standards on customers for the sole purpose of monetary gain. These standards assure customers that, as long as they purchase equipment that follows the established set of criteria for the functioning of communication equipment, they will be able to connect the equipment to their networks and should expect it to work properly. The set of criteria or standards is formulated by country representatives that have grouped together and formed the International Standards Organization for Standardization.

Current Standards

The computer industry is dominated by standards that are the result of several companies forming committees to ensure that the equipment they produce will be compatible. These sets of standards minimize the risk of creating networks that use equipment from different vendors who may follow different protocols. Also, by designing a network with equipment that complies with a set of standards, the users of these networks are assured that they will be able to share information from different sources and over different network schemes.

Additionally, the use of standards in network design and installation helps in managing the system by creating common management processes. At the same time it insulates the network operators from changes at low levels of the standard. Although there are several types of standards in the communication industry, the two most commonly implemented are those established by the Open Systems Interconnect subcommittee or OSI, and IBM's System Networking Architecture, or SNA.

Open Systems Interconnect (OSI)

Network evolution has been toward standardized networking and internetworking technology. One of the most important standards-making bodies is the International Standards Organization or ISO, which makes technical recommendations about data communication interfaces. Standardizing the interfaces and the format of the data flowing through them ensures that, regardless of the equipment manufacturer, the entire network will work as long as the equipment in it adheres to these standards.

History

In 1978, the ISO created the Open Systems Interconnect (OSI) subcommittee, whose task was to develop a framework of standards for computer-to-computer communication. The result from the subcommittee is referred to as the OSI Reference Model. It serves as the model around which a series of standard protocols is defined. Using this model, hardware and software companies can develop their products to work within certain parameters that are the guidelines of the model. The resulting product is then able to communicate with other products that follow the same parameters.

The OSI Reference Model is known as a layered protocol, specifying seven layers of interface, wherein each layer has a specific set with functions to perform (see Fig. 9-4). Each layer has standardized interfaces to the layers above it and below it, and it communicates directly with the equivalent layer of another device.

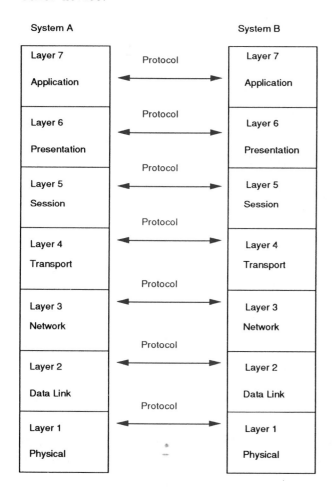

Fig. 9-4. The OSI Reference Model.

As a result of the OSI Reference Model, the communications industry has concentrated on making products that comply with the interface guidelines, making them OSI compatible. Among the best known customers of OSI products is the federal government, which is commited to purchase large quantities of OSI compatible products through the Government Open System Interconnect Profile or GOSIP. By basing their networks on OSI compatibility, users can discuss product relationships, compatibilities, and capabilities in the same working framework.

The OSI Model divides the communication process into seven-layered processes. These processes are as follows:

1. The first layer is the physical link control.
2. The second layer is the data link control.
3. The third layer is the network control.
4. The fourth layer is the transport control.
5. The fifth layer is the session control.
6. The sixth layer is the presentation layer.
7. The seventh and final layer is the application layer.

When a company refers to one of its products as working at level two, it means that their product works at the second level of the OSI model and it is "transparent" to any other products that work on layers 3 through 7. The word transparent means that the product in discussion will not affect negatively the operation of any other products that work in higher level layers. The lowest level layer is one and the highest level is seven.

Benefits

Having a layered framework, the OSI model offers several benefits:

1. Network hardware and software designers can allocate tasks more effectively among network resources.
2. A network layer can easily be replaced by a layer from another network vendor.
3. Processes from mainframes can be offloaded into FEPs or other network control devices.
4. Networks can be upgraded more easily by replacing individual layers instead of the entire software system.

The user and network designer are not restricted to using the product of a specific company. If they are not satisfied with the performance or the service of a product provider, they can simply replace the product in question by another of a different company that is OSI compatible and works in a similar manner. To better understand the individual layers, let's take a closer look at the function of each.

Functional Layers

The seven OSI layers define the following standards in the field of data communications.

1. Physical layer. This layer defines all the standards that provide guidelines on how to physically move data bits between modems and perform circuit activation and deactivation. The specifications on this layer define the electrical connections between the transmission medium and the computer. The layer describes how many wires will be used to transmit the signals, the size and shape of connectors, the speed of transmission, and the direction of data transmission.

2. Data link layer. The standards in this layer establish and control the physical path of communication to the next node. This includes detection and correction of errors, handling flow control between modems, and the proper message sequence. This layer is basically responsible for the accuracy of the data transmitted between two locations on the network and the control mechanism for accessing the network.

3. Network layer. The standards defined for this layer provide the necessary control and routing functions to establish, maintain, and terminate communication links between transmitting and receiving nodes.

4. Transport layer. The standards established by this layer are responsible for generating addresses of end users and ensuring that all data packets are received. A packet is a block of data that is sent from an originating point to a receiving location.

5. Session layer. It provides the necessary standards to define the interface to manage and support a communication dialog between two separate locations. It establishes a session, manages the session, synchronizes the data flow, and terminates the session.

6. Presentation layer. The standards for this layer define how products may accept data from the application layer and format the data. If there are any data preparation functions, the functions are not embedded into the data; rather, they are performed by this layer. The types of functions that can be performed are data encryption, code conversion, compression, and terminal screen formatting.

7. Application layer. The standards defined by this layer provide guidelines for network services such as file transfer, terminal emulation, and logging into a file server. This layer is functionally defined by the user, and it supports the actual end-user application.

Systems Network Architecture (SNA)

Another standard proprietary to IBM is the Systems Network Architecture or SNA. SNA was introduced in 1974, and today there are over 36,000 SNA compatible network installations. This large installed base warrants the study of SNA and some of the standards established by it.

The SNA strategy is conceptually similar to the OSI model but it is not compatible with it. Like OSI, SNA is divided into seven layers, but these layers are defined differently from those found in the OSI model. In the SNA scheme, the seven layers are as follows:

1. The first layer is the physical layer.

2. The second layer is the data link control layer.

3. The third layer is path control.

4. The fourth layer is transmission control.

5. The fifth layer is data flow control.

6. The sixth layer is the presentation layer.

7. The seventh and final layer is the application layer.

Remember that, although these layers seem compatible to the OSI layers, the standards are not compatible with each other.

Concepts

The SNA definition divides the network into physical units (PUs) and logical units (LUs). The physical units constitute the hardware on the network such as printers, terminals, computers, and other processor devices. There are four types of physical units defined as 1, 2, 4, and 5. Presently there isn't a physical unit 3. These four types correspond to the hardware in the following manner:

PU	Hardware
1	Terminals
2	Cluster Controllers
4	Front end processors
5	Host computers

The logical units are the users logged onto the network and the application programs running in the system. The logical units or LUs are implemented through software in the network. The communication between users is a communication between logical units called a session. Notice that a physical unit can support many logical units.

The sessions mentioned above need to be established before two LUs can communicate with each other. Sessions occur between terminals and programs, terminals and terminals, and programs and programs. They can also be classified as interactive, batch, and printer sessions with each user having multiple simultaneous sessions, each with its own LU. This provides users of SNA systems the ability to communicate with two or more computers or with two or more programs simultaneously.

The SNA standard specifies that each device uses a 48-bit-long network address that identifies the LUs and PUs, also called network addessable units or NAUs. Each NAU has its own unique address which, due to its 48-bit format, can be a large number, giving SNA compatible networks access to a large number of nodes.

Each of the NAUs in an SNA compatible network uses the Synchronous Data Link Control (SDLC) protocol as its primary data link protocol (see chapter 8). In addition, SNA can operate with the BISYNC and X.25 protocols (see chapter 7). This was implemented in response to a large number of IBM customers requesting access to other networking standards.

SNA networks are normally designed to maximize the network connecting the centralized mainframes that serve as hosts for all data processing activities. The network itself is not as intelligent as other standards in the market. In the SNA architecture, the mainframe is the main processor of data and the network is just an avenue for getting the data to the mainframe.

To manage the SNA network, IBM and other third party vendors provide software to aid in this task. One of these products that is commonly found in many installations is called Netview. Netview becomes an interface between the network administrator and the network itself. This product provides statistics about transmission errors, circuit problems, difficulties with modems, response time, and other network problems. In addition, the Netview product is an "open" product that allows third party manufacturers to create products that interface with it.

Two other common standards in the field of networking and data communication are the X.25 and X.400 standards. The X.25 standard is used for data transmission using a packet switching network and it covers the first three layers of the OSI model. The X.400 standard is used for creating definitions and compatibility in the electronic mail industry. These two standards were discussed in chapter 7. Refer to them as necessary.

Network Topology

The configurations used to describe networks are sometimes called network architecture or network topology. Networks can have many different logical and physical configurations. However, regardless of how they are implemented, networks can be placed into one of the general categories below. The most common network topologies are

1. Ring
2. Bus
3. Star
4. Hybrid

Regardless of the configuration used, all networks are made up of the same four basic components:

1. The user workstations that perform a particular operation. In newer implementations, the user workstation comes in the form of a microcomputer.

2. The protocol control that converts the user data into a format that can be transmitted through the network until it reaches the desired location. These are the rules that govern how the data will be moved through the network from the originator of the message to the receiver of it.

3. The interface that is required to generate the electrical signals to be moved on the medium. This interface can be in the form of an RS-232 with its associated signals. In most cases it is handled by an interface board that connects the computer to the transmission media.

4. The physical medium that carries the electrical signals generated by the interface. The physical medium can be twisted pair wire, coaxial cable, optical fiber, microwaves, or some of the other media explored in previous chapters.

In addition to categories mentioned above, networks can be further categorized into narrowband networks and wideband networks. A narrowband is a cable whose characteristics allow transmission of only a small amount of information per unit of time (see modes of transmission in chapter 4). Larger bandwidth capabilities of a cable mean larger data carrying capacity. This carrying capacity is controlled and enhanced by the use of different transmission techniques such as multiplexing.

On narrowband networks only one device on the network can be transmitting at any point. This means that only one user can be communicating through the network at any given time. The typical transmission speed for this type of network is up to a maximum of 10 megabits per second. In wideband networks multiple users can be communicating at the same time. Most of the microcomputer networks such as Novell and IBM's PC LAN are considered narrowband whereas many of the newer wide area networks are wideband networks.

Ring Network

The ring architecture is depicted in Fig. 9-5. This configuration is typical of IBM's Token-Ring network. Each device in the network is connected sequentially in a ring configuration that is

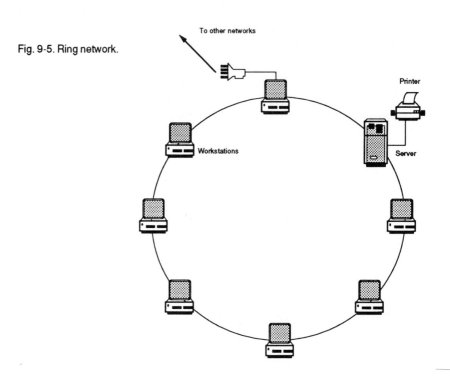

Fig. 9-5. Ring network.

shown in Fig. 9-5 as the solid line connecting all devices. The actual physical configuration is such that the beginning and end of the network link are attached so it forms a circle.

In a ring network, each node (receiving/sending station) can be designated as the primary station and the others as secondary stations. Also in this type of network, the wire configuration is a series of loop-type connections from a centralized location called a multistation access unit (MAU). This is done so that if a station on the network malfunctions, the ring will not be broken. The MAU provides a short circuit to ensure the integrity of the network in case of a malfunction in any location on the ring.

In this type of network, data travels around the ring in one direction. Each of the workstations or nodes on the network receives and examines the message transmitted to see if it is for the workstation. If it is, the workstation receives the message and takes appropriate action. If the message is not for the station that is examining it, then it regenerates the signal and sends it through the network again. The time required for the data to travel around the ring is called the walk time. The message knows the destination because each workstation in the ring network has a unique address.

Reliability is high in ring networks, assuming that the integrity of the ring is not broken. Also, expanding a ring network is easy to achieve by removing one node and replacing it with two new ones. Finally, the cost of the ring network is usually less than that of the star and hybrid networks.

Bus Network

A network based on the bus topology (also called a tree topology) connects all networked devices to a single cable (called the bus) running the length of the network. Fig. 9-6 depicts this configuration. Cables running between devices directly connect them to the bus. Therefore, data may pass directly from one device to another without the need of a central hub, as in the star configuration. With some applications, however, the data must first be moved in and out of a central controlling station, as in the case of a Novell network.

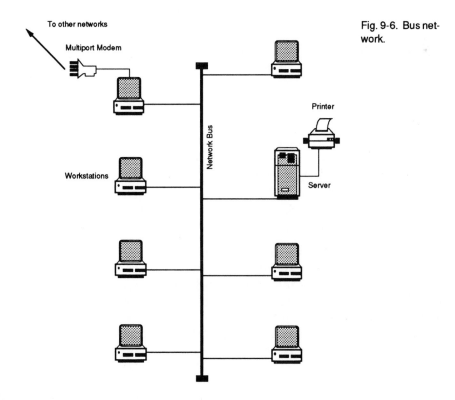

Fig. 9-6. Bus network.

In the typical implementation of the bus configuration, all nodes on the bus have equal control. One end of the bus is called the head end. The two ends of the cable or bus are carefully terminated so the data can be absorbed, preventing it from traveling the opposite direction and interfering with other signals traveling through the bus. Without these terminations the data moving through the bus could be lost when interference from incoming reflected waves cancels the electromagnetic waves that carry the signal.

Bus networks are, in essence, multipoint networks, in that a single cable extends through the length of the network with many nodes or stations attaching to the bus at different locations. Most personal computer networks use the bus topology. However, the distance that one of these networks can encompass is limited. This is because each time a node taps into the bus, some of the signal is lost on the cable. Because of this signal loss, typical cable distances are 2,500 meters and the practical number of nodes is 100 as in the case of Ethernet.

The reliability of bus networks is good unless the bus itself malfunctions. Losing one node does not have an effect on the rest of the network. But expandability is the strength of the bus topology. A new node can be added by simply connecting it to the bus. Because of the number of nodes and travel distance limitations, bus networks are normally limited to local area network installations.

Star Network

In a star network (sometimes called a hub topology), all devices on the network are connected to a central device that controls the entire network (see Fig. 9-7). The central location receives messages from a sending node and forwards them to the destination node. This central location becomes a hub that controls all the communication in the network.

The star topology is a traditional approach to interconnecting equipment in which each device is linked by a separate circuit through a central device such as a PBX. In this case the PBX receives a message from a workstation and switches it to a receiving station.

Workstation

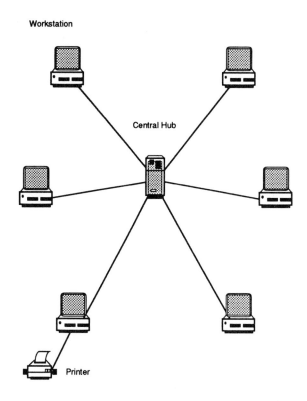

Fig. 9-7. Star network.

Central Hub

Printer

Star networks have several advantages. They provide the short-est path between nodes in the network. Messages traveling on the network must pass through one hub to reach their destina-tion. Therefore, the time required to get a message from the source to its destination is short. A star network also provides the user with a high degree of network control. Since all messages must pass through a central location, this station can log traffic on the network, produce error messages, tabulate network statistics, and perform recovery procedures.

Expanding a star network is relatively easy. To add a new node, a communication link is attached between the new node and the central device, and the network table on other nodes is updated. However, the reliability of star networks is low. If the central station malfunctions, then the entire network fails. This type of topology is common among networks designed by AT&T.

Hybrid Networks

A network with hybrid topology (Fig. 9-8) contains elements of more than one of the network configurations outlined above. For example, a bus network may have a ring network as one of its links. Another type of hybrid topology is a star network that has a bus network as one of its links, where a workstation is normally found.

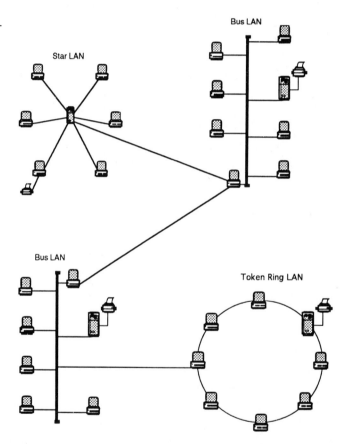

Fig. 9-8. Hybrid network.

This type of network is becoming more common in the workplace due to the capability of many protocols to interact with each other. In addition, the creation of standards promotes the design of multiple topology networks, since one topology may be more efficient or effective in a given situation than the other topologies. Yet, at some point in time, the different network topologies need to allow their users access to each other's resources.

Packet Data Networks

Packet switching is a widely used technique for exchanging data between computers over local area networks that may be in diverse geographical locations. Networks using these techniques are called packet data networks or PDNs. Packet switching is a store-and-forward data transmission technique in which messages are split into small segments called packets.

A packet is a logical container in which messages are transported from one originating location to their destination. Each packet is assembled at a workstation by a packet assemble/dissassemble facility or PAD. Then it is transmitted through the network independently of other packets, whether or not the other packets are part of the same transaction. The packets belonging to different messages travel through the same communication channel. When the packets that contain a message arrive at their destination, the PAD facility examines them and assembles the data contained in them into the original message.

Each packet in the network has a predetermined length that ranges from a few hundred bits to several thousand bits. This length is determined by the data transmission characteristics of the network through which the packets are moving. If a message is longer than the number of bits that the packet can store, several packets are sent, each identified with a sequence number. The communicating terminals or workstations that send the packets are connected via what is called a virtual circuit.

Virtual Circuits

A virtual circuit is a communication path that lasts only long enough to transmit a specific message. Virtual circuits are controlled by software that connects two nodes as if they were on a physical circuit. The address of the destination node is contained in the packet of data. When a workstation begins to send packets of data, the network is responsible for ensuring that the packets arrive at their destination. By knowing the originating and destination addresses of the packet, the network establishes the virtual circuit. When all the packets are sent, the virtual connection is broken. This avoids hardware problems that arise due to data speed mismatches and helps in retransmitting the packet in case of errors.

Example of a PDN

To better understand how these packets move through a network, let's follow a message as it is sent from a terminal to its destination address using a virtual switched connection (see Fig. 9-9).

Fig. 9-9. A message sent using a virtual switched connection.

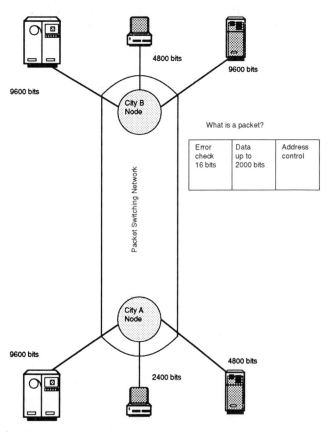

The first step is for the user to connect to a packet switching network. After the physical connection is made, the login procedure takes place. After the login procedure, the address of the receiving node is provided. The PDN then performs a call request packet from the sending node to the receiving node. The call request is delivered to the receiver as an incoming call packet. If the receiver accepts the call, it sends a call accepted packet that the sender node receives as a call connected message. Then the data exchange begins.

After the data is transmitted, either node can transmit a clear request to the other node. The receiver of the request acknowledges the disconnect with a clear confirmation control packet and the transmission is completed.

During data exchange, the process of splitting messages into individual packets is called packetizing. Packets are assembled and disassembled either at the sender's terminal or the receiver's terminal, or sometimes by the packet assembly/disassembly (PAD) facility mentioned above. In either case, packetizing is performed almost instantaneously, and data is transmitted in a virtually uninterrupted stream.

By using PDNs, users are charged only for the amount of data transmitted and not for the amount of connection time. In addition, PDNs provide access to many different locations without the cost of traditional switched connections. However, since PDNs are usually shared networks, users must compete for access. Therefore, it is possible for traffic from other users to block the transmission of a message. Also, if the number of data packets to be transferred is large, the cost of using a PDN can exceed that of leased lines.

Network Interconnectivity

As networks proliferate in the workplace, homogeneous networks are no longer the rule, but rather the exception. Heterogeneous or hybrid networks have become prominent in the workplace. They are composed of several network segments that may differ in topology, protocol, or operating system. For example, some networks contain a mixture of personal computers running on a bus network using Novell's NetWare, UNIX workstations using Ethernet on a token ring, and minicomputers running any of the several large-platform protocols.

During the first years of networking and data communications, these systems were designed to communicate with devices using the same topology and protocol on a homogeneous networked environment. Modern design strategies may include many different topologies in a communications solution that encompasses large geographical areas. To network these types of topologies into a single seamless environment is not an easy task, yet there are many combinations of hardware and software that can provide the connectivity solutions for interconnecting hybrid network designs.

Connecting Hybrid Networks

Before any attempt is made to interconnect a mixture of network configurations, some basic network characteristics need to be understood. One of these characteristics is network topology. The network topology is the way a network is configured. Different topologies were outlined previously in this chapter.

Another network characteristic is the protocol. Recall that the protocol is a set of conventions or rules for communication that includes a format for the data being transferred and the procedures for its transfer. When interconnecting networks, the protocol, as well as the topology, must be considered. Two networks that use the same topology but different protocols cannot effectively communicate without help. We call these heterogeneous networks.

Heterogeneous networks can be thought of as being made of building blocks connected by "black boxes." The building blocks are self-contained local area networks with their own workstations, servers, and peripherals. Each consists of a single topology and a single protocol.

To connect two of these boxes, a boundary must be crossed. A connection must be established between both boxes either by a physical cabling scheme or by radio waves. The device that makes the connection, the black box, does not change either interconnecting network. It simply transfers packets of data between the networks. It not only satisfies all the physical requirements of both networks, but also transfers the data safely and securely from one network to the other.

The ability to connect two heterogeneous networks depends on two requirements. The first requirement is that the topologies must be able to be interconnected. Second, there must be a way to transfer information between dissimilar systems of communication (protocols). This means that at some point a common protocol must be employed. There are several ways to accomplish this. Most solutions use high level protocols for moving data and employ tools for internetworking such as bridges, routers, brouters, and gateways. Each of these devices has distinct characteristics and specific applications.

The type of device used in connecting dissimilar networks will depend on the amount of transparency desired and the cost that a company is willing to pay for such devices. A rule of thumb is that the more sophistication a device has, the higher the transparency will be to the users and networks and the more expensive the equipment will be. With this in mind, let's take a closer look at some of these interconnectivity devices.

Bridges

Bridges are normally employed to interconnect similar networks. Both interconnecting networks must have the same protocol. The end result is a single logical network (see Fig. 9-10). A bridge can also be employed to interconnect networks that have different physical media. For example, a bridge may be used to join an optical fiber-based network to a coaxial cable-based network.

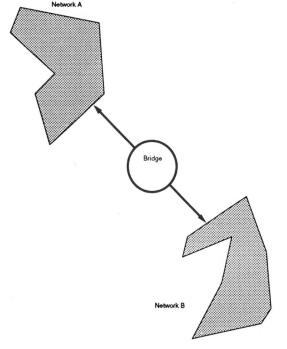

Fig. 9-10. A bridge connecting two networks.

Bridges may also be used to interconnect networks that use different low level communication protocols. Therefore, under the right circumstances, a bridge may be used to connect a token-ring network and a star network running different communication protocol software.

Bridges feature high level protocol transparency. They can move traffic between two networks over a third network that may exist in the middle of the others, and that does not understand the data passing through it. To the bridge, the intermediate network exists for the purpose of passing data only.

Bridges are intelligent devices. They learn the destination address of traffic passing on them and direct it to its destination. They are also employed in partitioning networks. For example, assume that a network is being slowed down by excessive traffic between two of its parts. The network can be divided into two or more smaller ones, using bridges to connect them. However, since bridges must learn addresses, examine data packets, and forward messages, processing is slowed down by these functions.

Routers

Routers don't have the learning abilities of the bridge, but they can determine the most efficient data path between two networks. They operate at the third layer of the OSI model (see Fig. 9-11).

Routers ignore the topologies and access levels used by networks. Since they operate at the network layer, they are unconstrained by the communication medium or communication protocols. Bridges know the final destination of data packets, but routers know only where the next router is located. They are typically used to connect networks that use the same high level protocol.

When a data packet arrives at the router, it determines the best route for the packet by checking a router table. The router sees only the packets sent to it by a previous router, where bridges must examine all packets passing through the network. The major use of routers is to interconnect networks of similar protocols but different packet sizes. Depending on the source,

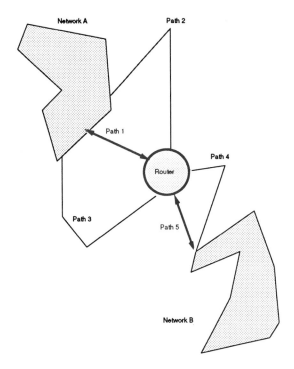

Fig. 9-11. Networks connected by a router.

routers are sometimes described as bridges and sometimes as gateways. Most large internetworks can make good use of routers as long as the same high level protocol is used.

Brouters

Brouters are hybrid devices that incorporate bridge and router technology. Often they are improperly referred to as multiprotocol routers. In fact, they provide more sophistication than true multiprotocol routers. Brouters provide the advantages of routers and bridges for complex networks. Brouters make decisions on whether a data packet uses a protocol that is routable. Then they route those that can be routed and bridge the rest.

Gateways

Gateways are devices that provide either six- or seven-layer support for the OSI protocol structure. They are the most sophisticated method of connecting networks to networks and networks to hosts (see Fig. 9-12). Gateways can interconnect

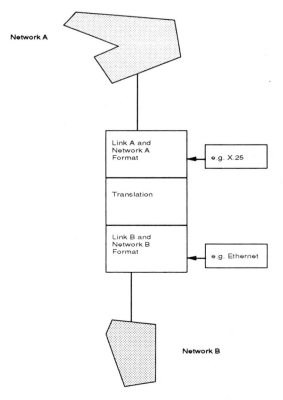

Fig. 9-12. Networks connected by a gateway.

networks of totally different architectures. With a gateway, it is possible to connect a Novell PC-based network with an SNA network or Ethernet network and make the sharing of resources transparent to the user.

Gateways do not route data packets within networks. They simply deliver their packets so the network can read them. When a gateway receives a packet from a network, it translates it and routes the packet to a distant-end gateway. Here the packet is retranslated and delivered to the destination network. A gateway is the most sophisticated method for interconnecting wide area networks.

Planning a Hybrid Network

Even though previous chapters in this book dealt with the different concepts of network design, this section provides a general overview of planning a heterogeneous network. For an in-depth view of network design fundamentals, read chapter 12.

Typically a network administrator or designer does not plan a network from scratch, but inherits one. However, if one can be planned from the beginning, several issues should be considered. The first of these issues is to decide on the objectives for the new system.

These objectives normally include interconnecting different work situations with different needs. Therefore it is a good idea to start by defining the individual needs of the users of the network. Each department that is going to be affected by the network will have different requirements that may be solved by different types of technologies. Instead of deciding at this point on how to interconnect networks, it is a better idea to understand the expectations of the department that will use them.

Once the needs of the individual users have been established, the commonalities can be identified. This can be done by considering how an individual topology, or set of topologies, and a single protocol may be used throughout the system. If possible, a single network topology and protocol will reduce the number of potential problems that may arise in the operation of the network. Additionally, the required technical knowledge of maintenance personnel is reduced, along with the amount of maintenance time required to keep the system operational.

After the individual workgroup and its related needs have been established, the designer must consider how best to incorporate the workgroups into individual local area networks or network segments. Once each of these segments is designed, the next step is to incorporate the individual network segments into a network at each location.

After individual segments are successfully connected into a single network, the interconnectivity needs of the different buildings in the office complex or campus should be considered. In this case the network designer must deal with traffic flow. Managing traffic flow includes two main issues. One issue is the speed of data transmission between locations. The other is the amount of congestion on the routes between locations.

Data speed problems can be addressed by employing a fast communication medium such as optical fiber, if the distance between buildings is short. Otherwise, high-speed dedicated links, such as T1 lines, may need to be considered since private companies don't have the rights to extend their own cables across thoroughfares or public right-of-ways.

Congestion of traffic in the lines becomes a concern when public data communication circuits are used. Since these lines may be shared by many devices, it is easier to exceed the capacity of the transmission medium, causing a slowdown in the overall speed of transmission. Alternative methods of traffic routing need to be considered. For example, if the network spans an area from Chicago to Dallas, alternate routes such as through Kansas City or Memphis are possible paths if the main route becomes congested.

Traffic problems are addressed by some companies by using a technique called the spanning tree algorithm. Using this technique, bridges can be placed between long-haul locations. Under the control of the spanning tree algorithm, the bridges making up the alternative routes, let's say, between Chicago and Dallas, conduct tests to determine the best communication path at any given time. The one with the best path becomes the forwarding bridge, and the others stay in a holding pattern. If the communication link begins to deteriorate, the other bridge starts forwarding messages and the original bridge stays on hold. This technique can also be used between buildings that are short distances from each other, in order to have a consistent throughput efficiency in the communication circuit.

Managing Hybrid Networks

Today's network managers have a large array of sophisticated tools to manage and correct problems in homogeneous and heterogeneous networks. The types of management tools available fall into three general levels of sophistication and flexibility of usage.

The first level consists of simple performance monitors. Performance monitors provide information on data throughput, node errors, and other occurrences. A product that falls into this category is Novell's LANtern. LANtern offers a cost effective way of monitoring individual networks or network segments and reporting the existence of problems. This solution is good for small to medium-sized networks.

The second level consists of devices or software that perform network analysis. These add meaning to the data generated by the network monitor. An example of a network analyzer is Novell's LAN analyzer. Network analyzers provide a large amount of information about the network operation, but require skillful and knowledgeable network operators to interpret the data. Also, network analyzers are very expensive.

The third level of network management tool is designed for wide area hybrid networks. These tools come in two different types. One is a new array of global network management tools that allow a network administrator to obtain a global and sometimes graphical view of the operations on the entire network. The other type of management tool comes in the form of two emerging standards called The Simple Network Management Protocol (SNMP) and the Common Management Information Protocol (CMIP). Both techniques have the same goal, that is, to move information across a network so the network manager can find problems in the system. However, they have different designs and reporting options, but they will play an important role in future management of wide area hybrid networks.

Summary

A computer network can change a group of isolated computers into a coordinated multiuser computer system. A network user can legally share copies of the software with other users. Data can be deposited in centralized locations or in different locations that are accessible to all users. Printers, scanners, and other peripherals connected to the network are available to all users. Additionally, a network allows users to share many different types of hardware devices. The most commonly shared devices are hard disks, printers, and communication devices.

Software designed for networks allows multiple users to access programs simultaneously and share the data produced and used by the application. The advantages of software sharing are many. The most important are cost reduction, legality of sharing the product, sharing data, and up-to-date upgrades.

The geographical area covered by the network determines whether the network is called a wide area network (WAN) or a local area network (LAN). Wide area networks link systems that are too far apart to be included in a small in-house network. They can be in the same city or in different countries. Local area networks connect devices within a small local area, usually within a building or adjacent buildings.

Network evolution has been in the direction of standardized networking and internetworking technology. One of the most important standards-making bodies is the International Organization for Standardization (ISO), which makes technical recommendations about data communication interfaces. The OSI Reference Model, created by the ISO, is known as a layered protocol, specifying seven layers of interface, where each layer has a specific set of functions to perform.

The configurations used to describe networks are sometimes called network topology. Networks can take on many different logical and physical configurations. However, regardless of how they are implemented, networks can be placed into one of four general categories. The most common network topologies are ring, bus, star, and hybrid.

One commonly used technique that networks use to transmit data to users' workstations is called packet switching. Packet switching is a store-and-forward data transmission technique in which messages are split into small segments called packets. Each packet is switched and transmitted through the network, independently of other packets belonging to the same transaction or other transactions. The packets belonging to different messages travel through the same communication channel. The communicating terminals or workstations are connected via a virtual circuit.

As networks proliferate in the workplace, homogeneous networks are no longer the rule, but rather the exception. Heterogeneous or hybrid networks are prevalent. They include several network segments that may differ in topology, protocol, or operating system. The ability to connect two heterogeneous networks rests with two requirements. First, the topologies must be capable of being interconnected. Second, there must be a way to transfer information between dissimilar systems of communication (protocols). This means that at some point a common protocol must be employed. There are several ways to accomplish this. Most use high level protocols for moving data and employ tools for internetworking such as bridges, routers, brouters, and gateways.

Questions

1. Why should individual microcomputers be connected into a network within an organization?
2. What is a local area network?
3. What is a wide area network?
4. What are the most common network topologies?
5. Describe the bus network topology.
6. What is a gateway?
7. What is a bridge?
8. What is a router?
9. What is packetizing?
10. Describe the operation of a PDN.
11. What is a hybrid network?
12. What tools are available to manage a hybrid network?
13. What is a communication protocol?
14. What is the first consideration in designing a hybrid network?
15. What is OSI?
16. What are the different layers of OSI?

Project

This project will familiarize the student with the software techniques required to transfer files and establish a two-way serial communication between computers using different operating systems but the same communication protocol. It is important that the student understand the individual concepts of basic file transfer and communication between two microcomputers using a direct serial or a modem connection. If two different computers are not available, then the project can easily be modified to accommodate two computers of the same type. In this case the student should be instructed that the process for dissimilar systems is the same and the process of file transfer among different systems will be simulated.

Communication between a Macintosh and an MS-DOS-Based PC through the Serial Port

Several methods allow you to connect a Macintosh and an MS-DOS-based PC or compatible through the serial port to provide file transfer capabilities. One of these methods is to purchase a commercial product specifically designed for this purpose, such as Maclink PC, and follow the instructions in the manual to perform file transfers. This package comes with all the cables and software required to perform the connection.

Another method is to use your existing communication software to perform the connection and the transfer. In addition, you will need to make a cable to physically connect the two machines. In this section we will take the second approach.

The cable can be constructed in two phases. The first step is to purchase a Mac-to-modem cable from your local computer store. This is done because of the small serial interface on the Macintosh side. The cable costs approximately $5.00, making this a simpler approach than working with the small Mac interface.

The serial cable by itself will not work (see projects in chapter 2). A null modem will be required to complete the circuit. To build a null modem refer to chapter 2 projects. Connect the serial cable and the null modem together and then connect one end of the serial cable to the Mac and the free end of the null modem to the PC (see Fig. 9-13).

Fig. 9-13. Connecting a Macintosh and an IBM PC.

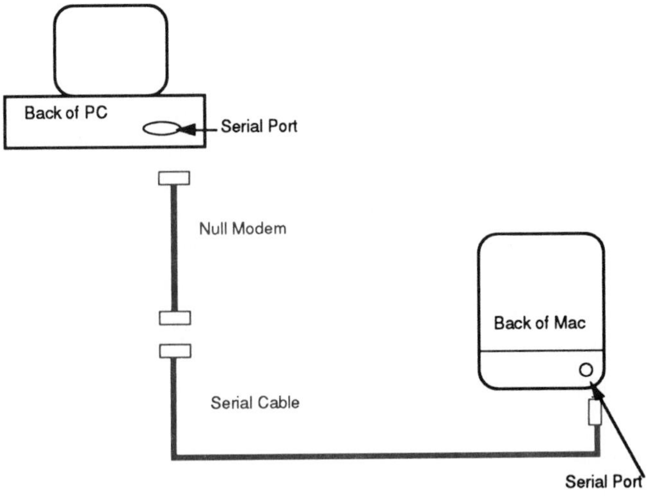

Back of PC

Serial Port

Null Modem

Back of Mac

Serial Cable

Serial Port

Now you are ready to establish the connection using whatever communication software is available. For this example, use the communication tool in Microsoft Works for the Macintosh and Microsoft Works for the MS-DOS-based PC. We have chosen Works on the Mac and the MS-DOS-based PC due to their popularity and availability. If your system does not have these two software products, use any type of communication software for both systems. The screens will look different depending on your communication software, but the procedures are basically the same.

Before the communications link can be established, both systems must have the same communications settings. Fig. 9-14 shows the communication settings that will be used for this project.

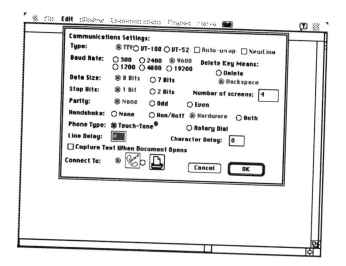

Fig. 9-14. Communication settings.

To set the right parameters on the Macintosh you will need to perform the following general steps:

1. Launch the Microsoft Works program (or your communication software).
2. Select New and choose the communications tool.
3. You will see a screen like the one shown in Fig. 9-15.
4. Click on the Communications menu and select Settings.

Fig. 9-15. Main terminal screen.

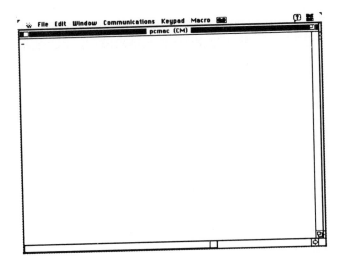

5. You should have a screen similar to the one shown in Fig. 9-14. At this point make sure that your screen has the same settings as those found in Fig. 9-14, regardless of your communication program.

On the IBM side you will need to perform the following steps:

1. Run the Works program or your communication application.

2. Select Create New File and then choose New Communications from the opening menu and press the ENTER key.

3. You should now have a screen like the one shown in Fig. 9-16. From the Option menu, select the communication settings..

4. Type 9600 for the Baud rate, and set the other parameters the same as those in Fig. 9-14. Now you are ready to establish communications.

5. Select the Options pull-down menu and choose Terminal. Here move the cursor to Local echo and press the ENTER key to place a check mark.

6. On the IBM PC side select the Connect pull-down menu and choose Connect.

7. Type the following on the MS-DOS-based PC side: "Now is the time for all good men to come to the aid of their country."

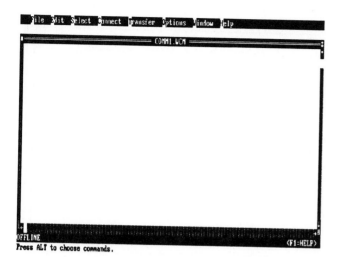

Fig. 9-16. Communication screen for the IBM PC.

You should see the same text you typed on the MS-DOS-based PC side displayed on the Macintosh side as you type. This is a successful connection.

Now we will transfer a file from the PC to the Macintosh. The file to be transferred can be of any type you desire. For this exercise we will transfer the file created by typing the following text using the word processing tool in Works for the PC and then save it as Letter.wps.

```
To whom it may concern,

This is a sample data file to test the communication
capabilities of the Works program. Files can be
transferred with any type of communications program
that supports uploading and downloading of text and
binary files.

We are copying the same paragraph again below this one.

This is a sample data file to test the communication
capabilities of the Works program. Files can be
transferred with any type of communications program
that supports uploading and downloading of text and
binary files.
```

To transfer this file from the PC to the Mac, follow these instructions:

1. Click on the Communications pull-down menu on the Mac and select Receive File. You should get a screen like Fig. 9-17. Make sure that you select Xmodem.

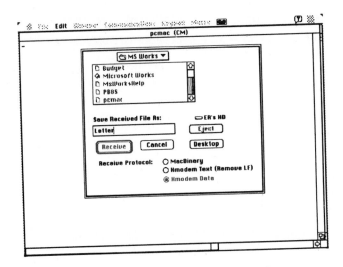

Fig. 9-17. Data receiving dialog box.

2. Type the name of the file that is going to receive the transferred data. Type Letter for the name of the file and press the ENTER key.

3. On the MS-DOS-based PC side select the Transfer pull-down menu and choose Send File.

4. Type the name of the file to be sent. In this case it is Letter.wps. Then press the ENTER key.

5. The Mac screen will look like Fig. 9-18 and will indicate the number of characters received after transmission is completed. The MS-DOS-based PC side will transmit and the Mac will receive the transmission, storing the data in a file labeled Letter.

Fig. 9-18. Transmission receiving screen for the Macintosh.

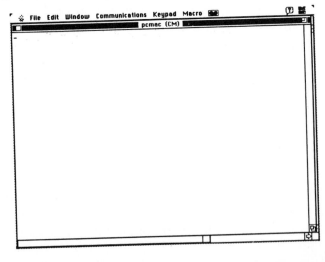

After the transmission is completed, the Mac will sound a short beep to indicate the end of transmission and you will have a file called Letter in the Works folder on the Mac. The same process can be repeated in reverse order to transfer files from the Mac to the PC.

To transfer files using a modem, the process is virtually the same, except that a modem connection must be made. The serial cable developed in chapter 3 can be used to connect the modem to the computers. One of the computers will be the host and its modem will be set to answer mode. This can be done by activating a switch on the modem. The software on the host will be indicated to receive and the sender will transmit using the procedure outlined above. Even though we used a Mac and an MS-DOS-based PC in the example above, the same procedure can be used to connect any types of microcomputers.

Local Area Networks

Objectives

After completing this chapter you will:

1. Understand the importance of a local area network.
2. Understand the function of a local area network.
3. Obtain a general view of the types of applications running on a local area network.
4. Understand the hardware and software components of a local area network.
5. Understand the different topologies of local area networks.
6. Understand the standards that guide the design of local area networks and their protocols.

Key Words

Bus Topology	CAD
CSMA/CD	File Server
Local Area Network	Novell
Office Automation	Ring Topology
Star Topology	Wide Area Network
Workstation	

Introduction

The rapid acceptance of local area networks has made networking a common event in the workplace, especially in education. The local area network allows individuals to share resources and offset some of the high costs of automating processes. An individual at any computer on a local area network can create a document and send it to another computer on the network for editing or printing purposes. The access provided by local area networks is controlled and, to some extent, secure.

These concepts, as well as some of the inner workings of the hardware that make up the local area network, are explored in this chapter. Additionally, the most commonly used protocols and the standards set up by the IEEE are defined, along with their impact on local area network design.

Local Area Networks

Definition

One of the largest growth segments of the communication industry since the early 1980s is local area network (LAN) technology. This growth has resulted in lower prices for the hardware and software required to implement a local area network. The lower prices of hardware components have translated into less expensive microcomputers, which have replaced terminals as the main hardware interface to the user. In addition, the increase in power of the processors that control the microcomputer has made the microcomputer a powerful work-horse, that in many instances has replaced the minicomputer. That is the reason most LAN workstations today are microcomputers. It is not intended to say that all LANs are composed of microcomputers, for many LANs contain a mixture of microcomputers, minicomputers, and mainframes. However, the microcomputer is well suited to be an active participant in local area networks. If we compare only numbers, the majority of the computing devices in local area networks are microcomputers.

Local area networks interconnect devices that are confined to a small geographical area. The actual distance that a LAN spans depends on specific implementations. A LAN covers a clearly defined local area such as an office suite, a building, or a group of buildings. To better understand LANs, it is important to know their uses.

Benefits

Most LANs are implemented to transfer data among users in the network and to share resources among users. A LAN implementation can provide high-speed data-transfer capability to all users without the need of having a system operator to facilitate the transmission process. Even when connecting a LAN to a wider area network that covers thousands of miles, data transfer between users of the network is time effective and in most cases problem-free.

Another reason for implementing a LAN is to share hardware and software resources among users of the network. Even though the price of microcomputers and their peripherals has dropped in recent years, it is still expensive to provide every user with a hard disk, printers, CD drives, scanners, plotters, and many of the other devices that are common in today's personal computers. Although the cost of some of these items is relatively inexpensive, it is not cost effective to purchase ten laser printers for ten workers in an office where the distance between workers is small, because the printers will be idle for large periods of times. Since not all workers will be printing at the same time and all the time, it is more practical to implement a local area network so all users can share one or two printers (see Fig. 10-1).

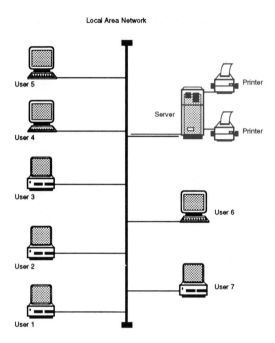

Local Area Network

Fig. 10-1. Users sharing printers over a network.

LANs also allow users to share software and the data produced by the software. Software for which a site license has been obtained can be placed on a shared hard disk drive. The software can then be downloaded to the individual workstation, provided that license agreements are observed. This type of sharing is efficient and has the additional benefit of facilitating backups of network-installed software and the installation of software upgrades as they become available.

In addition to the benefits outlined above, local area networks encourage security of data and software from physical disasters as well as computer viruses. Since all the workstations on the LAN are connected to each other and in most cases the bulk of the data and software resides on a file server, it is easier to perform frequent and complete backups of all important data and programs. Additionally, modern network monitoring software has sophisticated virus detection mechanisms that help in preventing the invasion of computer viruses into the workstations and servers.

Some of the more compelling reasons for installing a LAN are:
1. Sharing of software
2. Sharing of data
3. Sharing system resources
4. Security and backups
5. Easier maintenance and upgrades

Sharing Software

Imagine an office that has 20 employees, all using personal computers with word processing, spreadsheet, and database software. If each user is to have individual copies of software, there must be a legally purchased copy of each package for each user.

Another solution is to purchase network versions of all software products and install a single copy of each on a local area network connecting all users. Purchasing a network version of a software product is, in many situations, less expensive than buying individual copies for each user.

Additionally, there isn't the need to keep track of 20 copies of the same software product. Only one copy needs to be administered.

Sharing Data

With network copies of software programs, the data generated by one user can be used by others in a "transparent" mode. That is, all users can work with the same data file as if it were their own. With individual copies of software, data generated on one workstation must be physically moved from one machine to another. Data for sales, inventory, and other departments must be moved often to keep it current, requiring additional processing and duplication of files.

Sharing System Resources

Network versions of software also save on hard disk space. Instead of using space on multiple users' hard disks, the software can be placed on the network server's hard disk. This allows the software and data to be shared by everyone on a local area network.

Individual copies of software on multiple workstations are difficult to safeguard from unauthorized individuals. It is relatively easy to go to a person's desk and damage or change data files.

Using the security resources of a network, software can be safeguarded by installing passwords, trustee rights, and file attributes. This enhances the safety of data files and programs in a manner that is almost impossible with individual software.

With multiple users working with stand-alone programs, backing up software becomes a difficult task. Users are not always prompt when it comes to backing up important software and data. Using the network resources, software and data can be backed up from a single location with a minimal amount of effort. This also enhances security since the latest copy of a file is assured when using the latter method.

Easy Maintenance and Upgrades

In many situations, users of a particular package do not have the latest updates or modifications. Sometimes this is due to a lack of time to install software upgrades, and other times there is a lack of funding to purchase the latest release of a product.

If network software is used, only one upgrade copy of the software needs to be installed and/or modified to get the latest features. Also, in large corporations with many users, the cost of upgrading a network version of a software product can be substantially less than purchasing individual copies of the same program.

Applications

Not only are local area networks a good mechanism for sharing hardware and enforcing security, but they promote the sharing of application programs that, in many cases, take advantage of the capabilities of the LAN to enhance the flexibility and usefulness of the programs. There are many of these LAN applications. Some of the more common types of applications are office automation, factory automation, education, computer-aided design, and computer-aided manufacturing.

Office Automation

Microcomputers have provided office workers the ability to automate their processing needs. The local processing power of the microcomputer, coupled with software such as electronic mail, calendar automation, shared databases, and document exchange, have changed the way offices conduct business. Offices connected by a local area network can now exchange documents electronically, schedule meetings electronically by finding the best hours that workers can meet, and share high-quality output devices such as laser printers at a fraction of the cost of stand-alone systems.

A LAN can provide office workers with the following capabilities:

1. Memo and document distribution to recipients using electronic mail.

2. Automatic meeting scheduling with electronic calendars. The scheduler can automatically find commonly available times and schedule the participants.

3. Downloading of software from a file server at speeds comparable to that of local hard disks.

4. Multiple user access to printers, plotters, facsimile machines, CD drives, and scanners.

5. Multiple user access to documents for editing purposes and for sharing among other users.

6. Centralized backup of all documents by the network administrator. This ensures workers that, in case of a disaster, their work and files are recoverable and safe.

7. Enhanced security of files and data by allowing the LAN to safeguard files residing on the file server.

8. Extracting data from a centralized database and manipulating the data locally on a microcomputer.

9. Composing parts of a document or project and submitting them to a centralized location for integration with other parts of the document produced by other workers on the network.

10. Entering transactions to be processed on other LANs.

11. Sending data from the LAN to other users on a WAN or other LANs.

Education

Educational institutions have found LANs to be an invaluable tool in the education process. Colleges and universities use LANs to provide students access to a centralized server from which they can communicate with faculty or other students through electronic mail, access software required for class assignments, and place assignments on a centralized disk for faculty retrieval and review.

Research faculty and students have access through LANs to the local library and through gateways to electronic libraries throughout the world. In addition, the academic community has access to information located in large geographical areas through wide area networks such as Bitnet.

CAD

Computer-aided design (CAD) software allows users to have a workstation to create drawings, architectural blueprints, and electronic maps without the need of pencil and paper. A LAN used to connect CAD stations allows designers to place notes and instructions to drafters on a centralized server. Each drafter can retrieve the information, ask for further clarification, and complete a portion of the drawing. Then the drawing can be sent to other workers on the LAN for completion and then to a plotter. In most cases, many engineers work on portions of a single project collectively. A LAN enables them to quickly exchange and share information in order to complete the project. CAD systems are used extensively by car manufacturers, aerospace workers, and computer corporations.

CAM

Computer-aided manufacturing (CAM) systems are used to control assembly lines, manufacturing plants, and machinery. A LAN in a computer-aided manufacturing environment allows the automatic control of scheduling, inventory, and ordering systems. Errors that are found by the individual system in the manufacturing process can be transmitted by the LAN to a centralized location for analysis and correction. Instructions can then be transmitted through the LAN to correct the problem and continue the manufacturing process.

All of the above application categories demonstrate the extensive and various uses of local area networks. However, it is important to understand that when we talk about LAN applications, there are three categories that these application programs fall into. Most software that needs to be used in a LAN can be divided into the categories of network incompatible, network compatible, and network aware.

Network incompatible software cannot be used at all on a normal LAN while it is stored on a file server. Usually the problem involves the program's use of low level operations to control the disk drive or access its own files. These low level operations access the hardware of the computer directly, rather than using the operating system function calls that network operating systems normally employ to access the resources managed by the file server.

Other problems can arise when the program is simply incompatible with the resident network driver programs (programs that allow the computer hardware and operating system to take advantage of network functions), although this situation is rare. In this case the program cannot be run on a computer that is attached to the network. When the software can be run with the network drivers loaded in main memory, but not on the network, it is necessary to install it on the workstation's hard disk. This makes the program an individual software application on the user's workstation and not a networked application.

Network compatible software includes all programs that can be run on the network, even though they might not be network-specific versions. Many programs have no install options that indicate which logical hard disk they are running on. These programs can simply be copied to a network directory. Others, such as older versions of WordStar, can be installed on any of the network server's hard drives using the appropriate install procedures. This is often the easiest type of program for the network supervisor to install. Still others may be programmed to always look on a certain disk drive for their files, for instance on drive C. In this case, the network operating system will typically have some types of commands or functions that can be used to direct drive letter C of the workstation to the appropriate network directory or location where the files to be executed are located. The programs in this category must be handled very carefully in regard to federal copyright laws. Under almost all license agreements accompanying the software, one copy of the software must be owned for each user accessing the program.

Network aware programs have been written to detect and sometimes take advantage of a network. Many programs released in the last few years are designed specifically to detect that they are running on a network and to allow only one user to access them. This prevents users from illegally using more copies of the software than they own. Usually, special multiuser versions of such programs are available that allow five, ten, or some other number of users to access the software simultaneously. The multiuser versions are always more expensive than single-user versions, of course. But they are less expensive than an equal number of single-user copies. Other programs are written to take advantage of the network environment. These programs offer electronic mail, quick messages, easy use of network printers, or network use of a common database.

As can be seen from this discussion, many applications can run on a network. However, it is important to be aware of the different types of programs available in the market and how they can interact with the network. Many of the newer applications in the market are network compatible products. Additionally, companies that produced individual applications for single-user computers also have multiuser and network compatible versions of their programs.

LAN Characteristics

Today's local area networks have a number of characteristics that are common among most of the topologies that form their configurations. When a LAN is purchased, the following characteristics should be considered. LANs can provide users with:

1. Flexibility
2. Speed
3. Reliability
4. Hardware and software sharing
5. Transparent interface
6. Adaptability
7. Access to other LANs and WANs

8. Security
9. Centralized management
10. Private ownership of the LAN

Flexibility

Many different hardware devices such as plotters, printers, and computers can be attached to a local area network. A station or node on a local area network can be a terminal, a microcomputer, a printer, a facsimile machine, or a minicomputer. In addition, individual local area networks can be connected to form a bigger data communication system than the individual LANs by themselves. In most cases, adding or removing one of these devices to or from the LAN is simply a matter of attaching or removing a cable from the device to the transmission medium. Afterwards, software takes care of the rest of the functions required to make the new device available to the system or to remove it from its "inventory."

In addition to the network operating system, which is required, other types of software applications can also reside on file servers on the LAN. In an automated office, as one person is using electronic mail, another can be accessing a database, while another may be manipulating data in a spreadsheet and sending output to a shared laser printer.

Also, local area networks can handle applications with different processing and data transfer capabilities. As an example, some users may be transferring text files through the network at the same time other users are transmitting high-resolution images from a CAD system. This flexibility is inherent on most types of LANs and is one of the reasons for their success.

Speed

LANs can have high-speed data transfer. This speed is required because of the large number of bytes that must be downloaded when a workstation requests a software application. A good rule of thumb is to have a LAN that downloads files at a speed comparable to the transfer rate from a hard disk to the memory of a microcomputer.

Speeds of local area networks range from a few hundred thousand bits per second for the inexpensive, parallel port-based, local area networks to several million bits per second. The cost and complexity of the local area network tends to increase according to the speed of transmission and the volume of data that it can handle.

Reliability

A LAN must work continuously and consistently. For a LAN to be considered reliable, all stations must have access to the network according to the privileges established by the network administrator. A single station shouldn't monopolize the capacity of the LAN, since that would inhibit access by other users and increase the response time experienced by network users.

Also, local area networks should be able to recover from a system failure without losing jobs or files located on the server. If a station malfunctions, the rest of the network should continue operating without problems.

Hardware and Software Sharing

Sometimes there is a specialized device called a server to facilitate sharing. A server is a computer on the LAN that can be accessed by all users of the network. The server contains a resource that it "serves" to the LAN users. The most common type of server is the file server. Using the office automation example, imagine that there is a node located in one of the offices where a file server resides. The file server can contain software applications and data files, and it may have printers, plotters, and other devices attached to it. Other users on the network access the application software and data files stored on the file server. When a user's workstation requests a file, the server "serves" the file to the user's workstation (also called the client).

Servers can provide users other services besides files or programs. Some servers, in addition to being file servers, are also printer servers. These servers have printers, plotters, or some other output device attached to them that can be used by any users on the LAN to send a document for output. In many cases, servers are used as printer servers only, leaving other computers to perform the tasks of file servers. When a document from a user needs to be printed on one of the printers attached to the file server, the document is printed from the user's workstation in much the same manner as if the printer were attached locally. The document reaches the file server and it is transformed into a file that is then "served" to the printer.

Additionally, when software upgrades become available, the upgrades can be placed on the server. When a user requests the software, the user automatically receives the latest release of the product. In this manner, file servers become repositories for software applications.

The software residing on the server consists of software products with a site license for a predetermined number of users. For example, a company may decide that, of their 200 employees, only 50 will be using a word processor at any given time. Therefore, instead of buying 200 copies of the same program, it can purchase one copy with a site license for 50 simultaneous users. The one copy of the software is placed on the file server and downloaded to a user workstation whenever it is requested. This avoids the need to pass diskettes or to keep large inventories of application software and hardware.

Transparent Interface

Having a transparent interface implies that network access for users should be no more complicated than accessing the same facilities using a different interface. A user should not be expected to learn a series of complicated commands to print a file. Instead, the system should use the same commands or similar commands to the ones that he or she used when the workstation was not attached to the LAN. For example, if an application is invoked from a local hard disk by typing its name and then pressing the ENTER key, then the same procedure should work when requesting the application from a file server.

Adaptability

A well-designed LAN has the ability to accommodate a variety of hardware and can be reconfigured easily. If a new device such as a plotter or a facsimile machine needs to be added to the network, it should be done without disruption to the users. Additionally, if a node needs to be removed, added, or moved to another location, the network should allow any of these changes without affecting existing users. A LAN should also be capable of expansion without regard to the number of users. That is, the number of users should not inhibit the need for expanding the services of the LAN.

Access to Other LANs and WANs

In many situations a LAN is just a small component of a much larger network distributed through the corporation facilities. A large corporation may have LANs of different topologies and use different protocols, including packet switching and wide area networks. A LAN should allow user access to the global facilities in the corporation by connecting the local area network to the wide area network facilities using some type of gateway. This connection should also be transparent to the user.

Security

Connectivity and flexibility of a local area network should not be accomplished at the expense of security. If data and user communication are allowed to be accidentally or intentionally disrupted, then the LAN loses its integrity.

The LAN should have provisions for ID and password security mechanisms. File security should be enforced with the use of read, read-write, execute, and delete attributes. These attributes act on files and directories to prevent the unauthorized copying, deletion, or modification of data. Many operating systems, such as UNIX, already have these types of attributes as part of their security mechanisms. LANs also implement them, and in many cases, take security a few levels higher than the methods employed by the operating system.

Additionally, virus detection mechanisms should always be in place. As users are added to the network and dial-in lines are made available, the potential for the introduction of a computer virus into the network increases. In many cases, the viruses act on the individual workstations and leave the servers alone, mainly because of the protection mechanisms available to the server through the network. However, other viruses replicate themselves through the network, creating an overload of traffic and shutting down practical implementation of the network.

Security should also be extended to hardware devices attached to the network. The LAN should be able to restrict access to hardware devices to only those users that have proper authorization. This can be accomplished through the use of software, mostly the network operating system, and hardware such as call-back units.

Centralized Management

Most LAN installations are intended to reduce costs and promote ease of use. A LAN should minimize operator intervention and contain several management tools that provide a synopsis of the operation of the network to the network operator. Additionally, the network operator should be able to perform backups of the entire system from a centralized station.

The network operating system has management utilities that enable the local area network operator to obtain a synopsis, at any given time, of the performance of the network and of traffic that flows through it. However, in this case, many LAN administrators find that such monitoring and management utilities are not enough to get a complete "picture" of the network and where some of the problems may be located. For this purpose, many third party vendors offer management and monitoring equipment and software that enhance the software available with the LAN.

Private Ownership

The hardware, software, and data carrying medium are normally owned by the corporation or institution that purchased the LAN. This is in contrast to wide area networks in which the hardware is owned by the corporation but the medium belongs to a public carrier. All repairs, maintenance, and new connections are the responsibility of the owner of the LAN.

In conclusion, the above are characteristics of local area networks that are found in successful installations. Although these may not be all of them, they represent the bulk of the characteristics of what industry perceives as a "good LAN." They can also serve as a comparison list when deciding on the type and configuration of the local area network that needs to be installed at a particular location. However, to obtain a better idea of the involvement required to install a local area network, its components must be understood.

LAN Components

There are two major items that must be considered when planning or installing a LAN: the network hardware components and the network software. There are three major categories of devices that make up the hardware components of a local area network (see Fig. 10-2). These are the server, the LAN communication system, and the workstations.

Fig. 10-2. LAN hardware components.

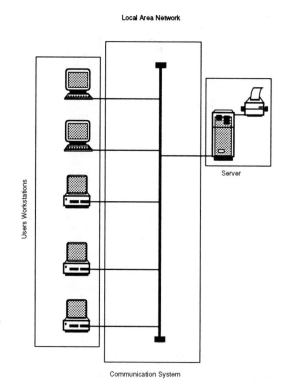

Servers

As stated before, servers are computers on the network that are accessible to network users. They contain resources that they "serve" to users who request the services. The most common type of server is a file server. Most LANs have at least one file server, and they often have multiple file servers. The file server contains software applications and data files that are provided to users upon request. For example, if a user needs a spreadsheet, a request for a specific spreadsheet package is sent to the file server. The server finds the requested application on its disk and downloads a copy of it to the requesting workstation. As far as the user is concerned, the spreadsheet behaves as if it were stored on a local disk.

The file server is simply a computer with one or more large-capacity hard disk drives. Normally it is composed of a minicomputer or a fast microcomputer. This is done since many users will be accessing the server at the same time, requiring a high performance machine with fast hard disks.

If a LAN relies on the server for all of its functions, then this technique is called a dedicated server approach. Other LANs do not require a distinction between a user workstation and the file server. This approach is called a peer-to-peer network. In a peer-to-peer network any microcomputer can function as the file server and user at the same time (sometimes called a nondedicated server).

File servers are not the only type of server that can be present on a network. Any computer that has a sharable resource is considered a server. For example, if users of a LAN need to have access to modems, it is possible to have a computer that contains several modems for user access. This is called a modem server. A gateway is also a type of server, a gateway server. Also, a network can have compact disk (CD) servers. These consist of an array (2 to 14) of CD drives attached to a microcomputer. Users can then access any of the CD disks on the server from their workstations.

As mentioned above, file servers can be nondedicated or dedicated. If a file server is dedicated, it can be used only as a file server and not as a workstation. This is typical when a LAN has many users. For small local area networks, a file server may function in a nondedicated fashion as a file server and as a user workstation.

Choosing Servers

If the network consists of only one server, the choice of where to install shared software is easy. However, if multiple servers are available, a decision must be made as to which server will hold the shared software.

There are several possibilities for multiple server networks. Assume that a network consists of two servers. One possibility is to purchase two copies of the software and install one on each server. Another possibility is to purchase a third server and place all shared software on it. A third option is to install the software on one of the servers and let users of the other servers attach themselves to that one. (see Fig. 10-3).

Fig. 10-3. Possible server configuration.

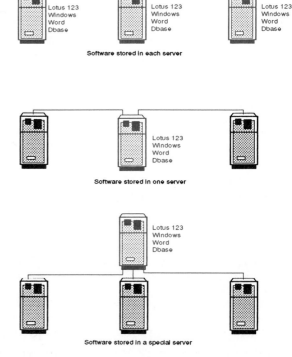

Each of these approaches has its pros and cons. If a copy is purchased for each server, the expense of the extra copy may be more than having a network version of the software and a license for all possible users. Additionally, there is the need to keep security and maintenance of the same software product on multiple servers.

Placing all shared software on a single server may prove to be too much for a computer acting as the server. Too many users can slow the response time of the server to unacceptable levels. In addition, hard disk space is quickly consumed by the large amount of software in the server, adding to the degradation of the response time of the system.

Acquiring a third server to place all shared software on and putting the data on the others is probably the most elegant solution. However, in many situations this is not economically feasible.

A final possibility is to spread all shared software among the available servers. This allows the purchase of a single network version of a software product, along with a license for the number of users involved. This method also allows the load created by the shared software to be spread evenly among all available servers (see Fig. 10-4).

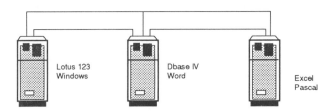

Lotus 123
Windows

Dbase IV
Word

Excel
Pascal

Fig. 10-4. Distributing software among servers is an efficient way to maximize the capability of the hardware.

Workstations

The typical LAN workstation is a microcomputer. For the remainder of this book it is assumed that file servers and workstations consist of some type of microcomputer. Terminals can also be used to communicate on a LAN, but the cost of a personal computer is usually low enough to be justifiable, since a complete computer is obtained.

Once the microcomputer is connected to a LAN, it is used in similar fashion to a microcomputer in stand-alone mode. The LAN just replaces the locations from which files are retrieved. Some LANs, such as those that use Novell NetWare, can have workstations from different vendors, such as IBM and Apple. Users of NetWare can attach an IBM PC or clone and a Macintosh, and use their machines the same way they used them in their stand-alone configuration.

The responsibility of the PC workstation is to execute the application served by the LAN file server. On most LANs the workstation typically does the processing. On distributed LAN networks, the file server and the workstation can share the processing duties. This scenario is typically found on LANs dedicated to database functions.

After an application is served to the PC workstation, the application begins execution. During the execution of the program, the user may want to store a file or print a file. At this point the user has two options. To save a copy of the file, the user can save it on a hard disk or floppy disk local to the workstation that he or she is using. The other option is to save it on the file server's hard disk. In the latter case, the file could be made available to all other users on the LAN, or kept for private use by using file security attributes. If the user decides to print the file, it can be sent to a printer attached to the server, or printed locally if the workstation has a printer attached to it.

All workstations and the server must be connected through some type of transmission medium. We call this the local area network communication system, and, as explained in previous chapters, it can consist of twisted pair wire, coaxial cable, optical fiber, and other types of communication media.

The LAN Communication System

When two or more computers are connected on a network, a special cable and a network interface board or card (NIC) are required in each computer and server. The cable is used to connect the network interface board to the LAN transmission medium. Most microcomputers are not equipped with an interface port that can be connected to a second microcomputer for networking purposes (except the Macintosh computer that has a built-in AppleTalk port). Although some networks are implemented through the parallel port or the serial port of personal computers, these networks operate at very low speeds making them unusable for most companies or situations where large volumes of data need to be transmitted. As a result, a network interface card (NIC) (see Fig. 10-5) or network adapter must be installed in the microcomputer. There are many different types and brands of NICs, but each performs the same function. It allows the microcomputer to be connected to a cabling system and transmits data between computers attached to the data transmission media at high speeds.

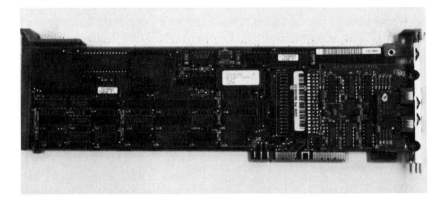

Fig. 10-5. Network interface card.

The speed of transmission will depend on the type of medium, the capabilities of the NIC, and the computer that the NIC is attached to. Typical speed ranges for LANs are from 1 to 16 megabits per second and a few are even higher. However, since the workstations on the LAN are connected by a cable, the geographic range the LAN can cover is limited to buildings or campuses where the cable can be laid.

Data is transmitted from a workstation to a file server and vice versa by packetizing it. When a file is requested from the file server, the NIC translates this file into data packets. Normally, the data packets are of fixed size, although they could be different sizes. Most adapters use packets of 500 to 2,000 bytes. The file server's NIC places the data packets on the network data transmission medium, where they are transmitted to the workstation NIC. Here the data packets are assembled back into the original data file and given to the workstation.

Each data packet contains the address of the workstation on the network that is to receive the data packet (see Fig. 10-6). The address of each node in the LAN is provided by the NIC. This

Error check 16 bits	Data up to 2000 bits	Address control

Fig. 10-6. A data packet.

address can be set with switches on the NIC when it is installed, although some NICs already have the address set at the factory before they are shipped to a customer.

The NIC address uses a combination of 8 bits, and therefore can have a value of from 1 to 256. This limits the number of users on the LAN to 256. Large LANs can be created by joining two or more LANs into a single network using one of the network interconnecting devices explained in previous chapters. Some new network adapters, such as 16 bit cards, have larger addresses by using more bytes to form the address. However, many LANs still use the system outlined above.

LAN Software

The processes that take place on the hardware devices of a LAN must be controlled by software. The software is the network operating system. One of the most widely used network operating systems is NetWare by Novell, Inc.

The network operating system controls the operation of the file server, and it makes the network resources accessible and easy to use. It manages server security and provides the network administrators with the tools to control user access to the network and to manage the file structure of the network disks.

The network operating system controls which files a user can access, as well as how the user accesses the files. For example, a user may have access to a word processor file, but it can only be read and not modified. At the same time, another user may have access to the same file and be able to modify it.

In most cases, the network operating system is an extension of the PC workstation operating system. The same commands used to retrieve, store, and print files on the microcomputer are used to perform these functions on the network. The network operating system also provides extensions to the PC operating system to do some functions more efficiently.

Choosing a Directory for Shared Software

In addition to choosing the server where the shared software is to reside, the directory structure of this server must also be decided. There are several possibilities. One is to place all shared programs under the main or root directory. The other possible solution is to create a directory under the root directory and name this subdirectory SHARESOF, PROGRAMS, or something that indicates its purpose (see Fig. 10-7 for two such subdirectories).

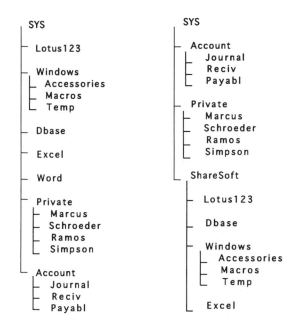

Fig. 10-7. Possible network subdirectories where applications can reside.

The first solution may not be the best approach. One problem is that the root directory may become cluttered as new programs are added to the server. This makes the task of maintenance and backup more difficult, since each shared program name must be identified during backups.

The second method is the better one. During backup procedures the entire shared software subdirectory can be backed up with a single command. Additionally, establishing security rights over one subdirectory is easier than over multiple subdirectories.

A more complex task is when some software is supposed to be "public domain" and other software is to be secured. The words "public domain" mean that all programs or data in the subdirectory are available to all users for downloading to their workstation, and there are no restrictions imposed on how they use it. Even though such software is shared, it should not share a parent directory with programs and data that require large measures of security.

LAN Configurations

Network topologies were introduced in chapter 4. Three of these topologies--the bus, ring, and star--are used extensively in LAN implementations. However, regardless of the topology used in the physical layout of the LAN, most LANs can be divided into baseband and broadband networks.

Baseband vs Broadband

Baseband local area networks are capable of carrying only one signal at any given time. The signal is the data that is carried by the media utilized to connect the different nodes in the network. Since there is only one signal traveling through the transmission medium, the entire bandwidth of this medium is used to move the digital bit that is part of the message from one node to another in the LAN.

Broadband networks don't suffer from the limitations of baseband networks. Broadband networks use frequency multiplexing techniques to send data through the transmission medium. The multiplexing techniques allow the network to divide the frequencies available in the cabling medium in order to create different paths or channels that can be used to deliver the data to the nodes. This allows the network to support many different information paths using the same cabling system.

Although broadband networks provide more capacity and flexibility to organizations, the typical local area network tends to be baseband. The reasons for such decisions are several, but cost, complexity, and the potential for failure are the most commonly cited.

Broadband networks, because of their larger size and the different signals they carry, are more complex to operate and maintain than baseband networks. This complexity also increases their cost. Additionally, assume that data and video signals travel through the same LAN. If the LAN fails, then not only are the data signals lost, but also the video signals. This increases the impact of a failure on the entire organization.

Broadband and baseband are terms use to classify the networks. However, within these two configurations, the physical layout of the network is also used to distinguish one system from another.

This physical layout was described in previous chapters when the general network was considered. But, the same physical layout or topology can be applied to local area networks.

Topologies

Bus Topology

As mentioned in previous chapters, in bus topology the micro-computer workstations are connected to a single cable that runs the entire length of the network. Data travels through the cable, also called a bus, directly from the sending node to the destination node.

The bus topology is the most widely used of all LAN configurations. The reason for its success is the early popularity of protocols, such as Ethernet, that used this configuration.

Ring Topology

A ring configuration uses a token passing protocol (see next section). It is the second most popular type of configuration. The ring topology connects all nodes with one continuous loop. Data travels in only one direction within the ring, making a complete circle through the loop.

Star Topology

The third major topology is the star. In a star configuration, each node is connected to a central server. Data flows back and forth between the central server and the nodes in the network.

LAN Protocols

Local area networks have a variety of configurations. However, regardless of the LAN configuration, every message transmitted contains within it the address of the destination node. In addition, each node in the network looks for its address in each message. If the address is present, the station picks up the message. Otherwise the message is allowed to circulate through the transmission medium. But, for this process to take place, the different hardware in the network must communicate under the control of some type of software.

The software that allows the hardware that makes up the network to communicate is called the protocol. The protocol is necessary so that all stations on the system can communicate with each other, whether they are from the same vendor or not. The protocol consists of the set of rules by which two machines talk to each other. It must be present, along with the LAN hardware and the network operating system. Some communication protocols were discussed in previous chapters.

Other common protocols used in LANs are the logical link control (LLC) protocol established by the Institute of Electronic Engineers (IEEE) 802 Standards Committee, the carrier sense multiple access/collision detection (CSMA/CD) protocol, and the token passing protocol.

LLC Protocol

The most important aspect of LAN protocols is the logical link control or LLC. This is a data link protocol that is bit oriented. An LLC's frame, also called a protocol data unit, contains the format shown in Fig. 10-8. The destination address identifies the workstation to which the information field is delivered, and the source address identifies the workstation that sent the message. The control field has commands, responses, and number sequences that control the data link. The information field is composed of any combination of bytes.

Fig. 10-8. Format of LLC packet.

Header (size is variable)	Destination Address (8 bits)	Source Address (8 bits)	Control Field (8 or 16 bits)	Data (8 x n bits)	Trailer (size is variable)

CSMA/CD Protocol

The carrier sense multiple access with collision detect (CSMA/CD) is a commonly used protocol that anticipates conflicts between nodes trying to use a communication channel at the same time. CSMA/CD was designed to deal with signal collisions inside the transmission media and resolve the conflicts that arise from such collisions. One of the older networking standards, Ethernet, uses this protocol as its controlling standard.

To understand how the CSMA/CD protocol works, let's look at an example of two nodes sending messages through the network transmission medium. If one of the nodes of the network sends a message and no other node is transmiting a signal, then the first node will sense that the communication channel has no "carrier" and that it is free. In this case, the node places the message on the communication medium and the message is allowed to travel through the network to its destination.

If two nodes transmit a signal at the same time, the signals collide, raising the energy level on the communication channel. This signals that the messages or data being transmitted are interfering with each other. In this case, both nodes stop transmission and wait a random amount of time before the transmission starts again. Since each node waits a random period of time, they will begin transmitting at different times, with one of the nodes gaining access to the communication channel before the other node, and therefore sending its message. After the first message is sent, the second node will sense when the communication medium is free and transmit its message.

The CSMA/CD uses frames as its basic data format. The header of the frame, also called the preamble, synchronizes the transmitter and receiver. A control field is used to indicate the type of data being transmitted. In addition, a 32-bit CRC field is used to prevent errors from getting through the system, providing good error detection capability.

Ethernet, AT&T's Starlan, and IBM's PC Network are three networking products that use the CSMA/CD protocol. Ethernet was one of the first commercially popular LAN protocols. Ethernet was developed by XEROX corporation in the early 1970s and has become one of the most widely used networking systems in the design and implementation of LANs. One corporation that uses Ethernet as its main networking solution to connect its terminals and microcomputers to its servers is Digital Equipment Corporation.

Token Passing Protocol

The token protocol is based on a message (token) being placed on the communication circuit of a LAN. Here it circulates until acquired by a station that wishes to send a message. The station changes the token status from "free" to "busy," and attaches the message to the token.

In the network, the token moves from station to station, with each station examining the address contained in the token. When the message arrives at the receiving station, the station copies it. The receiving station passes an acknowledgment to the sending station. The sending station accepts the acknowledgment and changes the token status from "busy" to "free." At this stage, the other stations or nodes in the network know that they can send messages. The token then continues looping on the circuit until another station places a message in it to be delivered to another node in the network.

LAN Standards

As in the general discussion of networks, the type of protocol and access method used depends on which LAN standard a specific vendor follows. The standards used in the design of local area networks are set by the Institute of Electrical and Electronic Engineers (IEEE) 802 Standards Committee. These standards have the headings of the subcommittee that created them. As such, the most important of these are as follows:

1. 802.1
2. 802.2: LLC Protocol
3. 802.3: CSMA/CD Baseband Bus
4. 802.4: Token Passing Bus
5. 802.5: Token Passing Ring
6. 802.6: MAN

These standards are used by equipment manufacturers to ensure that their equipment is compatible with any other equipment that is manufactured by other vendors, but follows the standards. In addition, it gives LAN implementors a frame of reference from which to work as they use different vendors to build their networks.

802.1

This is known as the highest level interface standard. This specification is the least well defined because it involves a lot of interfacing with other networks, and some of the specifications are still under consideration.

802.2: LLC Protocol

It is equivalent to the second layer of the OSI model and was described previously in this chapter. It provides point-to-point link control between devices at the protocol level. Many of the applications designed for data on LANs use the 802.2 standard so that they can interface with the other layers of the OSI model.

802.3: CSMA/CD Baseband Bus

This is known as the carrier sense multiple access/collision detection (CSMA/CD) baseband bus. It describes the techniques by which any device on a bus can transmit when the medium interface determines that no other device is already transmitting.

This type of LAN uses coaxial cable or twisted pair wire as the transmission medium. At the physical level, this standard also defines the types of connectors and media that can be used.

The 802.3 standard is based on research originally done by the Xerox Corporation. Xerox called this type of local area network Ethernet. It is among the most popular and is widely used.

802.4: Token Passing Bus

This standard describes a method of operation whereby each device on a bus topology transmits only when it receives a token. The token is passed in a user-predetermined sequence and guarantees network access to all users. Since the bus topology does not provide a natural sequence of stations, each node is assigned a sequence number, and the token is passed from one station to another following the sequence numbers assigned to the stations.

802.5: Token Passing Ring

This is the mechanism utilized on IBM's Token-Ring LAN. It uses a token to pass messages between workstations as outlined previously. Several types of cables can be used for token-ring LANs, but twisted pair and coaxial cable are the most commonly used.

802.6: MAN

This is the metropolitan area network standard. The specifications were developed to create standards for networks whose stations were more than five kilometers apart. The criteria include standards for transmitting data, voice, and video.

Summary

Local area networks are networks that interconnect devices that are confined to a small geographical area. The actual distance that a LAN spans depends on specific implementations. LANs are implemented in order to transfer data among users in the network or to share resources among users.

A LAN implementation can provide high-speed data-transfer capability to all users, without a system operator to facilitate the transmission process. Even when connecting a LAN to a wide area network that covers thousands of miles, data transfer between users of the network is time effective and, in most cases, problem-free. The other reason for implementing a LAN is to share hardware and software resources among users of the network.

There are many LAN applications. Some of the more common types of applications are office automation, factory automation, education, computer-aided design, and computer-aided manufacturing.

When a LAN is purchased, the following characteristics should be kept in mind. LANs can provide the user with:
1. Flexibility
2. Speed
3. Reliability
4. Hardware and software sharing

5. Transparent interface
6. Adaptability
7. Access to other LANs and WANs
8. Security
9. Centralized management
10. Private ownership of the LAN

There are two major items that must be considered when planning or installing a LAN: the network hardware components and the network software. There are three major categories of devices that make up the hardware components of a local area network. These are the server, the LAN communication system, and the workstations.

A file server is a computer with some added hardware and software. The main components of the server that will affect speed are the central processing unit, the hard disk and disk controller, and the random access memory installed in the server.

To effectively provide file sharing services, the software that controls the file server must provide security, concurrent access controls, access optimizing, reliability, transparent access to the file server and peripherals attached to the server, and interfaces to other networks.

LAN servers are computers on the network that are accessible to network users. They contain resources that they "serve" to users who request the service. The most common type of server is the file server. Most LANs have at least one file server, and many have multiple file servers. The file server contains software applications and data files that are provided to users upon request.

When two or more computers are connected on a network, a special cable and a network interface board are required in each computer. Connect the server to the cable and then connect the cable to the board. Most microcomputers are not equipped with an interface port that can be connected to a second microcomputer for networking purposes (except the Macintosh). As a result, a network interface board (NIC) or network adapter must be installed in the microcomputer.

The processes that take place in the hardware devices of a LAN must be controlled by software. The software comes in the form of the network operating system. One of the most widely used network operating systems is NetWare, which is provided by Novell, Inc.

The network operating system controls the operation of the file server, and it makes the network resources accessible and easy to use. It manages server security and provides the network administrators with the tools to control user access to the network and file structure.

Network topologies come in many different configurations. The bus, ring, and star topologies are used extensively in LAN implementations.

The LAN protocol is the set of rules by which two machines talk to each other. It must be present in addition to the LAN hardware and the network operating system. Some communication protocols used in LANs are the logical link control (LLC) protocol established by the Institute of Electronic Engineers (IEEE) 802 Standards Committee, the carrier sense multiple access/collision detection (CSMA/CD) protocol, and the token passing protocol. The type of protocol and access methodology used depends on which LAN standard a specific vendor decides to follow.

Questions

1. What is a LAN?
2. What types of applications can be found on most LANs?
3. Describe the major characteristics of LANs.
4. What are protocols?
5. What is the LAN communication system?
6. Briefly explain two different LAN topologies.
7. What is the 802.2 IEEE standard?
8. What is token passing?
9. Describe three characteristics that affect file server efficiency.
10. Describe four characteristics of server software.

Project

This project provides hands-on knowledge of software that allows remote access of a personal computer from another personal computer. This type of software is becoming more common in the workplace to provide assistance to users from remote locations. It helps users run programs that reside in computers located at remote sites. It can also be used to transfer files between computers that have incompatible disk drives. (Note: the software used in this project can be found in the shareware market. There are several other programs that will perform the same function as the one here employed. Any of them could be used for this exercise; however, the commands will differ.)

Remote Access to a PC

There are situations in the workplace in which, for instructional or error checking needs, it would be desirable to control the functions of one personal computer (host) from another personal computer (remote). The remote computer can be located next to the host computer or miles away in a different geographical location.

To perform the operation, the host and remote computers need to run special software that allows the host to become a "slave" or extension of the remote system. There are several commercial programs available to perform such functions. One of these programs is a shareware program called The TANDEM Remote System (TTRS).

The TANDEM Remote System is shareware software. It can be acquired free of charge in most cases from local user groups or dealers who sell public domain software at nominal prices. The software can be tried, and, if found satisfactory, the user is expected to send a contribution back to the author of the program. In return, the author provides, in most cases, program documentation and enhancements to the software.

The main components of TTRS are two programs, TANDEM.EXE and TMODEM.EXE. TANDEM.EXE is the host program and TMODEM.EXE is the remote program. The function of the system varies slightly depending on whether the remote and host systems are connected directly with a null modem or through telephone lines.

Direct Connection

Before the remote computer can access the host system, the proper hardware must be connected to both computers using the standard RS-232 port. Follow the steps below to see if you have all the required items:

1. Write down the port number (COM1 or COM2) that you are going to use on the host computer.
2. Write down the port number (COM1 or COM2) that you are going to use on the remote computer.
3. Using a null modem cable (see chapter 3 projects), connect the two computers using serial port 1 (COM1).
4. Boot up both systems.
5. Make two copies of the original software. One copy will be used in the remote system and the other in the host computer.

With the TTRS diskettes in the computers' A drives or installed on their hard disks you will need to launch the TMODEM program in the remote computer and TANDEM in the host computer. The command lines are as follows.

For the remote computer the command line is

```
d:>TMODEM port, baud-rate, , D
```

d:> is the drive where the program is located

port is the serial port

baud-rate is the baud rate of the serial port

D indicates that the two computers are connected directly

For the host computer the command line is

```
d:>TANDEM port, baud-rate, , D
```

d:> is the drive where the program is located

port is the serial port

baud-rate is the baud rate of the serial port

D indicates that the two computers are connected directly

6. In the host computer type TANDEM 1, 9600, , D

7. In the remote computer type TMODEM 1, 9600, , D

At this point a password will be required. The passwords available are in a file called PASSWRDS.DAT that is on the original distribution disks.

8. Type any of the passwords provided on the original disk.

Telephone Line Access

To access the host computer through the telephone lines, a modem must be present at the host site and at the remote computer. You may want to refer to projects in previous chapters that show you how to connect a modem to a microcomputer.

1. Write down the port number (COM1 or COM2) that you are going to use on the host computer.

2. Write down the port number (COM1 or COM2) that you are going to use on the remote computer.

3. Make sure that the host system is attached to a modem set in "answer" mode, and that the modem is connected to a telephone line.

4. Make sure that the remote system is attached to a modem set in the "originate" mode, and that the modem is connected to a telephone line.

5. Boot up both systems.

6. Make two copies of the original software. One copy will be used on the remote system and the other on the host computer.

With the TTRS diskettes in the computers' A drives or installed on their hard disks, you will need to launch the TMODEM program in the remote computer and TANDEM in the host computer. The command lines are as follows.

For the remote computer the command line is

```
d:>TMODEM port, baud-rate
```

d:> is the drive where the program is located

port is the serial port

baud-rate is the baud rate of the serial port

For the host computer the command line is

```
d:>TANDEM port, baud-rate
```

d:> is the drive where the program is located

port is the serial port

baud-rate is the baud rate of the serial port

7. Assuming that the host's modem is connected to COM1 and that your modem can transmit with a speed of 1200 baud, in the host computer type TANDEM 1, 1200.

8. Assuming that the remote's modem is connected to COM1 and that your modem can transmit with a speed of 1200 baud, in the remote computer type TMODEM 1, 1200.

9. The remote modem program will ask you to enter the phone number of the host modem. Type the number correctly without spaces or extra characters. If the connection is successful you will see a CONNECT message on the screen.

For Both Cases

At this point a password will be required. The passwords available are in a file called PASSWRDS.DAT that is on the original distribution disks.

10. Type any of the passwords provided on the original disk.

At this point the two computers should be connected together. Under the TTRS control several commands can be used to control the host system, run programs on the host from the remote computer, and transfer files. These commands are as follows:

CLS. Clears the screen.

DIR. Displays directories of the host computer. It uses the same specifications as the DOS DIR.

DOS. Takes you to the operating system. This allows the remote computer to run programs that reside on the host computer.

BYE. Hangs up the phone and waits for the next call.

SHUTDOWN. Terminates TANDEM on the host computer from a remote location.

CHAT. Provides a clear screen so that the remote computer can communicate with someone at the host computer.

SEND. Transfers files between the host and the remote computers.

To transfer files between the host and the remote, the command line is as follows:

```
TANDEM:>SEND direction d:FILE.EXT
[d:FILE.EXT]
```

The direction parameter uses the symbol ">" to indicate "to" or the symbol "<" to indicate "from." In addition, the words "HOST" and "REMOTE" are used to establish the direction in which the file is to be transmitted. For example, if a file named "data.dat" resides on the host main directory and it needs to be transferred to the remote computer and placed in a subdirectory named "c:\datafile," the command line is as follows:

11. TANDEM:>SEND>REMOTE c:\data.dat
c:\datafile\data.dat

This procedure can be used to transfer files between desktop computers and portable computers.

To run a program from the remote computer that resides on the host computer the process is as follows:

12. Type DOS and press the ENTER key.

You will be taken to DOS and any DOS commands you type will affect the host system but will be displayed on the remote computer.

13. Type the name of the program that you wish to run and press the ENTER key.

14. When you are ready to return to the TANDEM environment, exit the program. Type EXIT, and press the ENTER key.

The TANDEM Remote System is useful in many situations in the work environment. It can be used to run demonstrations simultaneously on two computers, to run programs that reside at the office from home, and to provide assistance to users at remote locations.

LAN Installation

Objectives

After completing this chapter you will:

1. Understand the importance of a local area network.
2. Understand the function of a local area network.
3. Obtain a general view of the types of applications running on a local area network.
4. Understand the hardware and software components of a local area network.
5. Understand the different topologies of local area networks.
6. Understand the standards that guide the design of local area networks and their protocols.
7. Have a general understanding of how to install a local area network.
8. Understand the components required to have an efficient local area network.

Key Words

AppleTalk	Local Area Network
LAN	Manager
NIC	NOS
Novell	

Introduction

Previous chapters introduced general concepts that applied to all types of networks. This chapter describes local area networks in detail. The rapid acceptance of local area networks has made networking a common event in the workplace and especially in education.

The local area network allows individuals to share resources and offset some of the high cost of automating processes. An individual at any computer in a local area network can create a document and send it to another computer in the network for editing or printing purposes. The access provided by local area networks is controlled and somewhat secure.

These concepts, as well as some of the inner workings of the hardware that make up the local area network, are explored in this chapter. Additionally, the IEEE standards are defined and their impact on network design is explained.

Finally, the chapter provides a general overview of the implementation of a local area network and a discussion of efficiency considerations for file servers and server software.

Commercially Available LANs

There are many vendors of local area network hardware and software. However, a few commercial vendors control a large segment of the LAN market, especially in the personal computer market. When a LAN is being designed or purchased, it is common to identify the LAN by the maker of the LAN operating system or the operating system name itself. For example, if a baseband local area network using Novell NetWare as the controlling operating system is to be installed, we tend to say that a Novell

LAN will be implemented. Saying that a Novell LAN is in place at a particular geographical location doesn't necessarily indicate that it has a particular hardware configuration, since many network operating systems work under many different hardware platforms and configurations. Therefore, using this type of terminology, some of the most prominent commercial products available are Novell NetWare, Microsoft LAN Manager, 3COM 3+ (not longer available, but many installations still remain), IBM LAN Server, AppleTalk, and Banyan VINES.

Novell NetWare

Novell NetWare was originally designed around hardware using a star topology to communicate with a single file server. In this star configuration, the file server simply allowed client computers to store and share files using it as the center hub for the network. Since its early days, however, NetWare has become largely hardware independent, allowing many topologies and file servers to be used simultaneously. But communication on the network is still handled almost entirely through a primary file server with all user's workstations, called clients, accessing the server to perform network functions. This is done whether the configuration is a star, a bus, or any other topology.

Netware's original structure has influenced all of Novell's products to date. Even in new NetWare configurations the file server manages the network. In other words, two client computers may be connected directly to each other by a network cable, but, for a file to be transferred from one to the other, that file must first be sent to the file server, then to the target client computer. Of course, the network provides many other functions, but they are generally centered around the idea of a client computer connected to a file server.

By far, the most common client on a Novell network is an IBM PC or PC-compatible computer running DOS. Compatible, in this case, means that other manufacturers have designed computers to work almost exactly like the original IBM product. Even IBM has produced computers with much more power and flexibility, while maintaining this compatibility with the PC. DOS (usually pronounced as a single word) stands for disk operating system (see chapter 2). It is the software that handles all of the low level functions of the computer such as reading and writing to the disk drives, loading and executing application programs, and handling input from the keyboard. When running an application program such as a word processor, DOS allocates memory, reads the program from the disk drive, and then allows the program to begin. The application program can then use the resources of the computer through what are known as DOS function calls. This system allows the application program, and the person who wrote the application program, to be freed from worrying about the messy details of operating all the peripherals attached to the computer. For instance, there are many different types of disk drives and dozens of companies manufacturing them. To the application program, this is irrelevant. It will simply make a DOS function call to read or write data to the disk drive and DOS will handle the input and output to the device.

NetWare runs on a large number of hardware platforms in addition to the IBM PC. These platforms include DEC's VAX computer under the VMS operating system, IBM's mainframes under the VM and VMS operating systems, and the Apple Macintosh personal computer. In the case of the Macintosh, NetWare allows Mac applications to reside on an IBM or compatible computer (the server) and uses Macintosh computers on the LAN to run the applications. This allows a single network and server to provide applications that are DOS specific and Macintosh specific. Additionally, NetWare has specialized programs called drivers available for nearly all network interface cards (NICs) currently available for PCs. The interface cards allow workstations to use the LAN communication medium to send messages from one machine to another. Among some of these interface cards, Novell has drivers for ARCnet, Ethernet, Token-Ring, G-Net, and ProNet. The support for this wide range of hardware manufacturers makes Novell NetWare the most widely used LAN operating environment in the PC market.

NetWare was designed and optimized as file server and network management software. It uses proprietary directory and file schemas designed for quick access. However, the strength of NetWare for DOS users is that the network functions of saving and retrieving files appear as DOS structures. Because of this feature, DOS users can access and use the network without having to learn a new operating environment. They can continue to use familiar commands such as COPY, PRINT, and others in the same way that they use them in a stand-alone configuration. This is also true for users of Macintosh computers. The network functions are extension of the computer operating system, making the transition from stand-alone to network computing a less difficult task.

In addition to the basic services that the workstation operating system provides, NetWare provides services for security, network printing, file server access, access to other networks, electronic mail, and communications. With the largest share of the LAN market, and new partnerships with IBM, Novell is the largest provider of LAN operating systems in the United States and in many countries abroad.

Microsoft LAN Manager/3COM 3+ Open

3COM's 3+ Open is a network operating system based on OS/2 LAN Manager developed by Microsoft Corporation and now under the control of IBM. Therefore, 3+ Open is related to IBM's OS/2 LAN Server since the LAN Manager is the core of IBM's LAN Server. Although not longer available, many installations remain in the market. Therefore, it will be briefly covered in this section.

Using the same concept as Novell NetWare, this operating system provides the basic services of a stand-alone workstation in addition to providing users with network services. The core of the 3COM system is based on its directory services which are provided through a Network Control Server (NCS). This is a different approach than the one taken by most other network vendors. While other vendors opt to have a distributed directory service, 3COM uses a centralized system. If the NCS goes down, the entire network goes down.

The workstations can be OS/2 or DOS based. However, to take full advantage of all the network functions, OS/2 should be the operating system on the workstation instead of DOS. In addition to the standard services expected, such as file management and printing, LAN Manager provides services for security and controls access to the network. It also provides services for accessing SNA, X.25, X.29, and other MS-Net networks.

IBM LAN Server

The IBM LAN Server, like 3COM 3+ Open, is based on Microsoft's LAN Manager. Like LAN Manager, LAN Server runs under the

OS/2 operating system. It supports OS/2 workstations or DOS workstations. However, DOS workstations cannot take full advantage of all features of the network operating system.

Even though LAN Server is based on LAN Manager, IBM has changed many of the features of LAN Manager, making the product different in the way it provides several of the functions of the network.

LAN Server provides services for security through a global Domain Controller. This is a technique that uses one server to provide security for all other servers. This is a departure from LAN Manager, where each server maintains its own security.

The other services provided by LAN Server are similar to those provided by LAN Manager, but many of the commands used by LAN Server are different from its counterpart, making the management of both systems difficult.

Banyan VINES

Banyan Systems developed VINES (VIrtual NEtwork System) in an effort to provide high-quality communications among personal computers and to link their LAN to minicomputers, mainframes, and other LANs. In order for their LAN to work properly, Banyan recognized that they needed a multitasking operating system. Banyan settled on UNIX V as its platform for connectivity strategy.

VINES includes file and print services, a global naming and access system called "StreetTalk," and built-in connectivity services that provide:

1. PC dial into the VINES network
2. SNA access
3. Asynchronous communication and file transfer
4. TCP/IP support
5. X.25 and X.29 support
6. Token-Ring bridge support

In addition, VINES provides services for security through VAN-Guard, as well as NETBIOS emulation, time service, and chat and backup facilities. Also, it includes some optional services such as electronic mail, network management, and communication services.

The core of the VINES system is StreetTalk. This is a directory and naming service that allows access to applications, files, printers, gateways, bridges, users, servers, hardware resources, and communications. StreetTalk is responsible for making the network transparent to the user by integrating all services and users. This allows users to use the network facilities as natural extensions of their own workstations.

As with the other successful vendors of LAN operating systems, Banyan's VINES LAN hardware supports a wide range of third party vendors that includes ARCnet, Ethernet, IBM Token-Ring, Omninet-1B, Pronet 4, 10, and 80, VISTA LAN-PC, and StarLan network interface cards.

AppleTalk

All Macintosh computers have built-in circuitry for connecting the machine to a LocalTalk network. LocalTalk is one of the network types available in the AppleTalk network system. The AppleTalk system is a way of connecting computers, printers, and other peripheral devices so that users can share information and resources in a transparent manner.

LocalTalk under AppleTalk works by using a file server approach. The server, which can be any of the computers in the network, provides services for printing, file sharing, and some security services.

Since every Macintosh comes with the capability of connecting to LocalTalk, it is relatively simple to use the network and to perform network functions. However, the network has limitations in the types of services that it provides, and the speed of data transmission is slow when compared to other networks on the market.

General Installation of a LAN

Once the topology and vendor of the local area network are selected and the network distribution is designed, the next step in the LAN evolution is the installation. The type and amount of personnel required for the installation of a LAN depend on the size, type, and scope of the LAN itself. However, they all share some common characteristics. Some of these characteristics are as follows:

1. Most LANs use a personal computer as the basic client.

2. Most LANs use one or several fast computers as dedicated servers.

3. All clients have to be provided with an interface card that allows the client computer to become an active member of the network.

4. All hardware in the LAN needs to be protected.

5. Although each LAN operating system is different in how it works and in the process of installation, they all require a network profile to be created and maintained.

6. All users must login to the network to have access to networking services.

7. All networks have legal issues regarding the use of software that must be dealt with.

The above characteristics are the same for all LAN implementations. Therefore, the next section covers the LAN installation process in a general format, in order to be applicable to as many LAN configurations as possible. The student is reminded that, although the processes outlined below may seem simplistic, network installation is a complex task that requires thorough preparation prior to installation. Therefore, before installation of the network takes place, the installers will need to follow a system development cycle or approach using systems analysis and design techniques as they are explained in the next chapter. Failure to follow these guidelines will most likely result in a network with poor performance or many other anomalies that will make the LAN unsuccessful.

Installing the LAN Hardware

Most LANs have what is call a LAN kit. It consists of the network interface cards, communication medium cables, and LAN operating system. Assuming that a complete LAN kit is available, the first step is to install the NIC in each microcomputer that is going to be part of the LAN. The NIC (refer to Fig. 10-5) is installed in one of the expansion slots inside the machine. The NIC will be responsible for all the network communications between the client computer and the rest of the system. For this purpose, it has a unique address that identifies the client system to any other devices that are part of the LAN.

In many cases the NIC already has a unique address "burned in" by its manufacturer. If the NIC's address was set at the factory, the NIC can be installed as is. Otherwise, a set of dip switches on the NIC must be set to a combination that has not already been used on the LAN. It is suggested that each NIC on the network follow a sequence. Then if something goes wrong during the operation of the network it will be easier to identify problems.

After the NIC is installed, each microcomputer must be connected to other microcomputers on the LAN. The most common way of doing this is to connect each microcomputer in a daisy chain configuration but this will vary according to the type of topology chosen. The first and the last of the microcomputers are given an ending plug. This indicates to the network that there are no more nodes in the network beyond these points. The cable used to connect the microcomputers can be optical fiber, co-axial, or twisted pair cable, depending on the requirements of the LAN and anticipated upgrades.

In a general format, that is all the basic hardware installation requirements. Of course, the level of difficulty in performing the above installation will depend on the wiring system layout and the distances involved. But, regardless of the neatness of the cable arrangement, once the NIC is installed properly and each NIC is connected with the right cabling system, the network is ready to accept the software. However, one important aspect that shouldn't be ignored is the protection of the hardware that has just been installed.

Protecting the Hardware

Electronic equipment is succeptible to power sags, power surges, and electrical noise. As described in previous chapters, a power surge is a sudden increase in power, which in many cases can destroy the microchips that make up the computer circuitry. A power sag is a loss of electrical power that can force a computer reset or a network shutdown. Information stored in RAM prior to a power sag is lost, and, in some situations, a network can't automatically rebuild itself to continue operating. Electronic noise is interference from other types of electrical devices such as air conditioners, transformers, lights, and other electrical equipment.

There are several devices that protect computers against the problems outlined above. These are power surge protectors, power line conditioners (PLCs), and uninterruptible power supplies (UPSs). The type of device used depends on the equipment to protect, the importance of the data stored in the equipment, and economics.

Power surge protectors are the least expensive of all protecting devices. They range in price from a few dollars to approximately $150. They protect equipment from short duration electrical surges (called transients) and from voltage spikes. Their price depends on the type of materials used to make up the device and how fast these components react to a power surge. Devices with faster reaction time are generally more expensive. Whenever possible, the protector with the fastest reaction time should be purchased. Power surge protectors are normally found at the users' workstations.

Power line conditioners (PLC) are more expensive than surge protectors. They protect equipment against electrical noise and interference from other equipment. Most PLCs also protect against surges and sags in electrical power. They tend to filter out electrical noise while maintaining power within acceptable levels for the computer to operate. Many user workstations and servers use PLCs to guard against temporary and very short duration power spikes and sags.

Uninterruptible power supplies allow a system to continue functioning for several minutes even when there is a total loss of power. Normally, the additional running time provided by the UPS is enough to safely shut the system or network down; on many occasions, the time is long enough that power is restored without having to shut the system down. They should be used by all servers to protect users' data and the network from a sudden and unexpected loss of power. Additionally, a UPS protects against power surges and electrical noise.

All network servers should be protected by a UPS, and at a minimum, each workstation should have a power surge protector. This will prevent the most common network problems associated with disruptions in the power required to keep the network operational. Once the hardware is installed and properly protected, the next step is to install the LAN software.

Installing the LAN Software

To install the LAN software, the network operating system must be installed, a station profile for each microcomputer needs to be created, and a profile for each microcomputer logging onto the LAN also needs to be created. The process required to install the network operating system varies according to the type and size of the LAN.

On networks such as Novell's, the network operating system replaces the workstation's native operating system. This involves reformatting the hard disk of the computer that is going to act as the file server. In this case, installing the network operating system consists of following instructions displayed on the screen after placing the network system disk in the drive and turning the computer on. The procedure consists of loading the LAN kit disks in the sequence requested. The entire process is normally self-explanatory after the first instructions are displayed on the screen.

On smaller networks, the network operating system is loaded when the user turns on the microcomputer, or it is done automatically by using a batch file that is executed automatically. The network operating system manuals that come with the LAN kit indicate which files must be placed in batch files and which files must reside on the file server.

The Network Profile

A network profile must be established for each microcomputer on the LAN. The profile indicates the microcomputer's resources that are available for other network users. This profile is set up once when the network is installed, but it can be changed later if necessary.

The profile contains information about user access privileges and password requirements. Additionally, it indicates which devices are printers, which hard disks are shared, and the access mechanisms for these. For example, if a user has a hard disk called C:, and it is not included in the network profile, this disk is not accessible to other users.

Also, each user has a profile which adds security to the LAN. Each device has a name code and each user has a name code. During normal execution of the network operating system, only users with the correct codes and security access can use specific devices.

Login to the Network

The last step in installing the local area network software is the login process. Assuming there are no hardware problems, each microcomputer on the LAN has, in its autoexecutable batch file, a copy of the network files required to incorporate the microcomputer into the LAN. When the computer is booted, these files take over the operation of the microcomputer hardware and make a connection to the file server through the NIC and the network cable.

The first network request found by the user is a login ID that is unique to each user, and then a password which may or may not be unique to each user. In some setups, the password may be requested from each user. If the user profile software on the server acknowledges an authorized user, the microcomputer becomes active on the network and can perform any functions authorized for the specific machine.

Remote LAN Software

Remote software offers microcomputer users the ability to operate programs and access peripherals on a remote system by using a modem. In addition, remote LAN software allows users to have node-to-node communications so users can share networked applications.

This type of software can be used for technical support, group conferencing, and training. Also, network managers can control network functions from locations other than a network station or the file server. Additionally, technicians at remote locations can access a LAN experiencing problems. This is done to conduct diagnostic tests and software repairs.

Legal Issues

Software installed on a LAN needs to meet certain legal criteria. Some network administrators feel that a single legally purchased copy of an application can be placed on a file server and made available to all users. This is illegal. An application software program can be used on a LAN only when a site license exists for the package. Furthermore, the number of users accessing the application program needs to be limited to the number of users stipulated in the licensing agreement. Honesty and integrity are the best paths to follow in this area.

There are several management tools available to aid network managers in enforcing the proper and legal use of software on the network. Among these, metering software is the most widely used. Metering software can be used to monitor the number of users who are running a specific application. The network manager can instruct the software to lock out of the application any users who will create a potential legal conflict. When a user releases the application back into the system, a new user can be added to the total number that have access to the program. Many of the metering programs can perform this process automatically. Additionally, many network aware programs have this type of capability built in.

The Network Server

Since most LANs that use PCs as the basic client use some type of server to provide networking functions to users, it is important to discuss some of the characteristics that make a good server. As mentioned before, in many LANs the server is another microcomputer that contains large hard disk storage and a fast CPU. But, the configuration of the server shouldn't be left to chance or given low priority. A poorly configured server can slow the response time of the network or require excessive maintenance.

Server Hardware

The primary function of a server is to provide a service to network users. Servers can provide files to users, printing, and communication services as well as other services. The most important server in a LAN is the file server. Because in most LANs all requests must be processed through the file server, it has a much higher workload than that of a typical stand-alone microcomputer. The stand-alone PC takes care of the needs of a single user. The file server takes care of the needs of all users on the network. Therefore, careful consideration must be given to the hardware that constitutes the file server.

First, a network designer needs to decide whether a dedicated or nondedicted file server is going to be used. Since a nondedicated server functions as a file server and as a user workstation, a dedicated server will outperform a nondedicated server. For example, assume that an MS-DOS-based PC is being considered as the server, and NetWare is the operating system. If the clone is not 100 percent compatible with the IBM PC, interrupts used by NetWare may conflict with the software.

For large networks, the file server should be a dedicated server, and the fastest and most efficient hardware should be considered. Also, to avoid execution problems, a new dedicated server should be compatible with the network software.

Since the file server is just a computer with some added hardware and software, the main components of the server that will affect speed are the central processing unit, RAM caching, the hard disk and controller, hard disk caching, and the random access memory installed on the server.

The Central Processing Unit (CPU)

The central processing unit performs the calculations and logical operations required of all computers. All programs running on a computer system must be executed by the CPU.

In the personal computer market, the CPU classifies the computer. In the IBM market area, the original IBM PC had a CPU that consisted of 16 bits with a bus consisting of 8 bits. This meant that 16 bits were used to perform the calculations, and data moved inside the computer 8 bits at a time. The processor used in the original IBM PC was the Intel 8088. When the IBM AT was introduced, it had a 32-bit CPU with a bus of 16 bits. Today, the fastest IBM microcomputers and compatibles use a CPU and data bus, both of which process 32 bits. Today, the processors of choice are the 80386 and the 80486, but recently announced faster Intel processors may change user choices in the future. One good alternative for a server is one where the processor can be upgraded in the future. This provides the best solution for the money at present, but preserves the investment in the hardware by providing an upgrade path.

The main difference between the CPUs in the market is the speed of processing that they are capable of. The size of the data bus and the CPU's clock speed govern the speed of a microcomputer. The bus is the pathway that connects the CPU with the network interface card and other peripherals attached to the microcomputer. The size of the bus determines how much data can be transmitted in each cycle of the CPU's clock. A larger bus size can move data faster and provide better performance.

The CPU's clock speed is the other factor that affects performance. The clock speed determines how frequently cycles occur inside the computer, and therefore how fast data can be transmitted. The clock speed is measured in cycles per second or Hertz (Hz). The original IBM PC had a clock speed of 4.77 MHz. Recently produced microcomputers have clock speeds of 50 MHz and higher.

If a new file server is being installed, a computer with a faster CPU clock and the largest possible data bus should be utilized. Of course, the computer with the faster CPU and the larger bus is going to be more costly. For small networks, clock speeds of 8 to 20 MHz and a data bus of 16 to 32 bits should be considered. For large networks, clock speeds of 25 MHz or more and a data bus of 32 bits should be considered. However, with the price of high-end CPUs dropping all the time, even small networks will eventually be able to utilize servers with CPU speeds of 50 MHz or at the price of yesterday's 20 MHz CPUs.

The Hard Disk and Controller

A fast computer with a slow hard disk will deteriorate the performance of a LAN. The hard disk is a mechanical device that contains metal platters where data is stored for later retrieval. The hard disk controller is a circuit board that directs the operation of the hard disk.

As data moves inside the server at speeds of up to 10 million bits per second, data moves to and from the hard disk at speeds of approximately 1/20th of that in the best of situations. This can create a bottleneck that slows the LAN for all of its users. A fast hard disk and controller are essential to the performance of a LAN.

The average time required for the disk to find and read a unit of information is called the access speed. Most drives today have access speeds that range from a low of 9 milliseconds to a high of 80 milliseconds.

Hard disk controllers come in four different categories with varying performance, and they vary in the size of hard disk that can be attached. These are the categories:

1. ST506. Standard on most IBM ATs and compatibles. This drive controller has a transfer rate of approximately 7 megabits per second and supports a maximum of two drives, each with a size up to 150 megabytes.

2. ESDI. Enhanced Small Device Interface. This is standard on many 80386-based computers. The controller has a transfer rate of 10 megabits per second and supports a maximum of four disk drives. Typical drives have 300 megabytes.

3. SCSI. Small Computer System Interface. This controller has data transfers of approximately 10 megabits per second and supports up to 32 disk drives. This type of controller supports drives having a capacity of 700 megabytes and more.

4. IDE. Intelligent Drive Electronics. IDE controllers combine features of the other three interfaces and add additional benefits. They are fast like ESDI drives, intelligent like SCSI drives, and look like standard AT ST506 interfaces to the system. With capacities of up to 300 megabytes and even larger disks, this type of controller is becoming increasingly popular. They suffer from a lack of standardization, but there are new proposals in the market that attempt to create a better standard for this type of drive.

In addition to considering the speed of the hard disk and the hard disk controller, drives with enough size to support future upgrades and expansion should be considered.

Random Access Memory

Random access memory (RAM) is used by the file server to store information for the CPU. The speed of the RAM installed in the CPU determines how fast data is transferred to the CPU when it makes a request from RAM. If the speed of RAM is too slow for the type of CPU in use, problems will arise and LAN deterioration will take place. Care should always be taken to match the speed of RAM to the speed of the CPU clock for optimum performance.

Some network operating systems, such as NetWare, use RAM as buffer areas for print jobs and for disk caching. Disk caching is a method by which the computer will hold in memory the most frequently and recently used portions of files, increasing the efficiency of the input/output process.

If a file server has only the minimum amount of RAM to run the network operating system, performance will deteriorate as users are added to the LAN, due to the increased access to the hard disk by the file server. Adding extra memory will increase the performance of the network by increasing efficiency of the input/output operations.

Server Software

To effectively provide file sharing services, the software that controls the file server must provide security, concurrent access controls, access optimizing, reliability, transparent access to the file server and peripherals attached to the server, and interfaces to other networks.

The file server software should provide user access to those elements necessary to perform job functions, while restricting access to items for which a user does not have access privileges. This means that some users do not know that more files exist. Other users are allowed to read them, and still others are allowed to delete or modify them.

Concurrent access controls allow users to access files in a prioritized fashion using volume, file, and record locking. These controls allow a file to be changed before another user reads the information. Otherwise, a user may be reading data that is no longer current.

Access optimization is achieved by having administrative tools in the LAN that allow the fine tuning of the network. This provides users with the best possible response time while safeguarding the contents of users' files. Some of these tools are fault tolerance, file recovery, LAN-to-mainframe communications, disk caching, and multiple disk channels.

The software in the file server and the server itself need to have a continuous and consistent mode of operation if users are to trust the network. In some situations, multiple servers offer each other backup services and increase the reliability of the LAN.

Transparent access means that using the LAN should be a natural extension of the user knowledge of the individual computer system. LAN users are typically not computer experts. Access to the file server should be no more difficult than accessing a stand-alone computer. This includes accessing peripheral devices such as printers, plotters, and scanners. Additionally, often the LAN needs to interface with other LANs. The server software should have extensions that allow this to take place.

LAN Security

As the network grows in size and importance, security will become one of the major concerns for the network administrator. The threats that can affect the LAN come from unauthorized users gaining access to sensitive volumes or data files, computer viruses corrupting users' files and programs, accidental erasure of data and programs by authorized users, power failure during an important transaction, breakdown of storage media, and others. Although security mechanisms are explored in chapter 12, the following is a general overview of some security measures that are common practice for many network administrators.

Volume Security

One of the most important functions of LAN software is the security of the network against accidental or unauthorized access. One methodology is to split the file server's hard disk into sections, or volumes. Each volume can be given public, private, or shared status. If a volume is made public, then everyone on the network has access to its contents. Private volumes can be accessed only by single users for read or write functions. Finally, shared volumes allow all authorized users to have read and write access to the contents of the volume. This type of security is set up by the network manager using network management tools and then it is enforced by the network operating system or NOS, every time a user logs into the network. Additionally, the use of script or login files can help in establishing better security controls. These types of files are executed every time a user logs into the network. They contain a combination of commands that takes the user to a specific path and locks him or her out of other areas of the network. Some file servers have more sophisticated security levels than the ones mentioned above. Network operating systems, such as Novell's NetWare, not only allow volume security attributes, but extend the security attributes to individual files on any volume.

Locking

Another type of security employed by LANs is volume, file, and record locking. Volume locking is a technique by which a user can lock all other users out of a volume until he or she is through with the volume. Some networks allow locking to be placed at the file level. Others allow locking at the record level. Record locking is preferred under normal circumstances, since a user can control one record while other users have access to the rest of the records and the rest of the network files.

Others

Additional types of security that LANs can provide are data encryption, password protection to volumes and files, and physical or electronic keys that must be inserted into a network security device to gain access. Also, antivirus protection software and network management programs provide network managers with additional resources to help protect users and network files.

A LAN Example: Novell NetWare

Overview of NetWare

Little remains constant in the world of networking. Network operating systems, hardware components, and topologies have changed rapidly over the last several years to keep pace with advancing technology and consumer demand. Novell, Inc. has performed better than most at maintaining a saleable product and a share of the market. Novell's original network product, however, did not do well. The system was a file server and network operating system software, with serial cables to connect to client computers running the CP/M operating system. The product line was expanded somewhat, but the company went bankrupt. Novell's reorganization, however, took place at an opportune point in history. The introduction of the IBM PC gave Novell an entirely new market. Novell's operating system was eventually rewritten to allow the IBM PC to be used as both the file server and the client. Novell has introduced many software and hardware products since then, and now controls the largest single share of the networking market with Novell NetWare. "NetWare" refers to all of Novell's network operating system products.

Novell NetWare was originally designed around hardware using a star topology to communicate with a single file server. The file server simply allowed client computers to store and share files. This structure has influenced all of Novell's products to date. NetWare has become largely hardware independent, allowing many topologies and file servers to be used simultaneously, but communication on the network is still handled almost entirely through a primary file server. Two client computers may be connected directly to each other by a network cable, but for a file to be transferred from one to the other, that file must first be sent to the file server, then to the target client computer. Of course, the network provides many other functions, but they are generally centered around the idea of a client computer connected to a file server.

By far, the most common client on a Novell network is an IBM PC or PC-compatible computer running DOS. DOS is the software that handles all of the low level functions of the computer such as reading and writing to the disk drives, loading and executing application programs, and handling input from the keyboard. When running an application program such as a word processor, DOS allocates memory, reads the program from the disk drive and then allows the program to begin. The application program can then use the resources of the computer through what are known as DOS function calls. For instance, there are many different types of printers and dozens of companies manufacturing them. To the application program, this is irrelevant. It will simply make a DOS function call to write data to the printer and DOS will handle the output to the device.

Since even DOS can't "know" the details of every peripheral device that one might attach to a computer, including a network, programs known as drivers are often used to help DOS provide a common environment for application programs to work in. Attaching a Novell network to a computer is a good example of this and essentially involves three components: the network interface card or NIC, a program called IPX, and another program called NET#, where # indicates the version of DOS already running on the computer.

The NIC is the hardware that is physically connected to the network, much like a telephone is the piece of hardware that is physically connected to the telephone network. It generates the proper electrical signal to communicate on the particular type of network being used. It may even use pulses of light or radio waves to send signals across the network.

IPX is an abbreviation for Internetwork Packet Exchange. The IPX program controls the operation of the NIC so that a common protocol is used throughout the network. Since there are hundreds of types and brands of NICs, IPX is built using drivers specific to each. IPX is actually hardware dependent, but, since drivers are available for all types of NICs, NetWare itself can still claim to be hardware independent.

NET# controls communication between DOS and IPX. Since there are several versions of DOS, NetWare comes with several versions of the NET# program: NET2, NET3, NET4, XMSNET2, XMSNET3, XMSNET4, EMSNET2, EMSNET3, and EMSNET4. The XMS prefix refers to Extended Memory System and the EMS prefix refers to Expanded Memory System. These are not different DOS versions, but significant extensions to DOS. The different versions of the NET# program allow it to take advantage of functions specific to each operating system version and memory extension. The NET# program is therefore operating system dependent. However, with the advent of DOS 5, Novell introduced a new version of these drivers named NETX, XMSNETX, and EMSNETX. They will work with all versions of DOS.

Together, the IPX and NET# make up the NetWare shell which is a complete interface between DOS and NetWare. The word "shell" refers to an interface provided to users to allow them to interact with the computer in a "natural" manner. This "shields" users from the complex low level operations of the computer and the network. Therefore, the network shell protects the user from having to know how to interact directly with the network.

The User Environment

Network Drives

The NetWare shell allows DOS and the user to treat the file server as a disk drive attached to the client computer. DOS assigns a drive letter to each of the disk drives physically attached to the computer. A and B designate floppy disk drives while C, D, and so on represent hard disk drives. On a typical system, with two floppy disk drives and a hard disk drive, DOS would assign A, B, and C to those disk drives. When the NetWare shell programs are loaded, another drive letter is made available to the user. Typically, F is used to designate the first network drive. Ordinary DOS commands like DIR (which displays a list of the files on the disk) and CHDIR (which changes the reference to a different area of the disk) can be used on the network drive F. In addition, application programs can make ordinary DOS function calls to carry out their functions on the network drive, as if it were a hard disk attached to the computer. The network drive is the hard disk on the file server, the same hard disk accessed by every other user on the network.

Fig. 11-1 shows three computers, a file server and two client computers. The first client has local disk drives A, B, and C. It also has access to drive F, which is actually on the file server. The second client has only one local disk drive, but can also access drive F.

DOS Directories

In DOS you can create directories to organize the data on a disk. A directory contains files grouped together on the disk. Every disk has what is called the root directory even though it is not referred to as "root" in a DOS command. Since a "\" (a backslash) is used to separate directory names, a backslash with no name is considered the root directory.

Fig. 11-2 shows how a hard disk might be organized. The files in the root directory could be listed by typing the DIR command. The DIR command lists the files in the current directory. In this

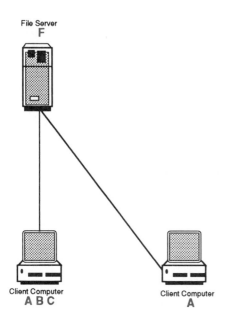

File Server
F

Client Computer
A B C

Client Computer
A

Fig. 11-1. Networked clients and file server.

case DIR C: would list the files COMMAND.COM, IPX.COM, NET3.EXE and a directory called WORD. The files in the directory WORD could be displayed by typing DIR C:\WORD and pressing the ENTER key. WORD.COM and LETTER.DOC would be listed. Another way to view the list of files in the WORD

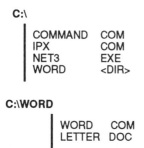

C:

COMMAND	COM
IPX	COM
NET3	EXE
WORD	<DIR>

C:\WORD

| WORD | COM |
| LETTER | DOC |

Fig. 11-2. Disk organization.

directory would be to use the CHDIR command. CHDIR stands for change directory and can be abbreviated further by using only CD. If you were to type CD C:\WORD, the current directory would be changed to the WORD directory and DIR C: would list the files WORD.COM and LETTER.DOC. In this way the drive letter C moves around the disk drive pointing to different areas. Just as the root directory contains a directory called WORD, the WORD directory could contain another directory, and so on.

The same commands can be used on the network drive F. In Fig. 11-1 the first computer could create a directory called F:\HISFILES by using the MKDIR command. MKDIR stands for make directory and can be abbreviated further by using only MD. By typing the command MD F:\HISFILES, the first user can create a place to store files on the file server. The user at the second computer could type MD F:\HERFILES. Now, if either computer user typed DIR F:, both directory names would be listed.

Drive Mappings

With directories containing directories and every user on the network creating directories, the directory structure can become quite complex.

Suppose a user on the network needed quick and easy access to files in both the F:\HISFILES directory and the F:\HERFILES directory. Rather than constantly using the CHDIR command to move drive F to the other area, he could use the NetWare MAP command to create a drive letter for one of the directories. Fig. 11-3 shows the result of the first user typing MAP G:=F:\HERFILES. This creates drive letter G which points to the HERFILES directory on the same physical drive as F:\HISFILES.

Fig. 11-3. Drive mappings allow access to files in the server.

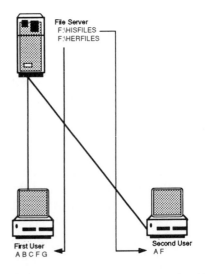

This arrangement does not affect the second user. Drive mappings pertain only to the client computer where the MAP command was issued. Each user still has access to the HERFILES directory through drive letter F. The first user simply has the choice of using drive letter F or drive letter G.

Paths and Search Drives

Drive mappings allow users to access data easily without worrying about the directory names. The DOS PATH statement allows the user to completely ignore the current directory when running programs. NetWare combines these functions in the search drive. Ordinarily, to execute a program, it must reside in the current directory or the full path must be used when referring to the program. The "path" is the complete directory name where the program resides. Referring to Fig. 11-3, the first user may have a program called WORD.COM in the HISFILES directory. If the current directory is F:\HERFILES, he would have to type F:\HISFILES\WORD to execute the WORD program. DOS provides a means to shorten this in the PATH command. The PATH command tells the computer where to look for a program if it can't be found in the current directory. If the first user types PATH F:\HISFILES he can use all the programs in the HISFILES directory without typing the entire path. He could simply type WORD and the computer would look in the current directory first, then look in the HISFILES directory and find, and then execute, the program. Multiple directories can be included in the PATH command to instruct the computer to search several areas for the program. The command PATH F:\HERFILES;F:\HISFILES would tell the computer to search the current directory first (as it always does), then the F:\HERFILES directory, and lastly the F:\HISFILES directory. A NetWare search drive is a drive mapping that is automatically inserted in the PATH.

In Fig. 11-4, the second user has typed the command MAP S1:=F:\HISFILES. This NetWare command automatically chooses a drive letter starting from the end of the alphabet and maps it to the directory indicated. But the drive letter is more than the pointer used in the other drive letters; it is also a PATH to the directory. The second user can use drive letter Z, just as she would any other drive letter. But if she is using drive A, for instance, she needs only to type WORD to run the program contained in the F:\HISFILES directory.

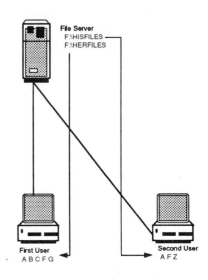

Fig. 11-4. Trustee rights. (Note: these rights are applicable to NetWare 2.15 and 2.2. NetWare 3.11 and 4.0 have the same type of rights but they use different names for some of them.)

Security

Trustee Rights

NetWare allows users to share data or to restrict access to data. Trustee rights allow access to specific directories on the file server. Without trustee rights to a certain directory, a user cannot access the data in that directory. Trustee rights are composed of several permissions a user may have to a specific directory. These permissions include Read, Write, Open, Create, Search, Delete, Modify, and Parental. Each of these permissions may be granted or denied to a user. The meanings of these permissions or rights are listed:

> Read. The user can read from open files in the directory.
>
> Write. The user can write to open files in the directory.
>
> Open. The user can open files in the directory.
>
> Create. The user can create files in the directory.
>
> Search. The user can search for files in the directory. This means he or she can also see the files in a directory list.
>
> Delete. The user can delete files in the directory.

Modify. The user can modify the Attribute of a file.
The Attribute of a file indicates what access anyone has to the file.

Parental. The user can grant the rights he or she
has to a directory to other users.

Fig. 11-5 shows the trustee rights each of the users has to the
file server using the first letter of the above listed rights. The first
user has all rights to the F:\HISFILES directory except Parental.
He can use all of the files there any way he wants, but he cannot
grant those rights to any other users. He only has Read, Open,
and Search rights in the F:\HERFILES directory. This means he
can only read from the data there, not change it or add to it. The
second user has all rights to the F:\HERFILES directory. She
could even grant additional rights in that directory to the first
user. Her access to the F:\HISFILES directory is restricted to
Write, Open, Create, and Search. This allows her to create new
files in the directory, but not to read or change the files already

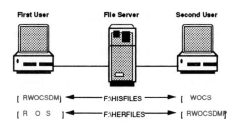

Fig. 11-5. Trustee rights.

there. (Note: the rights outlined above are applicable to NetWare
2.15 and 2.2. NetWare 3.11 and 4.0 have the same type of rights
but they use different names for some of them.)

Batch Files and Login Scripts

Many of the commands described above could become quite
tedious if you had to type them every time you used the
computer. This is why DOS provides a means for storing these
commands in a file known as a batch file. A batch file is a list of
commands that can be executed by entering the file name.

For instance, if a user needed to execute the commands listed in Fig. 11-6, those commands could be stored in a file called START.BAT. The ".BAT" portion of the name is called the extension and, in this case, indicates that the file is a batch file.

Fig. 11-6. Batch file commands.

```
MAP G= F\HERFILES
CHDIR F:\HISFILES
PATH G:
WORD
```

With this file in the current directory the user only needs to type Start. The computer will read the file and execute the commands listed in it.

NetWare provides a similar function in the form of login scripts. Login scripts are lists of commands that are executed when a user logs into NetWare. Logging in identifies the user to the network so trustee rights can be established. A user might type LOGIN USER1, then a password. NetWare would verify the password is correct, establish the trustee rights for the user, then execute the login script for that user. Each user may have a different login script and the login script may execute batch files.

Together, batch files and login scripts free the user from a great deal of typing each time she or he starts working on the computer. Additionally, the user may not need to know many of the DOS and NetWare commands if the login scripts and batch files are already installed.

Installing the Network

As outlined before, a local area network links two or more computers and other peripherals together for the purpose of sharing data and equipment. A Novell NetWare-based local area network normally is considered a dedicated file server network. That is, the network has at least one computer whose job is to act as a central data storage system.

Novell networks can consist of one or more file servers, each with dozens of workstations, multiple shared printers, and other devices that can be attached to the file server or workstations.

A small office network or a teaching laboratory can be established easily by creating one for the first time or by using existing networks. The basic components are as follows:

1. A file server (IBM AT or higher model or IBM-compatible computer) with at least 2 megabytes of RAM and a hard disk (preferably with a minimum of 80 megabytes of storage).

2. Network interface cards (NICs) for the server and the workstations.

3. Transmission media (twisted pair, coaxial, or other type according to the type of NICs used).

4. Novell NetWare 2.2 or higher.

5. A printer should also be added to the network (preferably more than one).

If a Novell NetWare-based network is not already available, the process to install one consists of the steps outlined below. (The list below provides a general review of the process.)

1. Find a location for the server.

2. Find a location for the workstations.

3. Configure each NIC to contain a unique network address.

4. Install the NIC in each of the workstations and servers that will make up the nodes of the network.

5. Connect each node with the medium chosen.

6. Write down all the hardware that makes up the network.

7. Install the NetWare network operating system and use the data from item 6 to answer NetWare's requests.

Fig. 11-7 displays a possible configuration for such a laboratory or work environment. If the network is used to provide instructions on the use of commands and network management, a program called LANSKOOL from Lan Fan Technologies, Inc. may be a good addition to the system. This program allows the instructor to project his or her workstation screen on the screen of other users for the purpose of answering questions or for instructional needs.

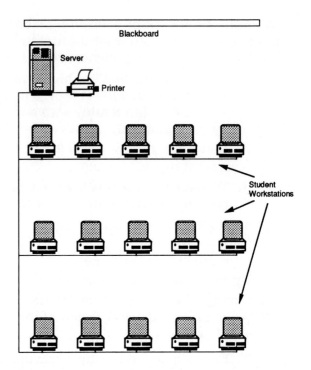

Fig. 11-7. Possible network configuration for instructional purposes.

The other scenario consists of a Novell network that already exists. It is expensive to purchase additional workstations, materials, and space if all that is required is a laboratory or room for providing training to users. If a current network is in place with user's workstations available, all that is needed is an additional server that can function as a training server for the users. This server can be connected to the existing wiring and, after NetWare is installed in it, training can be conducted using existing workstations. Fig. 11-8 shows this scenario. The equipment required for this situation is as follows:

1. A file server (IBM AT or higher model or IBM-compatible computer) with at least 2 megabytes of RAM and a hard disk (preferably with a minimum of 80 megabytes of storage).

2. A network interface card (NIC) for the server.

3. Novell NetWare 2.2 or higher.

4. A cable to connect the new server to existing wire.

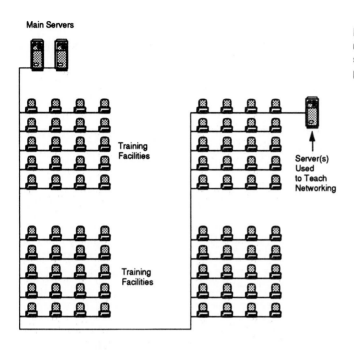

Main Servers

Training Facilities

Training Facilities

Server(s) Used to Teach Networking

Fig. 11-8. Shared networks for instructional purposes.

The process to install the server is as follows:

1. Find a location for the server. If it is going to be used for training, then probably the classroom is a good place. After a training session is over, the keyboard should be locked for additional protection.

2. Install the NIC in the server and, if required, provide a unique address.

3. Connect the server to existing network transmission media.

4. Install NetWare in the server and provide a unique server name.

The process to install NetWare is beyond the scope of this book. However, after the server goes on line, users who need training will simply attach their workstation to the server. Any commands issued, and any modifications to the environment stay in the training server without affecting the rest of the users and file servers. The server can be configured so that users can attach themselves to other servers.

Before NetWare can be installed on a system, a listing of hardware, users, and other resources must be recorded. Also, all steps taken during the installation process must be recorded in case something goes wrong and an audit needs to occur.

Additionally, knowing the applications, directories, users, and workstations on the network will help in maintaining the network, and in performing future upgrades or expansions that may be required.

Summary

There are two major items that must be considered when planning or installing a LAN: the network hardware components and the network software. There are three major categories of devices that make up the hardware components of a local area network. These are the server, the LAN communication system, and the workstations.

LAN servers are computers on the network that are accessible to network users. They contain resources that they "serve" to users who request the service. The most common type of server is the file server. Most LANs have at least one file server, and many have multiple file servers. The file server contains software applications and data files that are provided to users upon request.

When two or more computers are connected on a network, a special cable and a network interface board are required in each computer. Connect the server to the cable and then connect the cable to these boards. Most microcomputers are not equipped with an interface port that can be connected to a second microcomputer for networking purposes (except the Macintosh). As a result, a network interface board (NIC) or network adapter must be installed in the microcomputer.

The processes that take place in the hardware devices of a LAN must be controlled by software. The software comes in the form of the network operating system. One of the most widely used network operating systems is NetWare, which is provided by Novell, Inc.

The network operating system controls the operation of the file server, and it makes the network resources accessible and easy to use. It manages server security and provides the network administrators with the tools to control the file structure and user access to the network.

A file server is a computer with some added hardware and software. The main components of the server that will affect speed are the central processing unit, the hard disk and controller, and the random access memory installed in the server.

To effectively provide file sharing services, the software that controls the file server must provide security, concurrent access controls, access optimizing, reliability, transparent access to the file server and peripherals attached to the server, and interfaces to other networks.

Questions

1. Name three commercially available LANs.
2. What is the most distinguishing characteristic of Banyan VINES?
3. What makes Novell NetWare a popular operating system for networks?
4. What is a file server?
5. What is the function of the network interface card (NIC)?
6. What is the purpose of the network operating system?
7. What is the purpose of the network profile?
8. Describe three characteristics that affect file server efficiency.
9. Describe four characteristics of server software.
10. Why is it important to have a fast hard disk and controller in a file server?
11. If given a choice, what CPU type would you choose for a network consisting of 20 users? Why?
12. Why is it important to use metering software?

Project

Creating a Network Log Book

A typical log book contains the information outlined below. One should be created for each server.

Name of the server.

Type of hardware.

Date of installation.

Name of installer.

Operating system:

> Name and version of the operating system in use.
>
> Installation date of the operating system.
>
> Name of the operating system installer.

Server:

> Purchase date of the server.
>
> Server's network address.
>
> Location of the server.

Volume:

> Volume(s) name(s) in the server.
>
> Volume disk number.
>
> Volume(s) size(s).

Users' workstations:

> Users' names.
>
> Users' locations.
>
> Users' network addresses.
>
> Users' workstation types.
>
> Users' workstation RAM.
>
> Users' workstation disk options.
>
> Users' workstation graphics boards and monitors.
>
> Users' workstation hardware options (other).

Applications:

> Name of the application in use.
>
> Application's vendor.
>
> Application's purchase date.

Application's version number.

Application's memory requirements.

Application's disk space requirements.

Additional log information.

Using the above as a guideline and a word processor, create a NetWare log book and fill in the information requested for the network that you will be installing during the hands-on portion of this class. Make sure that all information is correct because once the network is set up, it is difficult and time consuming to correct major errors or omissions in the setup process.

Network Design Fundamentals

Objectives

After completing this chapter you will:

1. Be familiar with the life cycle of network design and implementation.
2. Understand the importance of response time, network modeling, message analysis, and geographic location in network design.
3. Know the different types of security threats to a data communication network.
4. Know some standard controls for unauthorized access to a network by users and by computer viruses.
5. Understand the basic principles for developing a disaster recovery plan.
6. Understand the basic principles for developing a network management plan.

471

Key Words

Computer Virus	Disaster Plan
Encryption	Feasibility Study
Life Cycle	Network Management
Network Modeling	Network Security
Password/ID	Response Time

Introduction

Designing or upgrading a network is a complex and time consuming task that must follow standard system analysis methods. The typical planning methodology includes following the system life cycle and its inherent phases. Although the phases are not always followed in the sequence provided, it is important that network designers follow the life cycle process if the end result is to be successful. This chapter describes the different life cycle phases of system analysis and correlates them to network design and planning. Also, some specialized topics of network design, such as response time and network modeling, are explored.

The introduction of computer processing, centralized storage, and communication networks has increased the need for securing data stored in these systems. This emphasis manifests itself in the increase of available techniques and methods for detecting and deterring intrusions into the network by unauthorized users. Several types of network security enforcement techniques are explained. Additionally, a discussion of viruses is presented.

An additional measure of network security is the implementation of a network disaster recovery plan. The plan must be implemented within the framework of the system analysis approach. Several ideas on how to design a recovery plan are presented in the chapter.

The Life Cycle of a Network

The life cycle of a network is an important planning consideration because of inevitable technological changes that will have to be dealt with during the development and operation of a network system. Each network is a representation of the technology at the time of its design and implementation. Eventually, the network will become obsolete. New technologies and services will emerge, making it cost effective to replace outdated equipment and software with newer, more powerful, and less expensive technology.

During its life cycle, a network passes through the phases outlined in Fig. 12-1:

1. The feasibility study involves the subphases of problem definition and investigation. The problem definition attempts to find the problems that exist in the organization that caused management to initiate the study. The investigation subphase involves gathering input data to develop a precise definition of the present data communication conditions and to uncover problems.

2. The analysis phase uses the data gathered in the feasibility study to identify the requirements that the network must meet in order to have a successful implementation.

3. During the design phase, all components of the network are defined so their acquisition can be made.

4. The implementation phase consists of the installation of the hardware and software that make up the network system. Additionally, during this phase all documentation and training materials are developed.

5. During the maintenance and upgrade phase, the network is kept operational and fine-tuned by network operations personnel. Additionally, updates of software and hardware are performed to keep the network operating efficiently and effectively.

The life cycle concept can be applied to network design as a whole or in part. As a network moves through these phases, the planner becomes more constrained in the alternatives available for increasing data capacity, in the applications available, and in dealing with operational problems that may arise. These restrictions are the result of increased costs and the difficulty in changing the operational procedures of the network. In addition, although the phases of the life cycle are presented here as a series of steps, the designer may have to go back through one or

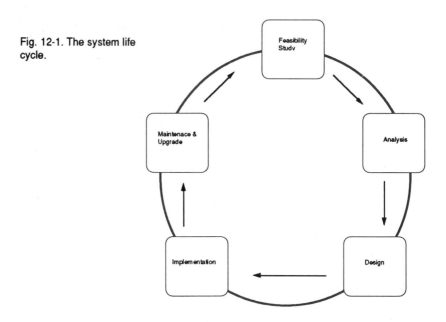

Fig. 12-1. The system life cycle.

more phases of the design process. This feedback mechanism is important in order to incorporate concepts or ideas that may surface during the design and installation of the network.

The Feasibility Study

The feasibility study is performed in order to define the existing problem clearly and to determine whether a network is operationally feasible for the type of organization that it plans to serve. This is not the place to determine the type of network that may be implemented. Rather, the designer needs to fully understand the problem or problems that are perceived by the management personnel who initiated the request for the study. This phase of the life cycle can be subdivided into problem definition, problem analysis, and solution determination.

Problem definition is the first step in the feasibility study. It is important to distinguish between problems and solutions. If a solution is made part of the problem definition, analysis of alternative solutions becomes handicapped.

The second step is problem analysis. The problems need to be analyzed to determine whether and how they may point to the formulation of a new network or the upgrade of an existing network. The investigation of the current system takes place by gathering input data from the personnel involved in the use of the network and from the personal observations of the designer.

Interviews with users help to develop a precise definition of current data processing needs and to identify current problems. This process emphasizes only the information that is relevant to the network planning and design process. Additionally, interviews involve personnel in the network design process, therefore facilitating its acceptance when the final product is implemented. This data gathering process concentrates on terminal or workstation location, the current type of communication facilities and host computer systems, and the future data processing and communication requirements that network users expect.

Aside from the interviews with current or potential network users, technical reports and documents can provide insight into the operation of an existing network. Research can provide exact locations of workstations, multiplexers, gateways, transmission speeds, codes, and current network service and cost. This information complements the interviews of personnel. It is essential in order to determine where potential problems may arise and to provide an effective solution to the corporation.

When extensive on-site interviews and surveys are not economically feasible, questionnaires can be used to gather information. Questionnaires and survey techniques can be combined with follow-up interviews to gather and validate data about the existing network. This helps ensure the success of the final design. Field personnel must always be encouraged to participate fully in developing accurate and complete data and in providing ideas and insights that cannot be provided in questionnaires.

The third aspect of the feasibility study is to examine possible solutions to the problem definition, identify the best solution, and determine if it's realistic based on the gathered data. This analysis provides a "best-scenario" solution, the one that offers the best all-around method for dealing with the problem.

At the end of the feasibility study, a report is produced for management. The report should contain the following items:

1. Findings of the feasibility study
2. Alternative solutions in addition to the best possible solution

3. Reasons for continuing to the next phase of the process

4. If a realistic solution was not found, recommendations for another study and the methodology to follow in order to arrive at a feasible solution

Analysis

This phase encompasses the analysis of all data gathered during the investigative stage of the feasibility phase. The end result is a set of requirements for the final product. These requirements are approved by management and implemented by the designer or designers of the network.

The formulated requirements must relate computer applications and information systems to the needs for terminals, workstations, communication hardware and software, common-carrier services, data input/output locations, data generation, training, and how the data will be processed and used. As a result, the formulated requirements identify the work activities that will be automated and networked. They relate the activities to the information input/output, the medium of transmission, where and how the data resides, and the geographic location where the information must be generated and processed.

Since data communication networks serve many types of applications, the volume of information for all applications must be combined to determine the final network design. Analyzing the raw data acquired in the investigation section of the feasibility study helps identify the total data volume that must be moved by the network.

The final product of this phase is another document, sometimes called a functional specifications report, which includes the functions that must be performed by the network after it is implemented. The report can include the following sections:

1. Network identification and description

2. Benefits of proposed network

3. Current status of the organization and existing networks

4. Network operational description

5. Data security requirements

6. Applications available for this network

7. Response time
8. Anticipated reliability
9. Data communications load that the network will support
10. Geographic distribution of nodes
11. Documentation
12. Training
13. Network expected life
14. Reference materials used in preparing the report

Many other requirements besides these can be incorporated into the report, but they provide a good basis to work from. The number and complexity of the requirements will vary according to the type and size of network being recommended.

Design

The design phase of the life cycle is one of the longest phases. The outcome of this phase depends on the expectations of management and the economics of the corporation. At a minimum it will include a set of internal and external specifications. The internal specifications are the "blueprints" of how the network operates, including modules used for building the network. The external specifications are the interfaces that the user will see when using the network. Both of these specifications may include data flow diagrams, logic diagrams, product models, prototypes, and results from network modeling.

At this point, designers should have a detailed description of all network requirements. These requirements should now be prioritized by dividing them into mandatory requirements, desirable requirements, and wish list requirements.

The mandatory requirements are those that must be present if the network is to be operational and effective. The desirable requirements are items that can improve the effectiveness of the network and the work of the users, but can be deferred until later if other priorities warrant it. The wish list requirements are those provided by workers who feel that such items could help them increase their individual productivity. However, when implementing wish list requirements, the network designer needs to be careful. Small increases in productivity might require a large cost, and the money might be expended more effectively in other areas.

The design phase will also indicate how the individual network components will be procured and the procedures for installation and testing of the network. The final document produced during this phase will become the "blueprint" for the remaining phases of the life cycle. Several items that network designers will have to address during this phase are response time, a network model, geographic scope of the network, message analysis, and some software and hardware considerations.

Response Time

One of the most important requirements in network design is response time. Response time is the time that expires between sending an inquiry from a workstation or terminal and receiving the response back at the workstation. The total response time of a network is composed of delay times that occur at the workstation end when transmitting a message, the time required for the message to get to a host, the host processing time, the transmission back from the host to the workstation, and finally the time required for the workstation to display the information to the user. Usually, a shorter response time requirement will dictate a more expensive system. A typical cost versus response time curve is found in Fig. 12-2. The graph shows that the cost of a network is exponentially proportional to the average response time required.

Fig. 12-2. Cost vs response time graph.

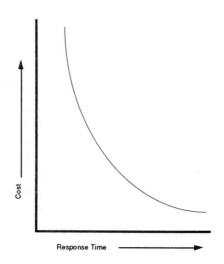

Cost

Response Time

To find the response time for a network that has yet to be implemented, the designers should look at statistics from other operating networks with similar work loads, a comparable number of users, and similar applications being run. Although the scenario may be difficult to find, comparing similar networks will provide statistics with approximate average response times and some indications as to pitfall areas for the network being designed. In situations where a similar network is not available, predicting techniques must be used. These techniques are based on network modeling and simulation methods.

Simulation is a technique for modeling the behavior of the network. The response time is viewed as an average of the time elapsed for certain discrete events. (Fig. 12-3 depicts some of the causes for increasing response times.) Simulation programs are written to emulate a series of real-life events, and the elapsed times for each event are added up to provide a measure of the response time and behavior of the network.

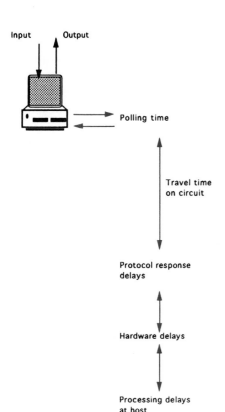

Fig. 12-3. Reasons for increasing response time.

Network Modeling

One of the major uses of the data gathering process is in developing a network topology. The load (the number of messages that need to be transmitted) and site data are used as input for network modeling programs. Network modeling programs are application software that model a network, using mathematical models.

The network design alternatives are mathematically modeled for performance and then for cost, using public network tariffs and the geographically distributed peak loads found during the investigation step of the feasibility study. The data that makes up the model can be placed in several commercially available software programs to better understand the behavior of the network under certain conditions. The model created, along with the simulation tool, provides an overall performance capacity and cost analysis for each network alternative. However, simulating a network is a complex task that requires a thorough understanding of networks and of the simulation program and its limitations. The advantage of having a model that can be manipulated electronically is that "What if" questions can be asked of the model, and the effect of any changes can be visualized and understood before any money and effort are spent in setting up the network. A good model will allow designers to find weaknesses in the design plan and to anticipate any problems that may appear during installation or operation of the network.

The output from the model is the basis for recommendations of a particular network design to be implemented. All aspects of the network should be included in these recommendations. Some of these factors are least-cost alternative, short response time, technical feasibility, maintainability, and reliability.

Once the overall network topology has been determined, the model is manually fine-tuned to achieve the levels of operational performance required. The modeled network may place hardware in locations where it is not cost effective, due to the time and cost of maintaining such equipment. In this case it would be better to incur the additional cost and place the items in a location where they are more accessible for maintenance purposes.

Network modeling tools are limited in their abilities to analyze the different data communication requirements. They normally model one aspect of the system, such as the speed link between workstations and servers. To model the other aspects of the network, subsequent iterations of the model are performed. The results of each analysis are combined to produce a final network configuration.

Geographic Scope

To better understand the geographic scope of the network, several maps may need to be generated. The geographic maps of the scope of the network should be prepared after the model is created and tuned. The geographic scope of the network can be local, citywide, national, or international. Normally, a map is prepared showing the location of individual nodes. The individual items that connect each node, such as gateways and concentrators, do not have to be indicated on the map (see Fig. 12-4).

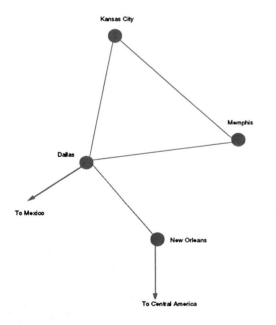

Fig. 12-4. Geographic scope of the network.

The next map to be prepared indicates the location of nodes within the boundaries of the country. It needs to show the different states or provinces that will be interconnected, and a line must show each connection from state to state.

The third type of map that may be required shows the location of the individual cities that are part of the network. The map should contain lines that connect each city in the network in the same logical fashion that the actual communication lines are distributed.

The last map shows the local facilities and the terminal or workstation location. It can be as wide as the boundaries of a city or as specific as the individual buildings and offices that are part of the network. Individual network connectivity items such as concentrators and multiplexers are not required to be displayed on the map. It is possible that, at this stage, the location of these items is not yet determined.

Message Analysis

Message analysis involves identifying the message type that will be transmitted or received at each terminal or workstation. The message attributes are also identified, including the number of bytes for each message. Message length and message volume identification are critical to determine the volume of messages that will be transmitted through the network.

The daily traffic volume is sometimes segmented into hourly traffic to provide the designers with the peak traffic hours. This information is used to identify problems with data traffic during peak hours.

It is important to note that most networks are designed based on average traffic volumes instead of traffic volume during peak hours. For most organizations it is not cost effective to purchase a network based solely on volume during peak hours.

Software/Hardware Considerations

The type of software purchased for the network will determine the operation of the network. It will specify the speed of transmission and whether the network will perform asynchronous or synchronous communication and full-duplex or half-duplex communication. Additionally, the software will determine the types of networks that can be accessed by the network being designed.

The network designer should select a protocol that is compatible with the OSI seven-layer model and one that can grow as the network grows within the organization. The protocol is a crucial element of the overall design, since the server architecture must interface with it. If the protocol follows accepted standards, the addition or replacement of multiple platform servers can be accomplished without many difficulties.

The pieces of hardware that are part of a network are:

1. Terminals
2. Microcomputers and network interface cards
3. File servers
4. Terminal controllers
5. Multiplexers
6. Concentrators
7. Line-sharing devices
8. Protocol converters
9. Hardware encrypting devices
10. Switches
11. PBX switchboards
12. Communication circuits
13. FEPs
14. Port sharing devices
15. Host computers
16. Channel extenders
17. Testing equipment
18. Surge protectors, power conditioners, and uninterruptible power supplies

Each of these devices has a unique graphical representation that varies slightly according to the designer (see Fig. 12-5). He or she should prepare a graphical representation of the network hardware using the symbols outlined in Fig. 12-5 or similar ones.

The final hardware configuration needs to take into account the software protocol and network operating system that are going to be implemented in the network. The results should be the least-cost alternative that meets all the organization's requirements. Additionally, before ordering any hardware, the designers should decide how to handle diagnostics, troubleshooting, and network repair. Most new network hardware has built-in diagnostics and testing capabilities.

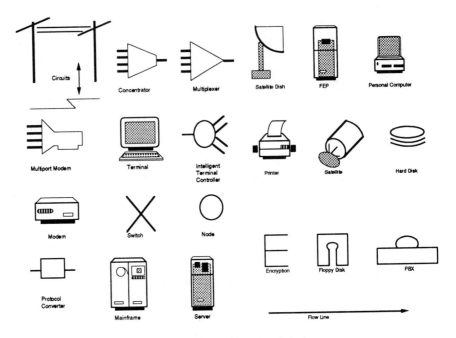

Fig. 12-5. Symbols used in network design.

Finally, selecting hardware and software involves selecting more than just a system. It involves selecting a vendor. The vendor's ability to maintain, upgrade, and expand the network components will determine the overall success of the network.

Implementation

During the implementation phase the individual components of the network are purchased and installed. This phase can be divided into:

1. Software acquisition. If a new network is being implemented, the necessary network operating system, application software, managing software, and communication protocols must be procured. A useful tool in software and hardware procurement is a request for proposal (RFP). The RFP is based on the network requirements produced in the investigation step of the feasibility study. Bids come from potential vendors in response to an RFP. The bids are evaluated, using specified criteria, and one is selected.

2. Hardware acquisition. Hardware procurement can be done from the same software vendor or a third party vendor may be used. Some software can run on a

multitude of computer hardware configurations (sometimes called platforms). Deciding on the software first helps narrow the selection of a hardware vendor.

3. Installation. During or after the hardware and software acquisition, the individual components need to be assembled into what will become the network. The final product of this phase is an operational network system.

4. Testing. Testing should be conducted in an integrated fashion. That is, hardware and software should be tested simultaneously as they are implemented, trying to process maximum work loads whenever possible. This will provide statistics that indicate the best and worst possibilities of network efficiency. It will also provide feedback for fine-tuning the network before it becomes fully operational. Integrated testing ensures that all parts of the system will function together properly.

   Testing should be performed using test plans developed during the design phase of the life cycle. There must be a complete and extensive test plan that produces predictable test results reflecting the operation of the network under real-life situations. These results are necessary if management is to trust and accept the network.

5. Documentation. Even though documentation is placed in the life cycle at this stage, it should be an integral part of each phase in network design. Reports that document every aspect of the network, from its conception until final implementation, must be present for audit trail purposes and must always accompany the network. These documents can take the form of reference manuals, maintenance manuals, operational and user manuals, and all the reference materials used in the feasibility study.

6. Switch-over. The switch-over step consists of moving all transactions from the old system to the new system. The final product of this step is the active working network. The switch-over plan must include milestones to be reached during the transition period and contingency plans in case the new system does not meet operational guidelines.

The Request for Proposals

Once the network has been designed, but before implementation can proceed, the specific vendors must be selected. A formal approach is to send a request for proposal (RFP) to prospective vendors. The RFP is a document that asks each vendor to prepare a price quotation for the configuration described in the RFP. Some RFPs give vendors great latitude in how the proposed system should be implemented. Others are very specific and expect detailed technical data in response from the vendor.

The format of an RFP can vary according to how specific the document needs to be. However, as a general rule, an RFP contains the following topics:

o Title page. This identifies the originating organization and title of the project.

o Table of contents. Any lengthy document should have a table of contents to provide a quick reference to specific topics.

o Introduction. This is a brief introduction that includes an overview of the organization for which the final product is intended, the problem to be solved, schedule for the response to the RFP, evaluation and selection criteria, installation schedules, and operation schedules.

o RFP response guidelines. The RFP guidelines for responding to it establish the schedule for the selection process, the format of the proposal, how proposals are evaluated, the time and place of proposal submission, when presentations are made, and the time for the announcement of the winner or winners.

o Deadlines. The deadline and place for submitting responses to the RFP must be stated clearly throughout the proposal. The deadlines should also include equipment delivery dates and the date to commence operations.

o Response format. The format of the response to the RFP depends on the user. Normally, responses come in two separate documents. One document contains the specific technical details of the proposed system. The other document has the financial and contractual details.

o Evaluation criteria. The RFP needs to include guidelines for the vendors as to how the responses will be
evaluated. It should include a prioritized list indicating the items that are the most important. This allows
the vendors to provide further information on these
items in their responses.

Typically, vendor responses include the following items:

1. System design
2. System features
3. Upgrade capabilities
4. Installation methods
5. Installation schedule
6. Testing methods
7. Maintenance agreements
8. Cost of items
9. Payment schedule
10. System support
11. Warranty coverage
12. Training options

This is the largest portion of the RFP. It describes the problems
that need to be solved. Solutions to these problems should not
be included in this section. Rather, the vendors should be
allowed to propose their own solutions.

Maintenance and Upgrade

The last phase in the life cycle of the network is the maintenance
and upgrade of the components of the network. During the
maintenance and upgrade period the system is kept operational
and fine-tuned to keep adequate performance levels and fix
system problems.

The products of this phase are change and upgrade requests,
updates to existing documentation to reflect changes in the
network, and reports and statistics from the monitoring and
control functions of the network.

At some point in the life of the system, the new network in its own turn will be replaced or phased out. This final stage in the life cycle leads to the beginning of a new life cycle as the organization goes through the same process to find a replacement or upgrade to the existing system.

Network Security

An important responsibility of network managers is maintaining control over the security of the network and the data stored and transmitted by it. The major goals of security are to prevent computer crime and data loss.

Detection of security problems in a network is compounded by the nature of information processing, storage, and the transmission system in the network. For example:

1. Data is stored on media not easily readable by people.
2. Data can be erased or modified without leaving evidence.
3. Computerized records do not have signatures to verify authenticity or distinguish copies from originals.
4. Data can be accessed and manipulated from remote stations.
5. Transactions are performed at high speeds and often without human monitoring.

The threat of the loss of the data stored in the network is sufficient reason for implementing methods and techniques to detect and prevent loss. It is important to incorporate the security methods during the design phase of the life cycle rather than add them later. Although no system is completely sealed from outside interference, the following methodologies will help in preventing a breach in network security.

Physical Security

The main emphasis of physical security is to prevent unauthorized access to the communications room, network control center, or communications equipment. This could result in damage to the network equipment or tapping into the circuits by unauthorized personnel.

The room or building that houses network communication equipment should be locked, and access should be restricted by network managers. Terminals should be equipped with locks that deactivate the screen and keyboard switch. In some situations, instead of keys and locks, a programmable plastic card can be used. The locking mechanism that accepts the card may be programmed to accept passwords, in addition to the magnetic code in the card.

Encrypting

With many networks using satellite and microwave relays for transmitting data, anyone with an antenna can pick up the transmission and have access to the data being transmitted. One method to safeguard the information transmitted through the airwaves, and even data transmitted through wires, is called encrypting or ciphering.

Encrypting involves the substitution or transposition of the bits that represent a known data message. The level of encrypting can be of any complexity, and it is usually judged by a work factor. A higher work factor indicates a more complex cipher or encryption.

As shown in Fig. 12-6, an encrypting system (also called a cryptosystem) between a sender and a receiver consists of the following elements:

1. A message to be transmitted and protected.
2. A large set of invertible cryptographic transformations (ciphers) applied to the message to produce ciphertext and later to recover the original message by applying the inverse of the cipher to the ciphertext.
3. The key of the cryptosystem that selects one specific transformation from the set of possible transformations.

A cryptosystem is effective only if the key is kept secret. Also the set of ciphers must be large enough that the correct key could not be guessed or determined by trial-and-error techniques.

The National Bureau of Standards has set a data encrypting standard (DES). The DES effectiveness derives from its complexity, the large number of possible keys, and the security of the keys used. The DES transformation is an iterative nonlinear

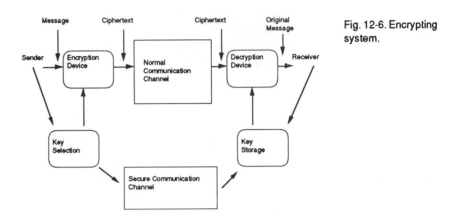

Fig. 12-6. Encrypting system.

block product cipher that uses 64-bit data blocks. It is implemented on special purpose microcircuits that have been developed for DES and are available commercially. The DES encrypting algorithm is used in reverse for decrypting the ciphertext. The key is also a 64-bit word, 8 of which are parity bits. Therefore, the effective key length is 56 bits.

The suitability of a type of encrypting algorithm for applications in a data network depends on the relevant characteristics of the applications running in the system, the characteristics of the chosen algorithm, and the technical aspects of the network. Even though the purpose of encrypting is to secure data, the effect of the cryptosystem on the network is equally important. A cryptosystem that provides excellent security may deteriorate the performance of the network to unacceptable levels.

User Identification and Passwords

User identification (ID) and passwords are the most common security systems employed in networks, and at times the easiest to break. The user ID is provided by the network manager when the user profile is added to the network. The password is normally at the user's discretion. Unfortunately, many users choose passwords that are too simple and that can be easily guessed by trial and error, such as their last name.

Some systems provide the generation of passwords for users. This technique is more effective than allowing users to define their own passwords. The user must keep the password available, but protect it from being accessible by others.

User IDs and passwords by themselves are not an effective security technique. When combined with call-back units, encrypting devices, and network physical security, they provide an effective deterrent to unauthorized users.

Time and Location Controls

The time and location of user access to the network can be controlled by software and hardware mechanisms. Some users may be allowed to access the system only during specific times of the day and on specified days of the week. Other users may access the system only from specified terminals. Although such measures are an inconvenience to users, they help in managing data flow and in monitoring the network usage.

Time controls are performed on individuals by having a user profile in the network that determines the day and time intervals during which the user can access the system. Location controls are enforced by having a terminal profile. The terminal profile identifies the terminal and sets up specific paths that the terminal can follow to access selected data. No matter who the user is on the terminal, the terminal profile can be given a higher priority to override the user profile.

Switched Port and Dialing Access

The most vulnerable security point on a network is switched ports that allow dial-in access. They are a security risk because they allow any person with a telephone and terminal to access the system. To enhance the security of switched ports with dial-in access, they should be operational only during the time when transactions are allowed, instead of 24 hours per day. A call-back unit can be used to deter unauthorized calls and to ensure that calls are made only from authorized locations.

The telephone numbers of the switch should be safeguarded and be available only to personnel who must have access to them. User identification and password enforcement take on a higher priority with dial-in access. In systems that contain critical data, a person-to-person authentication as well as application-to-user authentication should be used.

Audit Logs

Transaction logs are an important aspect of network security. Every login attempt should be logged, including date and time of attempt, user ID and password used, location, and number of unsuccessful attempts. In some situations, after a number of unsuccessful login attempts are made, the data described above may be displayed on an operator console for immediate action.

Many of the above methods can be incorporated into a system including extensive audit trails that collect the necessary information required to determine who is accessing the system. However, audit trails are worthless unless network managers study them and monitor the network.

Viruses

A computer virus is an executable computer program that propagates itself, using other programs as carriers, and sometimes modifies itself during or after replication: It is intended to perform some unwanted function on the computer system attached to the network.

Some viruses perform simple annoying functions such as popping up in the middle of an application to demonstrate they are there. Other viruses are more destructive and erase or modify portions of programs or critical data. They are typically introduced into network computers by floppy disk-based software that was purchased or copied. Many of the known viruses enter networks through programs or data downloaded from electronic bulletin boards. Some are deposited on networks by the creator of the virus. Other viruses migrate from network to network through gateways and other interconnecting hardware.

Viruses can be monitored and eliminated at the user level with the use of antivirus software. This type of application program searches files and looks for known computer viruses, alerting users to their presence. At this point, the user has the option to eliminate the virus or take some other security action. This process can take place on a stand-alone machine before introducing the application in the network. Additionally, the user can also run a virus scanning program from a directory in the network. The program will then scan the user's floppy disk and report any suspicious files.

At the system manager level, virus protection can be accomplished by using a network statistical program with a virus detection component that is designed to run as the network operating system is active. This type of application watches for signs of a virus and alerts the LAN manager at the first symptom. The program warns the LAN manager when application or data files show any change from the original. An example of this type of application is TGR Software's SCUA Plus.

It is important to note that antivirus software does not identify all viruses circulating. This type of software can work only on known viruses and offers little protection against new or unknown viruses. On a regular basis, the makers of antivirus software provide upgrades that contain protection against new computer viruses, introduced since the last release of the virus protection program.

Disaster Recovery Planning

The increased use of computer systems and data communication networks has expanded the need for a realistic disaster plan. The network manager needs to be involved in such planning and should have knowledge in the areas that follow:

1. The need for disaster planning
2. Computer backup approaches
3. Network backup approaches
4. The characteristics of a disaster backup strategy
5. Planning processes of the organization
6. The impact of a data network disaster on the organization

Planning for a disaster is much like planning for a new system. It requires goals, objectives, design, implementation, testing, documentation, and maintenance. Producing a good disaster plan requires significant organizational skills. However, LAN developers and LAN managers should also concentrate on disaster prevention measures. Good prevention measures may allow the disaster recovery plan not to be used.

The measures below and others will make the recovery process easier and protect users' information.

1. Adequate surge protectors. All computers in the network should be protected with surge protectors that can react to a large voltage spike in as little as one or two nanoseconds. This type of device normally costs about $100, so it can be expensive to outfit a network with many workstations. However, when compared with the cost of a workstation, it is worth the price.

2. Servers must be protected with a UPS. A UPS protects against voltage surges and drops. In many networks, the server contains invaluable data that a company needs to function. Protecting the data is one of the most important functions of the LAN manager. Additionally, the UPS allows the proper shutdown of the network in case of a loss of power.

3. Communication line protectors and filters. Computers connected to modems and telephone lines also need protection from incoming noise and surges that may travel through the phone lines.

4. Protect cables. All cabling must be protected and placed in locations where a user cannot accidentally tamper with the line.

5. Adequate backups. Continuous and comprehensive backups will ensure that all data and programs are safeguarded. If possible, during a period of network inactivity, the backup and recovery plans outlined below should be rehearsed.

Characteristics of the Disaster Recovery Plan

A disaster plan must meet certain criteria, including:

1. Reliability
2. Operability
3. Response time to activate the plan
4. Cost effectiveness

Reliability

Whatever the strategy taken to safeguard the network and the data stored on it, the organization must be confident that, in case of a disaster, the plan will work. Confidence can be achieved by using proven techniques to replace network media in case of a failure.

The best plans are those that are kept simple. The plan needs to be tested in order to ensure that the information in the system is secured. Any disaster plan is suspect without proper testing.

Operability

The methods used for recovering from a disaster should be consistent with the normal methods of backup and restore that are used in the routine management of the network. This ensures that, in case of failure, trained personnel will be able to restore the system quickly and without errors. Additionally, the plan should be well documented and distributed to appropriate personnel.

Response Time to Activate the Plan

The recovery plan must be capable of being activated within the time constraints imposed by the network. In some cases, backup networks are activated on a temporary basis until the stricken facility is restored to an acceptable operational level. The network design must be flexible to allow for time-sensitive considerations.

Cost Effectiveness

The recovery plan must be cost effective since it will be idle for most of the network life. However, in a disaster situation, the backup system must also be flexible enough for long-term use, if necessary.

Disaster Recovery Methodologies

Extensive planning and research are required to produce an effective disaster recovery plan. Some of the concerns that a manager may want to address in preparing a recovery plan follow:

1. Create a list of the critical applications. This will require involvement from top management. The items on the list should be prioritized, and their impact on the firm should be analyzed.
2. Determine the required recovery time for the organization.
3. Determine the critical nodes in the network.

4. Analyze the critical work load for each node, and create a transaction profile for it.

5. Analyze the use of shared communication facilities and alternate methods of information transfer.

6. Obtain best vendor and carrier lead-time estimates for a backup network.

7. Identify facilities that exceed the recovery time. That is, these facilities are critical and the recovery time exceeds the allowable down time. These must be restored first.

8. Determine costs.

9. Have the vendor develop a plan to connect users with planned backup networks.

10. List all cable and front end requirements.

11. Make a list of equipment that can be shared, such as modems.

12. List all facilities that can be provided at the recovery site in case of a prolonged downtime.

13. List all support personnel available for recovery.

14. List all dial-up facilities at the recovery site.

The Planning Process

The disaster recovery plan may be divided into strategic and implementation sections. The strategic section lists the goals, design objectives, and strategies for network recovery. The implementation section describes the steps to take during the recovery process. Some of the major items to be included in the plan are provided below.

1. List all assumptions and objectives, and the methodology for implementing the objectives.

2. List all tasks to be performed before, during, and after a disaster.

3. Put together a technical description of any backup networks.

4. List all personnel involved in the recovery phase and their responsibilities.

5. Describe how the recovery site will be employed.

6. Make a list of critical nodes and their profiles.

7. Make a list of vendors and carriers who will supply facilities and backup.

8. Make a list of alternate sources of equipment and supplies.

9. Create all necessary network diagrams.

10. Make a list of all required software, manuals, testing, and operational procedures of backup networks.

11. Diagram all backup circuits.

12. Describe procedures for updating the recovery plan.

A commitment to an effective disaster recovery plan must have the support of top management. They must be aware of the consequences of the failure of such a plan. A team consisting of a coordinator and representatives from management is required to continually upgrade the plan as facilities are added and modified, if the firm is to be protected.

Network Management

For a network to be effective and efficient over a long period of time, a good network management plan must be created. The network management plan must have two goals:

1. The plan should prevent problems where possible.

2. The plan should prepare for problems that will most likely occur.

A comprehensive plan needs to include the following duties:

1. Monitor and control hard disk space.

2. Monitor network workload and performance.

3. Add to and maintain user login information and workstation information.

4. Monitor and reset network devices.

5. Perform regular maintenance on software and data files stored in the servers.

6. Make regular backups of data and programs stored in the servers.

The server's hard disk is one of the network's primary commodities. Files for network-based programs are stored on the hard disk. Print jobs that are sent from workstations to network printers are stored on the hard disk in a queue before they are printed. And in some networks, personal files and data are stored on the network hard disk.

If the hard disk space fills up, then print jobs can't be printed and users can't save their data files. Data files may also be corrupted since data manipulation can't be accomplished.

Disk space must be available at all times for legitimate users of the network. The hard disk space must be checked every day. Growth of users' files should be controlled to ensure that a single user doesn't monopolize the hard disk. Unwanted files must be deleted, and when heavy disk fragmentation occurs, all files could be backed up and the disk reformatted. This will allow defragmentation of files on the hard disk and provide for more efficient access to data on the server's hard disk. Some networks allow the use of software to repack files on the hard disk and eliminate file fragmentation. When possible, such tools should be used. However, all files should be backed up before using a defragmentation software application, in case something goes wrong.

Monitoring Server Performance

The performance of the LAN's server will determine how quickly the server can deliver data to the user. The servers must be monitored to ensure that they are performing at their peak.

Several factors determine the response of a server. One of these factors is the number of users that are attached to the system. Working with more users will slow the server response time. If a specific application has a large number of users, the server that contains the application could be dedicated to serve only such a program. Other servers could be used to distribute the load of other programs on the system.

Additionally, the server's main memory (RAM) should be monitored to make sure that it is used efficiently. Many servers use RAM as disk buffers. These buffers cannot function if there isn't sufficient memory to run the network operating system and the buffers. If a server has to reduce the number of buffers required for I/O, the overall performance of the network will suffer.

Most networks provide tools that show statistical data about the use of the network and outline potential problems. An experienced network administrator uses these statistics to ensure that the network operates at its peak level at all times.

Maintaining User and Workstation Information

Network users have network identification numbers that can be used to monitor security and the growth of the network. A network manager must keep a log of information about the network users such as login ID, node address, network address, and some personal information such as phone, name, and address. Also, network cabling, workstation type, configuration, and purpose of use should be kept in records. This information can be stored in a database. It can be used to detect problems with data delivery, make changes to users' profiles, workstation profiles, accounts, and support other tasks.

Monitoring and Resetting Network Devices

A network consists not only of servers and workstations but also of printers, input devices such as scanners, and other machines. Some devices may need to be reset daily (such as some types of gateways), while other devices require periodic maintenance. Some types of electronic mail routers may need to be monitored on an hourly basis to make sure they are working properly. In any case, all devices should be monitored periodically, and a schedule of reset and maintenance should be created to ensure that all network devices work when a user requests them.

Maintaining Software

Software applications, especially database applications, need regular maintenance to rebuild files and reclaim space left empty by deleted records. Space not used must be made available to the system, and in many cases index files will have to be rebuilt.

Additionally, as new software upgrades become available, they need to be placed in the network. After an upgrade is placed in the network, file cleanup may have to take place. Also, any incompatibilities between the new software and the network will need to be resolved.

Old e-mail messages will have to be deleted and the space they occupy made available to the system. The same type of procedure will have to be performed as users are added to or deleted from the network.

Making Regular Backups

Backups of user information and data must be made on a periodic basis. If a server's hard disk fails, a major problem could occur if backups are inadequate.

Backups of server information are normally placed on tapes or cartridges. Tapes and cartridges offer an inexpensive solution to backup needs and can hold large amounts of information. Their capacity ranges from 20 megabytes to as much as 2,200 megabytes.

Writing information from the server's hard disk to a tape or cartridge is a slow process. Network managers should have automated backup procedures and a tape system that offers 1 to 3 megabytes of transfer speed per minute.

Summary

The life cycle of a network is an important planning consideration. One significant aspect is the technological changes that will have to be dealt with during the useful life of the network. Each network is a representation of the technology at the time of its design and implementation.

During the course of its life cycle, a network passes through the following phases:

1. The feasibility study involves the subphases of problem definition and investigation. The problem definition attempts to find the problems that exist in the organization that caused management to initiate the study. The investigation subphase involves gathering

input data to develop a precise definition of the present data communication conditions and to uncover problems.

2. The analysis phase uses the data gathered in step 1 to identify the requirements that the network must meet if it is to be a successful implementation.

3. During the design phase, all the components that will comprise the network are developed.

4. The implementation phase consists of the installation of the hardware and software that make up the network system. Also, during this phase, all training and documentation materials are developed.

5. During the maintenance and upgrade phase the network is kept operational and fine-tuned by network operations personnel. Additionally, updates of software and hardware are performed to keep the network operating efficiently and effectively.

One of the most important requirements in network design is response time. Response time is the total time that expires between sending an inquiry from a workstation or terminal and receiving the response back at the workstation.

One of the major uses of the data gathering process is in developing a network topology. The load and site data collected are used as input for network modeling programs. These programs are application software that model a network using mathematical models.

The network operating system and the protocols that the host can handle limit the number and types of application software programs that can be used on a network. These limitations can be overcome with the acquisition of protocol converters and FEPs.

The type of software purchased for the network will determine whether the network uses asynchronous or synchronous communication, full-duplex or half-duplex communication, and the speed of transmission. Additionally, the limitations imposed by the software will determine the types of other networks that can be interfaced with. The network designer should select a protocol that is compatible with the ISO seven-layer model and one that can grow as the network grows. The protocol is a crucial element of the overall design, since the server architecture must interface with it.

Once the network has been designed, the specific vendors must be selected. A formal approach is to send a request for proposal (RFP) to prospective vendors. The RFP is a document that asks each vendor to prepare specifications and a price quotation for the configuration described in the RFP.

An important responsibility of network managers is maintaining control over the security of the network and the data on it. The major goals of security measures are to prevent computer crime and data loss. Some of the data losses can be the result of computer viruses. A computer virus is an executable computer program that propagates itself, using other programs as carriers, and sometimes modifies itself during or after replication. It is intended to perform some unwanted function on the computer system attached to the network. Viruses can be monitored and eliminated with the use of antivirus software.

Another method to safeguard the information transmitted is called encrypting or ciphering. User IDs and passwords by themselves are not an effective security technique. When combined with call-back units, encrypting devices, and network physical security, they provide an effective deterrent to unauthorized users.

The time and location of user access to the network can be controlled by software and hardware mechanisms. Although such measures are an inconvenience to users, they help in providing access to data by monitoring communication sessions and access during critical times. The most vulnerable security point on a network is switched ports that allow dial-in access. To enhance the security of switched ports with dial-in access, they should be operational only during the time when transactions are allowed. A call-back unit can be used to ensure that calls are made only from authorized locations.

The increasing use of computer systems and data communication networks requires that managers need a realistic disaster plan. The network manager needs to be involved in the planning and should have knowledge in:

1. The need for disaster planning
2. Computer backup approaches

3. Network backup approaches
4. The characteristics of a disaster backup strategy
5. Planning processes of the organization
6. The impact of a data network disaster on the organization

Planning a disaster recovery system requires goals, objectives, design, implementation, testing, documentation, and maintenance. A disaster plan must meet certain criteria, including:

1. Reliability
2. Operability
3. Response time to activate the plan
4. Cost effectiveness

For networks to be effective and efficient over a long period of time, a good network management plan is needed. The network management plan must have two goals:

1. The plan should prevent problems where possible.
2. The plan should prepare for problems that will most likely occur.

A comprehensive plan needs to address the following tasks:

1. Monitor and control hard disk space.
2. Monitor network workload and performance.
3. Add to and maintain user login information and workstation information.
4. Monitor and reset network devices.
5. Perform regular maintenance on software and data files stored on the servers.
6. Make regular backups of data and programs stored on the servers.

Questions

1. Briefly describe the life cycle phases for network design.
2. Name four items that should be included in the report produced at the end of the feasibility study.
3. Why is network response time important?

4. What is network modeling?

5. What is the purpose of message analysis?

6. Name ten hardware items that are part of a network.

7. What are the steps of the implementation phase?

8. What are the major sections of an RFP?

9. Briefly describe encryption.

10. Why are passwords and user IDs not enough security for a network?

11. What is a virus? How can it be detected?

12. Why should there be a disaster recovery plan for a data communication network?

13. Name four characteristics of a disaster recovery plan.

14. Name four major items that should be included in the recovery plan.

Projects

There are two different projects in this section. The first project provides some general guidelines for troubleshooting a small local area network. Before expensive testing methods are used to find problems with LANs, the guidelines provided below may find and correct a problem in a more efficient manner. The second project is the study of the design and installation of a local area network for the computer laboratory.

Troubleshooting a LAN

Troubleshooting a LAN is accomplished by using an established methodology of problem determination and recovery through event login and report techniques. Some troubleshooting techniques will be explained in later chapters in this book. However, sometimes the best planned approach does not work. The following suggestions may accomplish what the scientific methods can't do. Try to follow them in the order they are listed.

1. If the problem appears to be on the network, try turning the power to network devices off and on in a systematic manner. Turn off the power to routers, gateways, and network modems. After turning the

power off, wait approximately 30 seconds and turn the power back on. Sometimes a device gets "hung-up" because of an electrical malfunction or an instruction that it cannot execute.

2. If the problem appears to be in your workstation, turn the machine off and reboot the computer.

3. Check for viruses on the file server and your workstation.

4. Reload the network software and any other software that controls devices such as gateways.

5. Swap out devices, cables, connectors, and network interface cards on your machine and then across the network.

6. Reconfigure the user profile in the network server.

7. Add more memory to the file server.

If the above suggestions do not work and the LAN manuals do not offer any other possibilities, call the LAN vendor.

Study of a Local Area Network

Go to the school's data processing center or any other site where a local area network may be in operation. Carefully document the following topics by questioning network managers and by observing the LAN in operation.

1. Describe the hardware that constitutes the LAN. Use the following check list as a guide.

    a. Is the network a peer-to-peer network or a dedicated file server network?

    b. What models of server(s) are available?

    c. What is the internal configuration of the server(s) (i.e., amount of RAM, disk space, processor speed, coprocessor speed, number of floppy drives and types, etc.)?

    d. What models of workstations are available?

    e. What is the internal configuration of the workstations (i.e., amount of RAM, disk space, processor speed, coprocessor speed, number of floppy drives and types, etc.)?

f. What make, model, and type of network interface card is being used?

g. What is the network configuration? Why was this type chosen?

h. What models and types of printers are available to network users?

i. Are there any gateways to other networks? If yes, what type and models are available?

j. What are the physical limitations of the network (i.e., number of users, maximum distance of transmission)?

k. What type of transmission medium is being used? Why was this type chosen?

2. What network operating system is in place? Why was this type chosen?

3. How do the users interact with the software stored on the network?

4. What type of work is normally accomplished by the workstations?

5. How do users perform network operations such as printing, copying files, and so forth?

6. What are the maintenance policies?

7. Are there any support fees? If yes, what type and amount?

8. What is the cost of adding stations?

9. What is the cost of adding a server?

10. What are the system management procedures in place and their cost?

11. How are software licensing agreements handled?

12. What types of upgrades or modifications are planned for the next three years?

After all the material is compiled, create a report indicating your findings about the status of the local area network. The report should consist of at least five pages, but it will probably be much longer.

After completing the report on the actual LAN, provide suggestions for improving the system without increasing the current costs. For each suggestion, provide evidence in the form of interviews, data compiled from magazines, or vendor specification sheets. Is there a way to provide a better service and lower the costs? What problems do you anticipate with this network during the next three years? How can a solution be in place before serious interruption of LAN services takes place?

Multimedia Technology and Networks

Objectives

After completing this chapter you will:

1. Understand some of the concepts associated with multimedia technology.

2. Have an understanding of digital video technology.

3. Understand the problems associated with distributing digital audiovisual technology on a network

4. Know some possible solutions and network arrangements required to have an effective network that can handle audiovisual data.

509

Key Words

Audio Board   CD-ROM

DVI   Media Player

Multimedia   OLE

Overlay Board   Sound Recorder

Video Display Board

Introduction

Multimedia is a broad and imprecise term that describes the various combinations of digital animation, graphics, audio, and video data combined with the capabilities of a personal computer. With the use of multimedia technology and a user-friendly interface, people are better able to communicate ideas to other individuals. Additionally, individuals are better able to quickly and easily access audiovisual information, which otherwise is difficult to handle.

Multimedia technology also enhances the usefulness of a desktop computer by helping people learn more by seeing, hearing, and interacting with the computer and the information that it contains. These capabilities are not normally found in today's personal computer technology.

Multimedia Today

Multimedia is currently used in training, education, advertising agencies, desktop videoconferencing, video electronic mail, and many other real-life situations. Additionally, consumers are beginning to see this technology in point-of-sale kiosks describing the different offerings of a company, at hotels displaying many of the services provided, at travel agencies describing possible vacation locations, and many other public places.

Multimedia for IBM PCs and compatibles is accessible to desktop computer users through a Multimedia PC. A Multimedia PC is a desktop computer that is equipped with the hardware and software necessary to read and execute the numerous multimedia software titles available in the market. In the market of IBM personal computers and compatibles, the de facto standard for using multimedia is based on a set of standard hardware that is under the control of Microsoft Windows 3.1 or higher. Although Windows 3.0 had optional multimedia extensions, it is version 3.1 that exploited the multimedia capabilities of the desktop computer.

The basic Multimedia PC consists of:

1. A personal computer based on the 80836sx processor or better. However, true 32-bit central processing units such as the 80386 and 80486 CPUs are better suited for this task due to their faster processing speed and their ability to transfer larger amounts of data quickly. On the Macintosh, a 68030- or better-based Macintosh is normally used for multimedia applications. The Quadra series of personal computers are the preferred platform for multimedia when dealing with Macintosh computers.

2. At least 2 megabytes of RAM. But, 4 to 8 megabytes is recommended.

3. A large hard disk. A disk of at least 120 megabytes of storage is recommended. Generally, larger is better.

4. A CD-ROM (Compact Disc-Read Only Memory) drive. This is one of the key components of a multimedia computer. Normally the information used on one of these computers is stored on a compact disk which is identical in size and appearance to an audio CD. A compact disk is capable of storing 680 megabytes of information and is a read-only device. Data can't be written on the CD by the user.

5. Audio board. This is another of the key components of a multimedia PC. An audio board is used to generate the sounds and music that much multimedia software uses as part of the delivery methodology. Because the speakers that are used in personal computers are poor in quality and don't have the range required to produce good sound effects or music, a sound board accomplishes this task. There are 8-bit and 16-bit boards. On the Macintosh, the Quadra line and most of the Mac II line of computers have sound

built into the motherboard. However, additional cards are available to enhance the sound capabilities of the Macintosh.

Eight-bit boards are capable of producing sounds that are half as good as those from an audio CD player, and most can produce only monophonic sounds. Sixteen-bit boards are capable of producing sounds that are as good in quality as those produced by a CD player, and they can produce stereo sound.

Sound boards not only can generate the sounds that a computer tells them to create. They are capable of recording analog sounds through a microphone and storing them in digital format in a file on the computer's hard disk. Once the sounds are stored digitally, they can be manipulated by the computer like any other file. Through inexpensive sound boards and with editing software, a computer can become a very capable recording device.

6. Video display board. The graphics capabilities of a multimedia PC are defined by the capabilities of its video display monitor and the video display board that drives it. Video display boards are characterized by their video resolution and color reproduction.

Video resolution is a measure of the number of horizontal and vertical dots or pixels that are contained on the screen. Larger numbers generally mean better resolution (the quality of the image) on the screen. Typical resolutions range from 640 by 480 pixels to 1280 by 1024 pixels.

Color reproduction is a measure of the number of colors the video display board can reproduce at different resolutions. More colors generally mean a better image. Typical color range is from 16 on low end boards, up to 16 million colors on more sophisticated boards. A typical VGA screen with a resolution of 640 by 480 has a color reproduction of 16 colors. Whenever possible, a sophisticated board capable of millions of colors at high resolutions should be used for multimedia applications.

Although the multimedia PC specification for IBM PCs and compatibles ends with the above mentioned hardware, another device that is gaining importance is an overlay board. An overlay board allows a computer to display video in a window on the computer monitor. These boards are required since additional processing capabilities are needed to reproduce quality video on a computer screen. The board does this, leaving the CPU to concentrate on the processing of data. Without an overlay board, output from a VCR or laser video disk player must be displayed on a television monitor instead of a computer monitor.

With one of these boards, interactive video is made possible by accessing clips of audio and video that are stored on a laser disk or VCR tape. This technology has given birth to a world of engaging applications. Although relatively new, it can provide information in a format that many users call "interactive television." Despite the many advantages of this traditional interactive video technology, it is still a hybrid technology. It uses videodiscs which are created with analog technology and can't be altered once they are created.

Additionally, since the output of videodisc is a signal that can't be processed by the computer, the distribution of these signals through a network remains a difficult task at best. This creates problems for real-time video applications such as video e-mail and cut-and-paste video editing.

Digital Video

A new type of technology has corrected some of these shortcomings. It is compressed digital video. Technically speaking, in the Windows world this new technology is called DVI (Digital Video Interactive) multimedia. Through the use of a DVI board, a computer can digitize analog video from a video camera or any other video source, and store it as 0's and 1's in a file on the computer's hard disk. Additionally, the file is compressed in order to reduce the amount of storage required. Compression is achieved through the use of hardware on the DVI board and software residing in the computer's RAM. Playback can be achieved without the use of the DVI board. However, better results are achieved when playback is done using the board as an aid in the processing of the digital data that makes up the video.

DVI is not the only compression technique available for personal computers. Many different compression techniques exist for storing digital video. Some of these are JPEG, MPEG, MPEG II, Apple's Quicktime, and P*64. Apple's Quicktime is also available for IBM-compatible computers running under the Microsoft Windows environment.

Through the use of DVI and similar technologies and multimedia, documents take on new dimensions, incorporating stunning full-motion video, photographic imagery, and stereo audio. Also, DVI multimedia technology will allow individuals to video-conference from their desks, share documents and images, and simultaneously edit and "mark up" documents through mutual "chalkboards." The end result is an increase in productivity.

Video Applications and Networking

There are many types of applications that are practical for incorporating video on the computer. One example is called "performance support systems." These systems are used by businesses and corporations to provide employee training on demand at the employee's desktop computer. This type of system requires servers that need to deliver audiovisual information to client computers to facilitate the employee learning sessions.

Another example of the use of digital audiovisual technology is in educational institutions. Most of the suppliers of educational software systems are now delivering complete integrated learning systems that include student modules and teacher management systems. With this technology, teachers are able to manage resources in a more effective and efficient manner by assigning courseware to students according to their abilities and needs. In this type of system, network video is a central part of the effectiveness.

Network video systems will allow businesses and other institutions to maintain multiuser audiovisual databases. Individuals can then access resources without leaving their desks and they don't need additional equipment on their desks such as VCRs or televisions. Also, video teleconferencing can be performed on the desktop. Through digital video technology, cost effective teleconferences can be performed, providing support for worldwide communications needs and increasing the productivity of employees.

Distance learning is another example of the use of networked digital video technology. Through distance learning, students and teachers can be in different geographical locations. Teachers can use video cameras, and analog video can be digitized and compressed using compression hardware and software. The digitized video is placed on the network and delivered to the students. The students may have another video camera or microphone for a two-way interaction with the instructor. This type of videoconferencing allows the teacher and student to interact as if they were in the same classroom.

Characteristics of Video-Based Applications

As outlined above, there are many types of applications that can benefit from the use of digital video technology. However, the video needs of these applications are different, and the needs dictate the type of computer required to run them. These characteristics can be categorized as

1. Requests for video files
2. Requests for video structures
3. Requests for video stream management

Requests for Video Files

This is the simplest level of request since it requires store-and-play capabilities which is a basic service provided by networks. This allows a network server to store video and retrieve it later for viewing. Although some access delays may occur with this type of service, most delays don't reduce the overall effectiveness of the application. An example of this type of application is on-line help videos.

Requests for Video Structures

The next level in sophistication is requests for video structure services. These services allow an application to be interactive by providing synchronized video and audio that can change quickly. Video editing is an example of this application. It requires video and audio to be combined and edited to create another video stream to be viewed or to be added to another document. This requires fast access to video structures and fast interaction among them. In the example of video and audio editing, users will need to access many different structures at the same time. The delays associated with simple store-and-play capabilities are not easily tolerated.

Requests for Stream Management

The last category of request is stream management services. These are required since many users will access live video simultaneously through the network. Examples of these are desktop videoconferencing and distance learning, as outlined earlier in this chapter. Video stream management can involve sending live video across the network to simultaneous users from many different sources and managing the streams of video in the network. Different users need these video streams at different rates. Users normally have devices such as DVI cards that compress and decompress video.

Challenges of Networking Video

To promote the wide use of digital video technology across networks, many factors must be considered. One is the large installed base of networks. Video technology must use these existing network connections rather than adding costly new networks dedicated only to these services. This can be done by centralizing video services and resources at a video server. The overall goal is to provide low cost digital audiovisual services using existing networking standards.

Existing local area networks are designed to handle the data and file sharing needs of offices and businesses. This involves the storing and transmission of text and graphic files. These files are transmitted in "burst" modes by packetizing the files and reassembling the packets at the client site. The packets arrive to the user at different times. The delay associated with the transmission is normally not detected by the user and doesn't affect the application running in the client computer.

Audiovisual files pose a different challenge to networks. They are large in size and the sources that make them are time dependent. If the audio and the video arrive at different times, then the overall quality of the video will suffer. Additionally, if the video segments don't arrive contiguously at the client side, the video will appear fragmented and "jerky."

The large file size of digital video files requires large disk drives or multiple-disk systems with a high data transmission and transfer capability. This type of file takes the form of a stream of data that must arrive on time at the client computer. This is in contrast to the burst mode that networks use for delivering data. Networks are inefficient when needing to transmit simultaneous, continuous large blocks of data that make up an audiovisual file. Additionally, a single microprocessor has difficulty in combining the bursty mode of normal data transmission and the continuous stream data transmission of audiovisual files.

Another problem arises in how network operating systems allocate resources. Current network OSs allocate resources in a "democratic" manner. All applications have equal access to the network. When a resource or the network is busy, everything slows down. No data has priority over other data. Other problems are the overhead required to manage the network to ensure that all applications have equal access to the network and detection of errors in the transmission of data through the network cabling medium. These factors are important for applications such as spreadsheets and databases, but not as important for audiovisual files. If a pixel is incorrect in a movie frame, the human eye will not be able to detect it. However, incorrect numbers on a spreadsheet are not tolerated.

Visual information can't slow down and speed up according to the traffic on the network. Video files need to arrive on time at the client computer. If the file can't be delivered to the user reliably and timely, then the server must provide an indication to the client application that the data is not available. It could reduce the amount of data that has to be transmitted by dropping frames, lowering the resolution, or changing the image size. Changing the audiovisual data to meet available bandwidth is called "scalable video."

Solutions

While distributing video information, the video files go through a series of bottlenecks as outlined in the figure. These bottlenecks occur in:

1. Drives that are slow or with poor transfer rates
2. Servers not optimized for the distribution of video and with traditional operating system software not designed to handle large continous streams of data
3. LAN access and protocols that are optimized for dealing with bursts of data instead of continuous streams
4. The internetwork access hubs
5. The client computer and the network interface

To see how these bottlenecks affect the network's overall efficiency in delivering audiovisual files, let's use an example. If a LAN site uses DVI to deliver video to the desktop, then approximately 1.5 Mbits per second per DVI stream are required to send the video properly. Therefore, each client computer must handle continuously 1.5 Mbits per second. If the server has 40 clients, then it must handle 60 Mbits per second simultaneously.

The example above shows that the server must handle all 40 users at the same time, with 60 Mbits of throughput per second. Also, the network must handle 60 Mbits per second from the server and 1.5 Mbits per second from the client. And lastly, the network interface will have to handle the video files and concurrently provide access to other network services. These are tasks that current networks can't accomplish.

The solutions to the above problem are as follows:

1. Increase the power and efficiency of bottleneck areas
2. Replace the bottleneck area
3. Install a parallel network

Increasing the power and efficiency of bottleneck areas is a cost effective manner to improve the general performance of the network. This process doesn't replace all the network components, it just increases their efficiency. However, increasing the power of the server or client computers may not address the time dependent nature of audiovisual files.

Replacing the bottleneck areas with more powerful and faster hardware can be costly. For example, the server could be replaced by a faster server with more storage. However, this solution still doesn't address the time dependent nature of digital video files and differences between this type of file and other data files in the network. A parallel system dedicated to video is an elegant solution only if it has a separate video server. This may mean a separate physical network that is cost prohibitive. However, if a separate software world is established for video while sharing the same hardware resources, the system is then able to handle all types of information.

The Hardware

The best solution is probably a combination of all three described above, using much of the existing network and providing a cost effective and efficient answer to current problems. This can be understood by analyzing the network-client transmission needs. A typical client will need only one or two streams at about 1.5 Mbits per second. This is normally less than the rate that most hard disks have and it supports standards such as Intel's DVI, MPEG, and MPEG II compression techniques. It is also within the range of the typical Ethernet network running at 10 Mbits per second.

When many clients require video streams the Ethernet cabling system could be overwhelming. Many installations are deciding on fiber optic as the cabling medium. However, despite its large bandwidth, this is also a shared resource, and it will have difficulty handling the time dependent nature of digital video. Many companies, such as Starlight Networks, Inc. have opted to base their solution on a star network such as 10BaseT Ethernet, with dedicated lines to each client computer.

To create a star topology, designers use "hubs." A popular hub device is the 10BaseT for Ethernet networks. Another popular star network is IBM's token-ring network. Although these networks use star hubs, they operate like a ring or bus. That is, all the workstations connected to the hub share a limited amount of the available bandwidth. Normally this bandwidth is 10 to 16 Mbits per second. This is not enough for applications that require digital video files if the number of users is large.

One solution to this problem is FDDI, but it is costly and doesn't necessarily address the time dependent nature of video files. Another solution is to increase the efficiency of the Ethernet hub by dedicating a 10-Mbit-per-second line per desktop. Sometimes this process is called "turbocharging the hub." Although this increases the cost of the hub, it doesn't replace the client hardware or the wiring on the network. The 10-Mbit-per-second connection reliably satisfies all the data and video needs of the user. These types of hubs are now available in the market for reasonable prices.

The Software

Although turbocharging the hub will help in handling the data transmission needs of the network, software will be required to work with the network operating system to handle the time dependent nature of video files. One possibility in handling video streams through software is to replace existing inefficient network protocols with new ones. But this destroys the compatibility with the company or institution software investment. What is needed is a network protocol for audiovisual data streams that coexists with current network protocols and operating systems.

By creating an environment as outlined above, users request network services in the same manner as they are doing it today. However, when a client calls for audiovideo services, the network should use the special audiovisual protocol to create a reliable connection between the server and the client. This provides for the uninterrupted distribution of large streams of data to the client. For nonaudiovisual data requests, the normal protocols would be used. With this type of parallel approach all data types are available to clients concurrently. Protocols that handle audiovisual data and coexist with such popular network protocols as NetWare and Vines are available in the computer market.

The Server

The last element of the network to address is the server itself. When dealing with audiovisual data, dedicated audiovisual servers need to be employed. These servers are optimized to handle the large continuous streams of data that make up audiovisual files. When dealing with audiovisual data, the server needs to ensure that all data for that stream is sent without interruptions to the client computer.

The storage system in the server will also have to be optimized and managed so that users can access data files at the same time. It needs to provide simultaneous access to large and continuous data files. Some setups try to use video laser disk juke boxes. However, for many simultaneous users accessing the same file, the access delays associated with these devices or CD-ROM arrays create problems for the application. The solution is to use arrays of Winchester disk drives. This provides for a low cost and effective solution to the storage needs of the video server.

The data served by the video server needs to look like ordinary data to the client's applications. To the operating system, the data from the server should look like any other file structure. This needs to be accomplished with a single copy of the data file and needs to support a wide range of platforms and operating environments.

Summary

Multimedia is a broad and imprecise term that describes the various combinations of digital animation, graphics, audio, and video data combined with the capabilities of a personal computer. With the use of multimedia technology and a user-friendly interface, people are better able to communicate ideas to others. Additionally, through the use of multimedia technology, individuals are better able to quickly and easily access audiovisual information, which otherwise is difficult to handle. However, in today's network enterprises, multimedia technology needs to become an integral part of the existing networks if it is to become an effective tool in business and education.

Networked digital audiovisual needs of a company or institution can be satisfied by using existing off-the-shelf solutions and by modification of the current hardware and network and the addition of software. The hardware comes in the form of an audiovisual server and turbocharged hubs in the case of Ethernet networks. The software is in the form of protocols that handle the audiovisual requests of the client computers while coexisting with the standard network operating system. This provides a cost effective, yet efficient solution for distributing digital video and audio files across a network.

Questions

1. What is meant by multimedia technology?
2. What is the purpose of DVI?
3. Why can't current networks handle digital video properly?
4. What is a turbocharged hub?
5. What is the major difference between the network data needs of a spreadsheet and the data needs of a digital movie?
6. Why is a star network a better configuration for distributing video?
7. Why is a Winchester disk better than a compact disk for storing digital data when multiple users need to access the same file?
8. Why is digital video compressed?

Project

Microsoft Windows and Multimedia

As stated before, for IBM personal computers and compatibles, the hardware and software are normally under the control of Microsoft Windows version 3.1 and higher. Windows can control hardware through the use of drivers that are provided by Microsoft or the hardware manufacturer. These drivers contain information that is provided to the Windows environment so it knows the different commands that the device can accept. To install a driver, the folder that contains the control panel is selected and the Control Panel icon is chosen. Then the Drivers icon is selected and a list of drivers appears, such as the one in Fig. 13-1. If a new driver is to be installed, the Add button is selected and the computer responds by asking for the path were the driver is located. After the path is provided, Windows loads the driver into memory and modifies the system files to reflect the new additions. After the driver is installed, software that controls the desired hardware can be used to perform any multimedia processing.

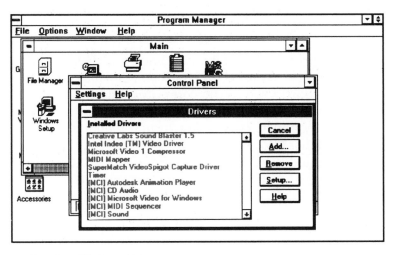

Fig. 13-1. Windows drivers.

If you want to perform some interactions with sound and video, Windows provides tools that you can start using right away, provided that you have the proper hardware. These are the Sound Recorder and the Media Player. These programs can be found in the Accessories group of Windows 3.1 and higher (see Fig. 13-2). Other products that provide additional multimedia functionality to Windows are the Media Browser, Videdit, Vid-Cap, BitEdit, PalEdit, and WaveEdit. These are provided with the Video for Windows package from Microsoft Corporation.

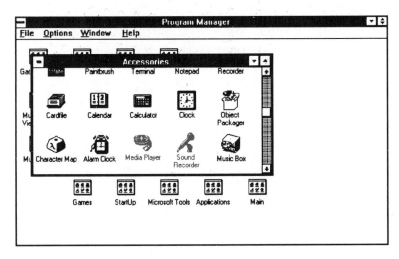

Fig. 13-2. The Accessories group.

The Sound Recorder

The Sound Recorder tool allows the recording of analog sound into a digital format. It can also play back any digital recording. The quality of recording and playback will depend on the quality of the sound board used in the computer. The sound quality is measured by the sampling frequency of the wave that makes up the sound. Frequency ranges are from 11 kilohertz up to 44 kilohertz. A higher frequency produces better-quality sound. For example, CD-quality sound is achieved at sampling frequencies of 44 kilohertz. Also, the board will determine if the sound can be recorded in stereo or mono.

To record a sound:

1. Attach a microphone to the sound board.

2. Locate the Sound Recorder application in the Accessories group and select the Sound Recorder icon.

3. Select the picture of a microphone (See Fig. 13-3).

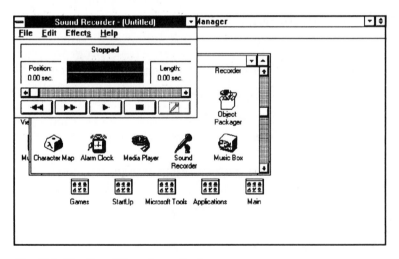

Fig. 13-3. The Sound Recorder application.

The computer will record the sound and will show the frequency spectrum on the screen as the sound is being recorded. After the sound is recorded, it can be saved to a file by selecting the File pull-down menu and then selecting a name for the file that will contain the digitized sound (see Fig. 13-4).

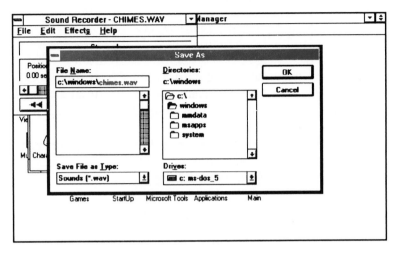

Fig. 13-4. Save As dialog box for the Sound Recorder.

To play back the sound,

    1. Activate the File pull-down menu.

    2. Select the Open option.

Files with the WAV extension are digitized sound files that can be played back with the Sound Recorder. Once a file is in memory, it can be played by clicking the "play" button on the sound recorder window. This is the button that shows the same "play" symbol found on many tape players and other audio equipment.

    3. Move the mouse pointer over the "Play" button and click the mouse button.

The Media Player

The Media Player is a program that allows you to play multimedia files such as sound, animation, and digital video files. It also allows you to control external devices such as laser disk players and CD-ROM players. However, you must install the appropriate hardware in your computer before the Media Player can control the operation. Additionally, once a device is connected or installed in the computer, Windows needs to be made aware of its existence by installing the appropriate driver in the driver section of the control panel. Most hardware devices contain optional diskettes that have the drivers required by Windows.

To execute the Media Player:

1. Select the Accessories group and locate the Media Player icon.
2. Select the Media Player icon.

You should see a screen similar to Fig. 13-5. If device drivers have been properly installed in Windows, then the device options available are selected from the Device pull-down menu, as seen

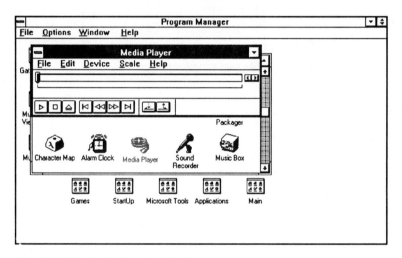

Fig. 13-5. The Media Player application.

in Fig. 13-6. Only one device at a time can be selected. Once the device is selected, the file that contains the information needs to be opened. For example, to play a digital video file the process is as follows:

1. Select the Device pull-down menu.
2. Choose the Video for Windows option.
3. Select the File pull-down menu.
4. Choose the Open option.

You should see a file open dialog box.

5. Find the subdirectory where the file is located, high-light the file name, and press the OK button.

Once that is done, you will see a screen similar to Fig. 13-7. Instead of the picture that you see in the figure, you may have a different picture.

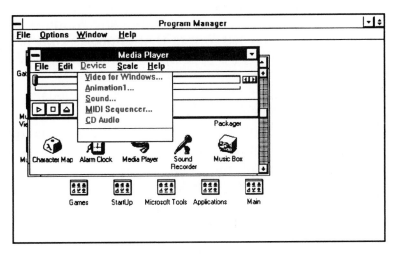

Fig. 13-6. The Media Player's Device pull-down menu.

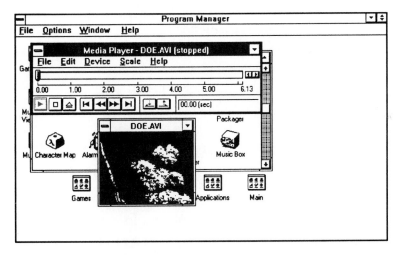

Fig. 13-7. A digital video being played on the screen.

To play the file:

    6. Move the mouse pointer to the "Play" button. This is the button that looks like the play button in most VCRs.

At this point the digital video will be played on the screen.

One of the advantages of using the Media Player is its ability to insert any of the objects played by it into any Windows-based product such as Microsoft Works that supports OLE (Object Linking and Embedding). As an example, insert the above digital video into an MS Works word processing document.

1. Activate the Media Player by moving the mouse pointer over it and clicking the mouse button.

2. If the file to be inserted is not loaded, load it using the procedure outlined above.

3. Select the Edit pull-down menu.

4. Choose the Copy Object option, as in Fig. 13-8.

5. Load Microsoft Works if you have this program. If you don't have Works loaded, you can load Microsoft Write from the Accessories group document.

6. Once inside the word processor, load the document where the video is to be inserted by selecting the File pull-down menu, choosing the Open option, and then selecting the document.

7. Move the pointer to the location where the video is to be located.

8. Select the Edit pull-down menu.

9. Choose the Paste Special option.

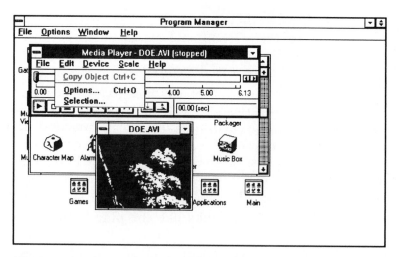

Fig. 13-8. The Copy Object option of the Media Player.

You will get a screen similar to Fig. 13-9. This is the Paste Special dialog box. Here you can select different objects from the Clipboard and insert them into your document. In this case, you will select the digital video clip.

10. Highlight the Media Clip option.

11. Press the OK button.

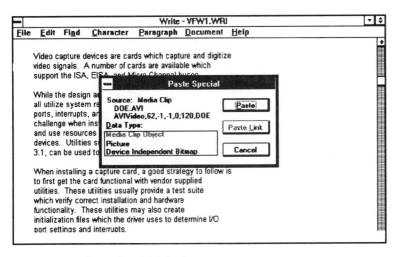

Fig. 13-9. The Paste Special dialog box.

The clip is inserted into the document and becomes a permanent component of it (see Fig. 13-10). Once the document is saved, the reference to the media clip is saved with it. To run the video clip select the picture that represents the clip.

In the same manner that the above digital video was loaded, played, and inserted into a document, any other type of files that can be executed by the Media Player can be inserted into a document. This includes audio clips, animation, graphical images, and others. In reality, the process of embedding a document into another is not limited to the Media Player. In Windows, any document that supports OLE can be embedded into another document as a "live" document.

Hands-On with Multimedia

Note to the instructor: before the following tutorial can be practiced, you must ensure that the student workstation has a Video for Windows driver installed in the driver section of the

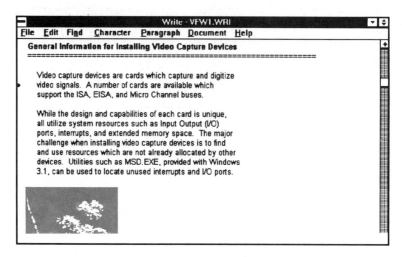

Fig. 13-10. A digital video placed inside a document.

control panel, and an audio driver needs to also be installed. Additionally, you will need to install the files LAUNCH.AVI in a subdirectory called TEMP. The digital video tutorial doesn't require hardware beyond Windows 3.1 requirements, but it will require the drivers. They can be obtained free from an information utility such as Compuserve or by purchasing the Video for Windows package. If the file LAUNCH.AVI is not available to you, then any AVI file will suffice for the exercise. The audio tutorial will require the addition of an audio board.

1. Locate the Media Player icon in the Accessories group folder.

2. Double click on the Media Player icon.

3. Select the Device pull-down menu and choose Video for Windows, as in Fig. 13-11.

4. Select the File pull-down menu.

5. Choose the Open option.

6. In the file open dialog box, type the following: C:\TEMP\LAUNCH.AVI

Note: Your instructor may have a different file name and subdirectory for you to use.

7. You should now see a small window on the screen that contains a still image of the first frame of the digital video.

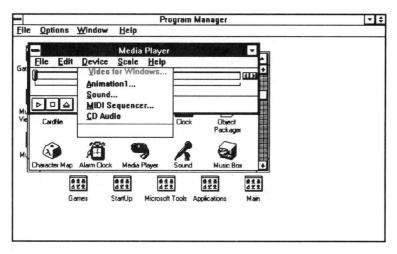

Fig. 13-11. The Device pull-down menu.

To play the video:

8. Move the mouse pointer over the "play" button on the Media Player program and click the mouse button.

The video will play and if you have an audio board installed, you will also hear the sound that accompanies the video.

To insert the above video clip into a document:

1. Load or create the document where the clip is to be inserted. In this case, create the document displayed in Fig. 13-12.

2. Find the Multimedia Player on the desktop and click the mouse button on it to activate it.

3. Select the Edit pull-down menu and choose the Copy Object option.

4. Activate the document that was created in step 1.

5. Move the pointer to the end of the first paragraph. You should have left a blank line between paragraphs.

6. Select the Edit pull-down menu.

7. Choose the Paste Special option. You should get a dialog box like the one shown in Fig. 13-13.

8. Highlight the Media Clip if it is not already highlighted.

9. Press the Paste button.

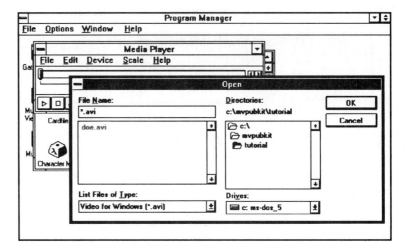

Fig. 13-12. The Open dialog box of the Media Player.

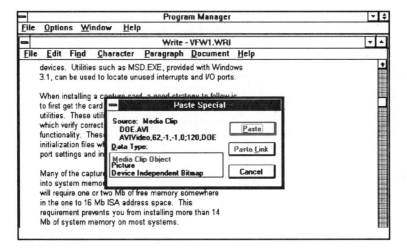

Fig. 13-13. The Paste Special dialog box.

The still image that you saw earlier is now inserted into the document as in Fig. 13-14. This creates a "live" link between the document and the Media Player and the file that was copied into the document. This process is called OLE. At this point, the video clip is part of your document in the same manner that words are part of your document. When the file is saved, a reference to the video clip is also saved. Therefore, when you load the file later on, the document will still contain the live link to the video clip.

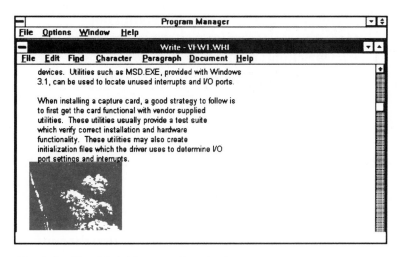

Fig. 13-14. The digital video pasted into the document.

However, a copy of the video is not included in your document, just a reference to it. This means that the same path used in copying the file from the Media Player must exist when the document is loaded later on. Otherwise, the system will not be able to find the video clip.

To play the video clip:

10. Double click on the still image that represents the video clip. The digital video will play.

To insert a sound clip into a document,

1. Make sure that you have the document displayed in Fig. 13-14 in memory.

2. Find the Media Player on the desktop and select it.

3. Select the Device pull-down menu.

4. Choose the Sound option.

5. Select the File pull-down menu.

6. Choose the Open option.

7. Find a file with the WAV extension. In this case we will use one provided by Windows located in the C:\WINDOWS subdirectory. It is called CHIMES.WAV. Your instructor may have a different file and path for you to use.

8. Move the pointer to the "play" button and press the mouse button to hear the sound once.

9. Select the Edit pull-down menu and choose the Copy Object option.

10. Activate the document that was created in step 1.

11. Move the pointer to the end of the last paragraph.

12. Select the Edit pull-down menu.

13. Choose the Paste Special option.

You should get a dialog box like the one shown in Fig. 13-13.

14. Highlight the Media Clip if it is not already highlighted.

15. Press the Paste button.

16. Double click on the icon representing the sound in the document. The sound will play.

To save the document:

1. Select the File pull-down menu.

2. Choose Save.

3. Type a name for the file containing the video and sound clips. In this case call it MULTDEM.

4. Press the OK button.

The document is saved and can be retrieved later for further use.

Appendix A
A Quick View of the UNIX vi Editor

Introduction

There are two important topics that you need to understand about the vi editor before using it. First, vi is case sensitive, meaning that an upper case letter does not represent the same command as a lower case letter. Second, vi operates in modes. It is very important to understand what you do in which mode. In edit mode, you input characters to your file. In command mode and last line mode, you send commands to vi. A more detailed explanation of the modes follows. Fig. A-1 shows a graphical view of how the vi editor works within the UNIX environment. Refer to this figure as you read and practice the commands explained below.

Input Mode

Input mode is the mode from which you enter all text into your file. When you are in input mode, everything you type will be entered into your work buffer and all printable characters will be displayed on your screen.

535

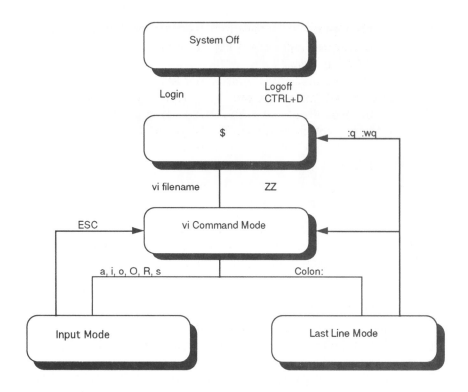

Fig. A-1. The vi editing system

How to Get into Input Mode

You may enter input mode by specifying a, i, o, O, or R from command mode. These commands are explained next.

i- insert. This puts vi into input mode and places the text before (to the left of) the cursor. Use i to insert a few characters or words into existing text or to input text in a new file.

a- append. This command is similar to the i command, except that it places the text you enter after (to the right of) the cursor.

o- open. This command puts vi into input mode and opens a blank line in existing text below the current line. Use the open command when entering a new line or several new lines within existing text.

O- Open. This command works just like the open command, except that it opens a line above the current line.

R- Replace. This command takes you into input mode and allows you to overwrite (type over) existing characters. Use R to make corrections where you need to overwrite characters. You can also use R to input new text in a file if you prefer working in an overwrite mode.

How to Get out of Input Mode

You can go back to command mode from input mode by pressing the ESC key. Moving with any of the arrow keys will also take you out of input mode and back to command mode.

Moving Around the Screen

You have a choice of the keys that you use to move the cursor around on the screen. You can use the arrow keys or the following letter keys to move the cursor:

Key	Direction
h	left
j	down
k	up
l	right

Using the letter keys has the advantage of allowing you to specify the number of times that you want the command repeated. For example, to move down four spaces you would type 4j. You have to be in command mode to use the letter keys for cursor movement.

If you use the arrow keys, you do not have to get out of input mode. You can use the arrow keys from either mode. If you are in input mode, however, and you press an arrow key, this will take you back to command mode. Then, you will have to get back into input mode before entering text.

Command Mode

Command mode is the mode from which everything you type is interpreted as an editor command. When you are in command mode, none of the characters that you type are entered into your work buffer.

How to Get into Command Mode

You can go to command mode at any time by pressing ESC. If you press ESC and you are already in command mode, your terminal will beep.

How to Get out of Command Mode

From command mode, you can go to input mode, to last line mode, or back to UNIX.

> To go to input mode, type a, i, o, O, or R.
>
> To go to last line mode, type a colon (:).
>
> To save your file and go back to UNIX, type the following:
>
> ZZ <press ENTER>

If you want to quit without saving, or save your file under another name, you will have to go to last line mode (see Last Line Mode).

Yank, Undo, and Delete

When you use any of the delete commands, the lines that you have just deleted are stored in the general purpose buffer. For this reason, you can use the undo (u) command to replace text that you have deleted.

Because the general purpose buffer stores your last deletion, you use one of the delete commands to move a line or block of lines. First, use one of the delete commands to put the text in the buffer. Then move the cursor to the point where you want to insert your text. Use one of the put commands to insert your text at that point.

If, instead of moving a line or group of lines, you want to copy the line, you would use the yank command. This command stores the specified lines in the buffer without deleting them. You may then put a copy of the line(s) where you want them by using one of the put commands. Use this command by placing the cursor at the beginning of the text you want to place in the buffer and then typing nyy (where n is the number of lines you want to yank).

Put

The put commands, P and p, copy text from the general purpose buffer into the work buffer. To use these commands, first use the delete or yank command to get the text you want to move or copy into the general purpose buffer. Then move the cursor to the point where you want to place the moved or copied text. Type P to put the text before or above the cursor, or p to put the text below KD or after the cursor.

The put commands do not destroy the contents of the general purpose buffer and may therefore be used to place the same text at repeated points in your file by using one delete or yank command and several put commands.

NOTE: Because vi has only one general purpose buffer, you should use only cursor movement commands between a delete or yank and its subsequent put or Put.

Putting Form Feeds in Your Program

If you want your program listing to form feed to a new page, use a commented-out control L.

List of Commands

Moving the Cursor

Use the arrow keys on the keypad on the lower right of your keyboard or the following keys to move around the screen:

h.	Moves cursor one space to the left
j.	Moves cursor one space down
k.	Moves cursor one space up
l.	Moves cursor one space right
nh.	Moves cursor n spaces to the left
nj.	Moves cursor n spaces down
nk.	Moves cursor n spaces up
nl.	Moves cursor n spaces right
$.	Moves cursor to end of line
H.	Moves cursor to top of screen
M.	Moves cursor to middle of screen
L.	Moves cursor to bottom of screen

Moving Around in Your File:

Ctrl+D.	Forward 1/2 screenful
Ctrl+U.	Backward 1/2 screenful
Ctrl+F.	Forward 1 screenful
Ctrl+B.	Backward 1 screenful
G.	To end of file if not preceded by a number
1G.	To beginning of file
numberG.	Takes you to the line specified in number

Adding Text:

i.	Inserts text before cursor
a.	Inserts text after cursor
O.	Opens line above current line
o.	Opens line below current line
r.	Replaces (overwrites) current character (1 character only)
R.	Overwrites until ESC

Deleting Text

Move the cursor to the first character of the area to be deleted. Then type in one of the following commands:

dd.	Deletes one line
x.	Deletes the character beneath the cursor
ndd.	Deletes the number of lines specified by n
nx.	Deletes the number of characters specified by n beginning with the character underneath the cursor
D.	Deletes to End of Line beginning with char qacter underneath the cursor

Copy and Move Blocks

nyy.	Copies n lines into buffer
ndd.	Deletes n lines into buffer
p.	Puts lines from buffer into your file below cursor position

Miscellaneous Commands

ZZ.   Saves your file and exits

J.   Joins the line below the current line to the
           end of the current line

Last Line Mode

Typing a colon from command mode puts vi into last line mode.
The cursor goes to the bottom line of your screen, waiting for you
to type in a command. From last line mode, you always press
Enter to execute the command.

The following are commands that are executed from last line
mode:

:q! <press Enter>. Quit without saving

:w filename <press ENTER>. Save your program
   under another name

:r filename <press ENTER>. Read a file into your
   current file

:set nu. Display line numbers

:set nonu. Turn off line numbering

Search for a String

To search for a string, from command mode type:

/text <press ENTER>. Search forward

n. Repeat original search

N. Repeat original search - opposite direction

Replace String

To replace strings in a document use the following command.

:g/string/s//replacement string/c. Prompts for y or
   n for each change

Appendix B
Hardware and Software Vendors

Vendors of Gateways and Related Products

C-Slave/286 and XBUS4/AT
Alloy Computer Products Inc.
165 Forest St.
Marlboro, MA 01752
508-481-8500

MultiComAsyncGateway
Multi-Tech Systems Inc.
2205 Woodale Dr.
Mounds View, MN 55112
800-328-9717

Telebits ACS
Telebit Corp
115 Chesapeake Terr.
Sunnyvale, CA 94089
800-835-3248
386/Multiware

Alloy Computer Products Inc.
165 Forest St.
Marlboro, MA 01752
508-481-8500

ComBridge
Cubix Corp.
2800 Lockheed Way
Carson City, NV 89706
800-829-0550

FlexCom
Evergreen Systems Inc.,
120 Landing Ct.
Suite A
Novato, CA 94945
415-897-8888

ChatterBox 4000
J&L Information Systems Inc.
9238 Deering Ave.
Chatsworth, CA 91311
818-709-1778

Access Server
Novell Inc. Comm. Products
890 Ross Dr.
Sunnyvale, CA 94089
800-453-1267

Vendors of EBBS and Related Products

Accunet
The Major BBS
Galacticom Inc.
4101 SW 47th Ave., #101
Fort Lauderdale, FL 33314
305-583-5990

Oracomm-Plus
Surf Computer Services, Inc.
71-540 Gardess Rd.
Rancho Mirage, CA 92270
619-346-1608

PCBoard
Clark Development Co.
3950 S. 700 East, #303
Murray, UT 84107
800-356-1686

RemoteAccess
Continental Software
195 Adelaide Terr.

Perth, Australia, 6000
USA contact 918-254-6618

Searchlight
Searchlight Software
Box 640
Stony Brook, NY 11790
516-751-2966

TBBS
eSoft Inc.
15200 E. Girard Ave., #2550
Aurora, CA 80014
303-699-6565

Vendors of Routers, Bridges, and Related Products

G/X25 Gateway & Bridge 64
Gateway Communicatons Inc.
2941 Alton Ave.
Irvine, CA 92714
800-367-6555

Microcom LAN Bridge 6000
Microcom Systems Inc.
500 River Ridge Dr.
Norwood, MA 02062
800-822-8224

LAN2LAN/Mega Router
Newport Systems Solutions Inc.
4019 Westerley Pl, #103
Newport Beach, CA 92660
800-368-6533

NetWare Link/X.25
Novell Inc.
122 East 1700 South
Provo, UT 84606
800-638-9273

NetWare Link/T1
Novell Inc.
122 East 1700 South
Provo, UT 84606
800-638-9273

POWERbridge
Performace Technology
7800 IH 10, W. 800
Lincoln Center
San Antonio, TX 78230
800-825-5267

Vendors of E-Mail Products

cc:Mail Gateway
Lotus Development Corp.
2141 Landings Dr.
Mountain View, CA 94043
800-448-2500

Beyond Mail
Beyond Inc.
38 Sidney St.
Cambridge, MA 02139
617-621-0095

@Mail
Beyond Inc.
38 Sidney St.
Cambridge, MA 02139
617-621-0095

MailMAN
Reach Soft. Corp.
330 Portrero Ave.
Sunnyvale, CA 94086
408-733-8685

Microsoft Mail for PC Networks
Microsoft Corp.
One Microsoft Way
Redmont, WA 98052
206-882-8080

Microsoft Mail
Microsoft Corp.
One Microsoft Way
Redmont, WA 98052
206-882-8080

Office Works Comm. Option
Data Access Corp.
14000 SW 119 Ave.
Miami, FL 33186
800-451-3539

WordPerfect Office
WordPerfect Corp.
1555 N. Technology Way
Orem, UT 84057
800-451-5151

Vendors of Fax Gateways and Related Products

NetFax Board
All the Fax, Inc.
917 Northern Blvd.
Great Neck, NY 11021
800-289-3329

FaxPress 2000
Castelle
3255-3 Scott Blvd.
Santa Clara, CA 95051
800-359-7654

GammaFax CPD
GammaLink
133 Caspian Court
Sunnyvale, CA 94089
408-744-1430

Facsimile Server
Interpreter, Inc.
11455 West 48th Ave.
Wheat Ridge, CO 80033
800-232-4687

Vendors of Network Management Products

PreCursor
The Alridge Co.
2500 City West Blvd., Suite 575
Houston, TX 77042
800-548-5019

StopCopy Plus
BBI Computer Systems
14105 Heritage Lane
Silver Spring, MD 20906
301-871-1094

Stop View
BBI Computer Systems
14105 Heritage Lane
Silver Spring, MD 20906
301-871-1094

SiteLock
Brightwork Development, Inc.
766 Shrewsbury Ave.
Jerral Center West
Trenton Falls, NJ
800-552-9876

Certus LAN
Certus International
13110 Shaker Sq.
Cleveland, OH 44120
800-722-8737

Saber Meter
Saber Software Corp.
Box 9088
Dallas, TX 75209
800-338-8754

EtherPeek
AG Group
2540 Camino Diablo
Walnut Creek, CA 94596
510-937-2479

LocalPeek
AG Group
2540 Camino Diablo
Walnut Creek, CA 94596
510-937-2479

NetPatrol Pack
AG Group
2540 Camino Diablo
Walnut Creek, CA 94596
510-937-2479

Net Watchman
AG Group
2540 Camino Diablo
Walnut Creek, CA 94596
510-937-2479

ARCserve for NetWare 286
Cheyenne Software, Inc.
55 Bryant Ave.
Roslyn, NY 11576
800-243-9462

ARCserve for NetWare 386
Cheyenne Software, Inc.
55 Bryant Ave.
Roslyn, NY 11576
800-243-9462

Network Supervisor
CSG Technologies, Inc.
530 William Penn Place
Suite 329
Pittsburgh, PA 15219
800-366-4622

Retrospect Remote
Dantz Development Corp.
1400 Shattuck Ave., Suite 1
Berkeley, CA 94709
510-849-0293

LANVista 100
Digilog, Inc.
1370 Welsh Rd.
Montgomeryville, PA 18936
800-344-4564

PhoneNET Manager's Pack
Farallon Computing, Inc.
2000 Powell St.
Emeryville, CA 94608
510-596-9000

NetWare Early Warning System
Frye Computer Systems, Inc.
19 Temple Place, 4th Floor
Boston, MA 02111
800-234-3793

NetWare Management
Frye Computer Systems, Inc.
19 Temple Place, 4th. Floor
Boston, MA 02111
800-234-3793

LANWatch
FTP Software, Inc.
26 Princess St.

Wakefield, MA 01880
617-246-0900

LANprobe
Hewlett-Packard Co.
5070 Centennial Blvd.
Colorado Springs, CO 80919
719-531-4000

Network Advisor
Hewlett-Packard Co.
5070 Centennial Blvd.
Colorado Springs, CO 80919
719-531-4000

OpenView
Hewlett-Packard Co.
5070 Centennial Blvd.
Colorado Springs, CO 80919
719-531-4000

ProbeView
Hewlett-Packard Co.
5070 Centennial Blvd.
Colorado Springs, CO 80919
719-531-4000

LANanalyzer
Novell, Inc.
122 East 1700 South
Provo, UT 84606
800-453-1267

Lantern
Novell, Inc.
122 East 1700 South
Provo, UT 84606
800-453-1267

Lantern Service Monitor
Novell, Inc.
122 East 1700 South
Provo, UT 84606
800-453-1267

Access/One
Ungermann-Bass, Inc.
3900 Freedom Cir.
Santa Clara, CA 95052
800-873-6381

NetDirector
Ungermann-Bass, Inc.
3900 Freedom Cir.
Santa Clara, CA 95052
800-873-6381

LattisNet Advanced Network
Management
Synoptics Communication, Inc.
Box 58185
Santa Clara, CA 95052
408-988-2400

LattisNet Basic Network Management
Synoptics Communication, Inc.

Box 58185
Santa Clara, CA 95052
408-988-2400

LattisNet System 3000
Synoptics Communication, Inc.
Box 58185
Santa Clara, CA 95052
408-988-2400

Network Control Engine
Synoptics Communication, Inc.
Box 58185
Santa Clara, CA 95052
408-988-2400

Vendors of Network Operating Systems and Related Products

LANtastic
Artisoft, Inc.
575 E. River Rd., Artisoft Plaza
Tucson, AZ 85704
602-293-6363

LANsoft
ACCTON Technology Corp.
46750 Fremont Blvd., Suite 104
Fremont, CA 94538
415-226-9800

VINES
Banyan Systems, Inc.
120 Flanders Rd.
Westboro, MA 01581
508-898-1000

PC/NOS
Corvus Systems, Inc.
160 Great Oaks Blvd.
San Jose, CA 95119
800-426-7887

LANsmart
D-Link Systems, Inc.
5 Musick
Irvine, CA 92718
714-455-1688

OS/2 Ext. Ed.
IBM Corp.
Old Orchard Rd.
Armonk, NY 10504
800-426-2468

EasyNet NOS/2 Plus
LanMark Corp.
Box 246, Postal Station A
Mississauga, ON
CD L5A 3G8
416-848-6865

LAN Manager
Microsoft Corp.
One Microsoft Way
Redmont, WA 98052
800-426-9400

NetWare
Novell, Inc.
122 East 1700 South
Provo, UT 84606
800-453-1267

Commercial Information Services

BIX
One Phoenix Mill Lane
Peterborough, NH 03458
800-227-2983

Compuserve
Box 20212
Columbus, OH 43220
800-848-8199

Dialog Information Service, Inc.
3460 Hillview Ave.
Palo Alto, CA 94304
800-334-2564

General Videotext Corp.
Three Blackstone St.
Cambridge, MA 02139
800-544-4005

GEnie
401 N. Washington St.
Rockville, MD 20850
800-638-9636

NewsNet
945 Haverford Rd.
Bryn Mawr, PA 19010
800-345-1301

Prodigy Services Co.
445 Hamilton Ave.
White Plains, NY 10601
800-776-3449

Quantum Computer Services
8619 Westwood Center Dr.,
Suite 200
Vienna, VA 22182
800-227-6364

SprintMail
12490 Sunrise Valley Dr.
Reston, VA 22096
800-736-1130

Public Communication Networks

Accunet
AT&T Computer Systems
295 N. Maple Ave.
Basking Ridge, NJ 07920
800-222-0400

CompuServe Network Services
CompuServe Inc.
5000 Arlington Centre Blvd.
Columbus, OH 43220
800-848-8199

IBM Information Network
IBM Corp
3405 W. Dr. Martin Luther King, Jr. Blvd.
Tampa, FL 33607
800-727-2222

Infonet
Infonet Services Corp.
2100 East Grand Ave.
El Segundo, CA 90245
800-342-5272

Mark*Net
GE Corp.
Information Services Div.
401 N. Washington St.
Rockville, MD 20850
800-433-3683

SprintNet Data Network
US Sprint
12490 Sunrise Valley Dr.
Reston, VA 22096
800-736-1130

Tymnet Global Network
BT North America Inc.
2560 N. 1st St., Box 49019
San Jose, CA 94161
800-872-7654

Vendors of Data Switches, PBXs, and Related Products

AISwitch Series XXX
Applied Innovation, Inc.
651-C Lakeview Plaza Blvd.
Columbus, OH 43085
800-247-9482

MDX
Equinox Systems, Inc.
14260 Southwest 119th Ave.
Miami, FL 33186
800-328-2729

Instanet6000
MICOM Communications Corp.
Box 8100
4100 Los Angeles Ave.
Simi Valley, CA 93062-8100
800-642-6687

Data PBX Series
Rose Electronics
Box 742571
Houston, TX 77274
800-333-9343

Gateway Data Switch
SKP Electronics
1232-E S. Village Way
Santa Ana, CA 92705
714-972-1727

INCS-64
Western Telematic, Inc.
5 Sterling
Irvine, CA 92178
800-854-7226

Slimline Data Switches
Belkin Components
14550 S. Main St.
Gardena, CA 90248
800-223-5546

MetroLAN
Datacom Technologies, Inc.
11001 31st Place, West
Everett, WA 98204
800-468-5557

Intelligent Printer Buffer
Primax Electronics Inc.
2531 West 237th St., Suite 102
Torrance, CA 90505
310-326-8018

Data Switches
Rose Electronics
Box 742571
Houston, TX 77274
800-333-9343

ShareNet 5110
McComb Research
Box 3984
Minneapolis, MN 55405
612-527-8082

Aura 1000
Intran Systems, Inc.
7493 N. Oracle Rd., Suite 207
Tucson, AZ 85704
602-797-2797

Logical Connection
Fifth Generation Systems, Inc.
10049 N. Reiger Rd.
Baton Rouge, LA 70809
800-873-4384

Vendors of Network Remote Access Software and Related Products

Distribute Console Access Facility
IBM Corp.
(Contact IBM sales rep.)
800-426-2468

PolyMod2
Memsoft Corp.
1 Park Pl.
621 NW 53rd St., #240
Boca Raton, FL 33487
407-997-6655

Remote-OS
The Software Lifeline Inc.
Fountain Square, 2600 Military Trail, #290
Boca Raton, FL 33531
407-994-4466

Vendors of TCP/IP Hardware and Related Products

Isolink PC/TCP
BICC Data Networks
1800 W. Park Dr., Suite 150
Westborough, MA 01581
800-447-6526

PC/TCP Plus
FTP Software, Inc.
26 Princess St.
Wakefield, MA 01880
617-246-0900

TCP/IP for OS/2 EE
IBM
Old Orchard Rd.
Armonk, NY 10504
800-426-2468

10Net TCP
Digital Comm. Assoc.
10NET Comm. Div.
7887 Washington Village Dr.
Dayton, OH 45459
800-358-1010
WIN/TCP for DOS
Wollongong Group, Inc.
Box 51860
1129 San Antonio Rd.
Palo Alto, CA 94303
800-872-8649

PC/TCP Thernet Comm.
UniPress Software, Inc.
2025 Lincoln Hwy.
Edison, NJ 08817
800-222-0550

Vendors of Zero Slot LANs, Media Transfer Hardware and Software, and Related Products

LANtastic Z
Artisoft, Inc.
575 E. River Rd.
Artisoft Plaza
Tucson, AZ 85704
602-293-6363

PC-Hookup
Brown Bag Software
2155 S. Bascom, Suite 114
Campbell, CA 95008
800-523-0764

Brooklyn Bridge
Fifth Generation Systems
10049 N. Reiger Rd.
Baton Rouge, LA 70809

LapLink
Traveling Software, Inc.
18702 N. Creek Pkwy.
Bothell, WA 98011
800-662-2652

FastLynx
Rupp Corp.
7285 Franklin Ave.
Los Angeles, CA 90046
800-852-7877

MasterLink
U.S. Marketing, Inc.
1402 South St.
Nashville, TN 37212
615-242-8800

Glossary

Account Boot Disk. A disk used to load DOS into the computer when it is turned on.

ASCII. The acronym for American Standard Code for Information Interchange. This is a standard code for the transmission of data within the US. It is composed of 128 characters in a 7-bit format.

Asynchronous. A method of communication that places data in discrete blocks that are surrounded by framing bits. These bits show the beginning and ending of a block of data.

Bandwidth. This is the capacity of a cable to carry data on different channels or frequencies.

Baseband. A network cable that has only one channel for carrying data signals.

Baud. The rate of data transmission.

Bit. An abbreviation for binary digit. A bit is the smallest unit of data.

BOOTCONF.SYS. A file on the file server used to indicate which boot image file each workstation will use.

Bridge. A device that connects different LANs so a node on one LAN can communicate with a node on another LAN.

Broadband. A network cable with several channels of communication.

Bus Topology. A physical layout of a LAN where all nodes are connected to a single cable.

Byte. Normally a combination of 8 bits.

CAPTURE. A NetWare utility program used to redirect output from a printer port on the workstation to a network printer.

Coaxial Cable. A cable consisting of a single metal wire surrounded by insulation, which is itself surrounded by a braided or foil outer conductor.

COMPSURF. A NetWare utility program that prepares a hard disk for use in a NetWare file server. Its name stands for COMPrehensive SURFace analysis.

Computer. An electronic system that can store and process information under program control.

CONSOLE. The file server.

Control Code. Special nonprinting codes that cause electronic equipment to perform specific actions.

CPU. Central processing unit. The "brains" of the computer; that section where the logic and control functions are performed.

Device Driver. A software program that enables a network operating system and the DOS operating system to work with NICs, disk controllers, and other hardware.

Directory Rights. Access attached to directories on a NetWare file server.

Driver. A memory resident program usually used to control a hardware device.

FCONSOLE. A NetWare utility program used to monitor file server and workstation activity.

Fiber-Optic Cable. A data transmitting cable that consists of plastic or glass fibers.

File Attributes. Access rights attached to each file.

File Server. A computer running a network operating system that enables other computers to access its files.

Full-Duplex. In full duplex communication, the terminal transmits and receives data simultaneously.

Gateway. A device that acts as a translator between networks that use different protocols.

Group. A collection of users.

Group Rights. Rights given to a collection of users.

Half Duplex. In half duplex communication, the terminal transmits and receives data in separate, consecutive operations.

Handshaking. A set of commands recognized by the sending and receiving stations that control the flow of data transmission.

Interface. A communication channel that is used to connect a computer to an external device.

Internetwork Packet Exchange (IPX). One of the data transmission protocols used by NetWare.

LAN. Local area network. A network that encompasses a small geographical area.

LOGIN. A NetWare utility program that allows users to identify themselves to the network.

Login Script. A series of statements executed each time a user logs into a NetWare network.

MAP. Association of a logical NetWare drive letter with a directory.

Modem. An electronic device that converts (modulates) digital data from a computer into analog signals that the phone equipment can understand. Additionally, the modem converts (demodulates) analog data into digital data.

NetBIOS. A network communication protocol that NetWare can emulate.

NETGEN. A NetWare utility program used to configure and load NetWare onto a file server.

NetWare. A network operating system produced by Novell Incorporated.

Network Address. A hexadecimal number used to identify a network cabling system.

NIC. The network interface card is a circuit board that is installed in the file server and workstations that make up the network. It allows the hardware in the network to send and receive data.

Node. A workstation, file server, bridge, or other device that has an address on a network.

Novell. A company based in Provo, Utah, that produces the NetWare network operating system.

NPRINT. A NetWare utility program used to send a file directly to a network printer. Its name stands for Network PRINT.

Packet. A discrete unit of data bits transmitted over a network.

Password. A secret word used to identify a user.

PCONSOLE. A NetWare utility program used to configure and operate print servers. Its name stands for Print server CONSOLE.

PRINTCON. A NetWare utility program used to create print job configurations.

PRINTDEF. A NetWare utility program used to create and edit print device files.

Print Devices. Definition files for different types of printers to be used on a print server.

Print Forms. Definitions of different types of paper size to be used on a print server.

Print Job Configurations. Complete descriptions of how a file is to be printed on the network.

Print Queues. Definitions of the order in which and where a file is to be printed on the network.

Print Server. A computer running the PSERVER program that allows it to accept files to be printed from other workstations.

Protocol. The conventions that must be observed in order for two electronic devices to communicate with each other.

PSERVER. The NetWare Print SERVER program.

RAM. Random access memory.

Remote Print Server. A computer running the RPRINTER program, enabling it to print output from other network workstations and operate as a normal workstation.

Remote Reset. The process of loading DOS and the network drivers from the file server.

Ring Topology. A network configuration that connects all nodes in a logical ring-like structure.

ROM. Read only memory.

RPRINTER. The program that allows other workstations to print to a workstation's printer.

Shell. Under NetWare, the network drivers.

SHELL.CFG. A file used on a workstation to configure the network drivers as they are loaded into memory.

Star Topology. A network configuration where each node is connected by a single cable link to a central location, called the hub.

Synchronous. A method of communication using a time interval to distinguish between transmitted blocks of data.

SYSCON. A NetWare utility program used to establish users and their rights on the file server. Its name stands for SYStem CONfiguration.

Token. The data packet used to carry information on LANs using the ring topology.

Topology. The manner in which nodes are connected on a LAN.

Trustee Rights. Rights given to users to access directories on the file server.

Uninterruptible Power Supply. A device that keeps computers running after a power failure, providing power from batteries for a short period of time.

User. Under NetWare, the definition of a set of access rights for an individual.

VAP. A value-added process to the NetWare operating system provided by a third party vendor.

Wide Area Network. A network that encompasses a large geographical area.

Workstation. A computer attached to the network.

X.25. A communication protocol used on public data networks.

Index